1993

Ideology and Development in Africa

A Council on Foreign Relations Book

COUNCIL ON FOREIGN RELATIONS BOOKS

Ideology and Development in Africa

CRAWFORD YOUNG

New Haven and London
Yale University Press

Published with the assistance of the A. Whitney
Griswold Publication Fund.

Designed by James J. Johnson
and set in Melior Roman.
Printed in the United States of America by
The Vail-Ballou Press, Binghamton, N.Y.

Library of Congress Cataloging in Publication Data
Young, Crawford, 1931–
    Ideology and development in Africa.
    "Council on Foreign Relations book."
    Includes index.
    1. Africa—Politics and government—1960–   . 2. Africa—
Economic conditions—1960–   . 3. Africa—Social conditions—
1960–   . I. Council on Foreign Relations. II. Title.
DT30.5.Y68   960'.32   81-15987
ISBN 0–300–02744–3   AACR2
        0–300–03096–7 (pbk.)

10   9   8   7   6

To Ralph A. Young, In Memoriam

Contents

Tables

Foreword

The Africa Project of the Council on Foreign Relations was designed to focus both on Africa and on its significance for the United States. Undertaken in response to a perceived need for greater knowledge about African realities on the part of the American foreign policy community, the Project aimed to produce and disseminate original research on Africa's changing role in the international community and to stimulate discussion and debate within the Western, and particularly American, policymaking communities.

The Project proceeded in two ways, each calculated to reinforce the other's impact: through a marked expansion of attention to Africa in the Council's regular activities during 1978–79 and 1979–80; and through a series of studies and publications. The process aimed at bringing together regional specialists with people in government, business, the professions, and the public media whose views are likely to have an effect on Africa policy. The Africa Project book series was designed to fill what the Council saw as a dangerous gap in information and public understanding, bringing a detailed knowledge of African issues to bear on the larger questions that confront United States citizens and policymakers. Its authors have sought to use their expert knowledge to interpret African developments in a way that addresses the concerns of an informed but largely nonspecialist audience.

This study by Crawford Young is the first of the series. Those to follow will deal with crisis management in Africa, United States policy toward southern Africa, African arms and armies, African economic development, and interstate relationships within the African continent.

The Africa Project was made possible by generous grants from the Ford and Rockefeller foundations. Their advice and assistance along the way has proved invaluable.

WILLIAM J. FOLTZ
Africa Project Director

JENNIFER SEYMOUR WHITAKER
Editor, Africa Project Book Series

Acknowledgments

The two decades of African postindependence development examined in this study coincide roughly with the period of my own close observation of African affairs. Those who have shared their perspectives and insights with me in the course of these years are so numerous that only a collective acknowledgment is possible. Government officials, political leaders, opposition critics, university staff, students, ordinary citizens: in the myriad encounters with Africans in all walks of life during twenty years of teaching and study, a frame of interpretation takes form, through which the sources referred to in the notes acquire meaning.

My first contacts with Africa occurred while I was studying in London and Paris in 1955–57; the attraction to the topic of ideology has much to do with the particularities of the African university student milieu of the time. Nationalism was acquiring its aura of invincibility; in this mood of impending political triumph intellectuals were beginning the quest for a definition of the economic and social purposes of independence. The unanticipated speed with which formal colonialism was crumbling opened exhilarating vistas; if the once-omnipotent imperial occupant could be defeated by the forces of liberation, surely the lesser dragons of poverty, ignorance, and disease could be put to rout. The moral energies so effectively mobilized in anticolonial struggle could now be directed toward the goal of development. All that was needed was a valid blueprint for the future; this quest for an ideology was the subject of endless and earnest debates in student restaurants, left-bank cafes, and diverse congresses. In the more somber hues of the mood of the 1980s, it is difficult to recapture, much less communicate, the excitement of this search. Yet, at the time, participant and observer alike were enthralled by the sense of boundless possibility in the adventure of independence.

In the quarter-century that has elapsed since that time, I have observed with special interest the most influential ideological projects that have emerged to give specific content to the somewhat formless visions of the mid-1950s. Thus, the invitation by the Council on Foreign Relations in 1978 to undertake a study on the theme of ideology and development choice, as part of a broader African project, was a welcome challenge.

Indeed, in the mid-1960s I had pursued this line of inquiry in less ambitious form with two colleagues at the University of Wisconsin, Charles Anderson and Fred von der Mehden. We had examined the diverse uses of the concept of developmental socialism as one of the themes in our jointly authored work, *Issues of Political Development* (Prentice-Hall, 1967). However, too little time had elapsed since African independence to permit much consideration of the impact of ideology on policy. In such crucial cases as Tanzania and Algeria, the relationship between theory and practice remained to be defined; no regime yet described itself as "Marxist-Leninist."

As invaluable prods and critics, special thanks are due successive generations of students at the University of Wisconsin-Madison, whose challenges have forced reconsideration of many assumptions over the years. In particular, the preliminary thoughts that formed the basis for the present work served as a topic for a graduate course in 1979; the vigorous exchange with students from a dozen countries and of diverse perspective was an invaluable stimulus.

The Council on Foreign Relations was unflagging in its support for the study. Of particular value were two critical discussion sessions on a rough draft of the manuscript, bringing together academic, public, and private sector specialists on African development. I am also grateful to the Council staff for its efficient and expeditious aid in various stages of the production process, from typing to editing. To William Foltz and Jennifer Whitaker go my special thanks for their continuing encouragement and support.

The final drafting of the manuscript took place while I enjoyed the inestimable hospitality of the Institute for Advanced Study in Princeton as a visiting member. The congenial and supportive environment for scholarship provided by the Institute is truly extraordinary.

The helping hand lent by so many to this work, as always, implies no guilt by association with whatever flaws the vigilant reader may detect. Defects in analysis, judgment, or interpretation are the exclusive responsibility of the author.

CRAWFORD YOUNG
Madison, Wisconsin
May 1981

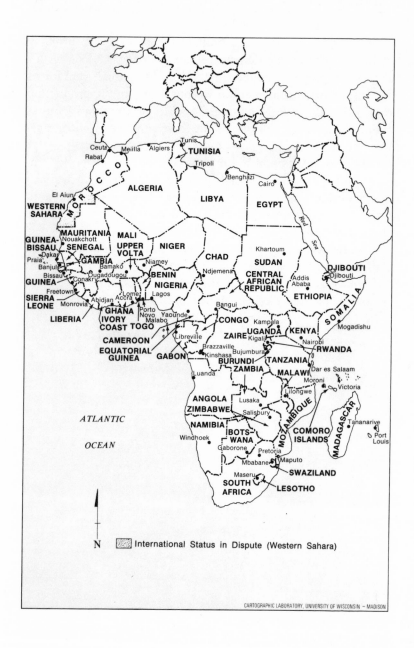

International Status in Dispute (Western Sahara)

CARTOGRAPHIC LABORATORY, UNIVERSITY OF WISCONSIN – MADISON

1

Ideology and Development Choice

THE WEST AFRICAN WAGER

In 1957, Kwame Nkrumah of Ghana offered a wager to Félix Houphouët-Boigny of Ivory Coast. Ghana, on the threshold of independence, had opted resolutely for the pathway of African nationalism; "seek ye first the political kingdom," went the oft-cited saying, "and all else shall be added unto you." Houphouët-Boigny, at this juncture, had opposed to "the mystique of independence" the alternative of fraternal association with France. The two countries were quite similar in resource endowment, dimensions, and level of development. Nkrumah challenged Houphouët-Boigny to a rendezvous of judgment in ten years; history would then render its verdict on the relative validity of the two pathways.

The wheel of fate did not permit Nkrumah a full decade of power; however, by the time of his fall in 1966, the outcome of the contest was clear.[1] Ghana was locked into a pattern of stagnation—which persists to the present—while Ivory Coast had enjoyed a remarkable rate of growth—though critics of its strategy pointed to the high ransom of dependency. Yet even during this decade the nature of the contest altered; in 1957, the salient distinction between the two lay in the more nationalist orientation of the Ghanaian design. From 1961 on, the concept of socialism was added in Ghana (though it was ambiguously applied), and

thus a new dimension was added to the wager: the evident contrast with the resolutely capitalist, if state-directed, model pursued by Ivory Coast.

THE EMERGENCE OF SOCIALISM IN AFRICA

Meanwhile, ideological discourse in Africa had been enriched
by a panoply of socialist designs. Some were associated with
leaders of exceptional charismatic force, such as Gamal Abdel
Nasser of Egypt. Others had prestige linked to the heroic circumstances of their birth: Algeria, whose liberation movement, the
Front de Libération Nationale (FLN), had carried out an eight-
year revolutionary struggle against overwhelming odds and at
enormous cost; Guinea, which had the courage to defy Charles
de Gaulle in rejecting his French Community in 1958. Yet others
attracted wide attention through the philosophic stature of the
ruler (Leopold Sédar Senghor of Senegal) or the originality and
ethical appeal of his analysis (Julius Nyerere of Tanzania).

Thus the Nkrumah shift to an apparently socialist strategy in
1961 appeared part of a much broader movement in Africa. Although the first influential socialist statement was published
only in 1956,[2] by the early 1960s what became known as "African
socialism" appeared to be on the march. These somewhat disparate socialist perspectives acquired commanding prestige for a
time, to the point where even the regimes that were most skeptical about socialist prescriptions solemnly adopted public documents that ingeniously redefined capitalism as socialism. Not
the least of the many ironies in this interesting phase of ideological history is that the most coherent intellectual statement of African socialism, by President Nyerere,[3] found serious application
only in 1967; by then, the prestige of "African socialism" was beginning to wane.[4]

Despite the tendency of socialism to dominate ideological

discourse, it was never in reality the most widespread guide to policy choice in the 1960s. Countries such as Nigeria, Zaire, Cameroon, Morocco, and Malawi, as well as Ivory Coast, quietly formulated their development choices in terms consistent with the modified version of the liberal market economy under substantial state direction and regulation characteristic of the West. Few voices, however, exalted this preference in esthetic terms. The reticence long ago noted by Schumpeter no doubt operated; nobody loved capitalism, and there was something shameful about openly espousing it.[5] Thus partisans of the market economy, if they did not find it prudent to don socialist camouflage, generally described themselves as "pragmatic," and therefore opposed to "doctrinal" formulation of development issues. Their critics, of course, were quick to point out that liberal Western economic theory might also be considered an ideology.

ENTER SCIENTIFIC SOCIALISM

As the 1960s drew to a close, the nature of the ideological debate began to change. "African socialism" was in retreat before an array of critics, especially from the left. They charged that the doctrine was formless and amorphous and failed to provide a clear blueprint for socialism. A more "scientific socialism," tied to the tradition of Marxist thought, was required.[6] Some went on to argue, as did Soviet critics, that socialism was a universal doctrine and could not accommodate geographical deviations. The stress upon the communitarian heritage of African society was held to be naive and the rejection of class struggle mischievous and wrong.

In 1969, the new military regime of Marien Ngouabi in Congo-Brazzaville went beyond the socialist commitment claimed since 1963 to announce an option for "Marxism-Leninism" as official doctrine. The army rulers of Somalia followed the same path the next year. In the mid-1970s, this new doctrinal trend of African Marxist regimes gained momentum when military regimes in Benin (1974), Madagascar (1975), and Ethiopia (1976) declared Marxism-Leninism to be their guide. Even more dramatic was the disintegration of the Portuguese colonial empire, whose successor states (Mozambique, Angola, Guinea-Bissau, Cape Verde, and São Tomé e Principe) held liberation creeds at least informed by Marxism-Leninism.[7] An important new dimension was added to the ideological dialogue.

Meanwhile, continuity jostled with change. Market-economy strategies were abandoned in favor of socialism in Benin, Ethiopia, Somalia, and Libya. In Ghana, the successors to Nkrumah dismantled the uncertain socialist apparatus of the Convention Peoples' Party (CPP) during 1966–72. While not admitting it, Sékou Touré seemed to veer away from socialism after the shock of the market women uprising in 1977. Socialism seemed to have exhausted its moral energies in Egypt with the passing of Nasser, and Anwar Sadat reverted without public outcry to a nonsocialist strategy. Although these cases suggest ebb and flow as norm, in other important instances there has been a remarkable degree of policy continuity, now extending over two decades. Tanzania and Algeria, while making occasional rectifications of their direction, were guided throughout by a socialist engagement. Ivory Coast, Cameroon, and Nigeria were equally consistent in their adherence to an essentially capitalist strategy.

THE CATASTROPHIC CASE

Not only was the ideological spectrum broadened during the first two decades of African independence, but events also unveiled a somber set of possible outcomes of the pursuit of prosperity. In the 1960s, the scope of conceivable variation seemed fixed by a scale extending from immobility to progress. The 1970s brought the specter of regression and even disintegration. To leaders of remarkable stature, such as Nyerere or Nasser, were added such sinister tyrants as Idi Amin of Uganda and Francisco Macias Nguema of Equatorial Guinea. Regimes might not only fail to achieve development, but might transform the state itself into a predator upon society. Amin's "state of blood"[8] was a paradigmatic case. His successors, when the Tanzanian army had finally removed this blight in 1979, accused Amin not only of killing an estimated 300,000 Ugandans, but of having cost Uganda a decade during which not a single school, hospital, or road was constructed. Coffee production, extorted from farmers to supply the terror apparatus of the regime with the bulk of its resources, fell by one-third, while cotton output dropped from 450,000 bales just before Amin to 60,000 by 1978. The copper mines had closed; tea, tobacco, and sugar output had dropped to the vanishing point; only the breweries prospered. Brett, writing on the eve of Amin's departure, captures the depth of the decay: "Ten years ago there seemed to be no reason to believe that the process of capitalist development would not be rapid and continuous; now it is difficult to see how the decline can ever be stopped."[9]

Nor, unhappily, was Uganda alone in its plight. While the first three postindependence regimes in Ghana failed to move the country beyond stagnation, the government of Ignatius Acheampong had been actually destructive. All-time record prices for Ghana's prime commodity, cocoa, extending over several years, should have provided an era of growth and prosperity; had Nkrumah been so fortunate, he might well have won his wager with Houphouët-Boigny. Instead, Acheampong and an inner ring of collaborators skimmed public resources at an extraordinary pace; *West Africa* cautiously noted a discrepancy of £500,000,000 in 1977–78 between reported state cocoa sales proceeds and prevailing world price levels.[10] Acheampong is reported to have accumulated a personal fortune of $100 million in six years of power,[11] a sum that apparently required five times as long for the Somoza family to amass. At the same time, hyper-inflation and massive shortages destroyed the livelihoods of most citizens. The depth of despair and anger was given full measure by the summary execution of eight leading military fig-ures, including three former heads of state, by the new regime of Captain Jerry Rawlings in June 1979—a traumatic departure for so deeply humane a country, which had never before known po-litical killing.

Crisis struck other lands. By 1979, Chad appeared on the verge of total disintegration. In Zaire, the government trade union issued figures in 1976 demonstrating that urban real wages had dropped to 26 percent of their 1960 level; with 80 percent inflation levels the following two years and only one 30 percent wage increase, the figure could have been little more than 10 per-cent by 1978.[12] An International Labor Organization survey in 1974 showed that in eleven of twenty-one African countries the real minimum wage had declined between 1963 and 1974.[13]

The sober mood of the Organization of African Unity sum-mit meeting at Monrovia in 1979 well reflected the sense that progress was not inevitable, though not all was unrelieved failure. Countries such as Algeria, Ivory Coast, and Cameroon could lay reasonable claim to positive performance. Some ob-servers found hopeful signs that revolutionary liberation move-ments in Guinea-Bissau and Mozambique were making some headway in overcoming extreme underdevelopment. But the dif-ficulties that beset so many countries could no longer be over-looked. As a report prepared for the OAU meeting concluded, "Africa . . . is unable to point to any significant growth rate or sat-isfactory index of general well-being" after two decades of inde-pendence. In many countries, what growth had occurred was ei-ther canceled by population expansion or benefited primarily the political-bureaucratic ruling strata and the foreign sector. The swelling urban centers could no longer be supplied with food from domestic production, and scarce foreign exchange had to be committed to grain imports. The rural sector had quite generally been a disappointment; only a few countries could point to real achievements for smallholder populations.

THE IDEOLOGY – PERFORMANCE NEXUS

By way of recapitulation, I suggest that African political economies, in two decades of independence, had become widely differentiated along two axes: one defined by ideology and the other by performance. At the point of departure, there were broad similarities in the economies resulting from the common legacies of mercantile colonial capitalism pursued by the different metropolitan states. Over the two decades, major differences both in ideology and performance appeared. The ideological contrast in 1957 between the fraternal association of Ivoirian dependent capitalism with France and the nationalist but liberal economy proposed by Nkrumah looks in retrospect not very great; the distance between Ivory Coast today and the extremely nationalist Marxism-Leninism of Ethiopia is immense. On the performance side, not until the 1970s did the really calamitous cases of mismanagement become evident, while the basic competence and probity of the state were in large measure sustained in Algeria, Tanzania, and Cameroon.

Evidently the adversity that afflicted many countries came partly from external factors. Dependency theorists in the 1970s have eloquently analyzed these facets of underdevelopment: the structural distortions of colonial economies; trade patterns based on primary commodity export to volatile Western markets; the dominant role of colonial and multinational capital; reliance on expatriate personnel and patents in high technology areas.[14] Catastrophic droughts in the early 1970s hit a vast zone from Somalia to Cape Verde. The sudden surge in oil prices after 1973 affected all but the producers. Soaring debt burdens became a major issue in the 1970s; though Zaire has been the most dramatic and indigent debtor, a number of other countries have been affected (Zambia, Sierra Leone, Sudan, even Ivory Coast). The spillover of the southern African liberation struggle badly hurt countries such as Zambia and Mozambique; closing of the Zimbabwe border between 1975 and 1980 cost Mozambique some $550 million of desperately needed transit earnings.[15] External aid, from West and East, has fallen far short of expectations and needs. The stinginess of the European Economic Community (EEC), dramatized in the bitter 1979 negotiations over renewal of the pact of association (Lomé II), was matched by the small and declining American aid contribution. Both Soviet and Chinese development aid has been dwindling in recent years.

All of these factors are important. Overall, however, they tend to operate in a uniformly negative manner and do not easily explain either the remarkable range of ideological preference or the diversity of performance. I would argue that both Afro-Marxist and Afro-capitalist regimes have emerged largely through internal processes, not through the machinations of external forces; the same holds true of all the regimes that lie ideologically between them. Ivory Coast and Ghana, Tanzania and Uganda are all heavily dependent upon and vulnerable to the Western-dominated international economy; this common pattern cannot explain the radically different state performance.

What then can account for the widening divergences of ideology and performance? A response to this question is the elusive quarry we will pursue in these pages. What are the policy implications of the ideological spectrum that now stretches from Abidjan to Addis Ababa? Is ideological preference a predictor of performance? Or are these two axes of differentiation quite uncorrelated? These issues too will be subjects of our inquiry.

While a time frame of two decades is brief, it begins to offer scope for at least provisional judgments. This holds particularly for those regimes that have retained an ideologically consistent perspective over the entire period: such socialist states as Tanzania and Algeria and countries of capitalist orientation such as Nigeria, Kenya, and Ivory Coast. In the broader sweep of history, twenty years is perhaps but a moment. Yet it is long enough for patterns to emerge, for at least some implications of choice to surface, and for a tentative reckoning of costs and benefits.

Most African regimes have not persisted so long; we would unduly narrow our field of observation if we considered only these cases. In particular, one important category—the Afro-Marxist states—emerged only after 1969. Factors that produce ideological mutation, in whatever direction, are of evident interest.

My objective, then, is to explore the interrelationship between ideological preference and developmental performance. I do not expect to find that ideology alone will explain relative success or failure in achieving the central goal of a better life for the citizenry. Simple political effectiveness, which cuts across ideologies, is one obvious factor. Nor do I assume that every policy choice is dictated by ideology; poverty and underdevelopment impose similar constraints upon choice for all but the oil states. However, I do believe that the nature of the objectives pursued and the hierarchy of priority accorded to them are influenced by ideological perspective. This in turn, in complex patterns, has an impact over time on developmental outcomes.

I wish also to examine the implications of the ideology—performance nexus for international linkages. At first glance, one might expect that the ideological spectrum from capitalism to Marxism-Leninism would largely determine external alliances and ties. In reality, I believe the interplay between ideology and external connections is much more complex, though affinities of ideology do have at least a predisposing impact.

DOES IDEOLOGY MATTER?

Some may question whether ideological preference really matters at all; in the final analysis is it trivial? From one perspective, all African states are tributary to the Western-dominated international economy; peripheralized and dependent, they have little real choice. Another argument holds that in the inner sanctums of power a practical calculus of survival and benefit exercises a uniform hegemony. Preservation or expansion of political power, economic advantage for the state, the national society, or its rulers supplant officially proclaimed ideologies when the crucial choices are made.

Both of these objections have some merit. Only major petroleum producers escape dependency and its associated constraints. Few rulers are such philosophically inspired kings as to apply ideology alone to policy reason. Indeed, many of the daily issues which reach the presidential desk or the cabinet or party central committee agenda are not formulated in terms that immediately evoke ideological perceptions.

Yet I believe that ideology is not to be dismissed as simple, evanescent rhetoric. The texture of the policy thinking of a Houphouët-Boigny is simply not the same as that of a Nyerere; nor does Samora Machel of Mozambique view the world through the same prism as Daniel arap Moi of Kenya. Overriding political or economic imperatives may force upon a regime choices that appear to be inconsistent with ideological preference. Such dissonance may be rationalized as either not truly inconsistent with ideology correctly understood or as a conscious and temporary departure from rectitude; it does not annul the world view with which it is in tension.

More than rhetoric separates Brazzaville and Kinshasa, Dar es Salaam and Nairobi, Cotonou and Lagos. Even the most casual visitor to these contrasting capitals will sense the divergence. Nor is this a mere illusion of intuition; over time, these various polities have come to differ from each other in quite significant ways, and these differences can be imputed in good measure to the variation in ideological persuasion.

AN IDEOLOGICAL TYPOLOGY: THE THREE PATHWAYS

If ideology is accepted as a pertinent consideration, there still remains the problem of classifying regimes. While few dispute that Nigeria, Kenya, or Ivory Coast are African capitalist states, some observers raise objections to the classification of socialist states. Was, for example, Nkrumah's Ghana a socialist state? Most analysts would agree that until about 1961 socialism was a nominal and verbal commitment and that a sense of socialist engagement did influence policy in the final five years of Nkrumah rule. Some, however, including persons who dealt regularly with the Ghanaian ruler during these years, would disagree. The most cynical whisper that Nkrumahism was merely the highest stage of opportunism.

The dispute has been even sharper where the African Marxist-Leninist states are concerned. Some analysts would exclude from the list those under military leadership (Benin, Congo-Brazzaville, Madagascar, Ethiopia, and Somalia). Ethiopia is extolled by some for experiencing the only true socialist revolution in Africa, based on class struggle; others revile the incumbent regime as a fascist military dictatorship. Still others cite Mozambique as the only serious venture in scientific socialism in Africa. A leading Soviet Africanist recently listed Ethiopia, Mozambique, Angola, Congo-Brazzaville, and Benin as belonging on the honor roll of aspirant scientific socialist states.[16]

I shall rely primarily upon the ideological self-ascription of a regime's leadership in classifying polities. This means accepting at face value the declaration of a regime that Marxism-

Leninism is adopted as state doctrine. The interesting question that immediately follows is, What precisely is understood by scientific socialist fealty? As we shall see, in practice there is considerable divergence within this set of regimes. This does not mean that the whimsy of petty tyrants such as Macias Nguema of Equatorial Guinea, who occasionally used the Marxist lexicon, need be given credence. But where, as for example in Benin, a Marxist-Leninist engagement is a deliberately chosen and sustained self-identification, I feel that it should be accepted as such, however unorthodox the application may seem to those who perceive the doctrine as permitting only a single correct interpretation.

While close inspection will reveal a whole array of ideological shadings, for purposes of analysis we feel that three major streams may be distinguished. From left to right, these are Afro-Marxism,[17] populist socialism, and African capitalism. The first set of regimes is distinguished by an official, explicit declaration for Marxism-Leninism as state ideology. The second group consists of states that espouse a socialist orientation but that either do not stress or expressly reject Marxism. The third cluster consists of regimes that pursue a market-economy, or capitalist, policy, though they generally deny any ideological attachments at all; "pragmatism," it is said, is their only creed.

The Afro-Marxist and populist socialist groups are small enough in number so that we can consider most, though not all, of the cases. In the African capitalist set, I shall pay particular attention to three, Ivory Coast, Kenya, and Nigeria, which have been the most visible and influential instances of the pattern. In all three clusters, I shall give careful consideration to those that enjoy particular standing and prestige within a given ideological stream.

EVALUATION CRITERIA: SIX MEASURES

Difficulties arise also when one attempts to evaluate a regime's performance and relate performance to ideological preference. Economists and political scientists have followed rather divergent paths to this goal. For long, per capita gross national product (GNP) held sway as the prime measure of economic efficacy; even today, the growth rate is a ubiquitous and most powerful single statistic. In recent years, this measure has come under increasing criticism because of its many anomalies. Taken alone, GNP offers no information about actual levels of well-being or income distribution; it is a mechanical index of physical output. Thus countries with relatively small populations and high volumes of mineral output record apparently imposing levels of prosperity that are belied by the briefest visit to any rural community.

Economic performance analysis that is tied to GNP has a further limitation: rising levels of mineral production, oil in particular, depend relatively little on either the ideology or the competence of a regime. Even though both capitalist (Nigeria) and socialist (Libya and Algeria) producers have frequently obtained majority interests in oil undertakings, the management remains substantially dependent upon foreign personnel, technology, and, usually, corporations.

The need for more discriminating measures was generally conceded and dramatized by the increasing evidence that growth, where it did occur, seemed to be frequently accompanied by widening levels of inequality. For a time, the influential Kuznets study on the economic growth process over long historical periods partly deflected this concern. It seemed to prove that in early phases of growth inequality might be accentuated, but that once higher levels were achieved corrective mechanisms appeared to ensure improving degrees of distributive equity.[18] Myrdal's massive tomes on Asian development, however, point in a different direction.[19]

An important inquest by Adelman and Morris into the impact of aid contributed much to the introduction of measures of distribution into the evaluative process.[20] The World Bank, in the 1970s, moved to incorporate employment and equality criteria into its powerfully influential development creed. A reflection of this shift was the important study by Chenery and associates, which argued the case for redistribution with growth.[21] Frequently, however, equality was seen to be an objective that stood in partial contradiction to growth—an analogue to the widely shared assumption that there is a trade-off between growth and employment in industrial economies, with inflation as mediating variable.[22]

On the political side, we may note efforts to define performance criteria by Eckstein and by the Social Science Research Council (SSRC) Committee on Comparative Politics. Eckstein was seeking a set of empirical measures that could be reliably assessed by quantitative indicators. The four central criteria were durability, civil order, legitimacy, and decisional efficacy. These standards were troublesome both conceptually and empirically. Survival and absence of collective disorder, in an authoritarian setting, do not seem very convincing indicators of developmental accomplishment. Legitimacy and decisional efficacy are more reasonable standards, though highly resistant to the kind of measurement Eckstein sought. This venture into performance measurement quietly expired; it is most interesting for its demonstration of the severe difficulties of the task.[23]

The SSRC comparative politics committee argued that the achievement of development could be understood as the resolution of a series of "crises" encountered on the pathway toward consolidation of the nation-state: identity, legitimacy, participation, penetration, and distribution.[24] Resolution of these crises entailed responding to the increasingly powerful normative claims for equality, expanding the capacities of the state, and coping with a growing differentiation of society; taken together, the latter three constituted the "development syndrome." These concepts were rather broadly defined, and no effort was made to translate them into measurable indicators.

The entire analytical tradition embodied in the SSRC comparative politics committee, often labeled "liberal modernization theory," has subsequently been challenged by writers of the dependency and neo-Marxist persuasion. Among the failings they recorded were the naive assumptions that the developing state was an autonomous entity and that it was a neutral and benevolent instrument for the realization of societal goals. Implicit in this often cogent critique were some rather different performance standards: capacity for self-reliant choice and a concept of equality that included in the analysis of distribution the relative returns to the country itself and especially to its popular sectors, as opposed to benefits accruing to foreign capital, expatriate personnel, and other interests of the developed world.

In suggesting an alternative set of criteria for assessing regime performance, I propose a list which at once draws upon these earlier contributions, both by economists and political scientists, yet validates these essentially deductive goal definitions by an inductive incorporation of aims commonly stated by African states. By this process, I arrive at a set of six criteria.

First, growth—even if dethroned as queen of development—must remain on the list, and probably at the top. Regimes of all ideological persuasions regard expansion as a central objective—excepting only those like Amin's Uganda, whose "supersonic" journey to oblivion was founded upon no consciously formulated policy direction at all. Even the regime most persistently and comprehensively concerned with egalitarianism—Tanzania—has always considered growth to be indispensable.[25]

But growth needs to be assessed in terms less mechanical than those offered by simple inspection of the GNP. Expansion that occurs simply through geological good fortune has much less impact than a broad-base rise in production in the rural sector. Both because the majority of the population in all African states remains in the rural sector and because rising rural productivity is very likely to be raising the incomes of the poorest fraction of the population, I believe that close examination of the growth record in the peasant agricultural sphere is a particularly valuable measure of a regime's effectiveness in achieving economic advance.[26]

Second, equality of distribution must be considered. Conventionally, measurement efforts focus on devices for illustrating the relative shares of national income accruing to the upper and lower ends of the social scale (Lorenz curve, gini coefficient). While such measures are quite useful, there are other sources of insight that may be examined. The nature of fiscal policy—particularly the true incidence of indirect tax mechanisms, which provide the bulk of state revenue in Africa—deserves careful examination, as do pricing policies for agricultural commodities, in a setting where a long tradition of state-fixed prices for major commercial crops is quite general. Another important measure of the egalitarian impact of a state's development policies is the degree of dispersion into the countryside of the most keenly sought state-provided amenities—schools, medical facilities, roads, piped water. Mortality rates and levels of infant mortality can be as revealing as the gini index. Another useful measure is the state-fixed urban minimum wage for unskilled labor, a category often covering the majority of wage earners.

Third, autonomy and self-reliance may deserve inclusion. This criterion is derived in the first instance from nationalist thought; it is espoused with equal fervor by capitalist Nigeria and socialist Algeria. While dependency theorists would argue that the goal is impossible, except through an undefined "socialist revolution" of a type yet to be encountered and "disengagement" from Western economic linkages, nonetheless the criterion partly responds to aspects of their critique.

In reality, this goal can be only very partially met; autarchy is beyond the reach of any country in the contemporary, interdependent world. The practical meaning is to enlarge—within the relatively narrow range of possibility—the range of choices available. Factors that foreclose choice include the need for foreign resource flows to meet current state commitments (in particular, the payroll), an excessive debt burden carrying all the disabilities of being in receivership, heavy reliance on expatriate personnel in high skill and technology positions, and unrestricted control over natural resources by foreign enterprises.

Fourth, the preservation of human dignity must be considered. At issue is not the transplantation of particular constitutional forms of governance or charters of human rights, but the absence of large-scale, state-directed repression of individuals or broad categories of persons. South Africa is a case in point; the buoyant growth rate cannot be considered apart from the system of racial oppression upon which its economic development has been based. The Uganda of Idi Amin, the Central African Republic of Bokassa, and the Equatorial Guinea of Macias Nguema are likewise instances of flagrant and extensive abuses of human dignity.

This issue becomes measurable at the point where abuse becomes systematic and widespread. A quite reliable indirect barometer is the emergence of a significant refugee population; only under the pressure of fear and acute deprivation do most people abandon their homes for an uncertain and usually precarious sanctuary in a neighboring land. Emigration here does not include wholly economic migration (Voltaics to Ivory Coast), the "brain drain" emigration of skilled persons to high income countries, or even the presence in foreign capitals of a small coterie of exiled opposition figures, which are to be found for most countries. Another possible measure of repressiveness is the size of the security forces relative to area and population for states facing no immediate external threat. Countries with only a few thousand police and soldiers evidently have neither the desire nor the capacity to pursue highly repressive policies.

While human dignity might seem at first view incontrovertible as a criterion, there are troublesome aspects to this standard. These have perhaps come into clearer focus in public debate since the Carter administration proclaimed a "human rights" yardstick in foreign policy calculations. Many have pointed out that the systematic imposition of degrading poverty upon large segments of the populace in societies whose resources permit a high degree of affluence to privileged social groups, or an outflow of wealth to foreign interests, is as offensive to human dignity as the overtly political repression involved in the liberal concept of civil liberties. I agree; this dimension of possible human rights deprivation is considered under the heading of social and economic equality. Some observers argue that the *purposes* of coercive state action need to be distinguished. If some measure of repression occurs in action designed to displace entrenched social hierarchies—as, for example, in Rwanda in 1959, Zanzibar in 1964, or Ethiopia since 1975—it may be momentarily justified as the birth pangs of a new social order. Further, the state can scarcely be expected to remain inactive if dissident movements fostered by external powers or committed to fragmenting the national domain take up arms. While these arguments have force, I believe distinctions are perfectly possible in this area. The question of human dignity can hardly be evaded when regimes persist in executing their opponents, relegating large numbers of persons to a *gulag archipelago*, or provoking by their actions a large-scale exodus of their citizens.

Fifth, I would add the admittedly problematic variable of participation. This must be broadly conceived to include a range of possible mechanisms for citizen access and involvement: party, administration, local government, cooperatives, presidential dialogues. The disabilities of the centralized, bureaucratic-authoritarian state unrestrained by any accountability have made it sufficiently clear that the concept of participation belongs among performance criteria. However, the meanings of the idea are sufficiently diverse and the devices for its realization so various that appraisal is possible only at a rather broad level.[27]

Difficult as the concept may be, differences in participation can be identified. Few would disagree, for example, that the

Chama Cha Mapinduzi (CCM) in Tanzania offers a higher degree of access than does the *Mouvement Populaire de la Révolution* (MPR) in Zaire. During the 1960s there was clearly a higher order of participation in Tunisia, both through the party and its ancillary organs, than in the 1970s. Participation has its potentially darker side, in the Huntingtonian nightmare of politization overwhelming a weakly developed institutional infrastructure,[28] or the Kasfirian demons of unleashed ethnic solidarities in uncontrollable collision.[29] In reality, there was no risk at all that any regime would permit, much less foster, a level of participation at which these fears might be realized.

Last and most difficult of all to evaluate, I would include as a criterion the expansion of societal capacity. Among other notions, this concept refers to the ability of the state to respond to new challenge and demand and to adapt to changing needs. As Coleman has phrased it, "developmental capacity" means "the power constantly to create and an enhanced capacity to plan, implement, and manipulate new change as part of the process of achieving new goals."[30] It incorporates as well the notion of "decisional efficacy" that figured on the Eckstein performance evaluation list.

The appeal of this criterion has been clouded by the rise of the bureaucratic-authoritarian state[31] and by the perverse conversion of the state into a predator upon society, as occurred in Amin's Uganda, Acheampong's Ghana, and Mobutu's Zaire.[32] The state is not necessarily a neutral and benevolent purveyor of development; when it is not, an increase in its capacity simply broadens the scope of its oppressive and extortionate potential. At the same time, there is no conceivable alternative to the state as prime organizer of change. Escape from poverty is impossible without collective societal intervention through the state. That the state itself may play an essentially destructive role and become an instrument of mass impoverishment is a grim but unescapable risk that—as I argued earlier—had been greatly underestimated. Probity, integrity, and responsiveness are not intrinsic

properties of the modern state, but problematic goals; yet competency, rationality, and efficacy—in short, capacity as we understand it—are indispensable attributes of a state if any of the other
aims are to be accomplished.

These six criteria offer an exceedingly broad normative charter for evaluation of regime performance. It would be utopian to
expect that any state can simultaneously optimize its achievement of all six objectives. Even if growth and equality are not
fundamentally incompatible, particular policy contexts may
force a choice between the two. Relatively extensive participation may exclude policy options that appear attractive by growth
criteria. The high growth strategy of Ivory Coast, in close alliance with the former metropole, does require some sacrifice of
autonomy.

Further, all six of these criteria are multiplex and not—in
my judgment—reducible to valid measurement by a single numerical indicator, or even a cluster of them. My appraisals will be
qualitative, based upon as broad a set of monographic, statistical,
and interview data as possible. The evaluation is thus indisputably subjective, not objective, as it might appear if concealed
by apparently rigorous but really quite unreliable mathematical
indicators.

To pursue the examination of ideology and performance, I
shall then turn successively to the three main streams I have
identified: Afro-Marxist, populist socialist, and market-economy
capitalist. For each of these, I shall delineate salient dimensions
of the ideological perspective, suggest the policy preferences
that flow from the doctrine, and then examine some representative cases. The international implications of ideological choice
will be explored by considering its effect upon external links
with the Soviet Union and the United States as leading representatives of East and West. In my conclusions, I shall return to the
six performance criteria to draw up a tentative balance sheet.

I am acutely aware of the inadequacy of any single analyst

for a task so broadly defined; these reflections—imperfect and tentative—are set forth as a contribution to an ongoing debate. I am likewise sensitive to the fact that my particular value premises—in this instance, a set of Western liberal perspectives—inevitably intrude upon much of the analysis. All the more important, then, is it for those who would approach the task with an alternative orientation to complete this appraisal.

2

The Rise of the Afro-Marxist Regime

THE NEW WAVE OF THIRD-WORLD
MARXIST-LENINIST STATES

A new era in the history of world socialism opened in December 1961 when Fidel Castro declared in Havana, "I am a Marxist-Leninist." In contrast to the revolutionary struggles in China and Vietnam, which were carried out by Communist movements, that of Castro had triumphed when the profoundly corrupt old order of Batista crumbled before the 26 of July Movement, which had never formulated its call to arms in Marxist language. The Cuban Communist Party, deeply compromised in the *ancien régime*, had offered only belated, eleventh-hour support to the Castro insurrection when its success seemed imminent. Marxism-Leninism was then simply declared from the summit, a fact that continues to flavor the Cuban experience to this day, however significant Soviet aid and the Moscow model of socialist transformation subsequently became.[1]

The proclamation of a Marxist-Leninist state in Congo-Brazzaville by the new military junta of Marien Ngouabi carried the process a step further. The declaration of revolutionary faith was made without the benefit of a regular Communist party or a revolutionary movement. It was simply the pronunciamento of a military junta. The same pattern appeared again, in Somalia (1970), Benin (1974), and Madagascar and Ethiopia (1975–76)—a trend seen as quite malignant by former Secretary of State Henry Kissinger. A roughly comparable process led to the emergence of self-declared Marxist-Leninist regimes in South Yemen and Afghanistan.

A somewhat different form of Marxist-Leninist state incubated in the long, bitter struggle against Portuguese colonial rule. (We may note the contrast with the Algerian revolution, where an equally prolonged and militarily even more intense combat did crystallize a strong socialist engagement, but never Marxism-Leninism.) The dominant liberation movements were not—as in Vietnam—Communist parties that launched an insurrection. They were nationalist movements that numbered some Marxist-Leninist intellectuals among their leadership and over time developed a Marxist-Leninist orientation. But Marxism-Leninism was not officially declared—in Mozambique and Angola—until the congresses of the ruling parties in 1977. Taking these two types of Afro-Marxist states together, we see that within the space of a decade nearly 20 percent of African states had adopted such a self-definition. While there have been no new instances since the major wave in 1974–75, there seems every possibility that such regimes may appear again in the future, not only in Africa but in West Asia and the Caribbean. This new species of polity is, accordingly, of considerable interest.[2]

THE STALINIST MODEL OF THE THIRD WORLD

If we compare this new third-world Marxist-Leninist polity with older Asian Communist states, major differences at once stand out. In the cases of Mongolia and North Korea, Soviet military force played a crucial role in the establishment of a Communist order. In Mongolia, extensive coercion was required in the first two decades to destroy and subdue what were seen as hostile sources of social power: the Buddhist monasteries and the herding clans.[3] In North Korea, the collapse of the Japanese occupation and its replacement by the Soviet army offered a clear field to the small and fragmented Korean Communist Party in its lunge to socialism; large landholdings and industrial ownership were primarily Japanese, so socialization of the economy could be undertaken without confronting powerful indigenous groups. Those who did oppose had an open gate to the American-occupied south, which further reduced potential resistance; the new order was created and consolidated quickly.[4]

In China, a hardened, dynamic, and powerful Chinese Communist Party had generated sufficient power and support during the two decades of struggle to carry through its revolutionary blueprint. The same was true in North Vietnam, which, like China, in its first years used a Leninist political superstructure to impose a Stalinist socialist economy. Throughout the period in which these new regimes pursued their revolutionary aims, the concept of a single world socialist movement and model still held sway. Accordingly, the Soviet model was of great influence—however much the Chinese were subsequently to deviate from it.

The Cuban experience in building a Communist society was not only unique in its origins, but also occurred in the context of the deepening fissures dividing the Soviet Union and China. In its early years, Cuban policy fluctuated considerably and experimented freely; it was by no means the conventional Stalinist model that had been used earlier by new Communist regimes. Until 1968, Castro exploited the Sino–Soviet rivalry and, while never wavering in his Marxist-Leninist commitment, retained substantial autonomy despite being totally dependent on Soviet aid. In 1968, the Soviets used the leverage of their oil supplies to impose a somewhat more orthodox (from their perspective) strategy of socialist development. What has become consolidated in the 1970s is an intricate symbiosis of Comecon prescription and Cuban distinctiveness.[5]

The family of Communist states in Indochina in 1975 emerged in a still different environment, with consequences that are only beginning to be apparent for the world socialist movement. In South Vietnam, the triumphant revolutionary leadership encountered a society not only ravaged but heavily transformed by the long war. Large and quite powerful social groups—the Sino-Vietnamese mercantile community, urban middle classes, capitalist rice farmers in the delta, Buddhist sects, and Catholic groups—were refractory to the Stalinist socialism that had been built in the north. The peculiarly distorted infrastructure of war capitalism that grew in the shadow of the enormous American military intervention proved difficult either to uproot or replace.[6] In 1964, flight to the south provided an escape valve. By 1978, the deepening crisis of socialism in Vietnam was reflected in the tragedy of the "boat people" and the revelation that a Vietnamese *gulag archipelago* held as many as 800,000 involuntary residents.[7]

Further questions about the viability of the Marxist-Leninist orthodox model in very underdeveloped societies with weak Communist parties were raised by the fate of Laos and Cambodia. While the quasi-Vietnamese protectorate regime in Laos could preserve its control, it found that building socialism was an arduous task. In Cambodia, the small cohort of Khmer Rouge cadres who seized power in 1975 attempted to impose their own vision of socialist transformation through unparalleled brutality and terror. The sanguinary socialism of Pol Pot was replaced in 1979 by a Vietnamese-imposed substitute whose prospects were at best problematic.

SCIENTIFIC SOCIALISM FACED WITH ECLECTICISM

Thus a crucial prologue to the birth of the Afro-Marxist state has been the decay of the once-authoritative, virtually compulsory Soviet model. The formerly monolithic Soviet bloc has fragmented. Once formidable machinery for enforcing ideological uniformity within the Marxist-Leninist world has disintegrated; Comecon is a pale reflection of the Comintern and Cominform. A diversity of patterns of the Marxist-Leninist state has emerged.

This is not to suggest that the Soviet version of Marxism-Leninism is of no consequence. On the contrary; not only is the Soviet Union by far the most powerful and internationally active Communist state, it is the only one that actively seeks to promote its own model. Though Yugoslavia, China, and Cuba have actively pursued foreign policy goals in Africa, they have never promoted adoption of their own particular blueprints for socialism.[8]

This fact has important consequences. The fabric of ideology is woven from many different threads. West European Communist parties—especially the French and Portuguese—have been an important source. Although both of these have been Stalinist in their party structure and fidelity to Soviet interests, the teachers and intellectuals who were the major intermediaries did not necessarily transmit Marxism-Leninism in its most ossified Soviet form. Further, Marxism was received through many more channels than simply Communist parties; African students and sojourners in Europe were attracted to the broad ideological discourse of the European left. Of increasing importance, in the last two decades, have been the currents of thought encountered in radical anti-imperialist third-world milieux. From these quite varied sources the ideology of the Afro-Marxist state took shape.

Indeed, the possibility of eclecticism may well have been a prerequisite for the emergence of the African Marxist-Leninist state. Jowitt makes this point:

. . . the particular designation "scientific socialist" or "Marxist-Leninist" may appeal to certain African elites precisely because an authoritative center no longer exists within the Leninist group of regimes. . . . The absence of an authoritative center of Leninism comparable to the Communist Party of the Soviet Union under Stalin allows self-designated "scientific socialist" African elites *to avoid the hard identity choice of bloc alignment internationally and exclusive political choices domestically* [emphasis in the original].[9]

By 1975, formal espousal of Marxism-Leninism neither implied an abandonment of official nonalignment, through exclusive and privileged relations with the Soviet bloc, nor did it require an automatic commitment to a particular set of policies.

THE COMMON THEMES IN AFRO-MARXISM

The triumph of eclecticism means that the new wave of Afro-Marxist regimes is not homogeneous in ideological interpretation or policy practice, as we shall see in examining the various cases. Several common themes, however, give some coherence to the experience, both in demarcating these regimes from most others in Africa, socialist and nonsocialist, and in distinguishing them from Marxist-Leninist states in other parts of the world. The most salient of these themes is the application of Leninist theory to the organization of state and party.

In sharp contrast to the populist mass single parties that characterized earlier African socialist (and some nonsocialist) regimes, the parties of the Afro-Marxist state are Leninist in conception: they are an organizational weapon theoretically manned by a revolutionary vanguard of the ideologically select, incarnating the will of the workers and peasants. The party is accorded supremacy over the state, which it dominates both through defining its political choices and penetrating its key organs through party cells.

In reality, the Leninist concept immediately encounters the contradictions posed by the origins of these regimes. For those germinating in military cliques, the army is quite ambivalent about placing full power in the hands of a party that is not a simple emanation of the junta. Further, the Marxist political field is partly preempted by radical civilian movements espousing leftist perspectives. It is in practice very difficult to disperse these formations, especially to secure their voluntary self-effacement before a monopolistic political instrument under military hegemony. In 1980, this problem had still prevented the formation of a single Leninist party in Ethiopia, and impeded its attainment of exclusive political leadership in Madagascar.

In the case of the national liberation movements, there was a wrenching identity transformation involved in the metamorphosis from mass populist organization into Leninist party. Indeed, the most effective of the liberation movements, the *Partido Africano da Independência da Guiné e Cabo Verde* (PAIGC), at the first postindependence congress in 1977 explicitly rejected a proposal to espouse Marxism-Leninism formally. It was the colonial experience that was the critical reference point for the liberation movements, and not class struggle per se—even though the most intellectually powerful of the heroes of this struggle, Amilcar Cabral, used Marxist categories of social analysis.[10] The mobilization of the entire population against colonial oppression is the essence of the national liberation struggle. Even the *Frente de Libertação de Mozambique* (FRELIMO), which did begin to move toward a Leninist self-concept from 1970 on, did not officially proclaim it until 1977.[11] The sharp distinction between the ideologically elect party militant and the mere supporter, on the one hand, and reactionary and retrograde elements within the society, on the other, ruptures the populist notion of an undivided people in arms.

In different ways, both the military and the national liberation Marxist-Leninist state faced the problem of according a central place to the armed forces far beyond what classical Leninism would admit. Neither army junta nor freedom fighters could be expected simply to efface themselves before a purely political and ideological set of cadres. Neither the barracks nor the guerrilla battlefield was likely to germinate philosophically pure ideological warriors.

The nature of the social base claimed for the Afro-Marxist state is one of its major ambiguities. While the concept of the worker and peasant state receives appropriate deference—probably most markedly in Mozambique, where the 1977 FRELIMO

Congress adopted the standard East European slogans extolling the proletarian dictatorship—in reality the working class is invariably small, lacking in class identity, and often dominated by state employees. Workers played little role in the establishment of the military Marxist regimes or in the armed liberation struggle in Guinea-Bissau and Mozambique. Guinea-Bissau—which does not speak of proletarian rule—is an extreme case; the industrial labor force was a mere 1,800, most of whom were employed in Bissau, which remained under full Portuguese control until liberation. Organized workers have proved to be a turbulent and refractory group in Congo-Brazzaville and Ethiopia.

The dominant social group in the Afro-Marxist states is what Soviet analysts have called "revolutionary democrats"—political figures, intellectuals, teachers—who are neither tied directly to capitalism nor allied with it as agents of multinational capital; they are prepared to lay the foundations for socialism by following a noncapitalist path of development.[12] To a significant degree, the pressures for ideological radicalism come from a "youth" phenomenon, particularly in Congo-Brazzaville, Benin, Madagascar, and to some extent Ethiopia. Relatively large, well-educated urban youth cohorts in the first three states are highly politicized and face an uncertain professional future. Marxist commitment may become interlocked with regional divisiveness as well; this relationship stands out clearly in Congo-Brazzaville and Angola and to some extent in Benin and Ethiopia.

In terms of socialization of the means of production, there is a consistent thrust to gain control of the "commanding heights" of the economy, thereby creating a "socialist sector" that is designed to serve as motor for state direction of the economy. Foreign ownership of banks and insurance companies is a universal target; socialization of these institutions is held to be critical to control and direct capital flows. These are ideologically appealing targets, and they pose only modest compensation problems because their actual assets are small. To a significant extent, the hostile referent is colonialism more than capitalism. Virtually all

the Afro-Marxist states have proclaimed their desire to attract
new Western capital, and large capital undertakings have frequently been spared; Gulf Oil in Angola is one spectacular example. In 1980, both Mozambique and Angola made dramatic new
overtures to external capital and even declared their welcome for
petty commercial traders.

Comprehensive central planning on the Soviet model is
completely beyond the administrative capacity of the Afro-Marxist state, even of those—such as Benin and Congo-Brazzaville—
that have a large and relatively competent pool of bureaucrats.
The overwhelming pressures of immediate economic crisis—
meeting the next state payroll, supplying the capital with foods,
coping with huge foreign exchange deficits—mean that the dream
of the command socialist economy is far removed from the reality of the desperately improvised crisis-management state.

With the exceptions of Ethiopia and Mozambique, the Afro-
Marxist state has been exceedingly cautious in promoting socialist agriculture. The well-known failure of earlier collective production efforts in Mali and Guinea, the evident lack of rural
interest in such measures, and the weakness of the bureaucratic
and coercive structures that would have to impose and manage
such policies are all incentives to prudence. The truly revolutionary land reform in Ethiopia was by far the most significant
experiment in rural transformation, though these measures were
undertaken in early 1975, more than a year before the regime announced its conversion to Marxism-Leninism. The model of Soviet collectivization played no part in inspiring this move. However, because it did strike at the economic underpinnings of
entrenched social hierarchies, Soviet diplomats, according to the
Ottaways, concluded that "the Ethiopian military were carrying
out a revolution very similar to the Soviet one, with its overthrow of a feudal monarch, its bypassing of a bourgeois revolution to plunge headlong into a socialist one, and with a real element of class struggle that was lacking in Somalia." [13]

There are several points on which the African Marxist-Leninist state is clearly deviant from the orthodox model. One list is put forward by a Soviet analyst, P. I. Manchkha, who chides "some revolutionary democrats [who] treat socialism not as a historically inevitable social and economic formation but only as the most effective method of eliminating age-old backwardness and bondage to the imperialist metropolitan countries." Afro-Marxists are said to lack an adequate appreciation of the centrality of the working class, the necessity for a party based on a "correct" line, the universal features of socialist revolution, and the requirement of a confrontational attitude toward religion.[14] Colonialism rather than class struggle remains the defining referent. The "revolutionary democrats" who are vehicles for African Marxism are rooted in the political-administrative bourgeoisie whose emergence was noted long ago by Frantz Fanon and René Dumont. Afro-Marxism has a vocation of eclecticism and is refractory to "correct" lines. The fraternal identity ties are with third-world radical anti-imperialism, not "proletarian internationalism." There is no taste for mortal combat with religion, though there may well be battles with church hierarchies (Angola, Mozambique) or Muslim notables (Somalia).

Afro-Marxist states generally have extensive ties with Communist states and adopt similar positions on many issues in international forums. Indeed, in some respects ideological orientation can have freest rein in the foreign policy sphere, particularly in United Nations votes. Relative to the painful choices in domestic policy, positions in the international realm may permit more cost-free expression of doctrinal orientation. However, none have abandoned the claim to be "nonaligned," even though this doctrine tends to be interpreted in ways close to the Cuban position in third-world forums.

In the economic sphere, there are severe limits to the possibilities for close incorporation in the "socialist camp." Soviet aid, always parsimonious, has been decreasing. The Soviets have little interest in most African primary commodities, and Soviet products are generally uncompetitive. Soviet technology lags and

is wholly deficient in such crucial areas as offshore oil development. Thus historical patterns of economic relationship, trade
necessities, and the desire for resource development schemes requiring capital and technology all reinforce the disposition of the
Afro-Marxist states to retain links with the Western economic
system.

CONGO-BRAZZAVILLE: DEAN OF THE AFRO-MARXIST STATES

With the portrait of the African Marxist-Leninist state thus
sketched, we may now begin a closer examination of particular
cases. I shall first consider the group of military Marxists, then
turn to those that issue from national liberation movements.
Congo-Brazzaville, as the dean of the Afro-Marxist states, is entitled to first treatment.

The sociological parameters of this Marxist republic are immediately striking.[15] There is a powerful youth culture in the
country, product of a high degree of urbanization, and a dense
educational network. By 1970, some 42 percent of the population
lived in towns with populations over 25,000.[16] Since the 1950s,
Congo-Brazzaville has had the highest rate of schooling of all the
former French territories. A 1972 urban survey showed that only
16 percent of the bottom social strata—the unemployed—were
illiterate.[17] The youth culture is thoroughly politicized, a phenomenon that extends into the countryside.[18] This politization is
both sustained by and reflected in a series of turbulent youth
associations, where the ideological tone is intense.

Even the casual visitor to Brazzaville is at once struck by the
innumerable contradictions of the People's Republic. The red
flag of socialism floats aloft, while the supermarket below over-
flows with Rhodesian beef and elegant French cheeses. Slogans
adorn the walls, as in Eastern Europe, but their content is
not very Marxist: eternal glory to the fallen comrade Marien

Ngouabi, down with corruption, long live the work ешис
rhetorical level of the state media is shrill; the private conversa-
tion of ranking government officials is relaxed and moderate.
Ideological spokesmen hurl thunderbolts at capitalism and imperialism, while economic delegations tour Western financial
centers, assuring would-be investors that these imprecations are
only verbal. Marxism-Leninism is at once ubiquitous and evanescent. Yet however detached they may seem from reality, Marxian dialectics are conducted on a highly sophisticated level.

The first independent government in Brazzaville was the
very model of neocolonialism: corrupt, incompetent, and a
toady to French interests. In August 1963, the Brazzaville youth
took to the streets, and in three days the Fulbert Youlou regime
dissolved, an embarrassment even to its Lari ethnic clientele and
French patrons. The successor regime, under Alphonse Massemba-Débat, declared itself to be socialist, aligned itself with
the more radical bloc of African states, and developed active ties
with the Soviet Union, China, and Cuba.

Though an apparently monist policy was achieved through
the imposition of a single national party, the *Mouvement National de la Révolution* (MNR), in reality the Massemba-Débat
period saw incessant conspiracy and unrest. While the regime
never declared itself to be Marxist-Leninist, there was a strong
Marxist left within the fluid constellation of factions. Factionalism, ideological, regional, and personal, was extended into the
armed forces and youth movements through indoctrination campaigns and clandestine scheming, abetted by a generous flow of
funds from interested foreign embassies. The MNR youth was a
particularly unruly body. Used as a power base by the ambitious
Interior Minister André Hombessa, it was involved in a 1966
putsch attempt and eventually became a Kongo-dominated paramilitary band of thugs, resented and feared.

In a curious and complex chemistry, ideological politics became intertwined with ethnicity. Cultural cleavage in the Congo
had initially become salient in the 1950s with the introduction of

competitive politics, and first revolved around the central duality in the capital itself between immigrants from the south
(Lari-Kongo) and north ("Mbochi"). The political conflict of
the 1950s did largely hinge upon this division, with Jacques
Opangault standing for the north and Youlou for the south. The
serious riots in Brazzaville in 1959 essentially pitted Lari against
Mbochi.

However, the ethnic reality was really much more complex
than this simple north–south dichotomy suggested. After 1960
competition was no longer carried out through electoral mobilization—which tended to polarize the populace along this single fault line—and was less dominated by the social arena of
Brazzaville itself, making underlying complexities of ethnic affiliation more manifest. The Kongo category in the south divided
into three major components: 1) the Lari, whose homeland lay in
the Brazzaville area itself and the nearby hinterland and who
recognized their affinities with Kongo language and culture but
always used the "Lari" self-label; they were heavily represented
in the ranks of the educated (and thus were numerous in the senior bureaucratic categories) and predominant among the small
Congolese merchant community; 2) the "Kongo" proper, who
considered their most direct linguistic and historical attachments to be with the ancient Kingdom of the Kongo (and Kongo
communities in neighboring Zaire and Angola); and 3) the Vili
and other coastal groups, for whom Pointe Noire was the major
social field; their historic attachments had been to the Kingdom
of Loango rather than Kongo, and their identification with the
concept of a greater Kongo culture was ambivalent, contingent,
and situational. Youlou was a son of the Lari; Massemba-Débat
was from a small Kongo subgroup close to yet distinct from the
Lari.

"Mbochi" is a somewhat synthetic label that in Brazzaville
came to refer broadly to northerners in general, whose urban language was generally Lingala. In reality, the north is inhabited
by several small groups that do not have the same degree of cul-

tural and historical affinities as the Kongo. These include Teke, Kouyou, Sangha, and Makaa, in addition to Mbochi per se. Of the three northern heads of state since 1968, Ngouabi and Denis Sasso Nguesso were Kouyou, while Joachim Yhombi-Opango was a Lari born in the northern regional center of Fort Rousset.[19] In Brazzaville, they were all considered northerners.

Ngouabi during much of the Massemba-Débat period was regarded as a moderate. In 1966, he had been demoted and rusticated for opposing moves to indoctrinate the army politically, provoking a mutiny by Kouyou-Mbochi soldiers personally loyal to him. The demotion was rescinded, and Ngouabi regained control over the Brazzaville paracommando faction. However, the Massemba-Débat regime—perhaps more accurately, some elements within it—began promoting two paramilitary formations, the JMNR (MNR Youth) and a party militia. While these revolutionary instruments were initially unpaid, soon many of the members, particularly the officials, were receiving salaries, housing, and subsidies from East European embassies. The JMNR, 35,000 strong by 1968, was an unruly but potent body. The party militia, which received Cuban military training, numbered 2,000, nearly matching the army itself. The Ngouabi takeover in August 1968 was above all a corporate response of the army to the increasing threat to its role and even its existence posed by the growing paramilitary strength of the JMNR and the party militia.[20] The seizure of power required a bloody assault on the hard core of the JMNR militia, with the result that 100 of its 300 members were killed. The coup was also a response to personal threat; on its eve Massemba-Débat, in a final desperate effort to purge his enemies, again arrested Ngouabi—who was promptly released by his Kouyou troops.

The new military regime of Ngouabi, who posthumously was the object of an extraordinary personality cult, survived its first years in an atmosphere of permanent conspiracy. In 1969, as part of the arduous task of consolidating his power, Ngouabi swept away the MNR and declared the Congo to be a People's Republic, guided by Marxism-Leninism, with a new Leninist party, the *Parti Congolais du Travail* (PCT). Ngouabi became an eloquent master of Marxist-Leninist rhetoric, which was a patina over his quite moderate personal convictions. As Decalo aptly puts it, "Ngouabi not only mastered the jargon but also the Byzantine intricacies of developing a radical dialectic while holding centrist positions and purging the true militants in the political system."[21]

The army remained throughout the uncertain pillar of the regime. Ngouabi moved to eliminate the fragmentation of armed force by dismantling the paramilitary political formations and absorbing some of them into the army. The gendarmerie, whose personnel were mostly Lari, became a focal point of dissidence. The unrest culminated in the coup attempt by Lari Lieutenant Ange Diawara, undertaken in defense of what was then generally labeled Maoism.

The new Marxist-Leninist republic reflected a sharp shift in the regional balance of power. The key organs of power since 1969, the PCT Politbureau and the army high command, have always been heavily northern, with nominal Lari and Kongo representation. Ngouabi sought to give himself a better foothold in the predominately southern civil service by purging a number of senior Lari and Kongo officials as "counterrevolutionaries" or "bourgeois deviationists," thereby opening slots for northern nominees.[22]

The ideological discontinuity between the Massemba-Débat and People's Republic eras was not as sharp as the shift to official Marxism-Leninism might suggest. Creation of the Marxist state was not really the triumph of one ideological socialist faction over another, but is perhaps better understood as a method by which Ngouabi could, in the symbolic domain, clearly demarcate his regime from its predecessor. It provided the pretext for the replacement of the MNR by the PCT and justified the claim that the military regime had ushered in a new order. It partially preempted the strident claims of the ultrapoliticized social

forces of the urban arena that incumbents were betraying socialism and compromising with imperialism.

However, regime affirmations of Marxist-Leninist faith never
sufficed to defuse and co-opt the turbulent youth culture. A student leader used the PCT Congress of 1974 as a forum to denounce the "neocolonial character of the state," which provoked
Ngouabi to denounce irresponsible "ultraleftism," dissolve the
student union, and threaten recalcitrant leaders with military
conscription.[23] The equally militant official union defied the government by calling a general strike on 24 March 1976; Ngouabi
angrily denounced the strike leaders as "opportunists, situa-
tionists, and bandits."[24] The PCT has never been able to really
control student, youth, or labor unions, though they are nominally its ancillary organs.

Despite the considerable efforts deployed to make the PCT a
dynamic, Leninist vanguard party, it remained a lethargic instrument. It did uphold Leninist principles of ideological selectivity;
a long probationary period and evidence of ideological purity
were required for membership. Its membership is in fact quite
small; in 1979 a ranking party cadre indicated there were only
3,000 full members. Endemic conspiracy necessitated frequent
purges of the party as well as the state. The most devastating of
these occurred in 1971–72 in the wake of the Diawara uprising.
No fewer than 176 persons were convicted of treasonous action,
23 receiving death sentences (subsequently commuted); the
party Central Committee was reduced to 5 members and the Po-
litburo to 3. Total membership at this juncture was no more than
160.[25]

Beginning in the Massemba-Débat years, a relatively extensive socialized sector was created. Import–export trade was
taken over, and state marketing monopolies were created for agricultural produce and forestry products: *Office Nationale de
Commercialisation des Produits Agricoles* (ONCPA) and *Office
Congolais du Bois* (OCB). Oil palm plantations were partly taken
over, as were petroleum distribution networks and the sugar in-

dustry. Meanwhile, a new socialist industrial sector was to be created, particularly with the help of Communist states. In the late 1960s, a cement, a textile, and a match factory were constructed; by 1979 the first two of these had suspended production and were bankrupt. In 1975, insurance companies and some banks were nationalized.

Another measurable impact of the socialist commitment, as well as of the potency of political pressures originating in the urban sector, was a relatively high level of wages. According to ILO figures, real minimum wages increased 75.5 percent between 1963 and 1974, a figure second only to that of Libya among the twenty-one African states surveyed.[26] The Congo had a per capita income of $510 in 1976, a figure somewhat inflated by significant oil production and a small total population.[27]

However, the practical limits of the socialist strategy were nowhere clearer than in Congo-Brazzaville. Despite the intensity of the ideological onslaught against the colonial legacy, in fact French influence remained quite strong. The number of French residents—about 10,000—was the same as in the 1950s. Offshore oil exploitation was dominated by the French corporation ELF, though AGIP also had a concession. Potash mines, which once were regarded with high hopes as generators of state revenue, were ceded to a mainly French corporation in 1969, with the Congolese state retaining only 15 percent ownership. The forestry industry, until the People's Republic era the largest exporter, remained essentially French despite repeated efforts to bring it to heel. In 1978, the four French logging companies produced two-thirds of the output, while the deficit-ridden state enterprises managed only 8 percent. The OCB, intended to secure for the Congolese states the trading profits once accruing to foreign producers and intermediaries, was not really capable of performing this task; many of the logs purchased from the French logging companies had to be simply sold back to them for export.[28] By and large, French firms that were taken over were marginal and ailing. French private interests continued to flourish in Brazzaville.

France has remained the major source of external aid. The Soviet Union has proved a remarkably stingy friend outside the security field: Soviet economic aid from 1963 to 1977 totaled only $14 million, and no new grants were made in 1976 or 1977.[29] Further, Congo-Brazzaville has remained within the franc zone, which means that monetary policy is largely beyond the reach of the state. In particular, the impossibility of obtaining forced advances from the central bank has shielded the country from hyperinflation, while the integration within a Central African monetary community (Cameroon, Gabon, Chad, Central African Republic, and Congo) has forestalled foreign exchange crises. French influence through the apparatus of the franc zone, while weaker than it once was, is still substantial.

The public sector, far from being an engine of socialist construction, was a calamitous drain. By the early 1970s, state corporations required annual subsidies of 4 billion CFA annually.[30] Bertrand, a Marxist scholar, delivers a harsh verdict on the socialist sector:

While the productive sector of the State began to take form from 1968 on, the hold of the bureaucratic and tribal oligarchy is such that, far from constituting for the political leadership an economic instrument permitting them to overcome foreign economic domination, it is rapidly becoming a source of financial strangulation which daily threatens the country with bankruptcy, tying more than ever the hands of those who would like to transform the country through the State structures.[31]

Ngouabi was no less forthright in denouncing the performance of public enterprise in 1976, imputing its abysmal results to "imperialism allied to the apathy of administrators. . . . corruption and embezzlement have reached disquieting proportions in these enterprises."[32]

In many respects, the fundamental contradiction of the People's Republic was the state itself. Not only was the parastatal

TABLE 2.1. Expansion of the State, Congo-Brazzaville

Sector	Number of employees		
	1960	1963	1972
General services	1,437	2,385	6,710
Infrastructure	136	299	1,266
Social services	1,300	3,940	10,347
Education	(500)	(2,890)	(6,853)
Economic services	170	359	2,230
Army, police	436	3,715	4,474
Total	3,479	10,698	25,027

SOURCE: Hugues Bertrand, Le Congo (Paris: Maspero, 1975), p. 255.

sector huge, but the machinery of the state itself expanded at a formidable pace; by the early 1970s the civil service accounted for 26 percent of all wage employment and the state corporations another 27 percent. The phenomenal rate of state expansion is shown in table 2.1.

A striking example of the pathological expansion of the state lay in the agricultural sector. There was a tenfold expansion in the number of people employed by the state agriculture service; in 1972, 636 of 1,677 extension agents lived in Brazzaville. By 1971, salaries for the agricultural service exceeded the total cash income of the 600,000 peasants.[33] The impact of this intensified encadrement on production appeared generally negative; as table 2.2 shows, recorded production of most cash crops fell during this period (although it improved subsequently). Meanwhile, output appeared to increase in such staples as manioc and palm wine, both of which fall outside the state encadrement, regulatory, and marketing network. Not only was the state encadrement a net burden upon the farmers, but the marketing monopolies also were a clear obstacle. Rather than transfer former private trader marketing profits to the state in new revenue or to the farmers in better prices, these resources simply accrued to the ONCPA staff. Faced with operating losses in spite of its monop-

TABLE 2.2. Agricultural Output, Congo-Brazzaville

Crop	Production (in metric tons)			
	1964	1967	1970	1977
Peanuts	6,400	6,300	4,000	24,000
Palm oil	4,400	4,100	3,300	5,400
Palm kernels	6,200	4,100	1,900	600
Coffee	1,500	1,900	1,400	1,000
Cocoa	900	1,200	1,300	2,000
Tobacco	470	750	740	
Rice	1,600	1,500	1,900	8,000
Value to peasants (millions CFA)	687	543	645	

SOURCE: Hugues Bertrand, *Le Congo* (Paris: Maspero, 1975), for 1964–70, p. 187; *Marchés Tropicaux et Mediterranéan* 1756 (6 July 1979) for 1977.

oly, the ONCPA retrenched by abandoning less profitable sectors and raising its own operating margins on the sectors remaining. From 1967 to 1971 the value of its sales rose from 582 million to 707 million CFA, while the total paid to peasant producers fell from 364 million to 321 million.[34]

In the face of the general stagnation of the productive sector, the growing numbers of people pouring from the educational system generate intense pressures on the state to provide employment. The precarious hold on power of successive regimes has intensified this pressure, which cannot all be decanted into ideological discourse. A major vulnerability of the state enterprise sector is the difficulty of avoiding overstaffing. Typical of the state enterprise plight was the Chinese-built textile factory, which in its first year of operation, 1970, had a value added of 210 million CFA but a wage bill of 320 million.[35] The timber industry was forced to employ the same number of workers in 1978 as in the early 1960s to produce half as many logs. Wages doubled during this period, while output per worker was half its earlier level.[36]

The consequence of the huge expansion of the state and the

mediocrity of public sector performance has been a chronic fiscal crisis. The monthly payroll was a recurrent trauma, requiring one desperate expedient after another. The payroll crisis began in earnest by 1969 and eased only briefly in 1974–75, when the sudden surge in oil prices, as well as new potash production, generated a sharp increase in state revenues. However, in 1976–78 oil output fell far short of expectations and the potash mines encountered serious technical problems, then were completely destroyed by floods in 1977. The failure of ELF to sustain anticipated oil production levels and the closure of the potash mines led to bitter recriminations. Congolese authorities charged that a capitalist conspiracy was afoot to strangle the socialist revolution.[37]

The tremendous pressures on the state to sustain a revenue flow forced it to turn anxiously to Western capital. With agriculture at an impasse and forestry in decline, only extractive mineral development schemes held any prospect of resolving the fiscal crisis. Thus the Marxist state proposed an investment code that was more liberal than those of many market-economy states. The overdeveloped state itself proved to be an engine of dependency, not of socialism, much less of development.

The Congo-Brazzaville leadership took seriously the task of self-criticism, and the most pungent and candid assessments of the difficulties faced by the state came from regime spokesmen. At the end of 1975, the PCT Central Committee devoted a week-long session to identifying the ills undermining the country. Their conclusions were a severe indictment, blaming "weakness of party leadership, lack of liaison between the leadership and the Party and between the Party and the masses, the irresponsibility of the trade unions, the inflexibility of the State apparatus, the weakness of the State economic sector, the frantic race for material advantages, the excessive number of workers in State enterprises and the incompetence and irresponsibility of cadres. . . ."[38]

BENIN: STABILITY UNDER SCIENTIFIC SOCIALISM

While the Congo-Brazzaville option for Marxism-Leninism was a gradual ideological deepening of a socialist trend that began in 1963, the proclamation of a worker and peasant republic in Benin in 1974 was both a dramatic ideological reversal and a complete surprise. Benin (formerly Dahomey) resembles Congo-Brazzaville in the size of its intellectual elite; Beninians, in the 1950s, were to be found in skilled roles throughout francophonic West Africa. As in Brazzaville, the pressures to absorb this abundant and talented elite have led to the formation of a large state apparatus. However, Benin lacks the extraordinary urbanization that marks Congo-Brazzaville. The coastal centers of Cotonou and Porto Novo are modest in size, and there are no other substantial cities.

In the first dozen years of independence, ideology played almost no overt role in politics; socialism was never a regime commitment, nor were significant differences discernible in the policy orientation of the five civilian and four military regimes that passed through the portals of power. Some were effective, some austere, some competent—but the permanent instability of the country was its most striking characteristic. With a relatively large bureaucracy and a very modest economy, the state was in chronic fiscal crisis. Unions, representing primarily the public sector, were aggressive in pursuing their claims; France, the primary financial sponsor of the deficit-ridden state, gradually reduced its subsidies. Governance was essentially the art of reconciling the contradictory pressures for budgetary austerity on the one hand and mollifying state employees on the other. Room for maneuver in this continuous balancing act was narrow, and success only fleeting.

Power was rendered all the more precarious by the pervasive impact of regional cleavages. Electoral civilian politics had crystallized a triangular regional power struggle, with Hubert

Maga (north), Sourou-Migan Apithy (Yoruba), and Justin Aho-
madegbe (Fon) as the three corners. The southern Fon and Yoruba, though bitterly antagonistic toward each other, shared a
relatively advantaged social status in comparison with the neglected north. Even in 1967, school attendance rates ranged from
90 percent in Cotonou to a mere 13 percent in the far northwest.
These figures necessarily translated into heavy southern predominance in the upper ranks of the state apparatus.[39]

Overlying the regional cleavages that shaped civilian political competition were the complex divisions within the highly
fragmented armed forces. Initially, the senior officer corps of the
small armed forces was primarily Fon, while the enlisted ranks
were heavily northern. The regional animosities dividing civilian politicians soon brought military intervention and the politization of the army hierarchy. Factionalism in the armed forces
was more fluid than in the civilian realm. Rank, generation,
ideology, and personal ambitions defined the shifting military
cliques, which yielded intramural struggles so intense that at
some points the military seemed on the verge of disintegration.[40]
The praetorian mood of the armed forces, in the years of instability, became steadily more salient. In Decalo's words, "Without
clearly defined garrison and defense duties and responsibilities, the very briefly ingrained colonial tradition of the army as
'grande muette'—the silent apolitical prop of legitimate political
authority—became transformed into the concept of the military
as arbiters of political power and, later still, the source of political legitimacy."[41]

Following the third return of power to civilian leaders, a
more permanent military power seizure occurred in October
1972, led by then-Major Mathieu Kerekou, commander of the key
paracommando unit based at the strategically located Ouidah
garrison. Kerekou surprised the government by leading his detachments along the beach into the heart of the capital. The army,
it was said, was not merely intervening to mediate a civilian impasse but taking back the power it had given to the civilians.[42]

Kerekou, who comes from the small Somba group in the far northwest, directed the coup partly against the mainly Fon army colonels. However, key coconspirators—particularly Captain Janvier Assogba and Captain Michel Aikpe—were Fon. The ruling military group became more heavily northern in coloration from 1975 on, when Assogba was eliminated for plotting, while Aikpe—initially viewed as the "strong man" of the regime—was killed in a sordid encounter in which purportedly he was discovered in a tryst with Kerekou's estranged wife.[43]

By the 1970s, the lexicon of dissidence, particularly among the unions and above all the leftist student union, the *Union Générale des Etudiants et des Elèves Dahoméens* (UGEED), had become radicalized. The union militants and students were drawn primarily from the coastal areas. Their more radical critique of the ills besetting Benin had percolated into some of the junior ranks of the officer corps and was shared by a small number of politicians and intellectuals. However, there was no sign of a new ideological departure when Kerekou seized power. Decalo, who interviewed a number of the ranking military officers a few months before the coup in 1972, found that none of these soldiers evinced any interest in socialism.[44]

Two years went by before socialism was declared to be the "chosen path" for Benin, with Marxism-Leninism as the "guide." The option was clearly not a carefully nurtured, long-standing intellectual commitment on the part of Kerekou, but rather born of more immediate contingencies: the permanent challenge of survival in this precarious polity. The choice for socialism is most comprehensible as an effort to lay claim to legitimacy for regime institutionalization. Disaffection with the endemic instability of Benin politics was high; Marxism-Leninism represented at least rhetorical innovation and a means of distinguishing the incumbent regime from the discredited past. It offered the hope of disarming the union and student militants, who decried the neocolonial subservience of successive Cotonou governments to French interests. It further might deflect southern resentments at the "northern domination" implicit in the Kerekou power configuration. In addition, the Marxist-Leninist option did not require, in the short run, a massive assault upon either domestic or external socioeconomic hierarchies. There were some Benin coastal mercantile interests, but nothing comparable to those in neighboring Nigeria; there was no really large foreign capital enterprise.

The Marxist-Leninist commitment was proclaimed on 30 November 1974 and was followed in 1975 by the creation of a Leninist party, the *Parti Révolutionnaire du Peuple Beninois* (PRPB). The guide to the future was inspired by such Marxist analysts of third-world "scientific socialism" as Charles Bettelheim, rather than by the classical Soviet texts.[45] In reality, the policies actually pursued fall well short of the prescriptions of Stalin, Mao, or Bettelheim.

The new Afro-Marxist state faced the same dilemma as Congo-Brazzaville. The military inner core of the regime had no intention of relinquishing power, though they did wish to acquire a civilian coloration; the first congress of the PRPB chose a civilian majority for the Central Committee.[46] Though union and student turbulence was reduced—there has been no rerun of the general strikes that brought down two former governments—restiveness continued. With a grand total of 5,500 industrial workers, a genuinely "proletarian" regime was out of the question.[47] The imposition of the "dictatorship of the militariat" brought a substantial exodus of intellectuals, civil servants, traders, and professionals to neighboring countries and to France. Most, however, remained, and found that the Kerekou regime had no stomach for class struggle and had neither the desire nor the apparatus to impose a harshly repressive political order.

In the economic sphere, the scientific socialist blueprint was partly implemented in 1975–76. In the industrial sector, the state wished to pursue a dual strategy: recuperate existing plant by forcible acquisition of 51 percent control, while enlarging the state role by creating new public corporations. In reality, the industrial sector was so inconsequential that there was little to nationalize; industry was a mere 7 percent of GNP.[48] Majority holdings were obtained in two textile factories, a ceramic plant, and a cement works; electricity and water, vegetable oil, and beverages were wholly nationalized. The state also took over banks, insurance, pharmaceuticals, oil product distribution, and hotels.

In the crucial trade sector—which accounted for a third of GNP—the state sought a commanding position by creating public monopolies in export and import commerce. In reality, these state offices were forced to operate through innumerable brokers, intermediaries, and agencies; the impact of socialized external trade was simply to insert a bureaucratic mechanism in what remained an essentially private domain. French and other mercantile interests were nudged over but by no means uprooted by these moves. Further, not all industries were caught in the nationalization net; small private enterprises remained in food processing, chemicals, construction, and shoes.[49]

While the scope of socialization was extensive in terms of the total size of the Benin economy, the modest scale of the latter is attested by the mere $8 million compensation bill.[50] By way of contrast, French aid from 1970 to 1974 totaled over $40 million. The performance of the socialized sector appears somewhat better overall than in Congo-Brazzaville, though mixed. Textiles and state trading have been problem areas, and the expectations of swelling revenue flow for the state coffers were soon disappointed.

The mobilization of the rural sector has been limited. An effort to extend the political infrastructure into the countryside was made by creation of new local councils by "consultation" (not election) under party supervision. By this Leninist tutelage, the regime hoped to root out those who sought to "sabotage the revolution."[51] In the agricultural realm, according to a sympathetic observer of the revolution, the regime had "moved from wish to intent," but not yet to action. Cooperatives were promoted as the opening wedge to a noncapitalist organization of

peasant agriculture, with the ultimate goal of collective production. Such a goal is far over the horizon, and the regime is much
too prudent and cautious to embark on an adventurous policy
that has little or no spontaneous village support and that the
state lacks the capacity to organize, much less impose.[52]

The first wave of socialist measures in 1974–75 was quite
far-reaching, given the small dimensions of the Benin economy.
However, the cruel limits to policy choice became swiftly apparent when France suspended its aid until compensation accords
on expropriated assets were in view. Relations with Paris remained chilly for some time, and the United States expressed its
hostility to the Marxist experiment by withdrawing its ambassador.[53] Even at the height of the socialization campaign, Kerekou
was multiplying his reassurances to private investors, claiming
that he "did not have particularly revolutionary motives."[54]
While the Soviet Union and Cuba enlarged their diplomatic and
military representation, their aid was negligible. From 1960 to
1977, Soviet aid was a mere $5 million, with no new commit-
ments in 1976 and 1977. This compared with $44 million from
China, with a sports complex in Cotonou being the largest single
project.[55] By 1979, it had become clear to the Kerekou regime that
its external economic relationships—aid, trade, and investment—could be only with the West, and especially with France.
The hopes entertained by the ideological members of the entourage for a socialist alternative had all but vanished.

Kerekou did make one major ideological pilgrimage, visiting
Somalia, North Korea, China, Rumania, and Algeria in 1976 to
make a personal study of the socialist pathway; this itinerary was
hardly calculated to generate Soviet enthusiasm. A ten-year accord with the Chinese was signed during this trip, but since that
time ideological fervor seems to have ebbed. Red banners pro-
claiming socialist slogans still span many Benin arteries, and
the media are tireless in their repetition of official Marxist
themes. Yet ties have quietly warmed with the West. Renewed
French interest in Benin as a route to Niger mineral wealth is in

evidence, and there may well be French financing for extension of the rail line to Niamey. A Norwegian company was to bring the small offshore oil deposits discovered some years ago into production in 1980. Some observers did detect minor ideological undercurrents in the preference for an oil partner which, though Western, was not one of the petroleum giants with their connotations of international imperialism. Benin never severed its ties with the franc zone and remains as dependent as ever on French assistance.

For all its difficulties, the Kerekou regime has outlasted all of its predecessors. The comic-opera mercenary airborne invasion in January 1977, apparently instigated by exiled opposition groups with the complicity of two or three foreign governments, proved a blessing in disguise. The ignominious failure of the operation gave a badly needed morale boost to the regime, which hastened to construct an imposing monument to the heroic popular resistance to this provocation. The 1975 exodus of the elite has been arrested, and the self-confidence of the bureaucracy enhanced. A respite from the turmoil of continuous coup and conspiracy has lowered the temperature of regional conflict, if only momentarily. In a subtle way, the regime's claim to legitimacy, by 1979, rested implicitly on stability and moderately competent governance rather than revolution and socialism. At the end of 1979, elections were held for the first time under the Marxist republic, and a more civilianized cabinet appointed, with only seven of twenty-two portfolios in military hands; previously, the army had dominated the council of ministers.

There is no economic miracle in view for Benin. The performance of the rural economy has not been very good, but neither has that of most of its neighbors. In the period 1971–75, real per capita income declined at an annual rate of 1.1 percent.[56] The prospect of oil production and some new capital inflow in the late 1970s provided a glimmer of hope. In spite of the heavy burden of public sector salaries, it was the Marxist republic that in 1976 balanced the state budget for the first time since independence.[57] The Kerekou regime has been scrupulous in meeting its external obligations, including the compensation payments for nationalized properties. By 1980, many observers believed that the would-be Marxist-Leninist state was able to sustain favorable comparison with its many predecessors.

THE INSULAR MARXISM OF MADAGASCAR

The intriguing Madagascar venture in Marxism-Leninism has some evident common points with Congo-Brazzaville and Benin. It was proclaimed unexpectedly by a military ruler, naval Captain Didier Ratsiraka, who, like Ngouabi and Kerekou, had no previous record of Marxist conviction. It likewise fits well the Jowitt model of scientific socialism as ideological vehicle for establishing distance and differentiation from preceding regimes. Originating under military auspices, the patrons of Marxism-Leninism are reluctant to create a genuinely political instrument that might escape their grasp. It fashions a very large public sector, but its thrust seems as much nationalist antagonism to neocolonial survivals as aspiration for a socialist economy. The sincerity and depth of the ideological engagement of the leadership is doubted both by nonsocialist foreign observers and the doctrinally pure scientific socialist intellectuals at home.

There are also significant contrasts. The Malagasy society is far more stratified socially and complex culturally than the other two francophone Afro-Marxist states. Neocolonialism under the *ancien régime* was pervasive, arrogant, and unreconstructed. The eclecticism of the Marxist-Leninist official ideology is even more marked, and the Soviet impact, whether as development model or diplomatic participant, is even less significant.[58]

In contemporary politics, cultural diversity on the island has tended to be expressed as a polarity between the Merina of the high plateaus of central Madagascar and diverse lowland groups collectively labeled *cotiers* (coastal people). The Merina ethnic identity crystallized in the centuries preceding colonial rule is associated with a centralized monarchy that emerged in the eighteenth century and extended its dominion to most of the island in the nineteenth. At the same time, Merina society became highly stratified, with castelike layers of nobles (Andriana), freemen (Hova), and servers (Andevo, Mainty). The Merina core of the historical state profoundly affects contemporary relationships, implying a vocation of leadership to the central plateau on the one hand and instilling a sensitivity to Merina domination on the other. Mission activity and school implantation occurred first in the highlands, and the Merina are heavily predominant in the ranks of the now extensive elite.

The *cotier* category breaks down into a large number of ethnocultural groups, united only in the rivalry with the Merina. They range from Antandroy pastoral herders in the south to Betsileo rice tillers west and north of the high plateau; expanding Tsimihety farmer-herders in the north to the more penetrated and fragmented Sakalava in the west, and the Betsimisaraka of the colonial plantation zone in the east. Several of those turned toward the sea had partly or wholly absorbed Arab mercantile communities, with the mark of Arab and Muslim culture strong at the top of the social hierarchy.[59]

Merina culture provides a unifying core for the island; their language, which enjoys official status, is spoken throughout the island, though there is some ambivalence among *cotiers* toward the national culture concept. Superimposed upon the Merina/*cotier* duality is a religious one. Protestant mission activity began well before the French conquest and won over the Merina royal court and a good fraction of the nobility. Catholic evangelization tended to focus on the *cotiers*. The centers of Muslim activity are also coastal. Merina number about two million of a total population of eight million.

French rule imposed upon the island a pervasive mercantile and plantation colonial presence. French settlers, who numbered 100,000 by the end of the 1950s, formed a self-contained, isolated, and reactionary community. The colonial citadels were the four great trading houses, the *Marseillaise*, *Lyonnaise*, *Rochefortaise*, and *Compagnie Générale*, which wholly dominated the colonial economy. An all-too-conspicuous French hegemony continued throughout the 1960s and contributed in no small part to the leftward shift in the 1970s.

Madagascar politics in the 1960s were dominated by Philibert Tsiranana, who was weakened by a stroke in 1970, then ousted by the military in May 1972. A Tsimehety, he was one of the few highly educated *cotiers* in the mid-1950s when electoral politics gained momentum. Early Malagasy nationalism had tended to be Merina-centered. The occasional invocation of the old Merina state as a symbol of island unity was disconcerting to some *cotiers*. The widespread 1947 uprisings had occurred in the coastal regions; the ferocious repression that followed stilled these zones for some years. Tsiranana was a man for the times: moderate enough to win support in Paris, yet vocal enough as spokesman for Malagasy interests to command a nationalist following; *cotier* enough to allay fears of the coastal groups whose large numerical majority would weigh in politics for the first time, but conciliatory in style, not aggressively anti-Merina, and finally, acceptable to large segments of the growing Merina bourgeoisie.

Tsiranana dominated electoral politics through his *Parti Social Démocrate*. The PSD always won large majorities; however, other political movements were never suppressed during the Tsiranana era, nor were they deprived of the liberty to diffuse their views. Ideologically, the PSD was ambiguous; verbally, the movement described itself as socialist. Tsiranana had very close ties with the French socialist party (PSU, formerly SFIO), and had benefited from quite decisive support by the socialist government of Guy Mollet in 1956–57.

At the time of independence, 80 percent of the apparatus of production was in foreign hands. Tsiranana seemed to hesitate in the early years of power. There were some experiments in the mildly socialist "rural animation" inspired by the model of Father Lebret in Senegal. From about 1966 on, Tsiranana appeared to shift toward a more capitalist model of development with substantial state intervention and public investment, on the Ivory Coast pattern. By this time, Tsiranana was a substantial magnate himself, enriched by fruitful land and urban property acquisitions.[60]

Compounding the ambiguity of the Malagasy variant of socialism was a somewhat divergent policy carried out under the aegis of the dynamic Minister of the Interior André Resampa, a Bara from southern Madagascar. Resampa, who became increasingly powerful in the latter Tsiranana years, wanted to create under his direction an important state sector, which would be the foundation for a future socialist society. By 1968, he attached to each of the seventeen prefectures a *Syndicat prefectoral de commune*; these were to offer tractor rentals and market food crops and to establish food processing plants. He also launched about ten state farms on abandoned settler estates and a cooperative network to displace private traders in peasant export crops. By 1970, the factional socialism of Resampa had foundered; the *Syndicats prefectoraux* had a collective debt of over $40 million, and the state farms and cooperatives were mostly bankrupt.[61]

The image of conservatism that Tsiranana acquired over the years was fostered both by the very close ties he retained with the former metropole and South Africa and by the unchallenged predominance of French interests on the island. Even within the state apparatus, a wide range of top posts continued to be held by French nationals throughout the 1960s; the personal entourage of Tsiranana was more French than Malagasy. Many believed the reluctance to localize senior state posts was attributable to the predominance of Merina among the pressing assortment of frustrated and ambitious young Malagasy elites who aspired to these posts. Educated Malagasy were keenly aware than an estimated 40 percent of the consumption, in the late 1960s, was accounted for by foreigners.[62]

Unlike most of the one-party dominant regimes in Africa, which by artifice, force, or law converted themselves into one-party states, the PSD always tolerated opposition movements; the most important, the *Antokon'ny Kongresin' my Fahaleovan-tenan' i Madagasikara* (AKFM) and *Mouvement National pour l'Indépendance de Madagascar* (MONIMA), were of the radical left. The AKFM, led by a Marxist-oriented Protestant pastor, Richard Andriamanjato, of Merina noble ascendance, appealed to the urban intelligentsia and included nationalists, socialists, and Communists among its following. MONIMA, led by Monja Jaona, an Antandroy from Tulear in southern Madagascar, was a rural populist movement, confined to the most impoverished and disinherited zones of the south. Even though MONIMA was associated with a brutally repressed southern peasant uprising in 1971, it remained a legal party.

The Tsiranana-Resampa regime was ousted by a military coup in 1972. The new regime, led by Gabriel Ramanantsoa—in a move again reflective of the unique features of Malagasy politics—legitimated its rule by permitting free elections the following year. The disgrace of Tsiranana was completed by the heavy defeat of his PSD; at the same time, at least lukewarm support from the left was gained by allowing them a parliamentary voice. AKFM won 34 of 144 seats, its strongest showing ever, and MONIMA 18. A large majority of deputies were nonparty backers of the military regime.

Ramanantsoa belonged to the first generation of Malagasy officers, trained in the French military academies. Like his peers, he was a scion of the Merina bourgeoisie and of aristocratic outlook. Tsiranana, as part of his cultural balancing strategy, had created outside the army framework a *Force Républicaine de Sécurité* and a gendarmerie, both predominately officered and manned by *cotiers*. As in a number of other African military interventions, army discontent over this proliferation of security organs was doubtless one predisposing element in the 1972 coup. Ramanantsoa himself may well have been a relatively neutral and prestigious "front man" for a cabal of ambitious colonels. The new orientation of the regime appeared to reflect less the personality of Ramanantsoa than the somewhat discordant nationalism of various influential officers who gained control over particular policy sectors.[63]

The Ramanantsoa regime distanced itself from the largely verbal democratic socialism of Tsiranana by de-emphasizing the word *socialism* and focusing upon nationalist and populist measures. The central pillars in the regime strategy were to assure primacy of the state in key sectors, especially the tertiary commercial sphere, which had been the bastion of colonial mercantile capital; to favor the rural economy; to associate national and foreign capital in the promotion of industry; and to alter the external image of Madagascar by a more radical foreign policy. The major target of the military regime was French colonial capital and those Malagasy elements tied to it; the prime beneficiaries were the Tananarive bourgeoisie and the educated Malagasy elite.[64]

A series of parastatals was created in 1973–74 to give effect to the first of these goals: SONACO (foreign trade), SIMPA (cash crop marketing), EEM (shipping), SOMAPAR (fishing), and SINEE (electricity). Madagascar officially left the franc zone, and the localization of senior bureaucratic positions was much more actively promoted. In the rural sphere, rice prices—which had been held stable since 1960—were nearly doubled. Above all, the military regime assiduously promoted a community development program based upon the traditional local rural community of Merina culture, the *Fokonolona*.

The *Fokonolona* was an idealized vision of the historical local community, which was to have its autonomy restored and to serve as the basic cell of a new self-reliant and decentralized rural society. In reality, the *Fokonolona* had already lost part of its autonomy to the centralizing Merina state in the nineteenth century. The colonial administration, perceiving the utility of these bodies as instrumentalities of local domination, extended them in name to the remainder of the island and denatured them in practice. They were then abandoned in favor of rural communes in a postwar reorganization of local government. To the military, their appeal lay not only in the populist mystique they embodied, but also in the opportunity they offered to outflank rural networks of the existing political parties. For that very reason they were viewed with skepticism tinged with distrust by MONIMA, which suspected they would become in practice new mechanisms for domination of the peasantry by the local administration. More frequently, it appears that the *Fokonolona* were dominated by traditional notables and prosperous farmers.[65]

However, the Ramanantsoa regime did have some egalitarian impact in improving rural income, which had declined some 30 percent per capita during the Tsiranana years.[66] The head tax was abolished and the minimum wages were raised for the first time since 1963. But the newly enlarged state sector encountered many operating difficulties; SIMPA and SONACO had problems of organization, finance, and honesty. The sharp rise in state outlays and a drop in revenue brought a large budget deficit in 1973, a foreign exchange shortfall, and an end to the price stability of the Tsiranana years. Though the French always maintained their official relationships, private investment all but ceased in the face of the nationalist thrust of the military regime.

An important part of the radical hue acquired by the Ramanantsoa regime came through its foreign policy, a sphere of action dominated by Foreign Minister Didier Ratsiraka. During the Ramanantsoa years, Ratsiraka enjoyed a remarkable ascension; beginning with neither a political nor an ideological base, he constructed both: politically, by mediating between the various Tananarive combines, while remaining carefully out of internal policy disputes; ideologically, by attaining visibility through flamboyantly nationalist speeches at the OAU and other international tribunes. A *cotier* (Betsimisiraka) by ascription, but of elite family (his father had served as governor of Tamatave), he used his ethnic and class attributes with considerable skill.[67] Ratsiraka as foreign minister engineered the shift from the Tsiranana stance as unconditioned enthusiast for French ties and active participant in the South African coprosperity sphere to radical third-world anti-imperialist desirous of expanding ties with the Communist bloc and rupturing South African links.

The Merina hue of the Ramanantsoa regime provoked growing tensions among the *cotiers*. MONIMA leader Jaona claimed that the Merina bourgeoisie had confiscated the benefits of the 1972 revolution—and many found Ramanantsoa and his entourage "most improbable revolutionaries."[68] The demise of the regime was triggered by the mutiny of a police unit on 31 December 1974. On 5 February 1975, unable to escape the impasse, Ramanantsoa handed over power to Colonel Richard Ratsimandrava.

Ratsimandrava, whose father was a teacher in Tananarive, was Merina but not of aristocratic antecedents. Tsiranana had placed him in charge of the predominantly *cotier* gendarmerie, to which had fallen the task of suppressing a MONIMA peasant rebellion in 1971 in the south. The task was carried out in brutal fashion. The reactionary image that Ratsimandrava thus acquired among the Tananarive radical intelligentsia was gradually effaced during the Ramanantsoa years, when, as minister of the interior, he became the principal architect of the *Fokonolona* program of rural populism. Thus, by the time Ratsimandrava took power, he had developed substantial linkages among the radical factions in Tananarive and had become a veritable hero of the left. By the same token, he was viewed with grave misgivings by an important spectrum of the aristocratic and mercantile elements in the Merina bourgeoisie. When, to general surprise, Ratsiraka was excluded from his cabinet, *cotier* apprehensions were also aroused. Only six days after assuming the presidency, Ratsimandrava was assassinated in a conspiracy whose full dimensions have never been unveiled. As the gendarmerie commander, he had been known only four years earlier as the scourge of peasant aspirations, but he died a veritable martyr of the revolutionary dream.[69]

Captain Ratsiraka was elected in his place by a military directorate. Though a spectacular judicial inquest was held—dubbed "the trial of the century"—with many leading Malagasy, including Tsiranana and Resampa, in the dock, the evidence presented was inconclusive. In the end only three policemen were convicted; they were given light five-year sentences. The dilemma facing Ratsiraka in giving ideological definition to his new regime is well stated by Philippe Leymarie: how to "revive a demoralized and fearful peasantry, a worn-out economy lacking in inspiring perspectives, and a morose and discouraged political class. But how could this be done when one is more a bourgeois intellectual and technocrat than a popular leader?"[70]

The response was a resolutely socialist commitment. It was given doctrinal definition in the Malagasy Red Book of October 1975, which proclaimed the Revolutionary Socialist Malagasy Charter. The Red Book, couched in Marxist-Leninist phraseology, appropriated the themes of the far left, which remained skeptical as to the real nature and objectives of the regime. While the phrases and categories of scientific socialism dominate the Red Book, a strongly nationalist undercurrent is visible. In August 1976, Ratsiraka organized a national seminar dedicated to the study of "Djoutche," an ideological contribution of North Korean leader Kim Il Sung, whose rather simple themes stress the marriage of intense nationalism and Marxism-Leninism.[71] At the same time, he warned the ultraleft elements of the intelligentsia against the excesses of the Khmer Rouge revolution.

The new socialist regime wanted to create a political movement to provide a popular base for military Marxism; however, it faced the insoluble problem that AKFM and MONIMA occupied the left end of the spectrum. While they were disposed to collaborate with the Ratsiraka socialist venture, they declined his invitation to efface themselves. It was not until March 1977 that a regime party, the *Avant-Garde de la Révolution Malgache* (AREMA) was launched; the party was more an administrative creature than a Leninist instrument, and AKFM and MONIMA showed no inclination to disappear—though some leaders from both parties participated in the government.

However, socialism was much more than mere words. In a wave of takeovers in 1975 and 1976, the strongholds of French colonial capital were stormed. Most dramatic was the expropriation, without compensation, of the four giant trading companies, the *Marseillaise, Lyonnaise, Rochefortaise,* and *Compagnie Générale*. The first of these had a turnover equivalent to one-third of the national budget. Also nationalized were French sugar companies, banks, insurance, shipping, oil refinery, and movie houses. By the end of 1976, the regime was able to boast that the socialized sector covered 61 percent of the economy, as compared to only 15 percent when Ratsiraka was elevated to power.[72]

The evidence is not yet in on the performance of the regime. Difficulties were manifest in the state sector, with some spectacular corruption cases. The tendency toward stagnation that was clear in the 1960s has certainly not been reversed. Problems in stimulating smallholders to produce enough rice for the domestic market remained, despite a more tangible commitment to rural well-being since 1972. While the commitment to the *Fokonolona* was officially maintained, its content changed to give it a more statist orientation. Ratsiraka believed that the Ratsimandrava populist conception placed too much power in the hands of village units. Firm state supervision and discipline, and intensive ideological instruction were required. Thus conceived, *Fokonolona* would seem destined for departicipation and bureaucratization.[73]

The regime has remained quite prudent in its financial policies. In 1977, the external debt remained low, requiring only about 3 percent of export earnings to service. Despite the non-convertibility of the Malagasy franc, it has not lost value as did the Guinea currency after withdrawal from the franc zone.

Similar caution is visible in the external policy of the regime. While maintaining cordial ties with Communist states, Ratsiraka has never broken with the French, who have maintained their aid programs. The size of the resident French community is down sharply—from 50,000 in 1972 to 12,000 in 1977—but the demise of the settler community is quite distinct from the dilution of cultural and economic ties with official France. Ratsiraka obtained a $14 million Soviet aid agreement in 1974 (flour mill, power and irrigation projects) while foreign minister, but has received only $6 million in additional Soviet credits (in 1978) since Marxism-Leninism became state doctrine; at the same time, the regime has resisted Soviet pressures for naval facilities at the old French base of Diego Suarez.[74] No doubt significantly, Madagascar never figures on Soviet lists of African states aspiring to a scientific socialist future. Nor is there any military connection in Soviet arms supply or training programs for Malagasy officers. Indeed, Chinese aid commitment, at $68 million (agricultural machinery plant, match factory, experimental farms, pharmaceutical plant, Tananarive-Tamatave road), is much greater than the Soviet.

The ambiguities of the Ratsiraka experience in scientific socialism are conveyed by the critical evaluation of it by a leading figure of the Malagasy intellectual left, Sennen Andriamirado:

Although now institutionalized, the revolutionary Malagasy State is perhaps a step toward the socialist revolution. This is what explains, doubtless, why Didier Ratsiraka seeks to rally in advance the nationalist bourgeoisie. A risk for revolutionary socialism. Provided that the boundary be maintained between compromise and being compromised.

Accordingly, the best policy for militants is not to support Ratsiraka as a new providential leader, but to oblige him to apply his program. If he is in the process supported by ricochet, this is only an accident of history.[75]

SOMALIA: IRREDENTISM AND AFRO-MARXISM

The Somalia experiment in military Marxism, second in se-
niority to that of Congo-Brazzaville, faces imposing obstacles: a
harsh and arid land whose minerals are as yet unexploitable. To
this ecological handicap have been added three calamitous af-
flictions: the 1973–75 drought, which forced 10 percent of the
populace into refugee camps; the 1977–78 military disaster in
Ethiopia, which cost the country most of its heavy military
equipment, and above all inflicted a national humiliation; and
the extraordinary Somali exodus in 1979–80 of the old, the
women, and the children from Ethiopia, which saddled the
country with an estimated 1.4 million refugees by mid-1980. And
yet, the Somali regime has received on the whole more uniformly generous appraisals than any other of the Afro-Marxist
military states; Le Monde Africa correspondent Philippe Decraene, who is not given to sentimental judgments, found that
the regime gave "an undeniable sense of progress. . . . The trans-
formations of Somali society now in course promise to be more
profound than those of any other African society." [76]

In the 1960s, Somalia enjoyed a certain prestige among external observers for a quite different reason: the maintenance of
open and competitive parliamentary politics during the 1960–69
period, in the face of the continental drift toward authoritarianism. There were two open and competitive postindependence elections, two peaceful and constitutional changes in the
premiership, and one for the presidency. The assassination of
President Abdirashid Ali Shermarke in 1969 produced a parliamentary impasse and military intervention. The manifold defi-
ciencies of the parliamentary order were laid bare by the coup.
The image of constitutional rectitude proved to be only external;
at home, cynicism over the clan basis for party divisions, the
absence of any development program, and the venality which
riddled ministerial ranks had long since corroded the legiti-

macy of the democratic order. The new military regime of General Mohammed Siad Barre had little difficulty in documenting through posthumous inquiry the corruption and malfeasance of the civilian regime.

Somalia would appear to be stony sociological soil for scientific socialism. The industrial sector is inconsequential, and the overwhelming majority of the population are nomadic herdsmen, whose most valued possession is their camel. While the population is linguistically homogeneous, solidarities are based upon the kinship idiom of clan and subclan divisions, as well as on Somali nationalism.[77] Islam is profoundly ingrained in the social consciousness as well. And yet, on the first anniversary of his coup, President Barre proclaimed that "in order to realize the interests of the Somali people; their achievement of a better life, the full development of their potentialities and the fulfillment of their aspirations, we solemnly declare Somalia to be a Socialist State."[78]

For a few, the distant origins of Somali socialism go back to contacts which Somali elites established with the Italian Communist Party or Fabian and other socialist milieux in Britain during colonial days. However, the proximate source lies in the military relationship that developed with the Soviet Union from 1961 on. The genesis of these ties had no relationship to the philosophical merits of socialism, but rather originates in the consuming passion uniting all Somalis to realize the irredentist dream of gathering in all of the Somali-speaking lands under other sovereignties. This imperative spawned the aspiration for a military force in scale and equipment far beyond what the small dimensions and overwhelming poverty of the country might otherwise dictate. The United States was approached first and declined to provide equipment that might eventually be directed against Ethiopia or Kenya. The Soviet Union was approached next, and thus began a relationship that provided little Somalia with a powerful air force and armored strike force and a Soviet military mission numbering 1,500 at the time of its expulsion in 1977. Some 2,400 Somali military personnel were sent to the Soviet Union for training (more than any other African state), as well as many hundreds of other students (695 in 1977).[79]

Another factor affecting the military option for Marxism-Leninism was the cold war competition that divided the security forces in the 1960s. The United States, unwilling to compromise its Ethiopian ties by aiding the Somali military, sought nonetheless to preserve some access by helping to train and equip the police, in partnership with West Germany. This force became a mobile and effective gendarmerie that played a critical role in rural administration. With the police a potent competitor to the army in the security domain, the military found its Soviet patron an indispensable support. The ideology associated with this alliance can be seen in part as a lexical weapon in the struggle for hegemony between army and police; the military takeover was swiftly followed by a subordination of the police into a circumscribed role.[80]

Through these extensive contacts, scientific socialism became widely familiar to the Somali officer corps. As an ideological rejection of the *ancien régime*, and formulation of a new ethos for Somali society, the logic of Somali socialism is clear enough. So also is the liberty that the military regime has taken with orthodox Soviet socialism. Laitin, who argues that the scientific socialist experiment in Somalia can be better understood through semiological analysis than programmatic impact, notes the elemental contradictions in Barre's thought. Barre joins Soviet analysts in castigating the concept of African socialism—there is only one universal "scientific socialism." In the same breath he denies its universality: "a Soviet socialist cannot tell me about Somalian problems, which must be put in an African context." The obvious absence of a proletarian base for Somali socialism is waved aside: "The Somali people as a whole are workers." With nomadic herdsmen thus proletarianized, the bourgeois class enemy can be similarly redefined as simply ex-parliamentarians, pseudoreligious men, and recalcitrant intellectuals.[81]

The adaptation of scientific socialist doctrine to Somali cultural metaphors is given interesting reflection in the terms chosen to translate key words. "Scientific socialism" is rendered as "hantiwadaag," literally, livestock sharing. "Scientific" became "kacaan," "standing up," "growing up." The concept of revolution is equated with prosperity, translated as "barwaaqo," the sweetest grazing grass—which in turn conveys the image of milk-laden camels.[82] In the process, Somalis acquire the capacity to conceptualize a counterreality.

The eclecticism and essentially military character of Somali socialism is attested in the long delay in launching a socialist political movement. Not till 1976 was the Somali Revolutionary Socialist Party established. Though the Central Committee had a large civilian majority, all five members of the initial political bureau were generals. The party has become an important organ for articulation of national policies; evidence is lacking as to its penetration of rural society. Decraene notes that its birth occurred at a moment of midsummer torpor; a significant fraction of the military leadership regarded it as still premature.[83]

With a minuscule industrial economy, the scope for achievement of a socialist productive sector is evidently quite limited. Yet significant nationalizations were undertaken in 1970. The target for these expropriations was a segment of Italian colonial capital. However, not all colonial capital was on the hit list; an intriguing distinction was made between foreign enterprises engaged in production, exempted from expropriation, and nonproductive ones, earmarked for takeover. Only "exploiters" would be nationalized, declared Barre. Another spokesman declared: "We do not nationalize for the joy of nationalization. We have a rational nationalization policy, aimed at liberating our country from parasitism. . . . We have no barriers against the private sector per se, provided it accepts our planned economy."[84]

Thus the state sector took possession of the airline, electricity, banks, insurance, Fiat distribution, and a sugar factory. Of these, only the sugar concern was an exception to the pledge of exoneration for foreign-owned production facilities. External trade was not taken over until 1975. A substantial foreign private sector was left untouched by these measures; most prominent among these were the Italian banana plantations, largest exporters in Somalia. Also spared were Italian soap, shoe, and meatpacking enterprises.[85]

None of this really provided the basis for a command economy, even if we set aside the crises of drought and war that have consumed the energies of the Barre regime for much of the decade. Even the nationalizations were accompanied by appeals for private investment, domestic and foreign; "clean business," investors were assured, had nothing to fear from scientific socialism. A moderately generous investment code was drafted in the vain hope of attracting foreign capital. Socialist agriculture for a pastoral economy was obviously totally out of the question; the kind of state expropriation of herds that occurred in Soviet Central Asia, Mongolia, and China was as unimaginable as it would have been suicidal. What the state did endeavor to promote was sedentarization of a fraction of the pastoralists on irrigated settlements, as a permanent response to the conjunctural crisis of drought. A handful of state farms, involving 7,600 hectares and 6,000 workers, were created, with undocumented results.[86]

The achievements of the Barre regime, however, lay elsewhere. There were noteworthy steps toward egalitarianism. In 1971, the courageous and decisive action taken to resolve the perennial dispute over an official script for the language eliminated the gap between state and subject imposed by administration in a language few ordinary citizens could speak or read. With the Roman alphabet as standard, an impressive year-long adult literacy campaign was mounted in 1974; secondary schools were closed for a year to permit students to serve as teachers. There was a marked shift in public investment allocations, away from urban-centered industry toward rural projects. The switch from English to Somali as principal instrument of education will eliminate the regional advantage that formerly accrued to formerly British-administered northern Somalia; figures from 1971 showed that 88 percent of northern Somalia pupils passed the standardized Standard Eight examination, compared to 54 percent in the formerly Italian-ruled south—a difference largely attributable to language skills.

Egalitarianism among men is a strongly held Somali cultural value; egalitarianism did not extend to women, however. Here the regime has made a real contribution, even if the results fall well short of its oratory. There has been measurable if limited progress in providing schooling opportunities for girls, and some of the more flagrant inequalities in customary divorce and bride-price custom have been reduced.[87]

The regime made effective use in its first years of some well-publicized symbolic gestures to reinforce its image of relative austerity and participation in the physical burdens of development. Civic work teams spent Fridays helping to fix sand dunes whose shifting threatened roads and valuable agricultural land and to rebuild the Hotel Juba in the capital, destroyed by fire. The spectacle of President Barre and senior officials shoveling sand alongside ordinary laborers impressed not only foreign observers but also the Somali public.

Barre had no inclination to interpret dialectical materialism as enjoining confrontation with Islam. Rather, he argued, "there is no conflict between Islam and socialism, as they both enshrine the principles of human dignity, mutual respect, cooperation, progress, justice and well-being for all." Reconciliation of the two was attainable through a progressive Islamic theology: "Our Islamic faith teaches us that its inherent values are perennial and continually evolving as people progress. These basic tenets of our religion cannot be interpreted in a static sense, but rather as a dynamic force, as a source of inspiration for continuous advancement. . . ."[88] Barre had no mercy for those who argued an incompatibility between Islamic theology and the secular faith; he executed ten Muslim notables who protested regime measures in favor of sexual equality.

An unavowed but probably not inconsequential function of the scientific socialist commitment was to legitimize a series of repressive measures undertaken by the military regime to eliminate open political debate. The democratic republic of the first independence decade was indisputably venal but also very open and tolerant. One of the first measures of the military regime was to shut down the Mogadiscio coffeehouses, focal points for an unending political debate and a favored haunt of the intelligentsia. This and related measures restricting free expression were highly resented in intellectual milieux and provoked the exodus of a certain number of educated Somalis. Expropriation of the revolutionary lexicon of the coffeehouse, regime foes claimed, was not true ideological conversion but the devaluation of ideas through their co-optation as instruments of military power.[89]

Scientific socialism was overshadowed in 1977 by the failed campaign to profit from the disintegration of the old order in Ethiopia by liberating the Ogaden. This led to a rupture with the Soviet patron. The Soviet aid commitment of $154 million—of which 60 percent had been drawn—had been substantial (far greater than that accorded any other Afro-Marxist state), and Soviet military supply and training was crucial. At the time of signing a twenty-year treaty of friendship and cooperation, the Soviets canceled all Somali debts. A large Soviet base complex had been accorded at Berbera. Thus the sudden shift in Horn alignments in 1977 and the thrashing applied to regular Somali army units in the Ogaden by Soviet- and Cuban-reinforced Ethiopians in spring 1978 sundered a far-reaching and multiplex relationship. By mid-1977, Somali overtures for a military relationship with the West began. By 1980, these had resulted in the establishment of American military facilities at the former Soviet base at Berbera. The reversal of external alliances did not involve public renunciation of the regime ideology. But it did make the Somali version of scientific socialism much less externally visible. While Afro-Marxism and a strong anti-Soviet position are not incompatible in theory, they may be to some extent in practice. The parade of foreign pilgrims who came to study Somali socialism and who gave such visibility to the Somali pathway in the mid-1970s came to an end; so also did the adulatory coverage in such influential reviews of the left as *Afrique-Asie*.

In the aftermath of the trauma of 1977 some unappealing aspects of the regime became more visible. Barre relied heavily on an inner core of trusted collaborators from his small Marehan subclan of the Darod.[90] In an effort to ingratiate himself with the West, Barre released a reported 3,000 political prisoners in October 1978, implying a more repressive nether side to the regime than had been generally recognized.[91] Despite the 1977–78 military debacle, however, the regime held together.

While the extravagant praise bestowed upon the Somali socialist experience in the mid-1970s may seem excessive at the end of the decade, there are many positive elements. The most serious miscalculation—the 1977 invasion of Ethiopia—originated in the pan-Somali nationalism, to which all regimes have been faithful. The bare statistical record does not suggest that scientific socialism has brought rapid economic growth, but neither did its liberal predecessor; World Bank figures show an annual per capita real income decline of 0.2 percent from 1970 to 1975— and 0.3 percent for the whole postindependence era, 1960–75.[92] The specifically Marxist-Leninist content of most Somali development policies, since the early wave of nationalizations, is difficult to discern. We would share the cautious conclusion of Laitin:

> The record suggests that a non-socialist but vigorous, development-conscious military in control of the Somali government would have acted in much the same way as the present socialist regime. While the Siyaad regime has made commendable progress along certain lines associated with socialist ideology, no radical transformations or

uniquely socialist programs have been essayed. But this achievement can be considered relatively successful in comparison with other socialist experiments in the third world.[93]

ETHIOPIA: FROM EMPIRE TO AFRO-MARXIST STATE

As a military Marxist regime, Ethiopia stands in sharp contrast to the other four. Soviet as well as Western observers have suggested that it is the only true African revolution to date; others that claim this designation, they suggest, are in reality mere national liberation movements.[94] There are in Ethiopia indisputably elements of internal class struggle and destruction of older indigenous social hierarchies that are absent in all other Afro-Marxist states. The sharpness of the conflict and the brutality that has accompanied these mutations have engendered much stronger passions. Far left Ethiopian critics, who object to the military monopoly of power, castigate it as simply a "fascist military dictatorship." Nonsocialist critics have been offended by the violence of the Red Terror and the heavy reliance on Soviet and Cuban armed support to impose the new regime on a restive periphery. Baxter, for example, dismisses the new regime as simply a misinformed Marxist minority with a Shoan center of gravity, ruling by terror.[95]

Ethiopia, as an African state, is distinctive in its genesis. The historical origins of the polity, rooted in a millennial kingdom rather than a colonial territory, have important consequences both for its class structure and cultural divisions. The revival of the Ethiopian kingdom in the late nineteenth century—led by the Emperor Menelik—permitted the ancient state not only to resist colonial conquest but also to participate in the imperial partition of Africa; the kingdom tripled in size during the last quarter of the nineteenth century. In the Amharic and Tigre core areas of the historic state, complex social hierarchies had evolved, related to differential rights to land and its products. In the contemporary period, most peasants in these regions, while they had rights to their land deriving from descent group membership, nonetheless paid what might be termed feudal dues in crops and services to either landlords or the Coptic Church. These payments have been estimated at 25 percent of the harvest (more if the landlord provided seeds and/or oxen), though some feel that in reality they were substantially higher.[96] Landlords owed their rights of tribute collection ultimately to the state, though some were hereditary. These benefices (gult) were distributed to royal favorites, imperial family members, military leaders, unpaid local government officials, or others the throne wished to reward.

In the newly conquered lands a more rigid pattern emerged. Here the state laid claim to all land; theoretically a third was attributed to local notables in return for their acceptance of the new suzerainty. The remainder was considered available to allocate to members of the conquering armies, government officials, or Amhara settlers. Peasants on these lands paid a higher share of their crops to the lords, who were often absentee, and were more like tenants than simply tribute-paying small farmers who had their own rights to possession of the land. This land spoliation was evidently not viewed with enthusiasm by its victims; settler lands came to be concentrated within reach and protection of government posts.[97] As the institutional infrastructure of the Ethiopian state was gradually extended under Emperor Haile Selassie from World War I on, and as the possibilities increased for marketing peasant crop tribute deliveries, the rural social hierarchies tended to become more sharply delineated.

Meanwhile, the growth of the Ethiopian state from a culturally specific core led to a polity that was not only multiethnic, as are most African states, but communally stratified, which is much more unusual. The contemporary state can be usefully conceptualized as a set of concentric cultural circles, where attachment to the symbols of the polity becomes progressively more diffuse as one moves outward; the outermost ring is totally hostile to the Ethiopian entity and is contained within it only by brute force. At the inner core was the Shoan Amhara group, who were associated with the last dynasty and who dominated the top ranks of the imperial establishment. A second circle, composed of other Amhara and Tigreans, falls within the zone of historical attachment to the Ethiopian kingdom. For a long time the center of the state was further north, in the Tigrinya-language zone. In the twentieth century, Amhara have been the core cultural community, and Amharic–Tigrean tensions have been frequent. The northernmost Tigreans, who were included in the Italian colony of Eritrea, are the most ambivalent members of the second circle, and many came to support the Eritrean secession movement. The first two circles also define the orbit of the Coptic Christian Church, which provided an important reservoir of orienting symbols to the empire.

A third circle consists especially of the numerically important Oromo (often labeled Galla by others), who are at least a third and possibly half the population. Most of the Oromo lands were added to the Ethiopian state by Menelik; however, there has been a long period of cultural interaction between Amhara and Oromo. A small number of Oromo were admitted, by marriage or co-optation, into the top spheres of the imperial state; some have also been incorporated into the second circle by assimilation. However, there is also a tradition of Oromo resistance to the empire, and in recent decades a new, pan-Oromo consciousness has been gestating, fostered by the increasing impositions of the imperial state, the cultural arrogance of Amhara settlers and officials who dominated the Oromo zones, and the humiliating encounters of Oromo schoolboys, soldiers, and clerks with the hegemonic culture.[98] Also included in this third circle of ambivalent incorporation would be such Islamic groups as the Harari and Afar.

A fourth circle is composed of groups that lie on the western periphery of the state, are only weakly related to it, and are neither participants in nor irreconcilable opponents of the Ethiopian state. These include such groups as the Anuak, whose linguistic and cultural ties are in southern Sudan and northern Uganda. Almost none were found in any significant position in the state apparatus, nor were they tied to the social hierarchy of tenantry.

The outermost circle consists of groups that have never willingly accepted the Ethiopian state and that, in the last two decades, have been in virtually permanent insurrection against its authority. These include nearly all Somalis and most Eritreans. In the Somali case, language, religion, and attachment to the pan-Somali cause yield an irreducible hostility to both imperial and revolutionary Ethiopia.[99] Eritrean dissidence is strongest in the northern Muslim areas but has also penetrated the Tigrean Christian areas.

This complex cultural mosaic could be quite differently viewed, depending on one's vantage point. Levine, who offers a sophisticated brief for Ethiopian unity, amasses linguistic, cultural, and historical evidence to demonstrate that the polity was not a subjugation of alien groups but rather "an ingathering of peoples with deep historical affinities."[100] For Somalis and most Eritreans, however, Ethiopia is a colonial power, and they are engaged in a people's war to bring national liberation.

To this deeply fissured society has come the rendezvous with socialist revolution. The slow unfolding of the revolution has some striking parallels with that of Cuba. The *ancien régime* of Haile Selassie, like that of Batista, had been slowly decomposing in its final years. The erosion of its legitimacy was not the work of an organized socialist movement, but rather the corrosion from within, brought about by its incompetence, corruption, and inability to transcend the narrow limits of patrimonial politics. Once the imperial state was swept aside by a creeping military coup, the new rulers—while not initially adhering to a consciously articulated socialist framework—undertook a sweeping land reform that profoundly altered the nature of rural power.

Like Castro, who did not declare himself to be a Marxist-Leninist until 1961, the regime did not declare for scientific socialism until 1976.

The trigger for the collapse of the old order lay in its callous apathy before the ravages of the drought that afflicted parts of the country, especially Wollo province. By 1973, awareness had gradually spread that a major tragedy had occurred; perhaps 100,000 peasants had starved, and the only government response was to suppress the information. The more particular grievances of many groups—students, teachers, civil servants, taxi drivers, soldiers—suddenly seemed to coalesce into a rising tide of protest.

In January and February 1974, mutinies occurred, first in Neghelle in the south, then in Asmara, Harar, and Addis Ababa. Junior officers and enlisted ranks rejected the authority of their commanders and drew up catalogues of material discontents. A wave of strikes and demonstrations by various civilian groups began almost simultaneously, which started, like the mutinies, with particular material grievances, then broadened into more general attacks upon the corruption of the system. In late February 1974, the emperor ousted Prime Minister Aklilu Habte Wold and named another trusted aristocrat, Endelkachew Makonnen, in his place: the first time ever that a prime minister had been driven from office by public pressure. The emperor sought to demobilize the mutineers, strikers, and demonstrators with concessions. A new constitution was promised. By May 1974, a military coordinating committee, whose members all had the rank of major or below, had come into being. This body, the *Derg* (Amharic for "committee"), whose composition was kept secret, numbered 120 at its numerical peak. By July, Endelkachew had been forced out; in September, the emperor himself was arrested by the *Derg*. Another civilian aristocrat, Michael Imru, held the premiership in August–September. From September to November, General Aman Michael Andom (a Christian Eritrean) was nominal head of government. Then, in November, the *Derg* unambiguously

seized full power, executing General Aman and sixty other leading figures of the old order.

This blood purge was an important turning point. Having
crept by degrees into power, the Derg now began to slowly radi-
calize. Its first real ideological proclamation, in December 1974,
mentioned socialism for the first time, but only in rather general
terms. The more central slogan, Ethiopia Tikdem, was essentially nationalist: it proclaimed the indivisibility and unity of
Ethiopia. General Aman had been shot not for opposing socialism but because he was suspected of seeking a compromise with
the Eritrean liberation movements.

The first and most crucial reform undertaken by the Derg affected land, the hinge of social power in Ethiopia. Virtually everyone in and out of Ethiopia had agreed for years that land
reform was indispensable. The top layers of officialdom and aristocrats, however, were not interested in any version of reform
that threatened their flow of revenue. Thus, as Farer aptly puts it,
in the last imperial years land reform was constantly on the
agenda, but, "like a child's toy car resting on its back while its
wheels spin, reform was noise without movement." [101] With the
decomposition of the old order, by late 1974 land reform that
went beyond cosmetics was in the air. A furtive debate on its
content was conducted in various milieux. The only one that
counted took place within the Derg.

The first indications that the reform might be radical came in
January and February 1975: the Derg first nationalized banks,
then thirteen insurance companies, followed by seventy-two
industrial and commercial concerns; it also took majority holdings in twenty-nine other businesses. In one swoop, the state
had seized virtually the entire productive infrastructure of the
country. Most of these enterprises, however, were quite small;
these commanding heights were mere foothills in the vast rural
economy.

The Derg was not of one mind about the scope of land reform; indeed, not only retrograde aristocrats but many ordinary

soldiers were beneficiaries of imperial land grants. The emperor customarily gave forty hectares to soldiers after five years of service; there were as many as 35,000 modest landlords in the army.[102] The consensus of the abundant advice from international agencies and experts—including Soviet and Chinese diplomats—as well as from bureaucrats was for a moderate reform, which would stress productivity as much as redistribution. The decrees published in March 1975, however, were sweeping.

The major provisions in the land decrees abolished private ownership of land and entitled peasants to usufruct rights to a maximum of ten hectares. Hiring of labor was forbidden; ownership of land was vested in the state. The *Derg*, however, was in no position to enforce such revolutionary measures. Its armed forces were tied down in combating the intensifying Eritrean liberation struggle, garrisoning the capital and large towns, and coping with local insurrections that were beginning to break out. Local administration remained in the hands of notables who stood to lose wealth and power by these measures. There were few technical specialists. The *Derg*'s solution to this dilemma was two-pronged: 1) peasants were directed to form associations themselves to organize, direct, and defend the land reform; and 2) some 50,000 university and secondary school students were to be dispatched to the countryside to assist in the execution of these decrees.

The difficulties of implementing so drastic a program were immense; the truly remarkable fact is that, by most accounts, the reform was in large measure carried out, and there was no severe dislocation of production levels, which many had feared. The decrees were most enthusiastically implemented in the conquest zones in the south, where Oromo and other peasants joyfully seized the occasion to drive out not only Amhara landlords but all other Shoan officials within their reach. In the north, the change was less far-reaching, with peasants generally confirmed in their land rights but freed of tribute payments.

Not all the poor were beneficiaries, it turned out. The prohibition on hiring labor resulted in the expulsion of immigrant workers, often Muslims, from coffee lands. Particularly in the northern zones, church patrons and some landlords were able to organize armed resistance by their clientele. Wealthy farmers denied use of their oxen to their former tenants, as well as seasonal advances, which had once been part of the reciprocity of patron–client ties. The estimated 18,000 peasant associations that had formed by 1976 were best organized in the south; their implantation was much thinner in the north.

The student role was not always a boon for the *Derg*. From the outset, students considered the soldiers to be usurpers of the revolution. While it was no doubt a source of secret satisfaction to the *Derg* to contemplate the rustication of these irritating self-appointed guardians of the revolution in the name of socialist duty, it was less exhilarating to discover the students preaching peasant resistance to the "fascist military dictatorship." While evidence suggests that in many areas students did play a valuable role in helping peasants establish their associations, their ideological zeal at times outstripped peasant understanding of the objects of reform. The more evangelical radicals tried to promote collective farming units, an idea that had a frosty reception. Many students found, as the months wore on, that revolutionary ideals were poor solace for the sparse amenities of the countryside. Less than a year after the student army of 50,000 was dispatched, no more than 18,000 remained.[103]

In 1979, announcements were made of a further stage in the agrarian revolution, with collectivization to be imposed. This move, which was privately opposed by East European advisers, seemed unlikely to move beyond the theoretical realm in the immediate future. Unlike the initial reform, it could not be enforced by spontaneous peasant action; the administrative or technical capacity of the *Derg* to implement collectivization is exceedingly dubious.

A special problem arose over the large capitalist farms

and internationally sponsored commercial farming projects that had emerged in the 1960s. Though they occupied only a small amount of land, their output was quite significant in supplying urban markets. Some of these were taken over by peasant associations, while others became state farms. The drop in output on these farms was serious and contributed to the shortfall in grain deliveries to the urban centers.

Although the evidence is far from complete on the land reform—and foreign appraisals extend over the entire gamut from euphoria to condemnation—the remarkable transformation of rural power is beyond dispute. The old local administration, based upon landholding notables, was undermined. The land nationalization had ruined the economic underpinning of the old social aristocracy. The relationship between peasant and state was also altered, perhaps only temporarily, as the necessity to delegate implementation to peasant associations implied an important decentralization. Finally, the fabric of Amharic domination over the conquest zones was greatly loosened, as was the economic power of the Coptic Church.

The other major component of the Derg's reform program was the nationalization of all urban land and rental housing in July 1975. Ostensibly to provide local management of urban land and housing rents, neighborhood associations (kebeles) were formed; they had broad theoretical powers but little practical capacity to fulfill them. The kebeles did prove significant in a rather different role, as local vigilante bodies for the Derg in the bitter struggle for control of the revolution between the Derg and its many civilian opponents in 1976–77. Urban property speculation had been an important source of revenue for the imperial establishment. However, these radical measures also ended rentals of rooms by more humble homeowners and compounded the shortage of low rental housing.

Only after its revolutionary program had been implemented did the Derg begin fully to define its doctrinal identity. Although

"Ethiopian socialism" had entered the regime's vocabulary from December 1974, it was not until 1976 that references began to be made to Marxism-Leninism. The leftward drift of the regime's rhetoric, interestingly, paralleled that of its civilian opposition of students, intellectuals, and labor.

This intensifying struggle was far more than verbal. By fall 1975, the Derg had dissolved the most important labor union, CELU. In August 1975, the Ethiopian People's Revolutionary Party (EPRP) was born; its leadership included many of the student, intellectual, and labor critics of the Derg. The essential similarity of the revolutionary programs proposed contrasted oddly with the ferocity of the antagonism between the EPRP and the Derg. The conflict degenerated into violent confrontation in 1976, and then in 1977 to an assassination campaign by the EPRP that was matched by the Red Terror of the Derg. According to Amnesty International, the latter claimed 5,000 victims, peaking in November 1977.

The Derg—despite strong pressure from its Soviet and Cuban allies in 1977–78—was not able in its first years of power to create a political movement to incarnate the revolution, above all because it was in the last analysis unwilling to share its power. The Derg itself was the antithesis of the vanguard Leninist party: entirely military, secret, and inaccessible, unable to overcome the contradiction between the widespread popular acceptance of much of its revolution and the illegitimacy of its own rule.[104] Only gradually did its existence become known in 1974, and the full list of its members has never been made public. They may have initially totaled 120, but have dwindled to perhaps half that number by death and defection. Conflicts within it periodically become apparent, but remarkably little is known about its inner workings, ideological divisions, or ethnic composition.

The first military leader chosen to serve as head of state by the Derg, General Aman (September–November 1974), was not a member, and his successor, Brigadier Teferi Bante (November

1974–February 1977), never really dominated the organization. When Bante was killed in a Derg shootout in February 1977, for the first time state and Derg leadership visibly coincided in the person of Major Mengistu Haile Meriam.

In late 1975, the establishment of a "Political Bureau" was announced, whose purpose was to form a Derg-controlled revolutionary movement. At first, it was announced that this would be based upon the peasant associations and urban kebeles. For a time, a former exile student leader and Marxist-Leninist intellectual, Haile Fida, served as ideological tutor and political organizer for the Derg Political Bureau. Fida, an Oromo, formed a Marxist movement of his own in early 1976, the All-Ethiopian Socialist Movement (MEISON). Before long, the Derg began to suspect (with good reason) that MEISON aimed at substituting its ideological leadership for that of the Derg and was engaged in a deadly contest for control of the kebeles. By 1977, Fida had been arrested, and MEISON cadres joined the EPRP members as targets for the Red Terror of Mengistu. In early 1977, the Derg encouraged the formation of another movement, the Revolutionary Flame (SEDED), as counterpoise to MEISON. SEDED, however, remained a movement of the military apparatus; its associates were mainly military figures or civilian bureaucrats. The continuously promised Leninist revolutionary party had still not appeared, an unmistakable sign both of the determination of the Derg to monopolize power and its uncertainties about its abilities to control a political movement, once fully launched. A preparatory commission to establish the long-awaited party was created in December 1979, but disputes over composition and ideology at once stymied its work.

Passionate nationalism is a centerpiece of Derg ideological convictions, and some of its most fateful choices—in particular, the Soviet alliance in 1977—are determined by the commitment to Ethiopian unity at least as much as by socialist affinities. The dislocations resulting from the land reforms and absorption of

Derg energies in the intensifying power struggle in the capital offered the occasion for widespread uprisings by disgruntled former landlords, supporters of the old order, and regionalist groups. By 1976, the situation both in the Ogaden and Eritrea deteriorated rapidly, with Ethiopian forces driven out of the greater part of both areas. The threat of a full-scale disintegration of the Ethiopian state loomed.

Initial contacts were made with the Soviet Union (as well as other possible suppliers) to seek new sources of military equipment to cope with the ramifying dissidence. The Soviet price was a full severance of the military relationship with the United States, which continued at a reduced level through the early stages of the revolution. The United States, however, declined to sell the amount of weaponry which the Ethiopian army believed necessary. The Soviet alliance materialized only after the February 1977 killings within the Derg and assumption of full power by Mengistu. The massive flow of an estimated billion dollars of Soviet equipment, and direct Soviet and Cuban logistical and even combat involvement proved decisive in turning back, in spring 1978, what had become a Somali military invasion, and then in permitting the Ethiopian military to regain control of the Eritrean cities.

The image of Ethiopian unity projected by the Derg has altered, and the association of the state with the Shoan Amhara aristocracy has ended. However, a subtle but pervasive identification with the core cultures remains. Brigadier Teferi Bante, though of Oromo background, altered the spelling of his name while in office to imply Amhara connections. The image of a more plebeian, non-Amharic cultural configuration of the state comes from the recruitment of the socially diverse junior officers and noncoms who composed the Derg. Mengistu himself is a case in point; often labeled an Oromo, in reality his father was a low-status Amhara night watchman, while his mother was from a servile southern ethnic community, probably Konso.[105] Many of the Derg members are from the Amhara and Tigre groups, and the military has exhibited little interest in formulas for the achievement of cultural autonomy for the conquered periphery.

The socialist revolution carried out by the military-Marxist state of the Derg has already produced a fundamental mutation in the inner three cultural circles of Ethiopian society. Its impact has been greatest in the countryside, where the social hegemony of the class of Amhara landlords seems permanently destroyed. What exactly will develop in its place remains to be seen; it seems likely that only a portion of the peasantry benefited, and that tenants and migrant workers as well as landlords were driven off land they once tilled. The phenomenal coffee price boom in 1976–77 provided, in the short term, financing for the revolution. In the coffee sector and apparently in the socialized industrial sphere the revolution has not disrupted production, though neither does it appear able to increase it. Grain deliveries to the cities have been uncertain, apparently because of higher rural consumption and marketing difficulties. The ransom of the Soviet–Cuban military support is high, not only in the pervasive military and diplomatic dependency but in the huge debt accumulated for the massive arms shipments.

While the rural sector may be considered a beneficiary of the revolution, the urban areas probably are not. Basic foodstuffs have become scarcer and their prices have soared. The urban land reform has reduced housing availability, and city dwellers find themselves caught in the bitter and deadly struggle between the Derg and its civilian opposition.

The failure of the Derg to define a viable formula for political relationship with the cultural periphery cast darkening shadows over the future of the regime, and even over the country itself in its present form. By 1980, well over a million ethnic Somalis had fled to neighboring Somalia; possibly a third of the Eritrean population took shelter in Sudan. Particularly ominous, for Addis Ababa, was the demographic profile of the refugee population: most were women, children, and old men. The young men of fighting age had remained behind to continue the war against Ethiopian overrule. In Eritrea, after a series of military successes in 1978 and early 1979 in which the Ethiopian army regained control of all towns but Nafca, repeated assaults on this last guerrilla redoubt failed, with heavy Ethiopian losses. In the south, the Oromo Liberation Front began to demand publicly the creation of an independent state of "Oromia."

The most basic contradiction is between the socialist ambitions of the revolution and the narrow military power base upon which it rests. The inability of the *Derg* to really legitimate its rule to the civilian intelligentsia or to the dissident periphery of the Ogaden, Eritrea, and Oromo country, means that the revolutionary state in its present form can survive only through raw military force. While the Red Terror had eased by 1979, this fundamental dilemma remained.

In the new context created by the Soviet military occupation of Afghanistan in December 1979, a chilling question arises: does the Brezhnev doctrine of the limited sovereignty of socialist states, enunciated in Czechoslovakia in 1968, now apply outside Eastern Europe? Would the Soviet Union, whose military support is now crucial to the survival of the *Derg*, permit an alternative regime to emerge, especially if new leadership wished to repudiate either scientific socialism or Soviet tutelage? The Soviets lack the leverage and probably the inclination to preclude ideological evolution or political change in other Afro-Marxist states. In Ethiopia, the Soviets, East Germans, and Cubans may be strongly enough implanted to forestall a change of orientation; the proximity of Ethiopia to the Middle East conflict zone may provide incentives in this direction. Of course, major changes in the configuration of regional and social forces in Ethiopia could occur without any alteration in the vocabulary of politics; in recent years, it is striking that not only the *Derg* but most of its adversaries (in Eritrea, the Ogaden, the south, and the civil intel-

ligentsia in Addis Ababa) formulate their political discourse in
Marxist-Leninist vocabulary.[106]

AFRO-MARXISM IN THE LUSO-TROPICAL ZONE

The other set in the Afro-Marxist array of states is found in the
rubble of the former Portuguese empire. As the liberation struggle gathered force in the 1960s, Marxist currents mingled with
nationalist ones in varying blends. Since these states became independent in 1974–75, all five have declared themselves socialist, but the saliency of Marxism-Leninism has differed substantially. Party congresses of the ruling movements in Mozambique
and Angola in 1977 elevated Marxism-Leninism to the status of
regime dogma, while in Guinea-Bissau doctrinal issues occupied
a much less central role—and in Cape Verde they virtually
disappeared.

The minuscule polities of São Tomé e Príncipe and Cape
Verde are too small and peripheral to weigh heavily in African
ideological discourse. Neither country experienced a real liberation struggle, and the postindependence ruling party in São
Tomé, the *Movimento de Libertação de São Tomé e Príncipe*
(MLSTP), scarcely existed at all on the islands before the Portuguese coup. The leadership has had fairly close intellectual
ties with Angola, which possibly influences their ideological
outlook. The economy is wholly tributary to cocoa plantations,
which have fared poorly since independence. Production has
dropped by half, placing the new state in an exceedingly precarious financial position. The impact of ideological preference
on either political choice or economic outcome is quite unclear,
and too little is known about the São Tomé experience to ap-
praise it.[107]

Guinea-Bissau enjoyed remarkable revolutionary prestige
during the liberation struggle years, both because of the virtual

defeat of the Portuguese colonial army and the striking originality of the political thought of the martyred hero Amilcar
Cabral. During the liberation war era, there was little to distinguish the doctrinal underpinnings of struggle in Angola,
Mozambique, and Guinea-Bissau. However, the latter explicitly
rejected Marxism-Leninism as official party creed at the first
postindependence PAIGC Congress, at about the same time that
the MPLA and FRELIMO made the opposite choice. Thus, although Marxist intellectual currents were important in shaping its ideological perspectives, we will categorize it among the
populist-socialist states and examine its experience in the next
chapter.

WAR SOCIALISM IN ANGOLA

The Angolan and Mozambiquan experiences are difficult to evaluate, though in the long run—because of the size of the two
countries—they are doubtless important and influential. Both
number among the party elite a large fraction whose intellectual
commitment to Marxist-Leninist doctrine is strong. Even so,
both are some distance from Soviet orthodoxy.

The Angolan revolution has been hobbled by the persistent
division of its liberation movements in the days of anticolonial action, and by the civil war, which has afflicted the country
since independence in 1975. During the 1960s, the three major
movements, the *Movimento Popular de Libertação de Angola*
(MPLA), *Frente Nacional de Libertação de Angola* (FNLA),
and the *União Nacional para a Independencia Total de Angola*
(UNITA), seemed to be divided more by ethnicity, external alliance, and personality than by ideology. The MPLA always had
a somewhat more radical image than the others and was the only
movement to have a significant cluster of Marxist intellectuals in
its entourage. But its major thrust was nationalist.[108]

While the classical tenets of Marxist-Leninist analysis of

capitalism and imperialism have been important in the evolution of MPLA doctrine, there is a pronounced infusion of specifically third-world themes. The Vietnamese war of liberation was an important influence; MPLA Party Secretary Lucio Lara stated that "The Vietnamese armed struggle was also very human, a blend of political and military action which became our model. In drawing up our MPLA program, we were strongly influenced by the Vietnamese experience."[109] The political thought of Cabral had a powerful impact on the late MPLA leader Agostino Neto, as did the flamboyant, charismatic, and third-world-oriented socialism of Fidel Castro.

The doctrinal tenets of the independent regime were well summarized by Lara to a sympathetic interviewer (Basil Davidson) in 1977:

> We are going to form an Angolan marxist-leninist party. But what does that mean in practice? It means that we are going to form a revolutionary party consisting of all those militants who have assimilated the teachings of marxism-leninism in relation to Angola, in relation to our own realities and experience, in relation to the needs and possibilities of our own people. We are not in the least concerned with persons who parrot extracts from the marxist classics as though these were some kind of magic. We are concerned with the enrichment of the ideas and methods of marxism-leninism through the revolutionary experience and aspirations of our own country now.[110]

In defining more closely the policy implications of the creed, Neto had told a gathering of trade unionists a few months previously that "The long period of transition from a colonial society to a socialist society will call for a multi-sided form of economic organization. The progress of our economic transformation towards socialism will be expressed by a steady growth of both the state sector and the cooperative sector in the rural areas, and by a steady reduction of the mixed sector, of the private capital sector."[111]

The actual application of socialist doctrine has been shaped more by circumstance than doctrine. The simple abandonment of a vast array of enterprises by the 440,000 Portuguese residents who fled at independence left no other possible manager than the state. In the same way a number of Portuguese farms in the Huambo area became state farms. In the field of oil production, the MPLA and Gulf have had no visible difficulties in maintaining a cordial working relationship. With the Cabindan oil wells accounting for the vast majority of both state revenue and foreign exchange, no other approach is feasible.

The pattern of external intervention in the civil war of 1975 brought about the dramatic Soviet-Cuban involvement on the side of the MPLA and contributed decisively to the triumph of the Neto regime. Continued resistance on the part of UNITA, and its access to external supplies, especially from South Africa, largely explains the continued deployment of the Cuban expeditionary force. Periodic raids on South West African Peoples' Organization (SWAPO) bases by South African troops contribute as well to the embattled mood of the regime. Once committed to its survival, the Soviet Union, East Germany, and other East Europeans have been deeply involved in supporting the security and administrative infrastructure of the regime. In 1980, in addition to approximately 20,000 Cuban troops there were an estimated 17,000 Communist state technicians and advisers (5,000 Soviet, 5,000 East Germans, and 7,000 Cubans). This heavy Communist bloc penetration of the Angolan state has created the appearance of a much higher degree of scientific socialist orthodoxy than in fact prevails.

Indeed, since independence adversity has crowded in from all sides: the spillover of the continuing Namibia impasse; the refusal of the United States to open diplomatic relations; periodic talk in Washington, extending in 1978 and 1981 into White House milieux, of providing support to UNITA; poor relations with Zaire until 1978. Despite frequent hopeful announcements of the imminent full reopening of the Benguela railway, with its valuable transit earning potential for Zaire and Zambia trade, the railway remains highly vulnerable to sabotage and unusable for the copper traffic. Coffee production by 1979 was only about 30,000 tons, compared to 240,000 in 1974; cotton production was a mere 15,000 tons, a quarter of preindependence levels.[112] The major commercial agricultural zones coincided with areas of strength of the rival political movements (FNLA in coffee country, UNITA in the food producing regions centered around Huambo). While the FNLA had collapsed as an effective force soon after independence, security conditions were unsettled in the Kongo areas, and worse in the Ovimbundu areas of central and southern Angola, where UNITA continued to operate. Under these circumstances, it was exceedingly difficult to create decolonized processing and marketing infrastructures in support of the farm sector or to define viable formulas to maintain output on former Portuguese farms.

Add to these obstacles the extremely negative colonial legacy: monopolization of the commercial and productive segments of the economy by the half million Portuguese settlers, slender possibilities for Africans to acquire the skills required for its operation, export or destruction of large amounts of equipment at the time of the 1975 exodus (especially vehicles). Policy was necessarily shaped by the daily struggle for survival. The eloquently articulated ideological superstructure rested lightly upon a substructure of ingenious improvisation.

Not only has the continuation of the civil war deepened Angolan dependency on the socialist camp, but the absence of any serious prospect of Western aid leaves no real alternative. While Soviet military and diplomatic support has been a vital asset to the regime in the face of its hostile surroundings, economic assistance has been neither generous nor particularly effective. Through 1978, Soviet economic aid amounted to only $17 million; Angola's most important Comecon aid agreement was with Rumania, in 1978 (with $75 million pledged).[113] Angola was required by the terms of a fishing accord that was consistent with the widely criticized Soviet pattern encountered in many littoral African states to concede to the Soviets 75 percent of the offshore fish offtake. A significant fraction of the oil earnings flows to the Soviet Union in payment for arms debts.

The sense of economic impasse pervaded the deliberations of a special session of the MPLA Central Committee in May 1980. While the basic ideological orientation of the regime was re-affirmed, the need for some doctrinal compromise, at least temporarily, was also recognized. The Central Committee resolutions appeared to parallel new policy declarations in Mozambique two months earlier: "The worrisome economic and financial situation of the country is due fundamentally to the drop in production and productivity—including other factors of a structural and organizational nature—as well as to the effects of the general capitalist crisis and continued South African acts of aggression. . . . the poor performance of some sectors of the state apparatus has contributed greatly to the existence of this situation." As a remedy, the party called for "studying ways of supporting and encouraging private and individual initiatives in the economic field, namely in the sectors of cattle raising, domestic trade and industry and services. . . ."[114]

The sense of ideological purpose that doubtless animates the inner corps of political cadres of the regime probably helps sustain the country in these years of privation and difficulty, when the shortages and dislocations in daily life inevitably demoralize many citizens. The lethal coup attempt by Nito Alves in May 1977 and the death of the revered President Neto in August 1978 were two major crisis points, both overcome by the MPLA. The continuous atmosphere of crisis within which the Afro-Marxist experiment in Angola has proceeded makes both premature and unfair any appraisal of its effectiveness and prospects.

However, the credibility of scientific socialism in Angola could probably not withstand indefinitely the stagnation of the postindependence years. Most visitors to Luanda sense a decreasing saliency to ideological pronouncements and a sober recognition of the difficulties of the economic problems; Angola cannot forever remain a rentier state subsisting on Gulf Oil.

Leading MPLA theoretician Lara, in a 1981 interview, reflected on his impressions on reading a harshly critical analysis of socialist agricultural experiments in neighboring Zambia by French agronomist René Dumont: "I read Dumont and saw my own country. We make big plans and we don't know enough to be realistic about our actual problems. For example, we made some plans with the Bulgarians or the Russians to grow cotton, and we bought their machines. But the machines turn out not to work here; they're not suitable for Angola. Again, I saw a giant machine for pineapple cultivation. It had never been used. You see that kind of thing everywhere. We need to do things our own way." [115]

MOZAMBIQUE: BELLWETHER FOR SCIENTIFIC SOCIALISM IN AFRICA

In Mozambique, the exceptional prestige earned by FRELIMO during the liberation struggle and its strategic location combine to spotlight this socialist experiment. After the failure of most of the first wave of socialist ventures in Africa in the early 1960s and the difficulties encountered in the 1970s by Tanzania, eyes are riveted upon Mozambique. The Mozambique regime has— quite unwittingly—become a bellwether for the future of socialism in Africa. Either remarkable success or resounding failure would reverberate throughout Africa. In the real world, of course, such clear-cut historical verdicts are the exception; more likely are ambiguous and contradictory results that permit each observer to find vindication for his preferences. [116]

The major resource that the new regime possessed was the relatively high coherence and well-articulated structure of its liberation movement, FRELIMO. While the formal commitment to Marxism-Leninism was made only at the 1977 conference, a substantial ideological consensus among the FRELIMO leadership had developed by the early 1970s. The assassination in 1969 of the first FRELIMO leader, Eduardo Mondlane, led to a period of factional struggle for succession, but these divisions had largely disappeared by 1972. While the rural infrastructure of FRELIMO was limited to the northern half of the country when independence suddenly came in 1975, the party was nonetheless a potent organizational weapon. The declaration that this highly structured body was to become a Leninist party in 1977 implied a less dramatic change in organization and style of operation than the similar decision for MPLA—or the rejected proposal in the sense for the PAIGC in Guinea-Bissau.

The evolution of FRELIMO into a revolutionary socialist party came only by degrees and was shaped both by the protracted struggle and the African context within which it evolved. When founded in 1962, with the quiet encouragement of Nkrumah and Nyerere, it was a coalescence of three preexisting organizations with rather disparate regional and ideological constituencies; its common denominator was nationalism and liberation, and its leader, Mondlane, was not of a Marxist intellectual formation. After two years of preparation, armed struggle began in 1964; formal ideological discourse took second place to the necessities of slow, patient permeation of the overwhelmingly rural northern belt, accessible from the Tanzanian rear bases. The revolutionary classroom, for this peasant audience, was the same as that in which Machel received his first political education; as he later described it, this came ". . . not from the writing in books. Not from reading Marx and Lenin. But seeing my father forced to grow cotton for the Portuguese and going with him to the market where he was forced to sell it at a low price—much lower than the white Portuguese cotton grower." [117]

When the factional struggles unleashed by the Mondlane assassination had been overcome, the socialist content of the Mozambique revolution gradually became more explicit. Some analysts argue that by 1972 FRELIMO was firmly moored to Marxist-Leninist doctrine; [118] other observers with sensitive ideological antennas, such as John Saul, who toured guerrilla areas inside Mozambique in 1972, found the common language of peasant and cadre to be essentially populist and nationalist.[119] But at the leadership level, scientific socialism increasingly predominated. This consensus of the revolutionary vanguard was consecrated as party doctrine at the third FRELIMO congress, held in 1977.

As in Angola, the political economy of Portuguese colonialism left Mozambique with enormous obstacles. Only in the final three decades of the colonial era did much development occur. The European population, which was only 27,500 in 1940 and only 60,000 in 1960, shot up to 200,000 by 1975. A large white farming area emerged in the south, with a substantial transformation of the African peasantry into tenants and farm laborers. This development was paralleled by the massive incorporation of Mozambique into the South African economic zone, symbolized most dramatically in 1969 by the groundbreaking for the Cabora Bassa dam, fourth largest in the world; the entire power output is transmitted by direct current line into South Africa, with a small fraction then relayed back to Mozambique. Prior to 1975, some 50 to 60 percent of the foreign exchange earnings came from South Africa, mainly through a gold premium paid for the 100,000 mine workers supplied annually, and the Transvaal transit trade, through Maputo port. South African management remains crucial to the hydroelectric station, the railways, and Maputo port installations.

The internationalization of the colonial capitalist economy and the swift expansion of the settler community brought few benefits to the African populace. No more than 15 percent of Mozambiquans knew Portuguese, a measure of the very limited scope of the African educational system.[120] Indeed, English may be more widely spoken than Portuguese, since hundreds of thousands of Mozambiquan miners have worked in South Africa. In 1975, of 2,000 students at then Lourenço Marques University, fewer than 30 were Mozambiquan Africans.[121]

To the negative colonial legacy were added the spillover

costs of the Zimbabwe struggle. Mozambique joined in the application of sanctions, at a cost of $550 million from 1975 to 1979 in lost transit trade. The sanctuary provided to the Zimbabwe African National Union (ZANU) guerrillas exposed the country to regular and deadly military incursions by Rhodesian security forces, who did not limit themselves to attacking only Zimbabwe guerrilla and refugee camps, but also hit Mozambiquan targets. The Smith government also provided bases, equipment, broadcast facilities, and logistical backing to Mozambiquan dissidents, who were a minor but not negligible nuisance.

Despite these many handicaps, FRELIMO in 1975 resolutely began building by its socialist blueprint. Extending the party organization into the as yet weakly penetrated south was an urgent priority. So too, for the leadership, was the challenge of winning rank and file acceptance of and commitment to FRELIMO ideology. "Dynamizing groups" were formed throughout the country, charged with the mission of political indoctrination. In 1977, an extended electoral process created, by indirect stages, a People's Assembly. These popular consultations, though within the single-party framework, were a novel experience and appear to have engendered active participation. Mass involvement, however, does not extend to debate over the basic options or policy orientations of the regime. Whether it will survive either the revamping of FRELIMO under more explicitly Leninist lines of "democratic centralism" or the bureaucratic centralism endemic to the Marxist-Leninist state remains to be seen.

Within a short period of time following independence, a huge state sector had been erected. In doctrinal terms, the regime distinguishes between a core of sectors deemed "vital to the maintenance of national sovereignty" (oil refining, coal mining, banking, and insurance), for which nationalization was imperative, and a much larger swath of the economy where it occurred by default, in response to the abandonment of enterprises by fleeing Portuguese.[122] The largest takeover of a foreign enterprise involved the British-owned Sena Sugar Estates, which employed

12,000 workers and had produced 173,000 tons in 1973 (but only 45,000 in 1978). The Mozambique regime tried hard to dissuade the British owners from withdrawing, but they considered the firm bankrupt. The regime is prepared to negotiate compensation for those foreign enterprises actually nationalized.[123]

In contrast to Tanzania, the Mozambique regime has declared that heavy industry is the imperative pathway for socialist development. The plans include an aluminum plant, a steel mill, and a paper factory, among others, though financing for the more ambitious schemes appears problematic. However, the country does possess a promising endowment of natural resources (iron, coal, uranium, copper, tantalite, bauxite, and natural gas, among others). The development of these is inevitably contingent on both the regime's stability and its ability to find formulas for collaboration with Western finance and technology.

In the rural sphere, the socialist thrust seems at first glance very extensive. The abandoned Portuguese estates, especially those in the south, have been converted into state farms, which numbered about 2,000 by 1979. Elsewhere, it is claimed that 1,500 peasant collectives involving up to 1,000,000 persons had been organized. Apparently most of these are accounted for by the conversion of the Portuguese-built strategic hamlets in the north into collectives and the resettlement of peasants uprooted by severe flooding in the Zambezi and Limpopo valleys in 1977–78.[124]

The impact of FRELIMO's rural policy on production has been varied. Some crops have recovered; a respectable cotton harvest of 80,000 tons was achieved in 1978. However, output for such crops as sugar and cashews remains far below preindependence levels. To what extent either the successes or the failures can be ascribed to the specifically socialist content of Mozambiquan agricultural policy is unclear.

The egalitarian commitment of FRELIMO is visible in a number of spheres. Civil service salaries have been held quite low. Emancipation of women is declared to be "a fundamental necessity of the Revolution, a guarantee of its continuity, a condition of its triumph."[125] Words alone do not alter entrenched sexual inequalities, but genuine regime backing for female equality makes a very big difference. Health policy stresses preventive medicine in rural areas, while in education major efforts have been deployed to extend adult mass literacy. The meager school system accessible to Africans has been tripled in enrollment since independence.

Close ties have developed with the Soviet Union, though during the liberation struggle FRELIMO was politically closer to the Chinese. Following the signing of a friendship treaty with the Soviet Union in 1977, there was a large influx of Comecon technicians. However, the actual aid has been primarily military. By the end of 1977, only $3 million in economic aid had been committed by the Soviets. Mozambique has found that Soviet goods are less attractive in price, financing, service, quality, and delivery times than those provided by traditional European sources, and the country apparently pays cash for most Soviet technical services. Despite the friendship treaty, Mozambique to date has steadfastly refused Soviet requests for base facilities.[126]

The transition to socialism in Mozambique has not been accomplished primarily by coercion. In part this reflects the legitimacy of party and leadership earned in the liberation struggle. Also, those most threatened by FRELIMO Marxism-Leninism were mostly among the European community, over 90 percent of whom fled. Despite the rigor of the official doctrine, there has been little class struggle in Mozambique; a triumphant national liberation movement found that the tentacular, war-bloated colonial capitalist sector simply vanished when its metropolitan support was withdrawn.

However, there are elements of repression. Their most visible form is the network of "reeducation camps," where foes of the regime are arbitrarily confined alongside hardened criminals for indefinite terms. Conditions in these centers are grim, and the detainees are incommunicado. Estimates of the population of the camps range from 5,000 to 12,000. Whether such centers accomplish their evangelical aims of ideological rehabilitation remains to be demonstrated.[127]

More important to the survival of Mozambiquan socialism than the modest levels of internal opposition now faced was the reconciliation of its doctrine with the measures required to salvage the fragile economy. In March 1980, Machel excoriated the state sector for its lagging performance and declared that private entrepreneurs, including former owners, were welcome back in much of the commercial and service sphere that had fallen into state hands by default. The state, the president asserted, should not sell matches; its energies should be reserved for the critical productive sectors. More broadly, the regime intensified its efforts to attract Western capital for its development programs.

Does this betoken the gradual erosion of Afro-Marxism in Mozambique? Such a conclusion would be premature. From the regime's perspective, the declarations of March 1980 are no more than a tactical adjustment to meet the specific immediate needs of the Mozambique venture in socialism: a step back today to permit two steps forward tomorrow. Yet surely the restoration of a thriving private commercial sector and an extensive partnership with Western capital on major resource development and industrial projects would affect the chemistry of ideological fermentation, not to mention its social environment. But the choices are few. Should socialism in Mozambique sink into a prolonged stagnation, cumulatively stigmatized as "failure," the consequences would be profound, not only for FRELIMO but for all those attracted by the Afro-Marxist pathway.

CONCLUDING OBSERVATIONS

We thus find that despite the claims of scientific socialists that their doctrine is of universal and singular validity the political uses of Marxism by incumbent regimes are quite diverse. Marxism in mufti is especially likely to yield quite eclectic and—from an orthodox Marxist viewpoint—deviant results, above all because the ideology serves in the last resort to legitimate the power of a particular military group. There is as yet no instance where Marxist-Leninist regimes in Africa have been able to achieve forced-draft economic expansion; on the other hand, no Marxist regime has yet mismanaged itself into bankruptcy, as have Ghana and Zaire. Nor have any been marked by high levels of venality. Some, such as Benin, have performed better than their predecessors. While the socialist world will on occasion provide substantial military force (Angola and Ethiopia) and will always sell weapons, the kind of economic generosity made available to Cuba in its years of struggle for survival is not forthcoming for Marxist rulers in Africa. Self-reliance is not only an ideological preference but a practical necessity. Equally imperative is a prudent maintenance of economic relationships with the Western world. The inspirational advice offered by some dependency theorists to "disengage from international capitalism" is nowhere heeded, if it is anywhere heard.

An ultimate verdict on the Afro-Marxist pathway will probably hinge on the political evolution and economic performance of Mozambique in the 1980s. Congo-Brazzaville, Benin, and Madagascar are too heterodox in their doctrine to serve as undisputed models, and Marxism there is too intertwined in military and regional factionalism. Scientific socialism in Somalia has been overtaken by the broader conflicts on the Horn and the ensuing reversal of strategic alliances. The embattled regimes in Ethiopia and Angola face the prospect of continuing civil war. Only in Mozambique are all the elements of the exemplary experience assembled: a sophisticated and united leadership; a relatively clear-cut ideological identity; a coherent political underpinning in FRELIMO. The 1980s will be a critical decade for this interesting experiment in political economy.

3

The Populist Socialist Pathway

THE EMERGENCE OF AFRICAN SOCIALISM

The publication in 1956 of *Les masses africaines et l'actuelle condition humaine* by Senegalese intellectual Abdoulaye Ly opened a new chapter in African ideological discourse.[1] Until that time, nationalist thought had been essentially anticolonial, preoccupied with establishing the claim to political independence and determining the territorial units to which self-determination would apply. As independence suddenly loomed on the horizon, the necessity for a definition of the postcolonial pathway became apparent. With striking swiftness, the kaleidoscopic doctrine of "African socialism" took form. By 1962, African socialism stood at the apogee of its continental prestige; in that year, one of its paramount philosopher-kings, Leopold Sédar Senghor of Senegal, convened a conference in Dakar to define its common themes.[2]

To those who transformed anticolonial nationalism into African socialism were added others who overthrew venal and discredited regimes, particularly in Egypt and Libya; from a starting point of intense nationalism and rejection of the previous ruling class, socialism gradually was assimilated into the ideological pronouncements of Abdel Gamal Nasser and Muammar Wanis al-Qadafy. Tunisia as well, whose initial doctrine was liberal nationalism, went through a phase of socialist self-identification during the 1962–69 period. The flamboyance and charisma of such leaders as Nasser, Qadafy, and Bourguiba enhanced the visibility of their doctrinal pronouncements.

While the diverse creeds loosely assembled under the umbrella of African socialism never had the coherence or uniformity of "scientific socialist" thought, there were some recurrent themes, which bore the mark of the most influential spokesmen, especially Senghor and Nyerere. Reflecting the roots of African socialism in anticolonial nationalism was the stress upon the common interests of the entire populace. Afirician societies were held to be relatively homogeneous, without sharply demarcated social classes; the social enemy was external, in the form of Western imperial structures. The doctrine of class struggle, accordingly, was held to be alien to socialism in Africa.

For Senghor and Nyerere, not only were contemporary African societies relatively free of class division, but the cultural heritage of rural Africa was founded upon a communitarian ethos. Resources—above all, land—were held by the community and production relations were suffused with a natural egalitarian solidarity. The capitalist instincts of individualism and acquisitiveness were held to be alien to the African heritage; in the classic formulation of Nyerere:

For when a society is so organized that what it cares about is individuals, then, provided he is willing to work, no individual within that society should worry about what will happen to him tomorrow if he does not hoard wealth today. Society itself should look after him. . . . This is exactly what traditional African society succeeded in doing. Both the "rich" and the "poor" were completely secure in African society. . . . Nobody starved, either of food or of human dignity, because he lacked personal wealth; he could depend on the wealth possessed by the community of which he was a member. That was socialism. That is socialism.[3]

Because it was ethically rooted in the African heritage, socialism in Africa was an original doctrine and thus had no obligation to follow the prescriptions contained in the universal corpus of socialist thought. For Senghor, the African road to socialism must be deduced within the ontological framework of *négritude.* Specificity must accordingly be its fundamental postulate.[4]

The distinctiveness of socialism in Africa, and in particular its non-Marxist basis, was a general motif. In Algeria and Tunisia, it was argued that Islam itself bore the seeds of socialism. In the words of Bourguiba, "even the companions of the Prophet . . . were socialist before the invention of the word, considering themselves members of the same family. . . ."[5] Nyerere, in a 1967 speech, took strong exception to the conception of socialism as a singular and universal theory:

Unfortunately, however, there has grown up what I can only call a "theology of socialism." People argue—sometimes quite violently—about what is the true doctrine. . . . Frankly, this seems to me to be absurd. I am a Christian and it is part of my belief that the word of God is expressed in the Bible. To me, therefore, in spite of—or even because of— the contradictions of the Bible, it is quite sensible to try to get its full meaning and, when I am trying to act in accordance with God's wishes, to refer to those who have given the Bible a detailed study. . . . But the books on socialism are different. They are written by men; wise and clever men perhaps—but still men. Consequently we should use their books as we use the work of living people—knowing that one individual may contribute greatly to the solution of a problem, but that no man is infallible. Indeed, I think that this idea that there is one "pure socialism" for which the recipe is already known, is an insult to human intelligence.[6]

The sundry forms of African socialism began to lose their intellectual ascendance in the late 1960s, encountering criticisms from all directions. The empirical soundness of the communitarian ethical heritage was questioned.[7] The thesis of the classless African society was challenged, both as historical fact and contemporary reality.[8] The diffuseness of the doctrine and the absence of a clear programmatic content blurred its appeal. The mediocrity of the economic performance of some regimes most closely associated in the public eye with the socialist pathway— Ghana, Guinea, and Mali—and the initial public enthusiasm at the overthrow of such respected spokesmen as Kwame Nkrumah

(1966) or Modibo Keita (1968) dulled its glitter. At one end of the spectrum the malaise was diagnosed as the deviation from universally valid principles of "scientific socialism." At the other, market-economy states such as Kenya and Ivory Coast pointed to a better economic performance than their socialist neighbors.

POPULIST SOCIALISM AS A DOCTRINE OF DEVELOPMENT

While the freshness of its allure is long gone, what Rosberg and Callaghy have termed "first wave" socialist regimes have not entirely vanished from the scene. Forms of socialism that belong to this generation of ideological discourse have informed the policy perspectives of Tanzania, Algeria, and Guinea for two decades—though Guinea after 1977 appeared to be seeking a different formula. The blend of radical Arab nationalism and socialism that—in differing combinations—characterized the eras of Nasser and Qadafy also belongs to this ideological family. While there are very substantial differences between, say, Nyerere and Boumedienne, I believe that the differing experiences of these "first wave" socialist regimes can be usefully considered together. I shall, in this chapter, give particular scrutiny to Tanzania, Algeria, and Guinea-Bissau, with briefer consideration to Nkrumah's Ghana, Keita's Mali, and Guinea. In all these instances a socialist perspective did shape—or at least legitimate—major policy choices. Further, the pathway was pursued for a sufficient period of time to make possible analysis of its implications and consequences. I shall not include either Senegal or Libya in this discussion. In the case of the former, despite the sheer intellectual elegance of the Senghor contribution at a philosophic level, it is not easy to distinguish clearly Senegalese development strategy from that of liberal market-economy states. In the case of Libya, while there is no reason to doubt the personal austerity or intellectual conviction of the leadership, the enormous oil revenues available to the state eliminate the factor of scarcity in policy choice and its evaluation. If the flood of public revenue is in fact used for societal purposes, it is difficult for any policy to fail.

Perhaps the best characterization of this set of regimes is populist-socialist. While their ideologies do not offer a comprehensive model of development, there is a syndrome of orienting perspectives that condition their policy choices. I would suggest five elements that define the populist-socialist perspective.

First, these regimes are intensely nationalist. In all instances, nationalism precedes socialism chronologically. Nasser, for example, had virtually completed the set of land reform and nationalization measures before beginning to invoke socialist doctrine as sanction. The Algerian revolution was well launched before a socialist option was declared. Tanzanian socialism remained very abstract until the 1967 Arusha Declaration. Assaults upon the citadels of foreign ownership and economic domination find as ready moral nurture in nationalism as in socialism.

Second, they are characterized by a radical mood. The term is vague, yet reflects a tangible reality. Radicalism translates into impatience with perceived injustice, a willingness to incur risks, international and internal, a more confrontational style in dealing with adversaries.[9]

Third, an underlying anticapitalism pervades policy thought. The historical linkage of capitalism and imperialism partly explains this perspective and joins it to intense nationalism. But more than this was involved; capitalism was believed to rest upon flawed and debased ethical principles. Acquisitiveness corrupts, because the accumulation of wealth rests upon "the comparative discomfort of the rest of society" and requires the exploitation "of the abilities and enterprise of other people."[10] Capitalism must be rejected both as an attitude of mind and a method of economic organization.

Fourth, there is an exaltation of the "people," hence populism. Ideology is pervaded with a moralistic celebration of the

virtues of the mass, above all the rural mass. Frantz Fanon, phi-
losopher of the Algerian revolution, celebrated the peasant, pu-
rified in the crucible of violence, as carrier of the moral values of
society. Populism is a loose ideological referent in and of itself;
its students have described it as being—like radicalism—more a
mentality than a creed. While populism is not an appeal to class
war, it does juxtapose the virtues and rights of rural folk to the
menacing encroachment of international capitalism.[11]

Last, socialism—though not orthodox Marxism—becomes a
diffuse yet important component of the syndrome. The sources
of socialism are diverse—Fabianism for Nyerere, the socialist
current of the French left for Keita or Touré, Middle East radical
thought for Nasser and Qadafy. Given the immense impact of
Marxism, directly and indirectly, in the overall evolution of socialist thought, it would be misleading to maintain that there are
no elements of Marxist thought in African populist socialism.
The Marxist imprint is clearly visible in several of the cases we
will examine, especially Guinea, Mali, and Guinea-Bissau. But
ideologists within this school generally describe themselves as
non-Marxists, or at least deny they are embracing Marxism as a
systematic doctrine.

Though populist socialism does not yield a very clear-cut
"model" of development, observation of these regimes, as well as
of comparable experiences elsewhere in the third world (Peru in
1968–75, Sukarno's Indonesia, the Ba'ath regime in Iraq), does
reveal some common policy patterns. There is a general stress
upon a large public sector, particularly through the nationalization of foreign holdings. The development strategy is usually
very statist in conception. Radical rural reforms characterize
most of these regimes: land reform in Egypt; *auto-gestion* in Algeria; *ujamaa* in Tanzania; socialist production experiments in
Guinea and Mali. However, comprehensive planning receives
rather less stress than in the Afro-Marxist states; there is a less
compulsive attachment to the command economy concept. Finally, the populist impulses that color regime ideologies exalt

‚ass participation in theory, usually through a single party intended to mobilize the entire populace. But in practice, participation tends to be quite limited, defined, and orchestrated
from the summit; Tanzania comes closest to being an exception
to this last trait.

TANZANIA: "WE MUST RUN WHILE THEY MAY WALK"

Of the set of populist socialist regimes that concern us, Tanzania
is the most important. While there has been some evolution in
Nyerere's political thought over the years and some alteration of
policy to accommodate shifting circumstances, nonetheless the
underlying ethical foundation of his political ideology—and by
virtue of his unquestionable ascendancy, that of the regime—has
been remarkably consistent over two decades. From the very outset, the unusual appeal of Nyerere's political personality—the
simplicity and modesty of his style, the generosity of his sentiments, the unwavering integrity of his leadership—won for the
Tanzanian experience an attentive and sympathetic audience
both inside and outside of Africa. Ali Mazrui noted a decade ago
the phenomenon of "Tanzaphilia," or the cult of uncritical adulation that surrounded the Tanzanian experience.[12] By this fact
Tanzania has become a critical test of non-Marxist socialism in
Africa: egalitarian in creed, generally honest in application, consistent in its adherence to its ideological charter.

   While the ethical foundations for Tanzanian socialism were
laid down with the publication of the doctrinal document *Ujamaa* in 1962, for the first years of independence its policy appli-
cations were limited.[13] The momentum of the welfare and development programs of the terminal colonial era carried forward,
and the country counted heavily upon Western investment and
aid to finance its first five-year plan. Cooperatives were expected
to assure peasant control over their major cash crops. Consider-

able energies were deployed to achieve genuine participation through a single-party framework. While the capitalist ethos was decried in the *Ujamaa* statement, little was done in practice to circumscribe it. Indeed, the principled nonracialism of Nyerere appeared to guarantee a more secure role for the main mercantile group, the Asian community, than in neighboring Kenya. Though the country had a satisfactory growth record during these years—4.5 percent real growth per annum, or 1.5 percent per capita[14]—there were a number of trends that Nyerere viewed as ominous. The flow of public and private Western capital fell far short of expectations, while at the same time political irritations multiplied in relations with Britain, the United States, and West Germany. Civil servants and politicians displayed distressingly acquisitive instincts in the pursuit of leisure time capitalist ventures in such spheres as urban housing, transport, and beverage distribution. The cooperatives were a bitter disappointment: farmers were outraged by their unreliable marketing services and occasional dishonesty, while party leaders were disconcerted by the autonomous mercantile fiefdoms that the leaders of the larger cooperatives constructed. A presidential inquiry in 1966 encountered a barrage of farmer grievances.[15]

In 1967, the socialist ethos was translated into concrete policy through a far-reaching program set forth in the Arusha Declaration. While this was ostensibly a party document, it reflected above all the moral vision of Nyerere himself. As Pratt observes, at the time, the Arusha blueprint did not embody the demands of either a revolutionary working class or a mobilized peasantry. Neither did it then reflect an ideology widely held by the elite. Nor, on the other hand, did it encounter strong resistance from the political and administrative class; there was no alternative body of thought to be displaced.[16]

As Shivji asserts with some acerbity,[17] Arusha was not a "proletarian ideology," but it nonetheless set forth a radical set of moral axioms: the aim was a "truly socialist society" where all people were workers, where no one lived on the work of others,

TABLE 3.1. Acquisition of Parastatal Assets, 1966–71, Tanzania

| Sector | (shs millions) | | | | | | |
	1966	1967	1968	1969	1970	1971	Total
Manufacturing		134	102	86	2		324
Mining							
Construction							
Electricity							
Transport							
Tourism		1					1
Commerce		11			86	250	347
Agriculture		120					120
Finance		96					96
Total		326	102	86	88	250	888

SOURCE: W. Edmund Clark, *Socialist Development and Public Investment in Tanzania 1964–1973* (Toronto: University of Toronto Press, 1978), p. 107.

where "all major means of production and exchange were controlled and owned by the peasants through the machinery of their Government and their co-operatives," and where the ruling party was "a Party of peasants and workers."[18] Pursuant to these principles, the public sector was to be speedily enlarged. First on the nationalization list were the financial institutions, whose control of capital flow was believed to be the jugular vein of the still-capitalist economy. A broad-front enlargement of the parastatal sector followed, as documented in table 3.1.

In reality, the mercantilist tradition of the colonial state had created a substantial public sector even before Arusha. Pan-African considerations also entered; a large fraction of public investment in the late 1960s was committed to developing the Zambian transport corridor, a political response to the Rhodesian crisis. However, the socializing thrust in the years immediately following 1967 placed the state in at least formal control of a large swath of the economy: banks, insurance, export–import, mining, most manufacture. The final major swoop in 1971 extended the parastatal domain into urban real estate, the

last retreat of Asian capital. This was added to earlier state control, direct or indirect, of electricity, railways, major hotels, and
agricultural marketing. The public sector was expanded not only
through nationalization but also through the creation by state investment of new enterprises, especially the National Development Corporation. Indeed, Reginald Green (an economic adviser
to the Tanzanian government in these years) argues that by the
mid-1970s, 80 percent of the medium- and large-scale economic
activity lay in the public sector, generating 44 percent of mone-
tary GDP; 80 percent of total investment was accounted for by
the public sector or its contractors. These figures, he maintains,
were higher than those for Soviet bloc states a comparable time
after the imposition of Stalinist socialism.[19] The private sector by
1971 was quite circumscribed, mainly in smaller-scale commercial spheres. However, a number of the parastatals were joint
ventures with private partners, especially in the manufacturing
sector; as of 1971, two-thirds of parastatal manufacturing assets
were in firms with at least some private equity.[20]

The phase of public sector expansion was accomplished sur-
prisingly painlessly, and the early doomsayers were confounded
by the skill with which ownership transfer of the major foreign
banks was negotiated and by the minimal disruption that attended their metamorphosis into parastatal agencies. Figures
through 1974 showed an overall profit rate for the parastatal sector of 17 percent,[21] although this was concentrated mainly in the
finance and commercial segments of the state realm. A sympathetic critic of the Tanzanian socialist strategy, writing in the
mid-1970s, chided the parastatals not for losses incurred or mismanagement but for their proclivity for capital-intensive operation, import dependency, and urban concentration (especially in
Dar es Salaam); thus, Clark argues, scarce management resources
are tied up in operations that have the same flaws as their private
predecessors.[22]

However, disenchantment with the performance of the public sector grew in the following years, partly as a spillover from

the agricultural crisis. In 1977, the government for the first time in a decade smiled upon small-scale commercial, manufacturing, and housing private expansion. The state would concentrate its efforts on the larger ventures. These, too, would be held more strictly accountable for profitability. Parastatals were warned that those that continued to lose money would face liquidation or transfer to the private sector.[23] These warnings now applied to a significant fraction of the parastatal domain.

The battle against capitalism was also pursued by the enactment of a strict leadership code. Party and state personnel were prohibited from holding private directorships or company shares and from owning rental housing. Further, civil servant salaries were sharply eroded over the years through inflation; between 1971 and 1974, senior salaries lost 25 percent of their value. The ratio between the official minimum wage and top civil service brackets fell from 80:1 in 1960 to only 11:1 in 1974.[24] Perquisites were curbed, and import restrictions on such consumption items as automobiles made virtually impossible a life-style modeled on the expatriate predecessors of Tanzanian administrators. The much more generous terms of service (and off-hour opportunities) available to the Kenya public service next door could hardly fail to leave residues of relative deprivation.

While the bureaucratic class was still privileged in comparison to most of their fellow citizens, few if any other African states have gone farther in impeding the translation of administrative status into mercantile affluence. The bureaucracy was no doubt more responsive to the nationalist thrust of public sector expansion than to the austerity inflicted upon it. There has always been some undercurrent of grumbling, but until 1974 the public morale of the bureaucracy was reasonably positive, primarily because of the continuing legitimacy of Nyerere himself. However, the palpable drop in material well-being during the 1974–75 crisis made discontent more manifest; Lofchie argues that the "demoralization of public-sector employees became one of the basic facts of political life that had to be taken into account by Tanzania's leadership in any calculation of future policy."[25] From another perspective, the leadership elite, political and bureaucratic, is seen by advocates of a more rigorous socialism as "an inevitably exploitative group, fitted into a network of foreign contact: while making minor practical concessions to Tanzania's socialist goals and major rhetorical obeisance, they are seen as the real obstacles to the achievement of that socialist policy."[26]

A transformation of the educational system was envisaged as a critical underpinning to the future socialist society. Nyerere, in an eloquently succinct pamphlet accompanying the Arusha Declaration, "Education for Self-Reliance," laid bare the contradictions of the inherited educational system and the goals of egalitarianism. Schools fostered elitism, alienated pupils from their rural backgrounds, and were a motor of inequality. Schooling was to be redirected to prepare youth for rural life and cooperative endeavor.[27]

These objections to the educational system were not novel and not confined to those of a socialist perspective. Nonetheless, new energies were deployed in refashioning this peculiarly resistant institution. There was continuing quantitative expansion and a redeployment of resources to the advantage of the more disinherited regions of the country, though the forward momentum of the educationally advanced zones such as Kilimanjaro and Bukoba was really impossible to arrest: local initiative in sustaining school expansion at once replaced government effort, as social elites from these areas could hardly be expected to accept foreclosure of mobility opportunities for their children as the ransom of egalitarianism.[28] There is reason to doubt, moreover, whether the post-Arusha educational reforms have fared better than earlier efforts in promoting a commitment to rural life and agricultural labor, when the rewards for this are so meager. One study in two districts shows that the agricultural work incorporated into the rural school curriculum is viewed by students as simply a source of revenue for the school and staff and by the parents as a waste of their children's time.[29] Political education has been more effective in diffusing socialist vocabulary than attitudes engendered by Arusha. The challenge of fundamentally transforming an education system is daunting. Court, while noting that patience and persistence may well have a greater impact over time than is so far visible, concludes that the educational component of the Arusha socialist strategy "aims to fit students into a type of society that does not yet exist, and places excessive faith in changing student attitudes as a means of producing the desired reality." [30]

The egalitarian social policy was also reflected in the health field. From 1971, there was a sharp reorientation of medical outlays away from high-cost, Western-model, curative medicine and toward rural, paramedical, and preventive health care. By 1974, the fraction of the health budget allocated to hospitals had dropped from 80 percent in the late 1960s to 50 percent. [31]

The political pillar of the egalitarian socialist society was the democratic single party, the Tanganyika African National Union (TANU, now Chama Cha Mapinduzi, or CCM, uniting Zanzibar with the mainland in one party). This aspect of Tanzanian populist socialism was developed before Arusha gave programmatic content to socialism. A carefully designed formula was developed for assuring a measure of debate and competition within the framework of the inclusive single party. The formula was a model for those later adopted by other states (Zambia, Kenya), which provided for limited competition for parliamentary seats within the party framework. [32] The striking turnover engendered by this formula in its initial application (in 1965) gave it real credibility; only twenty-one of eighty-one outgoing mainland MPs won reelection. [33] Subsequent elections in 1970 and 1975 had less dramatic results but did confirm the turnover pattern; in the latter year only forty-three of eighty-six former members retained their seats, while in 1970 38 percent of the deputies were reelected. The important limitations in the party's capacity to serve as a vehicle for rural participation have been thoroughly documented by a number of authors. [34] Nonetheless, in both

ethos and structure the party provided elements of access to the
citizenry at large that were substantially greater than in most African parties; this fact forms part of the texture of populism that
characterizes the Tanzanian political style.

In the early 1970s, the coterie of scientific socialists (mainly
expatriate) at the University of Dar es Salaam agitated for the
transformation of TANU into a true Leninist vanguard party; the
reasons for Nyerere's refusal to countenance such a change il-
luminate the issues that separated Tanzanian regime ideology
from Afro-Marxist thought. TANU, Nyerere believed, had been
formed as a mass party, and acceptance of the Leninist vanguard
concept would require renunciation of its most central values.
The Leninist party was seen as a vehicle for ideological elitism,
all the more since the version of socialism sought by the vanguard party advocates was supported by very few Tanzanians.
Finally, the Leninist party eliminates any meaningful accountability of the leadership to the mass.[35]

A crisis in participation occurred in the early 1970s, when a
wave of worker unrest, perhaps catalyzed by the generally radicalized mood, affected a number of factories, especially in Dar es
Salaam. Workers rose against their managers and tried to operate
the enterprises as collectives. Government reaction to this development was at first ambivalent, tolerating—even encouraging—
some of the initiatives. By 1973, however, government acted to
restore managerial authority in the plants. The cluster of scientific socialists greeted this factory effervescence enthusiastically,
as a harbinger of the new age. The Nyerere decision to restore
workplace discipline was a point of rupture with scholars of the
far left; from this point forward, increasingly ferocious attacks
upon the Tanzanian regime charged that Tanzanian socialism
was simply a class ideology of the African petty bourgeoisie.[36]

The sharp disappointment felt by Tanzania in the limited
flow of public and private Western funds in the early 1960s
and no doubt a sense of admiration for the seemingly imposing

achievements of the People's Republic of China led to the forth-right assertion that self-reliance was to be a cornerstone of Tan-zanian development policy. "We made a mistake in choosing money—," declared Nyerere, "something we do not have—to be the big instrument of our development. We are making a mistake to think that we shall get the money from other countries; first, because in fact we shall not be able to get sufficient money for our economic development; and secondly, because even if we could get all that we need, such dependence upon others would endanger our independence and our ability to choose our own political policies." [37]

The self-reliance motif, tirelessly repeated in the following years, was partly belied by the remarkably high levels of external assistance. This aid reflected the glistening prestige accorded the Tanzanian experiment, not only among social democratic Scan-dinavian governments, who saw their own ideals mirrored in the Nyerere experiment, but also by the World Bank and other do-nors not normally mesmerized by socialist incantation. The eco-nomic crisis of 1973–75 created an additional aid imperative that in 1975 brought an inflow of external assistance totalling $300 million, or $20 per capita. [38] Nyerere himself ruefully con-ceded, in his address marking the tenth anniversary of the Aru-sha Declaration, that self-reliance was far from a reality; indeed, the proportion of public resources derived from aid had in-creased after 1968. Yet the paradox of self-reliance awash in a sea of aid should not lead us to conclude that the concept was a mere empty slogan. On the contrary, the value attached to the goal of self-reliance permeated development thought. In particular, the inward-regarding orientation of a self-reliant vocation led di-rectly to a quite exceptional stress on the rural sector. "Industries will come and money will come but their foundation is *the peo-ple* and their *hard work*, especially in AGRICULTURE. This," de-clared Nyerere, "is the meaning of self-reliance." [39] Not only self-reliance but the entire Tanzanian vision of socialism came to be founded on the rural sector; thus the policies pursued in this sphere are critical to an appraisal of the Tanzanian experience and merit our close attention.

For socialism to serve as a constitutive principle of society, in the Nyerere view, it had in the first instance to form the basis of the rural sector, where 90 percent of Tanzanians drew their livelihood. As a point of departure, the resources of the cultural heritage could be invoked, in the premise of *ujamaa*, or kinship communalism. Yet the perspectives and values of petty capitalism had been inculcated by colonial agricultural policy; hence the *ujamaa* ethos had to be reactivated. In 1967, Nyerere followed the Arusha Declaration with a statement called "Socialism and Rural Development," or *ujamaa vijijini*—socialism in the villages. The ideal formulated was the construction of rural communities where nascent capitalism was transcended through cooperative production: "We shall achieve the goals we in this country have set ourselves if the basis of Tanzanian life consists of *economic and social communities where people live together and work together for the good of all.* . . ."[40]

As backdrop to the *ujamaa vijijini* program stood the failure of an earlier village settlement scheme, launched on the morrow of independence. Although presented as a progressive rural development strategy, only twenty-four settlements had been created, involving about 15,000 persons and costing an average of £150,000 per village. By 1966, the scheme had been abandoned as a costly fiasco that squandered far too many resources on too few people; only four of the settlements were considered successful.[41] Most were ephemeral congregations of persons attracted by the short-lived shower of subsidies. These costly creatures of bureaucratic paternalism could not possibly serve as the foundation for rural socialism; Nyerere envisaged the reformed *ujamaa* as voluntary, self-constituted, and self-reliant cooperative communities.

It was recognized that the full-fledged *ujamaa vijijini* cooperative village could be achieved only by stages. Indeed, considerable time passed before the general principles enunciated in "Socialism and Rural Development" were completed by detailed administrative instructions and legal definitions. Some points were clarified in a presidential circular of 1969, but the Villages and Ujamaa Villages Act was not adopted until 1975.[42] In practice, by 1970 a threefold distinction had been established:

1. formative communities, which might request government help in land clearing, provision of access roads, and building materials;

2. communities cooperating in some spheres but generally cultivating individually, eligible to register as an agricultural association for access to credit;

3. full cooperative communities, producing primarily on collective fields, organized into a multipurpose village cooperative.[43]

During the first five years, the *ujamaa* program went forward at a slow but steady pace on a voluntary basis. By the end of 1968, 350 villages had been registered; a year later, the figure rose to 650, with 300,000 persons. In 1970, the totals were 1,100 villages, with 500,000 persons; in 1971, 2,668 and 840,000. By early 1972, 1,600,000 inhabitants in 4,500 villages took part; in mid-1973, some two million persons, or about 15 percent of the population, were grouped in 5,000 villages. However, very few of these villages were full *ujamaa vijijini* communities; of the 4,500 in existence in 1972, 4,125 were in stage one, 261 were in stage two, and only 160 were functioning primarily as producer cooperatives.[44] Of these, 37 percent were in Iringa District. Some 70 percent of all the *ujamaa* activity was concentrated in only five districts in 1972, generally in the poorer regions of central Tanzania. The export crop areas of northern and southwestern Tanzania exhibited little interest in this new vehicle of rural socialism.

While these results were far from inconsequential and did not appear to provoke significant dislocations of production, a mood of impatience crystallized at the summit. The massive villagization campaigns of 1974–75 were foreshadowed by a display of energetic *ujamaa* promotion in Dodoma in 1971 and

TABLE 3.2. Expansion of *Ujamaa* Villages and Cooperative
              Production, Tanzania

Year	% of rural population living in ujamaa villages	% of ujamaa villages registered as cooperatives (with communal production)
1967	0.0	0.0
1968	0.7	0.0
1969	1.7	0.9
1970	4.4	0.5
1971	12.5	1.8
1972	15.6	5.8
1973	15.5	6.1
1974	19.1	7.8
1975	66.6	n.a.
1976	91.3	n.a.

SOURCE: Dean McHenry, "The Struggle for Rural Socialism in Tanzania," in
Socialism in Sub-Saharan Africa, ed. Carl G. Rosberg and Thomas M. Callaghy
(Berkeley: University of California Institute of International Studies, 1979), pp.
43–48.

Kigoma in 1972. When, in November 1973, in a speech in Kigoma, Nyerere declared that swift villagization was an immediate imperative and that the country had no time to wait for
voluntary choice by the farmers. For the reluctant and the recalcitrant, force would be necessary.[45]

There followed a turbulent period of massive villagization,
which by late 1975 had brought 65 percent of the population
within the now very diffuse *ujamaa* framework. The notion of
voluntaristic, grass-roots, cooperative socialism virtually disappeared as the full resources of the bureaucracy were mobilized to
require abandonment of scattered peasant homesteads in favor of
administration-designated village settlements. Some material in-
ducements were offered—pledges of schools, dispensaries, and
water supplies—but the frantic pace of implementation far outstripped the government's capacity to deliver on these promises.
Peasants had learned through long experience that, when confronted with such a display of bureaucratic determination, dis-

simulation and minimal compliance were the safest responses; as Boesen puts it, peasants retreated into the "ndiyo bwana (yes sir) attitude towards the bureaucrats, agreeing to their advice, but doing as little as possible to do anything about it." [46]

The imposing quantitative achievements were a poor description of the real changes wrought. Particularly in the export crop zones, such as the coffee areas of Kilimanjaro or Buhaya, dissimulation frequently took the form of redesignation of existing coffee farms as village settlements. In other regions, peasants found themselves clustered in imposed settlements lacking in infrastructure; sometimes water supplies were inadequate. The bureaucrats, under the lash of the sweeping national goals, had no time for persuasion and no funds for amenities. When the dislocations inevitable in such a crash program were compounded by a widespread failure of the rains in 1974, Tanzania was engulfed in full-scale agrarian crisis.

During this phase, when the country was convulsed with the villagization campaign, the voluntaristic principle largely vanished. It is doubtless true, as Maeda has argued, that overseas press reports exaggerated the degree of coercion used in the campaign.[47] However, it had been made abundantly clear that there was no choice; resettlement was mandatory. *Ujamaa*, in this phase, had indeed become socialism imposed from above. Yet one choice was left to the peasants: whether or not to plunge into collective production. The overwhelming disinclination to make this leap amply demonstrated the gap in understanding between summit and base as to the socialist pathway.

This contrast in orientation is captured by a survey of some 500 peasants conducted by a Tanzanian scholar on the eve of the all-out villagization campaign. Queried as to the meaning of *ujamaa*, only 12 percent associated it with joint production. The great majority understood it as a vague sense of cooperation; only a handful linked the term to the "self-reliance" that was so important to Nyerere.[48] The author concluded that communitarianism as a folk concept was "true enough at a high level of generality. . . ." Further, "with regard to the communal ownership of the means of production (land), it must be remembered that . . . land was communally owned . . . but *individually held*. . . . It remained *his* land and could be inherited as long as it was properly used. Furthermore, the traditional forms of cooperation . . . were based on the principles of *reciprocity* rather than *joint production*" (emphasis in the original).[49]

Meanwhile, in the center voices far more radical than Nyerere were calling for an even more rigorous socialism in the countryside. True socialism, it was claimed, could be forged only in the crucible of class struggle; in the countryside, this meant relentless war against *kulaks*, or petty capitalist farmers.[50] Neither Nyerere nor the bureaucracy had much use for this view; on the ground, the *kulak* was quite difficult to distinguish from his fellows. In 1967, only 13,400 African farmers were found to hire any labor; Van Velzen reported that in Rungwe District the most prosperous farmer earned less than the lowest paid civil servant.[51] Farmers themselves were equally unmoved by the class struggle appeal; only 1 percent of the respondents in the survey noted above associated *ujamaa* with ending exploitation or combating rural stratification.[52]

Peasant reluctance to participate in joint production can best be understood in the context of the security-centered moral economy of the peasant.[53] There were far too many uncertainties in the collective formula. How would the crop proceeds be distributed? Would all share equally, irrespective of the effort contributed? Would those who frequently absented themselves to work on their own plots have the same share of the harvest as those who threw their lot entirely with the joint fields? The individual farmer lost all control of his or her labor in the collective, with the proceeds coming first into the hands of local officials, whose behavior and dispositions could not be precisely calculated. These preoccupations translated into carefully hedged participation in those villages that did embark on joint production. One study in Morogoro in 1972 showed that while all private

TABLE 3.3. Estimated Scope of Communal Production and
             Income in *Ujamaa* Villages, 1973/74 Crop Year,
             Tanzania

Region	% of ujamaa villages with communal production	Average annual participation per adult (days)	Average income per day in most productive quarter of village with communal production (in cents)
Dodoma	37	3.5	8
Iringa	52	26.4	18
Kigoma	7	5.3	3

SOURCE: Dean McHenry, "The Struggle for Rural Socialism in Tanzania," in *Socialism in Sub-Saharan Africa*, ed. Carl G. Rosberg and Thomas M. Callaghy (Berkeley: University of California Institute of International Studies, 1979), p. 50.

plots were weeded, only 42–80 percent of the communal fields were. Turnout for communal work ran between 20 percent and 50 percent rather than the 80 percent anticipated. In some instances, the communal fields were secretly subdivided into individual plots.[54] The productivity of the collective fields was remarkably small, as table 3.3 demonstrates. Peasant skepticism about this form of activity was at once entirely rational and a self-fulfilling prophecy.

The 1974 plunge into rapid villagization necessarily enlarged the role of the bureaucracy; the results demanded by the center could not be achieved through community-by-community persuasion. Site selection was primarily determined by the administration, whose criteria were by no means the same as peasant preferences. The concern for control and ease of supervision, implying proximity to a road, predominated over considerations of soil and water. The required speed of implementation overwhelmed not only the peasants, but also the bureaucracy; there were neither organizational nor material resources to coax farmers into these settlements or to reward them with instant amenities. Legal uncertainties as to the statutory basis for the villages gave free reign to extravagant rumors that family life was about to be collectivized or new local taxes imposed.[55]

The limitations of the communal farming formula are given interesting treatment in a sympathetic study of the early phases of *ujamaa*. The study involved the examination of a number of villages where collective production enjoyed some success. Of the six cooperative villages examined in detail, the majority arose in rather special circumstances: former employees of abandoned European plantations assuming control of the farm, a road construction team settling on a new bloc of land. In half the villages, growing pressures were felt for conversion of communal land into individual plots. Discord over handling of finances was quite general. Leaders and members were at odds over the extent to which proceeds from communal field harvests should be distributed or invested.[56] While the author reaches generally favorable conclusions, the evidence not only illuminates the practical difficulties to be overcome, but also raises doubts about the generalizability of the communal formula.

By the late 1970s, most outside observers of the Tanzanian scene—and many within the country—had concluded that the experiment in populist rural socialism had failed, though widely divergent explanations were offered of precisely what was flawed and why. From a liberal perspective, Lofchie asserted that

It is now generally acknowledged that Tanzania's policy of rural collectivization has been abandoned as a failure. Villagisation without socialism is, in effect, the current policy.

The *ujamaa* village programme . . . failed to gain ideological acceptance among the vast majority of the peasantry . . . and as a consequence . . . made only the barest headway in disseminating socialist practices in agriculture.[57]

Marxist critics imputed the failure to the absence of true socialist content. Shivji maintains that *ujamaa* was simply a class action by the petty bourgeoisie that extended their control over the rural economy in alliance with the *kulaks*.[58] Samoff discerns "little socialism in the officially socialist villages" and decries the bureaucratic dominance of rural transformation.[59] A few more sanguine commentators dissented from the "failure" consensus: Green, for example, places blame mainly on climactic misfortune in the rainfall deficiency from 1973 to 1975.

Amid the welter of conflicting interpretations, several points do seem to emerge. First, the village settlement aspect of *ujamaa* was substantially implemented and was probably irreversible. This in and of itself is a major restructuring of the rural sector, though not necessarily socialist in content. Second, the collective production aspect of *ujamaa* has found little peasant support and has encountered very great difficulties. While the bureaucracy was able to impose resettlement, its capacity to enforce from above what clearly will not be freely adopted from below is dubious. Third, Tanzania, like many other African countries, has experienced an overall stagnation in its agricultural production in the post-Arusha years, after substantial increases in output of major marketed crops in the first two postwar decades. Fourth, the production problems cannot be attributed to collectivization, which occurred on so small a scale that it could have had little impact.

The severity of the food production shortfall placed Tanzania in a desperate foreign exchange position. During 1974, the country was forced to import over 400,000 tons of grains; heavy external purchases continued through 1975. Yet historically Tanzania had been self-sufficient and had even exported small amounts of maize on occasion.[60] After 1975, production did improve and the crisis eased—although the $500,000,000 campaign to remove the scourge of Idi Amin in 1979 again unhinged national finances and brought the country to the verge of financial catastrophe.

The agrarian crisis in 1974–75 seems attributable to several causes. In 1973–74, the rains were poor, though Lofchie challenges the widespread belief that precipitation was also deficient in 1974–75.[61] In the decade after independence, the producer

TABLE 3.4. Marketed Production of Major Export Crops, 1945–75, Tanzania

Crop	1946	1950	1955	1959	1965	1970	1971	1972	1973	1974	1975
				(000 tons)							
Sisal	1.2	12.0	17.4	20.9	214.2	202.2	181.1	156.9	155.4	143.4	120.5
Coffee	10.0	15.0	18.5	19.6	28.1	49.7	45.8	51.4	54.9	44.7	62.4
Tea	.6	.5	1.7	2.7	6.3	8.5	10.5	12.7	12.7	13.0	13.7
Tobacco			4.7	5.5 (1958)	5.7	11.1	12.0	14.2	13.0	18.2	14.2
Cotton (lint)	10.0	7.0	20.4	30.7	74.8	76.4	65.3	76.9	65.1	71.5	59.2
Sugar				21.5 (1958)	66.3	87.3	85.8	88.5	105.1	96.2	103.2
Pyrethrum			.3 (1953)	.7 (1958)	4.1	2.3	3.7	4.3	3.5	3.3	4.6
Cashew nuts	3.2	6.5	18.2	33.2	63.7	111.2	121.5	125.6	145.1	121.7	80.3

SOURCE: Joel Samoff, "Crises and the Transition to Socialism in Tanzania" (Paper delivered at Conference on International Relations and Third World Development, University of Denver, June 1979); *Africa Research Bulletin*, 16, no. 6 (31 July 1979); International Bank for Reconstruction and Development, *Economic Development of Tanganyika*, (Baltimore: Johns Hopkins Press, 1961); United Republic of Tanzania, *Tanzania Second Five-Year Plan for Economic and Social Development, 1st July 1969–30th June 1974* (Dar es Salaam Government Printer, 1969).

TABLE 3.5. Government Purchases of Major Food Crops,
1970/71–1975/76, Tanzania

Crop	(000 tons)					
	1970/71	1971/72	1972/73	1973/74	1974/75	1975/76
Maize	186.4	43.0	106.4	73.8	23.9	91.1
Wheat	43.0	56.7	46.8	27.9	14.4	24.5
Rice	93.6	68.6	73.1	59.6	22.7	18.4

SOURCE: Joel Samoff, "Crises and the Transition to Socialism in Tanzania" (Paper delivered at Conference on International Relations and Third World Development, University of Denver, June 1979), p. 15.

price per ton of maize was perversely reduced from 374 to 270 shillings per ton (in current prices); when inflation is factored in, the real exchange value of officially marketed maize was certainly less than half of its 1961 level.[62] Not only were prices unattractive, but the cooperative marketing channels were often unreliable; persistent problems with the marketing cooperatives led to their abolition in favor of state marketing in 1976. To all these factors was added the tumultuous *ujamaa* campaign and its attendant dislocations. The precise weighting of these various elements will never be known. While bad weather certainly played its part, the impersonal wrath of the elements shares the blame with the human agency of the state. What few had foreseen was the potent riposte open to the apparently powerless peasantry: exit, through evasion of official marketing channels, increased local food consumption, or diminished output. For the 1974–75 crop season, government maize purchases were only 18 percent of the 1970–71 levels, and 24 percent for rice.

In the following years, the food production crisis subsided. The rains returned, and there were major policy rectifications. Prices were dramatically increased, nearly tripling for maize from 1973 to 1977 and more than doubling for wheat and rice. The settlement phase of *ujamaa* was over, and propagation of communal farming had all but ceased. Consolidation of the settlements permitted repair of some of the worst errors; the most poorly chosen sites could be abandoned, and some headway was made in extending amenities to the villages. A Zairian scholar interviewing in several *ujamaa* village settlements in the Kigoma region in 1977 found a basically positive response to the villages, but strong skepticism of communal fields.[63]

On the tenth anniversary of the Arusha Declaration, Nyerere delivered a somber assessment of the previous decade. With the engaging candor that has sustained his personal luster, he conceded that Tanzania had achieved neither self-reliance nor socialism. But while this speech was a sober litany of errors, it was by no means a funeral dirge for socialism. The indifferent performance of the public sector, the mediocrity of agricultural achievements, and the heavy sacrifices to ransom the Ugandan people from the predatory tyranny of the Amin regime impose a period of consolidation. A respite from the "we-must-run-while-they-may-walk" mode of policy determination analyzed by Hyden seems probable.[64] The well-publicized agrarian crisis of 1974–75 dimmed the once luminous prestige of the Tanzanian experiment—though it was already under attack from both left and right. But the sense of disappointment of the Tanzaphiles was in part a reflection of their unreasonably high hopes.

More serious is the mood of diffuse disappointment and even demoralization that many observers detect in the Tanzanian populace at large. There has been little in recent years to sustain the spirits, no tangible success to offset a wave of setbacks. While the state ideology of neighboring Kenya is perhaps not seductive, the unmistakably more buoyant economy stands in stark contrast. That life is more abundant to the north is widely accepted; those who live close to the Kenya frontier participate illicitly as best they can by smuggling part of their produce. Socialism, Green argues, must deliver a stream of benefits to sustain its appeal;[65] in recent years, it has failed to do so.

In some respects, the current dilemmas of development choice in Tanzania reflect a broader crisis of the state itself. The fraction of the GDP collected by the state as revenue rapidly in-

creased in the independence years, from 15 percent in 1961 to almost 35 percent by 1974.[66] This compares with a third-world
average of less than 17 percent in 1970, calculated by the IMF.[67]
The unhappy marriage of the utopian socialism of Nyerere,
Boesen argues, and the bureaucratic "modernization theory" that
predominated in the civil service begat a state ideology that
could be financed only by growing extraction from the peasant
sector. Boesen continues:

. . . the steady expansion of the state sector and its failure to generate
sufficient surplus to maintain its own growth . . . has led to government
penetration into the operation of the peasant sector in an effort to increase production of surplus, as evidenced by the reintroduction of coercive agricultural legislation, the establishment of tightly regulated
crop schemes, and the forced implementation of villagization. . . .

. . . however, if it extracts additional surplus it reduces producer
incomes and lessens the incentives for greater production. Coercion is
then introduced as a means to avoid this destructive cycle. . . . But experience—also from Tanzania—amply demonstrates that peasants find
hundreds of ways to evade coercive measures, even at the cost of falling
production.[68]

Add to this the somber assessment of an astute student of agrarian bureaucracy in East Africa, Jon Moris: "Contemporary rural
administration has reached a genuine point of crisis—a point
where the ineffectiveness of major public services has become so
obvious that it becomes difficult to justify further public investment in these sectors."[69] These two observations combined bring
into view a full vista of the crisis of the state. I hasten to add that
this impasse is not unique either to Tanzania or the populist socialist state, but rather is part of a general pattern.

But the matter cannot rest there. An overall balance sheet
would need to consider the overpowering constraints of poverty
and resource limitations. Some signal accomplishments deserve
mention. The ethos of austerity and egalitarianism has inhibited
the formation of a venal and mercantile political class. A reasonable case can be made for the effectiveness of the nationalized
financial institutions in promoting public goals.[70] The villagiza-

tion has been largely accomplished and may yet provide a framework for more effective provision of rural amenities. While self-reliance remains a distant dream, yet Tanzania has winkled remarkably high levels of aid from Western powers (especially the Scandinavians), international agencies, and China. Nyerere has achieved this without ideological or political concessions; while critics of the regime argue that the meshes of dependency are only tightened, it can be equally maintained that Tanzania has played well the diplomacy of an inevitable dependency to maximize extraction of external resources. The economic crisis of 1975 was weathered with remarkably little damage to the political system; the regime was not driven into repressive strategies to sustain itself. While the manifest shortcomings of populist socialism in Tanzania as an instrument for growth make it impossible to classify the experiment as a success, neither is the contrary verdict of failure fully demonstrated.

ALGERIA: POPULISM VERSUS TECHNOCRACY ON THE SOCIALIST PATH

Algeria stands with Tanzania as an example of the populist socialist pathway. While no Algerian leader has had the global prestige of Nyerere, the Algerian revolution has enjoyed a special saliency since the days of guerrilla struggle; indeed, the independence of all francophonic Africa was really won in the Algiers casbah and the Aures mountain fastnesses. Through two changes of leadership—by coup in 1965, and by death in 1979—there appears a remarkable constancy to Algerian socialism; viewed over two decades, oscillations that appeared to be of momentary significance become small squiggles in a quite consistent policy direction.

While Algeria may be reasonably paired with Tanzania in the persistence of its dominant ideological perspectives, there are also some obvious contrasts. The socialist option of Algeria

was much less the reflection of the political vision of a remarkable leader than the product of a revolutionary armed struggle.
The resource context is totally different as well. Algeria's huge
hydrocarbon revenues provide a much greater range of choice
than that open to Tanzania: not so much, as in Libya, that only
colossal venality or incompetence could cause any chosen development strategy to fail, but more than enough so that ambitious industrialization is a feasible option and a much more aggressive confrontation of Western capital can be contemplated.
At the same time, Algerian society was far more deeply penetrated by colonialism, which lasted half a century longer and
was carried by an occupying host of one million settlers.

We can view Algerian developmental ideology as containing
three constitutive elements: Islamic and Arabist nationalism,
radical socialism, and technocracy. These three components became sequentially incorporated in the political consensus. The
first, quintessentially nationalist, sought authentication of the
right to revolution in the religious and linguistic cultural heritage of the country, faced with the profoundly alienating assim-
ilationist theses of *algérie française*. The second had as incubus
the bitter years of armed struggle and was given relatively clear
articulation in the Tripoli Program of the *Front de Libération Nationale* (FLN). The third, stressing rationality and competence in
translating nationalism and socialism into policy, became a predominant motif from the time of the Boumedienne coup in 1965.

The assertion of nationalism necessarily came first, as the
very existence of an Algerian people was denied, not only by the
French, but by some Algerian intellectuals themselves. Among
the small group of middle-class elites spawned by colonialism,
the oft-cited affirmation of self-rejection by Ferhat Abbas, later to
become titular head of the Algerian revolution during part of the
war years, illustrates the scope of the identity-building task in
the 1930s:

If I had encountered the Algerian nation, I would be a nationalist and, as
such, would have nothing to be ashamed of. . . . And yet I will not die

for the Algerian fatherland, for this fatherland does not exist. I have not
encountered it. I have questioned history. I have questioned the living
and the dead. I have visited the cemeteries. No one has spoken to me of
such a thing. . . . You cannot build upon the wind.[71]

Rediscovery of the Islamic and Arabist moorings of society was
thus an imperative legitimation of the claim to liberation; denial
of these led implacably to the early Abbas position. Thus, even
though the first major nationalist leader, Messali Hadj, had close
ties to the French Communist Party for a time, his nationalism
gave little place to socialism.[72] The resurrection of a cultural
heritage was no small task; many of the intellectuals who rallied
to the FLN neither spoke Arabic nor were practicing Muslims.

The first official proclamation of a socialist engagement by
the FLN appeared in the Tripoli Program, adopted on the eve of
independence in 1962. But the announcement of a socialist vocation was only vaguely formulated and was eclipsed at the time
by other parts of the document and by the debates surrounding
it, which made visible the savage factional strife within the Algerian nationalist movement.[73] The newly identified socialist
perspective was not in real dispute; power struggle consumed
the energies of the welter of contenders: internal and external
military wings, exiled and imprisoned political leaders, workers,
youth, and student groupings. During the war years, a socialist
perspective—albeit not closely defined—became quite general
among nationalist intellectuals. For the dispossessed rural mass,
wartime promises had more to do with material blessings: a 30
percent rise in living standards within two years of independence and the first plan for full employment; universal education within five years; health facilities for all; new housing.[74]

With Ben Bella initially triumphant in the contest for leadership, the first national congress of the FLN in April 1964 was
fixed as the occasion for full doctrinal definition. The ideological
text was prepared primarily by the most leftist elements in the
Ben Bella entourage, in particular Trotskyite Mohamed Harbi.
The Algiers Charter was intended to consecrate the "continuous

development of the people's national revolution into a socialist revolution." With colonialism defeated, the FLN was to be the instrument of peasant and worker to crush through class struggle the mercantile and especially bureaucratic bourgeoisie that aspired to sabotage the revolution.[75] While the Marxist tones of the charter were somewhat diluted in debate, the document—though unanimously adopted by the congress—went well beyond the consensual populist socialism. Indeed, critics of Ben Bella claimed that he had never read the document.[76] In particular, the army leadership was angered by the Algiers Charter, which appeared to them a doctrinal coup that detached the Algerian revolution from the nationalist moorings that had anchored the guerrilla struggle.

Even before the Boumedienne coup, the Algiers Charter was stillborn. When the army seized power, the Marxist themes evaporated, as did the array of cosmopolitan doctrinal councillors self-recruited among the European left (the *pieds rouges*). As if in reprisal, a wave of studies appeared declaring the ideological bankruptcy of the Algerian revolution.[77] Cultural authenticity joined to renovation reappeared; socialism was fused with nationalism through the Islamic-Arabic heritage. Boumedienne insisted that Islam was not an impediment to radical change; those who deduced arguments against state socialism from theological texts were, in his view, alien to Islam. While Islam was not per se a moral charter for the regime's economic and social policies, as an indissociable component of national culture it was a necessary dimension of a populist perspective. Indeed, Islam was, according to Boumedienne, the world's first socialist movement.[78] In 1974, he declared that "We need a socialist party with a definite program and a unified line. . . . We are socialist and Muslims, and we are not Marxists."[79]

In the early Boumedienne years, what seemed most conspicuous was the retreat from the more doctrinaire socialism of Ben Bella. In the 1970s, with the regime no longer preoccupied with factional struggle and survival, there was a distinct ideological

resurgence. A cluster of documents appearing in October–
November 1971 gave renewed saliency to socialist doctrinal engagement, with a new Charter of the Algerian Revolution and allied declarations of "agrarian revolution" and "socialist industrial management."[80] The flavor of these documents is conveyed
by the opening paragraph of the socialist management text:

Having recovered its sovereignty, established solid foundations for the
institutions of the state, improved the health of the economy, and recovered its national riches, Algeria is setting out henceforth on the process of construction of the material bases of socialism, within the framework of rational planning and by the elaboration of structures which
will rapidly transform the previous situation with a view towards in-
stalling a new order, directed by the laws of socialist democracy. . . . The
new socialist organisation of enterprises marks a decisive stage of revolutionary construction.[81]

The third constitutive element in Algerian regime ideology
was a state-centered claim to rationality and competence—or,
otherwise put, a technocratic thrust, which appeared with the
Boumedienne coup. While the fatal cleavage between Ben Bella
and Boumedienne can be traced to the Algiers Charter with its
Marxist overtones, the specific indictment of Ben Bella that legitimated power seizure was not Marxism but improvisation and
incompetence. "Socialism," declared Boumedienne on 1 November 1965, "is not this incoherent collection of improvised measures and personal reactions that for three years gave the people
only an erroneous idea of socialism. Socialism is a long and la-
borious (process) of construction that requires the elaboration
and application of a comprehensive plan, rationally established
in the light of all the political, economic, and social 'givens' of
the country."[82]

This technocratic thrust was necessarily statist. It implied
central direction and bureaucratic control. These rationality
themes serve as the principal basis for the frequent critiques of
the Algerian experience as mere "state capitalism," or—worse—

a class action of the bureaucratic bourgeoisie in alliance with prosperous farmers and the urban mercantile groups.[83]

Technocracy has secreted the powerful administrative state, by now thoroughly institutionalized. Equally entrenched is the ideological synthesis of radical populist socialism: nationalist, socialist, and rationalist, as evidenced by its unchallenged continuity with the Boumedienne succession in 1979. The choice of Ben Jedid Chadli as new president was made within the narrow confines of the *Conseil de la Révolution*, a body created by Boumedienne in 1965 as a ruling organ above both state and party; though originally this body had twenty-six members, by death and purge it had diminished to eleven.[84] The selection of Chadli symbolized the stability of state, ideology, and regime. The apparent legitimacy of his succession, in both process and outcome, is a reasonable measure of institutionalization.

The emergence of a totally dominant state sector occurred in two distinct stages: the improvisations of the Ben Bella years, under the slogan of worker self-management and affecting essentially abandoned French enterprises; and the systematic expansion of the state industrial domain from 1966 on, culminating in the virtually complete takeover of major natural resource exploitation and industrial enterprises. The first phase was an ad hoc response to a given situation, subsequently given ideological gloss by a marriage of the Yugoslav model with Trotskyite ideals. The flight of nearly all the million *pieds noirs* (settlers) upon the termination of French sovereignty on 3 July 1962, and an initially chaotic political situation, created an enormous pool of abandoned properties and enterprises: 450 to 500 industrial undertakings (the only large ones being a metallurgical plant, a glassworks, a textile factory, and a flour mill; about half employed ten or fewer workers); 16,000 farms covering 800,000 hectares and employing 70,000 laborers; 200,000 apartments and houses; and hundreds of small commercial establishments (hotels, restaurants, shops).[85]

The regime's first step, taken on 24 August 1962, was to announce a temporary tutelage of the state over these properties; the owners were at first invited to return. In October–November, the first measures were taken to bring about a resumption of operations of the businesses, but not yet challenging ownership rights if the proprietors returned. In a sweeping series of socializing decrees in March 1963, temporization gave way to more ideologically inspired policy. Any enterprise or property left unoccupied for more than two months was declared vacant (and thus not nationalized, to avoid compensation claims). Production units would be managed by the workers under state tutelage. An assembly of all permanent workers was to adopt an overall production plan, approve financial plans, and allocate tasks. Enterprises with over thirty workers were to elect a workers' council to be charged with similar functions and hiring/firing. The council elected a management committee charged with monitoring operations and making immediate business decisions; the management committee elected a president, whose countersignature was required on all of the firm's documents. State tutelage was carried out by a government-appointed director, who was responsible for daily operations, and a member of the management committee.

The *auto-gestion* (self-management) conception, while it responded to the practical reality of worker occupation of the premises in many instances, also had two ideological sources. The Yugoslav model of socialism, which had become identified with worker self-management, held potent appeal to a broad spectrum of the Algerian revolutionary elite. At the same time, a coterie of Trotskyite intellectuals, Algerian and foreign, enjoyed excellent access to Ben Bella; their brief for *auto-gestion* was grounded in antipathy to bureaucracy and a pervasive fear of a betrayal of the revolution by a new class of state apparatchiki.

The practical difficulties of self-management in the commercial and industrial sector are self-evident. The directors evidently had the weight of the state behind them and were soon the dominant force. The businesses were not ongoing concerns, but disrupted and dislocated entities, often left in disarray (if not sabotaged) by the fleeing proprietors. Substantial financing was required for equipment, parts, and materials to restore operations. Many faced sharp competition from an Algerian private sector of 2,500 enterprises. Distribution of enterprise revenues between wages and investment was a controversial point. Little attention had been given to all of these practical aspects in the elaboration of the March 1963 self-management decrees; indeed, a major architect of these measures told the Ottaways that "he had categorically refused to discuss the economics of self-management at meetings of the special commission appointed by Ben Bella." The objective was above all political: to institutionalize worker power.[86] The utter naivete of this viewpoint provided the opening for the state bureaucracy to progressively assert its control over the *auto-gestion* sector.

However, *auto-gestion* had become a pillar of developmental ideology and could not be lightly abandoned. The advent of Boumedienne and the creed of rationality did not efface the dogma of self-management. Rather the new regime suggested the possible fusing of efficiency and worker control; Boumedienne declared in 1968, "We are for self-management, but a viable self-management that yields a profit, that results in an efficient organization of work and an increase of production. To liberate the worker . . . is a revolutionary principle, but to produce is also a necessity."[87] One can well understand the preoccupation with organization and solvency; at the time of the Boumedienne takeover, some 20 percent of the self-management industrial enterprises could not even produce accounts.

In an assessment of the Ben Bella stage, it is important to recollect the disruptions attending independence. Not only did the eight years of war exact a heavy price, but the fleeing settlers took with them an estimated 4 billion francs of assets. European personnel had monopolized skilled positions in colonial Algeria; among those departing were 15,000 members of the liberal professions, 33,000 managerial cadres, 35,000 skilled workers, and 200,000 technical or vocational workers.[88] By the mid-60s, some of these losses began to be made good. The still-French hydrocarbon industries were beginning to generate rising state revenues; by the end of 1967, Algeria had $400 million in foreign reserves.

These resources gave the new regime the means to enter a second phase of state-directed public sector expansion, in the 1965–71 period. This came about in several ways: through the creation of new industrial ventures with public investment; through the takeover of foreign firms; through the absorption of a portion of the *auto-gestion* sector into state enterprises. In 1966, the banks, insurance companies, and some mines were socialized. In 1968, the state took over the marketing of gas and oil products and nationalized sixty-six of the three hundred French enterprises that were operating in 1966 in such fields as construction materials, fertilizers, electrical supplies, textiles, and foods. The first steps toward state control of the oil and gas industry were taken in 1968, and takeover was completed in this crucial sector in 1971.[89]

Beginning with the creation of SONATRACH, the Algerian national petroleum corporation, in 1965, a network of state industrial combines was created as the key technocratic realm. There followed in short order a National Steel Company, the National Textile Company, the National Glassworks Company, the Algerian National Insurance Company, and in 1967 nine other state corporations, which taken together absorbed a sizable chunk of the *auto-gestion* sector. These and related state corporations formed later constituted the underpinning for the Algerian development strategy: secure full control over the natural resource base and convert the oil and gas revenues into a broad-based industrial sector. By 1971–72, 90 percent of Algerian industry was within the state sector, and other takeovers since then have further reduced the residual private sector. Nearly sixty parastatals operate Algerian industry.[90] By 1974, there were no large foreign firms, though some continued as minority partners in parastatal ventures.[91]

The fading ideal of worker participation was dramatically rejuvenated in 1971 by the new set of "socialist management" decrees. The parastatal sector was to be progressively reorganized to incorporate this principle. The cornerstone of these measures was that "the condition of the producers becomes, henceforth, that of active managers, no longer to be compared to that of salaried workers. At the same time concerned and interested, they are thus permanently associated with the decisions which involve their own future."[92] Workers through participation would regard themselves not simply as wage earners but as partners in production, and the factory as "their property." All contradiction in the interests of workers and managers vanishes; all are at once managers and workers. The socialist management charter stresses the purported harmony of interests of laborers and cadres from another perspective: "It is obvious, however, that in a socialist enterprise, this management does not represent the exploiting boss, but the popular state, the guarantor of the interests of the laboring masses. It is therefore in the interests of the working masses that management direct the firm in association with the workers."[93] At the same time, socialist management is different in ethos from the earlier *auto-gestion* philosophy. As one official source put it, ". . . socialist management is neither *auto-gestion* nor *co-gestion*. The workers do not directly run the enterprise, as they cannot suspend the decisions of management, taken in the framework of its prerogatives. . . . It is a question, rather, of a control of management by the workers which completes and reinforces that of the state."[94] The last word still belongs to the managers, and beyond them the state tutelary authority. Yet the powers of the elected worker assemblies, to be established in each production unit, are not trivial and do offer potentially meaningful leverage.

Not until 1974 were detailed ordinances issued prescribing modalities of application. By mid-1976, a significant start in implementation had been made, covering 550 production units in 40 parastatals, involving 150,000 workers.[95] A thorough assessment of this experiment must await more ample documentation; Nellis, however, offers solid arguments for his tentatively positive evaluation—at least in the sense that the reform is much more than mere sham to camouflage technocratic state capitalism. Criticisms of the slowness and timidity of application that have crept into the Algerian press attest both to the difficulties and to the seriousness of the regime's intent. At a minimum the socialist management reforms do reflect the permeation of policy choice by the underlying populist socialist perspectives.[96]

In the rural sector, a parallel pattern is observable, though statist paternalism is perhaps more pronounced in application.[97] Here as well there were two quite distinct operations: the sudden appearance of an *auto-gestion* section in 1962–63, composed essentially of the former European estates, and the creation of an "agrarian revolution" sector from 1971 on, based on Algerian-owned holdings exceeding 110 hectares. The first was an improvised response to a crisis situation; the second was a reasoned extension of populist socialism by a consolidated and self-confident regime, but limited in impact by the control-oriented impulses of the administrative-technocratic state.

The quite unanticipated flight of the European farmers in 1962 created a void quickly filled by the workers employed on their estates. The European farming zones, subjected to thorough military and administrative control, had not been major battlefields during the revolution; indeed, settler agricultural production had been little affected by the war through 1960. The work force was intact and in a position to assume immediate control over the farms. Settler agriculture was highly capitalized and not easily subdivided among the workers. Doubtless the farm workers themselves, faced with this sudden opportunity, generally believed their welfare would be best served if they shared the benefits of capitalist agriculture rather than assumed individual control over peasant plots. At any rate, during the chaotic summer of 1962, when the state was in no position to exercise control, there was no widespread move toward subdivision. State interests as well were best served if these farms remained as large, mechanized units producing an exportable surplus rather than small plots oriented to local consumption.

The first state action in August 1962 placed abandoned farms under the legal tutelage of the prefects. The March 1963 decrees organizing *auto-gestion* placed the lands under state ownership, with management of the farms in the hands of elected committees. At the same time, these measures provided the entering wedge for state control, through provision for a state-appointed director. In practice, the state-appointed directors quickly gained the upper hand on most of the *auto-gestion* farms. Not only did the March decrees arm them with ample legal authority, but their knowledge of finance and French were decisive advantages in the face of generally illiterate farm workers.

Some other little-noticed provisions that accompanied the March 1963 decrees further reinforced state dominance. The farms were, in effect, obliged to utilize state marketing channels and required to seek credit exclusively through the official *Office Nationale de la Réforme Agraire* (ONRA). Thus, as the Ottaways observe, "just one month after the publication of the March Decrees, the so-called self-management farms had lost all right of decision over two crucial matters—financing and the marketing of their produce."[98]

The immediate impact of rural *auto-gestion* was a sharp drop in production; by 1964, output on these farms was only half the 1960 level. This drastic shortfall was partly made up in succeeding years, yet overall production results were mediocre, with output stagnant and yields disappointing in relation to the fertility of the land and inputs supplied. Some useful restructuring of output occurred, in particular through the steady conver-

TABLE 3.6. Rural Structure in 1963, Algeria

Land category	Estimated active males	Hectares (millions)
Large holdings (over 100 hectares)	8,500	1.7
Medium large holdings (50–100 hectares)	16,600	1.1
Medium small holdings (10–50 hectares)	167,000	3.2
Small holdings (1–10 hectares)	332,500	1.3
Tiny holdings (less than 1 hectare)	105,000	.4
Auto-gestion lands	150,000	3.0
Agricultural laborers, sharecroppers	60,000	0
Landless peasants	1,000,000	0

SOURCE: Thomas L. Blair, "The Land to Those Who Work It": Algeria's Experiment in Workers' Management (Garden City, N.Y.: Doubleday & Co., 1969), p. 128. Copyright © 1969 by Thomas L. Blair. Reprinted by permission.

sion of vineyards into other crops; nonetheless, this sector has never lived up to its productive potential. By 1969, their yields were still 30 percent below colonial levels.[99]

The main beneficiaries, therefore, were the workers themselves. The auto-gestion sector was not a source of surplus generation for development. Within these structures, there was a built-in conflict of interest between the permanent farm workers, who were full members of the unit (an estimated 220,000 by 1970), and the much larger number of seasonal workers on these farms, who totaled 440,000.[100] The latter not only were not considered participating members, but did not share in the profits. Further, the socialized sector, in this phase, covered only the former European farms. It offered nothing to the numerous peasants who either had less than the ten hectares seen as a minimum for subsistence in most of Algeria or no land at all.

While robust ideological claims were made for auto-gestion through the 1960s, the reality of state domination of this sector and its modest productivity performance engendered rural skepticism as to government intentions. As one writer in the Algiers daily El Moudjahid put it, "Who of us does not bear, like a secret wound, the suffocation of the self-managed sector by the bu-

reaucratic structures?"[101] Knauss, summarizing the impact of the
first wave of agrarian reform, concluded:

The inability of the Ben Bella government to make real a broadening of
agrarian reform between 1963 to 1965 and the gradual takeover of this
bold experiment in democratic decision-making by state technocrats
was almost certainly a rude shock to all politically conscious peasants,
self-managers or not. It is likely, furthermore, that many of the small and
middle peasants were, by the end of the decade, already conditioned to
be cautious, even cynical and suspicious, of the Boumedienne government's plans to embark on a new project of agrarian reform. Many of
them fear they are merely being controlled or contained as a political
force.[102]

The second wave of agrarian socialism, the Agrarian Revolution decrees of 1971, were targeted upon the larger private Algerian holdings (over 110 hectares); these covered approximately
20 percent of the arable surface, though the number of individual
large landowners is believed to have dropped by half from 1962
to 1968.[103] The ultimate goal of the Agrarian Revolution was the
creation of communal socialist villages, furnished by the state
with housing, water, and electricity. By 1974, some thirty to forty
of these model socialist communities had been created; they
were inhabited mainly by former sharecroppers. Those involved
surrendered what livestock they possessed, and were assured a
monthly salary of about $75.00; however, they were wholly at
the mercy of the state. As one member put it, "Before we were
khames (sharecroppers) of the great landowner. Now we are the
khames of the State. And all the workers know it."[104] Defection
rates were reported to be 20 percent.

A larger component of the Agrarian Revolution consisted of
distribution of the large estates to small peasants, who were
grouped into cooperatives. Beneficiaries received roughly ten-
hectare plots and were supposed to pool their harvests and
incomes, for sharing with other cooperative members. The government claimed that 60,000 farmers were grouped into 4,000
cooperatives by 1974, and 100,000 by 1979, though other reports

set the figure of cooperatives at 2,500. Some 80 percent of the land previously held in estates exceeding 110 hectares was effectively redistributed; for the remaining 20 percent, owners succeeded in evading the legislation by themselves redistributing to family members.[105]

Agrarian socialism in Algeria is thus a maze of contradictions. The sheer scope of redistribution is imposing; roughly half the arable land—and doubtless the better half at that—was involved. The wealthiest landed proprietors were eliminated from the rural scene. Capitalist agriculture remained a significant force; a hundred-hectare tract of good land with access to urban markets was an attractive venture. The ranks of the middle farmers were joined by members of the politico-bureaucratic class, who have actively sought outlets for their savings in landholding or commerce. The socialized sector has undoubtedly raised the revenues of the quarter-million beneficiaries and their families, while placing them under state tutelage, with rhetorically impressive but empirically weak participatory structures.

Participation has been, more generally, the great paradox of the Algerian revolution. Populist in spirit, yet exclusionary in fact; mobilization is an ever-recurrent value, just as consistently denied in practice. The FLN was capable of organizing and directing the eight-year guerrilla war that kept the half-million-strong French army at bay. At the very moment of its greatest triumph, its factional divisions burst into full view in the chaos of the early weeks of independence. Since independence, the FLN as a single party has been the weak point of the regime. A debilitating series of feuds and conspiracies among its top ranks decimated the first generation of leaders. After 1967, the hegemony of Boumedienne was consolidated, but repeated reform efforts failed to breathe life into this moribund organism. Its ample bureaucracy—8,000 party functionaries labored in Algiers[106]—was a head without a body. The inability to convene regular congresses was a telling measure of party weakness. The first congress in 1964 adopted unanimously a charter that was never really accepted and was quickly abandoned by Boumedienne; the second met only in 1979, to ratify the Chadli succession. The contradictions of the FLN are captured by Leca:

Cut off from a base which lost interest in its fate . . . trapped in an ideology rigorous in its principles, but increasingly diffuse in political practice, torn by . . . disparate currents emanating from fragile coalitions, victim of a superleader busier with playing on rivalries than in consolidating and legitimizing power, incapable of breaking with the habits of pseudo-unity acquired in earlier days . . . the party is at once the sick man of the regime, and the reason for its failure. Too weak a support for too strong an ideology, the FLN has not been able to become the organization upon which the whole of the Algerian system can be supported.[107]

Relations of the state with such organs of corporate participation as the *Union Générale des Travailleurs Algeriens* (UGTA), the *Union Nationale des Etudiants Algeriens* (UNEA), and the *Union Nationale des Paysans Algeriens* (UNPA) were uneasy. Skirmishes were particularly frequent with the UGTA, which chafed under state and party tutelage. The first major confrontation occurred in 1963, the state, through the FLN, imposing its will and its personnel. Symptoms of restlessness were frequent, but the union was kept on a short leash. Domestication of the UGTA had as its logical corollary a declining and apathetic membership; by the early 1970s, UGTA had roughly 200,000 members, or no more than 10 percent of the work force.[108]

Yet, however great the chasm between populist proclamation and daily reality of the tutelary administrative state, the regime would appear to maintain a fair measure of legitimacy. Informed observers thought otherwise in the late 1960s; Charles Gallagher wrote in 1967:

There is no party except for the facade. . . . labour unrest has grown to the point where . . . urban workers must be counted among the active opponents of the regime. . . . Given the complexity of the economic and social problems confronting the country, and the limited abilities of not only most of the leadership but also of many middle and lower-level cadres, it would seem likely that matters will not improve for some time to come—and they may get worse before they get better.[109]

Moore, in 1970, reached similar conclusions:

A party apparatus still exists, but it no longer is permitted to intervene in administrative affairs, and there is little evidence that it even in a general way animates, impels or supervises state policy. Thus the gap grows between political realities and the rational legitimacy that is sought. . . . The resulting paralysis, often, in Algerian decision-making was thus not a consequence of structured conflict, as in Morocco, but rather of the weakness of all political structure, in the absence of a rational formula synthesizing theory and practice as in Tunisia.[110]

The fruits of technocratic, statist socialism have doubtless been disproportionately harvested by public sector managerial cadres. Entelis draws our attention to

another reality, more somber and less hopeful, behind the facade of stability and success. In the cities and countryside, among average men and women life is a continuous struggle, filled with despair. A microcosm of the enormity of the problem facing the society and its 18 million citizens is found in Algiers. . . . Scattered across its sidewalks and in hallways of apartment buildings are mounds of filth, garbage and debris; colonies of rats and vermin roam freely in basements and cellars; urban transportation is erratic and crumbling; potable water is turned on for an average of one hour a day; . . . brownouts and power shortages occur daily; inadequate housing has reached crisis proportions and what is available is dilapidated and unsafe; modest consumer goods are impossible to find except under the most outrageous black-market conditions; . . . education is a sometime thing, with an enormously over-crowded school system providing an average of two hours of classroom instruction per pupil per day; the program of free medicine is a sham. . . .[111]

These rather pessimistic assessments are partly belied by the apparent resiliency of the regime in the 1970s. The reflex of national solidarity attending Boumedienne's death in 1979 and the intriguing pattern of brokered and mediated factional conflict in the succession issue, which contrasted so sharply with the lethal rivalries of the early 1960s, are suggestive of a higher order of regime legitimacy. No doubt the intense nationalism and radical anti-imperialism of the Algerian international stance have a positive resonance among most milieux. Tensions clearly remain, both within the political class and the society at large. One reflection of them was the 1976 manifesto signed by former provisional government leaders Ferhat Abbas and Youssef Ben Khedda, among other old-line politicos, denouncing Boumedienne for "totalitarian rule and personality cult."[112] Another was the riots at Algiers University the preceding year and the 1980 disorders in Tizi-Ouzou over Berber cultural rights. But the regime in recent years has not required a high order of domestic repression to sustain itself.

There are some elements of simple good fortune. Above all, Algeria has been a major beneficiary of the soaring oil prices since 1973; it was possible to raise the state operating budget no less than 54 percent in 1975. Some 60 percent of state revenues in the mid-1970s derived from petroleum taxation.[113] The upward valuation of its hydrocarbon resource base lends credibility to the whole development strategy, even though part of it merely pays the growing food import bill (two-thirds of domestically consumed cereals are purchased abroad). It also compensates for the flagging efficiency of the huge parastatal sector; in the mid-1970s, only SONATRACH, of the whole sprawling public sector, operated at a profit.[114] Also some of the heavy industrial investment has yielded low returns; the first gas liquification plant cost $2.46 billion, or four times the projected figure, and now has uncertain prospects. The continuing outlet for Algerian workers in France was a critical safety valve; in 1972, there were still 400,000, which exceeded the total number of nonagricultural jobs outside the state bureaucracy in Algeria itself (300,000).[115] With *fortuna* placing an invisible weight in the scales, the balance of evidence was in many respects positive for radical populist—and statist—socialism in Algeria.

GUINEA-BISSAU: SOCIALISM AND UNDERDEVELOPMENT

A recent addition to the roster of populist socialist regimes is the minuscule state of Guinea-Bissau. The extraordinary effectiveness of its liberation struggle and the originality of the political philosophy of its martyred leader, Amilcar Cabral, have created in and out of Africa an attentive audience for its socialist experiment that is out of all proportion to its diminutive scale. In the first years of its independence, the close fraternal relationships with MPLA and FRELIMO dating from the days of the liberation struggle led many to include it among the Afro-Marxist ranks. However, the ruling PAIGC, after extended debate, decided in 1977 not to declare Marxism-Leninism as the state ideology. I thus consider its experience under the populist socialist heading.[116]

Guinea-Bissau is a remarkable amalgam of the inspirational and the ordinary, revolutionary aspiration and intractably non-revolutionary underdevelopment, socialist orientation and cautiously moderate policies. The parameters of choice are fixed by the enormously undeveloped state of the country as bequeathed by Portuguese rule as well as by the smallness of its territory (14,000 square miles) and population (less than a million). Schools for Africans were almost nonexistent, health facilities virtually limited to Bissau, and the up-country commercial infrastructure rudimentary. There were only a few thousand Portuguese residents, almost all either state officials or small traders. In fact, much of the small state apparatus was staffed by Cape Verdians, who were more numerous in the ranks of the colonial elite than the Portuguese themselves. There was neither dependent colonial development nor the "development of underdevelopment" argued by dependency theorists. Portuguese rule had the effect of preempting development; unlike the Algerian revolutionaries, who were confronted with a densely organized and distorted colonial economy, the PAIGC faced conditions much closer to a developmental *tabula rasa*. The only really important colonial infrastructure was the urban complex of Bissau itself, swollen by the war to 100,000.

This small country was the improbable setting for a particularly dynamic revolutionary liberation movement. The Algerians exhausted the French, but won few military victories; the PAIGC had all but ousted the Portuguese by force of arms. The 50,000-man colonial army held only the garrison towns, the capital hinterland, and a few rural zones where the PAIGC lacked a local base by the time that the Caetano government collapsed. Further, the PAIGC had created its own revolutionary administration and the beginnings of an educational, health, and commercial network in the large areas where its dominance was assured. The effectiveness of its revolutionary mobilization profoundly impressed various Western scholars and journalists who visited the PAIGC zones.[117]

The Guinea-Bissau revolution had as ideological guide its creative and original leader, Cabral.[118] His definition of the Guinean revolution falls in the third-world tradition of Che Guevara and Frantz Fanon, yet goes beyond most others in offering not only strategy and tactics for destroying colonial imperialism but ways and means of building the new order. His thought is molded by the analytical categories of the Marxist tradition, but far from being imprisoning metaphors of a dogmatic sociology, the categories are instrumental to a wholly novel and specific examination of Guinean realities. Indeed, Cabral rarely used the word *socialism* per se and never described himself as a Marxist. His response (made in 1971) to a question on this topic is quite revealing:

Is Marxism a religion? I am a freedom fighter in my country. You must judge from what I do in practice. If you decide that it's Marxism, tell everyone that it is Marxism. If you decide it's not Marxism, tell them it's not Marxism. But the labels are your affair; we don't like these kinds of labels.[119]

Cabral was, however, concerned that the future society toward which the liberation struggle was pointed would end—decisively—"the exploitation of man by man." To this end, he saw that the critical postindependence problem was not class struggle as such but who controlled and manipulated the state and to what ends. Crucial in the outcome would be the role of the African petty bourgeoisie, which would necessarily inherit command of the state apparatus. This petty bourgeoisie would be asked to commit class suicide—an unlikely but possible choice—by choosing to ally itself, indeed reincarnate itself, alongside the popular masses. For this to be possible, an unshakable revolutionary faith, forged in struggle, was indispensable.[120]

Cabral also stands out in the specificity of his thought and his willingness to examine ethnicity as well as the reified sociological categories of conventional socialist revolutionary thought, *worker* and *peasant*. He is able to recognize both the significance of ethnicity as a form of social consciousness and the differential receptivity to the revolutionary call of the more important cultural communities. The coastal Balante (32 percent) and Mandjak (14.5 percent) were the critical support groups, while the Fula (22 percent) were distinctly cool and—through favors granted to their chiefs by the Portuguese—open to recruitment for the colonial army. The one important ethnosocial group that Cabral does not analyze very directly is his own Cape Verdian community; during the colonial period, the term *African petty bourgeoisie* was almost synonymous with Cape Verdian. His political thought was totally grounded in the particular contours of Guinean society and in the praxis of the Guinean revolution. "In general," Cabral once said, "we have certain reservations about the systematisation of phenomena. . . . We greatly admire the scheme established by Che Guevara essentially on the basis of the struggle of the Cuban people and other experiences, and we are convinced that a profound analysis of that scheme can have a certain application to our struggles. However, we are not completely certain that, in fact, the scheme is absolutely adaptable to our condition." [121]

Cabral himself did not live to see the difficult transition from liberation struggle to organization for development. He was murdered in January 1973 by agents of the Portuguese. He was in no doubt, however, that if the revolution was to sustain its hold on mass loyalties, the obstacles of poverty and dependency would have to be surmounted and practical steps would need to be taken to bring concrete improvement to the ordinary Guinean. In a statement that foreshadowed the essentially pragmatic choices that were made, he declared,

Always remember that the people do not fight for ideas, for things that exist only in the heads of individuals. The people fight and they accept the necessary sacrifices. But they do it in order to gain material advantages, to live in peace and to improve their lives, to experience progress and to be able to guarantee a future for their children. [122]

The party itself had to undergo the metamorphosis from armed liberation movement to administering power. The potential for division and conflict was great; the temptations of embourgeoisement were evident as the leaders moved from the rigors of the forest camps to the relative comfort of the ministries. The Cape Verdian–mainlander cleavage lay just below the surface. The city of Bissau itself, despite the fact that the opening scene of the armed struggle occurred there when dock workers were massacred in 1959, was initially hostile terrain; the capital was in some respects a miniature replica of Saigon, transformed by the colonial war economy.

One important choice was whether the party was to remain a mass movement or transform itself into a Leninist organization on the FRELIMO model; there was some pressure in the latter direction from some in its entourage who were more committed to a Marxist-Leninist orientation than Cabral himself had ever been. The exclusionary option of a "vanguard" party was in the end not adopted. Rather, the 1977 PAIGC Congress concluded there was not "a proletariat in the sense of a class conscious of its interests and prepared to assume its historical responsibilities." The PAIGC, therefore, could not be a vanguard party but had to rely upon the "mobilization of all social forces" and to practice "a policy of national unity."[123] This conclusion appears to be dictated by implacable sociological logic: the industrial work force totals only 1,800; the total number of regularly employed persons numbers no more than 24,000, of whom 15,000 belong to the bureaucracy.

National unity itself was far from assured, even by the revolutionary success of the PAIGC. There were some 17,000 demobilized African soldiers of the former colonial army, the majority Fula. In the elections for regional councils held in 1976, while only the PAIGC lists were in the field, the party won only 80 percent of the votes nationally and only 50.6 percent and 56 percent in the two Fula regions.[124] The party has been very cautious in dealing with the Fula zones; its extant chiefly hierarchy has not been confronted. A party official told Hodges that chieftaincy would be allowed to erode of its own accord. "Islam teaches the people to respect the state. That is why we have no problems in the Fula areas."[125]

The Verdian issue has also been approached with circumspection. Of the six founding fathers of the PAIGC, Amilcar Cabral, Luis Cabral, Rafael Barbosa, Aristides Pereira, Fernando Fortes, and Inana Carvalho, all but Barbosa were Verdians. During the liberation struggle, Verdians provided much of the political leadership and organizational skills, while the actual military combat was almost wholly carried out by mainlanders. Some estimate as much as 70 percent of the colonial bureaucracy was staffed by Verdians; many remained to offer their services— which were accepted. The first president, Luis Cabral, was a Verdian, while the prime minister in the late 1970s, and president in November 1980, João Bernardo Vieira, is a mainlander. About a third of the cabinet in 1979 was Verdian. The virtually total exclusion of mainlanders from educational opportunity until very recently made inevitable a large Verdian contingent in the bureaucracy. Tensions inherent in this situation were always just below the surface and were reflected in such questions as what criteria to use in nominating personnel to state posts: formal qualifications, a criterion favoring Verdians, or military contribution to liberation, the basis for frequently disappointed claims of freedom fighters.

These contradictions finally brought about the downfall by military intervention of the Cabral regime in November 1980, and with it the elimination of the Verdian component in the national leadership. The issues that brought the smoldering resentments to the surface included the long-deferred project for political union with the Cape Verde Islands, the status of Barbosa, army reorganization, and a stagnant economy. The liberation struggle, while limited to the Guinea-Bissau mainland, had always been carried out as if Cape Verde and Guinea-Bissau had a vocation of unity; the PAIGC was, in theory, a single party ruling in two separate countries. From the perspective of mainlanders, however, one can understand that the amalgamation proposals— which had again been under active debate earlier in 1980—had many disadvantages. The overpopulated, barren, and drought-stricken islands had a far better educational system: an influx of educated Verdians threatened to flood the limited mainland employment market for skilled positions.

New irritations surrounding the amalgamation issue appeared in 1980. Some senior PAIGC officials were placed on trial on charges of opposing the union. Just before the coup, a new constitution was published that permitted both mainlanders and Verdians to hold presidential office; the Cape Verde constitution, however, limited the office to those born on the islands. To boot, the new constitution extended the powers of (Verdian) President Cabral, making him head of government as well as chief of state.

Plans to reorganize and professionalize the army upset the guerrilla fighter contingent, predominantly mainlanders. Such schemes carried overtones of supplanting those whose rank was won on the battlefield with those of higher technical and educational qualifications. Also, the Barbosa treason conviction in 1977 still rankled, even though the death sentence was not carried out; one of the first acts of the new regime was to release him, though he was not readmitted to the PAIGC.

The inability of the Cabral government to impart any real momentum to the economy played a part as well. There were persistent food shortages during 1980 and prolonged power failures in the capital. Criticisms were increasingly heard that the substantial foreign aid funds benefited only the Bissau area.

However, the coup did not alter the formal political structures of ideological orientation of the country. The PAIGC was retained, and even a nominal commitment to eventual union was reaffirmed. Former guerrilla leaders were prominent among the new leadership, which pledged to uphold the heritage of Amilcar Cabral.[126]

The most visible socialist institution is the network of *Armazens do Povo* (People's Stores) in Bissau and the small upcountry towns. These endeavor to make available the five basic necessities: rice, flour, cooking oil, sugar, and soap. However, there has been no effort to oust private traders, who operate mainly in Bissau. By 1980, the *Armazens do Povo*, which worked well during the liberation struggle, were encountering growing difficulties, with widespread charges of corruption.

The handful of tiny factories that comprise the industrial sector is too small to make public ownership a crucial issue. The leadership is anxious to encourage any potential investor who might consider establishing a factory. Overtures by a Portuguese shoe manufacturer in 1979 were warmly greeted.

Socialist agriculture is not a major issue of policy debate either; far more crucial is inducing peasants to increase their marketed production. The material resources and administration capacities of the state are so restricted that any policy in the rural area that must rely on encadrement and coercion has no possibility of being implemented—and virtually any conceivable initiative toward socialist agriculture would fail at this stage.

Policy choice is wholly constrained by the elemental exigencies of survival. Exports, in 1975, 1976, and 1977, covered only 19 percent, 17 percent, and 35 percent of imports—themselves severely curtailed, with a rigorous limitation on consumer imports. With an independent, nonconvertible currency, the payments deficit was a major constraint. Marketed rice production, which ran about 100,000 tons in the 1950s, leaving a margin for export, fell to below 30,000 tons at the time of liberation, thereby requiring substantial imports. Peanuts, which accounted for about 60 percent of export value, had fallen by more than half.

These harsh realities had an important impact in discouraging ideologically defined external ties. During the liberation struggle, the Soviet Union and Cuba had provided extensive and deeply appreciated military aid as well as educational opportunities for many young Guineans. However, economic aid fell far short of expectations; from 1975 to 1977, aid, nearly all in the form of loans, totaled $36 million, compared to $88 million from Western countries. Only 7.7 percent of Guinea-Bissau's imports came from the Soviet Union in 1978, while the Soviets bought almost none of its exports. A severe drought in 1977 brought a catastrophic fall in rice output; during 1978, the country did not have to pay for any of its food imports, though these tripled in volume and value over 1977. The donors were all Western countries, supplemented by UN agencies; the Soviet Union contributed only a token amount. The contrast was not lost upon the PAIGC leadership.

There have been other irritants in the Soviet relationship. A joint fishing venture whereby ownership is shared but management is essentially Russian has become viewed as exploitative; the Guineans have thrice demanded its renegotiation, to no avail. There is widespread suspicion that the Soviets have manipulated the agreed division of the catch and in particular have undervalued the take of the delectable Bissau shrimp. There has been vexatious pressure exerted for alignment on such international issues as recognition of the Vietnamese-imposed Cambodian government and the Chinese invasion of Vietnam, both of which Guineans see as peripheral to their concerns.

All of this has altered the texture of Guinea-Bissau's external linkages, although not its formally proclaimed goals nor its commitment to nonalignment and radical third-world causes. The disappointment with Soviet performance does not automatically extend to other Communist states. Cuba continues to enjoy admiration and affection; no one expects that Cuba would have the material resources to enable it to extend much economic aid. The Cuban ambassador in 1979 was an old guerrilla fighter who fought alongside the PAIGC troops during the liberation struggle—a solidarity not effaced by time.

In the first years of independence, only modest headway was made in addressing the daunting tasks of development; given the obstacles, it could hardly have been otherwise. The cynical and disabused gossip about corruption in the upper strata, frequent in many African capitals, was less pervasive in Bissau; overseas observers detected little repression, though after the 1980 coup Vieira claimed his predecessors had secretly executed five hundred persons. The 1980 coup came as a shock to some of the external authorities on the Guinea-Bissau socialist experiment, who were perhaps still captured by the euphoria of the guerrilla triumph. The change of leadership does add a new element of uncertainty, but it does not alter the judgment that, during the first five years of independence, the PAIGC generally provided prudent and—within the limits of reason—competent governance.

NKRUMAH AND THE SOCIALIST
JM

in Tanzania, Algeria, and Guinea-Bissau socialism con-
s as state ideology, in the three remaining cases, Ghana,
лea, and Mali, the phase of socialist experiment appears to be
er. In contrast to the three preceding cases, socialism in Ghana,
Juinea, and Mali became associated with the derelictions of particular regimes and thus was stigmatized as a "failure." The
shock waves of the street celebrations that greeted the demise of
the Nkrumah regime in February 1966 were felt round the world.
The overthrow of Modibo Keita in 1968 was followed by a partial
repudiation of his ideological orientation. In Guinea at the close
of the 1970s, the durable Sékou Touré himself, in a shift that had
important ideological repercussions throughout West Africa,
managed to lead a retreat from socialism.

The inquest that followed the sudden death of the Nkrumah
regime yielded an intriguing variety of interpretations. Soviet
analysts, who in the early 1960s had nourished the hope of a
noncapitalist pathway to development led by "revolutionary
democrats" such as Nkrumah, began to back away from this new
gloss on orthodox Marxist-Leninist thought. Fitch and Oppenheimer concluded that Nkrumah's political movement, the Convention Peoples' Party (CPP), was in reality a viper's nest of petit
bourgeois and capitalist elements who never seriously desired
the rupture with international capitalism and smashing of neocolonial structures indispensable to a true socialist strategy.[127]
Genoud maintained that the socialist orientation was never more
than verbal camouflage for conventional anticolonial nationalism.[128] Green argued that a sensible socialist strategy was indeed
pursued and was compromised only by a few poor decisions and
weak implementation; Berg asserted that grave miscalculations
were an ineluctable consequence of socialist preference.[129] Killick made the engaging claim that the Nkrumah strategy was not

only socialist prescription, but also a distillation of the conventional wisdom of development economics of the 1950s: ". . . the congruence of Marxian and non-Marxian economic thought on the development issue was a rather remarkable and mutually reenforcing one."[130]

Nkrumah had toyed with Marxism during his overseas student years and considered himself a socialist, but in his first years of political activism in Ghana his practical ideology was populist nationalism. The CCP triumphed through the perfection of a political idiom that was directed over the heads of the coastal professionals and hinterland chiefs and aimed at articulating the hopes and discontents of school leavers and commoners. However, during his six-year apprenticeship as leader of government business in the final colonial years, 1951–57, he cooperated with the moderately statist British version of a market economy joined to a rapid expansion of social amenities. In the preface to his political testament of these years, Nkrumah did make the revealing comment that "Capitalism is too complicated a system for a newly independent nation," and that socialism was thus required.[131] However, socialism played little role in public statements and had no visible impact on policy content. Of more immediate importance were the expectations kindled by the populist pledges made by CPP organizers; their flavor is conveyed by a statement Nkrumah made in 1949: "If we get self-government we'll transform the Gold Coast into a paradise in ten years. . . ."[132]

During the initial postindependence years, no basic alterations in development strategy were made, though the pace of infrastructure and amenity expenditures was stepped up; government expenditures rose from £60.5 million in 1975 to £113.7 in 1961. However, pressures built as CPP followers clamored for immediate benefits, the opposition carped, the cocoa price slid, and the comfortable hoard of £174 million in foreign exchange at independence vanished. Nkrumah was convinced that an evil combine of malevolent internal and external forces labored to thwart his dreams: the incurable neocolonial machinations of Western powers, laid bare in the Congo crisis; the iniquities of international capitalism, again revealed in the falling prices offered for Ghana's rising cocoa crops; state machinery hobbled by the bourgeois attitudes of the civil service; hostile scheming by such unreliable social groups as retrograde chiefs, greedy businessmen, and sullenly capitalist cocoa farmers. In the April 1961 Dawn Broadcast, a shift to a more explicitly socialist strategy was announced. The CPP program for 1962 laid strong emphasis on socialism, declaring it to be the "principle around which the Party is pivoted."[133] A new seven-year plan that confirmed the socialist commitment was unveiled in 1964:

The building of socialism imposes especially heavy responsibilities on the state in the field of economic policy and development. . . . As the state finances each year out of budget surpluses a large proportion of the productive investment made in the country the economy will become progressively socialised until by the end of the transition period the state will be controlling on behalf of the community the dominant share of the economy.[134]

During the final phase of Nkrumah rule, from 1961 to 1966, major policy choices were conditioned by an a priori set of principles, loosely deduced from socialism. Certainly not from scientific socialism: though from 1962 to 1966 Soviet Ambassador Georgi Rodionov was the most influential diplomat in Accra,[135] there was little resemblance between orthodox Marxism-Leninism and the Ghanaian developmental creed. The content of the socialist option never had the kind of clear articulation that the Arusha Declaration supplied in Tanzania. Yet, however elusive, it was nonetheless present as a mind set. Socialism can perhaps best be understood as a montage of several policy premises, none of which individually was distinctively socialist but which in assembled form constituted a socialist perspective—and, more important, were viewed as such. Nkrumah described himself as a Marxist on occasion but shrank from a systematic application of Marxism. He really sought an ideological formulation that at once would be an epitaph to his personal contribution and that could claim a distinctively African pedigree. At moments, socialism was presented in the personalistic garb of Nkrumahism. In 1964, he reached for a more metaphysical formulation with the publication, under his name, of *Consciencism*,[136] a pretentious and jargon-laden statement that discovered socialism immanent within the African cultural heritage. In the final bitter years of exile, he turned to a scathing and vulgar Marxism to stigmatize the malignant forces that destroyed him.[137]

Beyond the contradictions and inconsistencies in Nkrumah's own thought, the ideological mirror is further clouded by the disparate doctrinal factions that swirled about the presidency. On the left, there was a small but committed Marxist-Leninist group, orbiting around the radical publication *Spark*. On the right were a number of senior civil servants, among them the most influential authors of the seven-year plan, E. N. Omaboe and J. H. Mensah; this group was perfectly willing to frame the royal writ in socialist terminology, if such were the pleasure of the palace. However, they were fundamentally more at home with the neoclassical discourse of development economists than with the radicals. Their seven-year plan at once declared its socialist fealty while denying that there is any incompatibility between a socialist state and a vigorous private sector; it charted a transition to socialism "without our ever having to resort to such expedients as nationalization."[138] Beyond those groups whose policy thought had philosophical structure one encountered numerous persons in the upper reaches of the CPP for whom intellectual conviction was infinitely malleable and subordinated to the greater goal of amassing personal fortune.

Further, the contingencies of immediate political survival and power consolidation weighed more heavily upon Nkrumah than upon the leaders in the other countries we have considered. In addition, the consuming dream of Pan-Africa was a potent factor. Nkrumah was well aware of the widespread grumbling and discontent, even though the energetic use of preventive detention legislation and the proscribing of opposition eliminated the risk of ouster by constitutional means. The nearly successful attempt on his life at Kulundugu in 1962 was a profound shock, to which his instinctive response was radicalization. Equally influential was the ouster and subsequent assassination of Patrice Lumumba in the Congo, with whom Nkrumah had a secret protocol pledging Congolese membership in the Ghana-Guinea-Mali Union, a Pan-African embryo. The anti-Western animus was strengthened by increasing resistance in the moderate African states—those most closely identified with the West—to his Pan-African diplomacy.

For this syndrome of premises that shaped the Nkrumah socialist phase to become reality, speed was of the essence. The promised land awaited, and the CPP followers wanted the gates to the pastures of plenty unlocked at once. Colonial capitalism had brought only very slow change; the accomplishments of the Soviet Union showed what economic mobilization under socialism could achieve. Thus, an audacious frontal attack on underdevelopment was required; falling cocoa prices and vanishing reserves dictated not retrenchment but an all-out forward thrust.

Second, industrialization was the spearhead. Agriculture was a codeword for bondage; its most prosperous sector, cocoa, was deeply contaminated by capitalism and was the very monoculture Ghana needed to escape. The flight from poverty was possible only by rapid construction of an industrial base. The focus of public investment should shift from social overhead to directly productive industrial undertakings.

Third, both nationalism and socialism demanded state control of the new industrial sector, which was to be created through public investment. The Ghanaian business class, to Nkrumah, was too small to take on the task and would become a political menace if it were expanded. While the cooperation of foreign capital was perhaps unavoidable, the creation through industrialization of a foreign-owned and -operated enclave was unthinkable.

Finally, Nkrumah harbored a deep-seated mistrust of cocoa capitalism. Ghanaian control over cocoa marketing was assured easily enough through the Cocoa Marketing Board and other state-related mechanisms. The major foreign cocoa-trading firms, Cadbury's and United Africa Company, had withdrawn from the rural cocoa trade by 1960. However, a number of the major cocoa-producing areas (especially Ashanti) were centers of opposition. The large farmer-traders in the cocoa zones were seen as the cutting edge of emergent rural capitalism in Ghana. Not all the larger cocoa operators were hostile to the CPP; indeed, a number of them enjoyed its patronage. But many were, and as the regime's pricing and fiscal policies became increasingly unfavorable to the cocoa sector, bitterness and disaffection became general.[139]

In the industrial sphere, little recourse was made to nationalization; the only major takeovers were five failing gold mines, where abandonment appeared to be the alternative to state ownership, and the Cypriot mercantile empire of Levantis. Rather, the state sector was constructed through a host of new undertakings: cocoa processing, pharmaceuticals, various food processing and construction materials plants, marble, furniture, glass, a tannery, a boatyard, a dry dock, cocoa silos, among others. All observers, whatever their ideological sympathies, agree that the mushrooming state sector soon became a disorderly shambles. Many of these projects were undertaken with only the flimsiest study of their feasibility; Accra for a time was a rendezvous point for international mercantile buccaneers offering contractor financing for dubious turnkey factories to any minister who could be induced to listen. Many did, as there were frequently handsome rewards for intermediary services in clinching such deals. By 1965, there were some fifty-three state corporations; nearly two-thirds of the industrial projects were undertaken with supplier credits.

The most permanent, though controversial, legacy of the industrialization strategy was the costliest venture of all, the Volta Dam. Its cheap energy was intended to be the basic foundation for all other industrialization, and Nkrumah was from the beginning of his reign absolutely determined to build it. He paid a very high price; with mainly American finance, Kaiser (90 percent) and Reynolds (10 percent) undertook construction of the dam, and in return were assured power essentially at cost (the lowest in the world) for the aluminum smelter they built as the essential major client for the power generated. The Kaiser syndicate was given a five-year tax holiday, a thirty-year exemption on import duty on inputs, and the right to import their own alumina rather than develop Ghanaian bauxite.[140] The dam was finished ahead of schedule and below cost estimates. The Volta River Authority, which now operates the dam, has exceeded forecasts both in power sales and profitability.[141]

Critics of the scheme point out that Kaiser, not Ghana, was the major beneficiary of the dam. The combination of concessionary power rates for the smelter and fiscal exemptions meant that the state derived little revenue from the dam, yet had to repay the foreign debts incurred to construct it. Power sales to the neighboring states of Benin and Togo were necessary to generate foreign exchange for debt amortization. Thus, paradoxically, by the early 1970s Ghana itself faced a power shortage, with a large fraction of the Volta Dam output mortgaged to Kaiser and foreign buyers. The terms of the Kaiser deal blocked the development of an integrated Ghanaian aluminum scheme, from bauxite to metal fabrication, which was the original Nkrumah dream. From this perspective, the Volta Dam project is a paradigm case of the multinational corporate enclave described by dependency theory, created with the financial and diplomatic support of the United States and producing the "development of underdevelopment."[142]

The tripronged rural strategy deduced from the Nkrumahist creed involved concentrating public resources upon the promotion of a state farm sector, stepping up resource extraction from the cocoa sector, and gaining political domination over it through the imposition of a CPP buying monopoly, the United Ghana Farmers Council (later United Ghana Farmers' Cooperative Council, UGFCC). Each of these moves was calamitous; cumulatively, they dealt Ghanaian agriculture a lethal blow from which it has yet to recover.

The state farm was envisaged as a socialist navigational stratagem to evade the Scylla of rural capitalism and the Charybdis of traditional peasant cultivation with its low productivity. High returns were expected from mechanized cultivation and skilled management. However, the state farms quickly foundered on the hidden shoals of high costs and low output. The State Farms Corporation, founded in 1963, absorbed the assets of the defunct Agricultural Development Corporation, a colonial venture that created a few rubber, oil palm, and tobacco schemes in the 1950s and was liquidated in 1961 after accumulating a $400,000 loss. Some former experimental stations were converted to farms, and many new farms were created. At the height of the state farm program in 1965, there were 105 farms covering 1 million acres, of which only 104,000 were planted. About 4,000 tractors were acquired, and a good fraction of the government extension staff were transferred to the state farms. Overall, the results were not just disappointing but devastating. From 1963 to 1965, the State Farms Corporation lost $19.8 million. The aggregate yields per acre, by Miracle's and Seidman's calculations, were less than a fifth of peasant agriculture, and a state farm worker produced a quarter of what the peasant farmer had.[143] The Killick data shown in table 3.7, derived from different sources, show slightly divergent figures from those of Miracle and Seidman, but the same orders of magnitude. The harsh indictment by Killick seems fully justified by the facts:

Bearing in mind that the State Farms Corporation had absorbed many of the Ministry of Agriculture's professional officers, that it had command over infinitely more capital assets and other modern inputs than the peasants, and that it was receiving favourable treatment in the way of

TABLE 3.7. Comparative Performance of Peasants and State
Farms, Ghana

	Peasants (1970)	State farms (1963–64)
Number of workers (000)	1,791	18
Area cultivated (000 acres)	6,361	49
Output (000 tons)	5,960	10.6
Yield (tons per acre)	0.94	0.21
Labor productivity (tons per worker)	3.33	0.59

SOURCE: Tony Killick, *Development Economics in Action* (London: Heinemann, 1978), p. 193.

financial support . . . import licenses . . . technical assistance, it is little short of staggering that it should have achieved lower yields and smaller outputs per man.[144]

Table 3.8 documents the steadily increasing fiscal pressure on the cocoa sector; from 1957 to 1965 state-fixed prices fell from 80 to 40 shillings a headload, while inflation during the same period was 100 percent. Part of this reflected negative trends in the world market; cocoa prices, which in prewar years were quite stable at about 10¢ per pound on the New York market, soared to over 70¢ in the mid-1950s, then dropped back to the 30–40¢ range, finally dipping to about 20¢ in 1965; then, in the 1970s, they rose to new heights, reaching $2 per pound by the late 1970s. In part, however, the lowered returns reflected a deliberate choice to divert surplus from the cocoa sector into industrial development. Farmers were hit by a special "development contribution" in 1959, followed by "forced savings" in 1961, then a 24 percent price slash in 1965. Heavy taxation of the cocoa sector had begun in the 1950s, when—in addition to export taxation— the government (through the Cocoa Marketing Board) withheld from farmers a significant fraction of the Korean War boom price surge on the grounds that a surplus was being accumulated for price stabilization purposes. In reality, the surplus was decanted into other public investment projects; in the process, the price

TABLE 3.8. Government and the Cocoa Industry, Ghana: Selected Indicators

| | Index: (1960 = 100) | | | | | | | | | | |
	1960	1961	1962	1963	1964	1965	1966	1970
Index of real producer prices	100	87	77	61	46	37	45	64
Index of real value of total payments to cocoa farmers	100	80	76	69	79	37	34	60
Payments to cocoa farmers as % of total export proceeds from cocoa	72*	58	60	57	71	41	55	37
Index of real value of budgeted government expenditures on cocoa industry	100	70	16	20	18	30	39	41
Index of quantity of insecticide sales to cocoa farmers	100	63	67	86	63	2	9	118

*Figure based on fiscal year, rather than crop year; thus 1960 ≠ 100.
SOURCE: Tony Killick, *Development Economics in Action* (London: Heinemann, 1978), p. 119.

stablization fund underwent metamorphosis into a tax on cocoa producers. To add insult to injury, the CPP cocoa organ, the UGFCC, loudly proclaimed farmer support for each successive amputation of their incomes they were called upon to endure.

The third dimension of Nkrumah's agricultural strategy, the determination to acquire full political control over the crucial marketing infrastructure of the cocoa sector, began well before the 1961–66 socialist phase. The UGFCC was launched in 1953, initially tied to a 1952 creation, the Cocoa Purchasing Company (CPC), which was designed to challenge and ultimately displace the European trading houses. CPP party finance committee chairman A. Y. K. Djin was placed in charge of the CPC, which was flamboyantly described in Parliament by a CPP spokesman as "the product of a master brain, Dr. Kwame Nkrumah, and . . . the atomic bomb of the Convention People's Party." [145] Large resources were vested in the CPC, which was both a purchasing and lending agency. Some $1 million in loan funds poured through the CPP-inspired spillways to irrigate the party faithful, served by 1,960 CPC buying centers. The highly political operating procedures of the CPC, seasoned with venality, brought it growing disrepute. By 1956, it was dissolved with a harsh indictment for corrupt performance by a commission of inquiry.

The UGFCC lived on, however, and with independence became the main CPP hope for acquiring political hegemony over the cocoa sector. With the withdrawal of the European trading firms from rural operations, the major remaining adversary was the cooperative movement, which at its peak in the late 1950s numbered 50,000 members and handled 30 percent of the crop. The cooperatives were always viewed with suspicion by Nkrumah, both because of their close ties with the colonial cooperative department, which had sponsored their expansion, and because many of them were headed by large farmer-traders, whom Ghanaian socialists saw as the spearhead of aggressive rural capitalism. [146] An important component of the 1961 shift to a socialist strategy was the forced liquidation of the cooperatives;

their assets, valued at $3 million, were confiscated and turned over to the UGFCC, now accorded a full monopoly of cocoa buying. While the UGFCC did succeed in actually handling the very large crops of the early 1960s, and even increased the percentage of the crop graded as top quality, it totally failed to offer the farmers either material benefits or a political voice. The beneficiaries were above all the UGFCC officials, who soon became a focus for bitter farmer hostility; Afrifa expressed a view widely heard in the cocoa areas that the UGFCC officials "comprised a pack of criminals who had been involved in the old Cocoa Purchasing Company scandal, and a band of new sycophants who became the functionaries."[147] Beckman, in a meticulous monograph devoted to the UGFCC, comes to similar conclusions in less trenchant terms:

It was only for the members of the urban based petty-bourgeoisie with its degree of education that a "non-capitalist" solution could hold up a credible alternative as a means of private advance. Only they could compete for the offices of the new party and state bureaucracies. The real losers were not the party businessmen who had fought in the National Assembly for free enterprise and free competition. Few of these had any private interests in the cocoa trade. The losers were the farmer-traders who had handled the bulk of the trade either as brokers or as cooperators. Recruited mostly from the upper stratum of the farmer community, these were the people with the most experience in organising the farmers, and those most likely to turn farmer organisations against the central government and its heavy appropriation of cocoa income.[148]

The official commission of inquiry appointed after the fall of Nkrumah to investigate the UGFCC concluded: "The effect . . . of the UGFCC on farmers has been sinister and the farmers' discontent and apparent hostility towards the UGFCC . . . is justified and hardly to be wondered at."[149] In these circumstances, it is no surprise that the UGFCC vanished after the fall of Nkrumah as swiftly as its CPP sponsor.

There can be little ambiguity about the verdict in this instance: whether the cause was the inherent unsuitability of the socialist option, the poor implementation of a denatured version of socialism, or its subversion by domestic capitalism and external imperialism, the consequences were clearly negative. A large foreign debt of $768 million had replaced the handsome reserves of 1957; in the last five years of Nkrumah's regime the net deterioration of exchange holdings was $1.1 billion. The state was saddled with a deficit-ridden public sector, including a large number of plants that had no prospect of profitable operation; in 1966, the government estimated that its manufacturing plant functioned at 20 percent of single-shift capacity.[150] While the lagged momentum from cocoa plantings induced by the boom conditions of the 1950s brought output surging to an all-time record of 546,000 tons in 1965, these production figures concealed an ominous trend reversal. New plantings all but ceased in the early 1960s in the face of heavy state extraction and poor returns; young persons fled the cocoa sector. Both trees and farmers aged: a survey made in 1974 showed that approximately 60 percent of cocoa farmers were over fifty years of age and 80 percent over forty.[151] By the early 1970s, most food crops brought a higher return than cocoa, not only because of the growing urban markets but especially because these commodities escaped state taxation.[152] Inflation, never before an issue, gathered force in the 1960s, reaching 40 percent by 1965; although this figure is dwarfed by the post-1975 catastrophe, at the time it was a major social shock. From 1960 to 1965, real urban wages fell by half. Worker and farmer, presumed beneficiaries of the new socialist commonwealth, had totally withdrawn their support by 1966.

Against these infirmities may be set the real gains in social infrastructure during the Nkrumah period. A partial posthumous rehabilitation of Nkrumah occurred in the 1970s, especially of his nationalist and Pan-African contribution. The shortcomings of the 1960s fade somewhat in the face of the inability of successive regimes to really restore prosperity to Ghana. The

steady decline of the cocoa industry has continued, with production falling below 300,000 tons by 1978. Neither the neoliberal-
ism of the National Liberation Council (NLC) and Busia regimes
from 1966 to 1972 nor the more assertive nationalism of the early
Acheampong regime reversed this trend. The decline of other export industries—timber, gold, diamonds—persisted, and no new
ones have taken their place. Whatever damage the Nkrumah experiment may have done pales into virtual insignificance compared to the stupendous corruption of the later Acheampong
years, which saw Ghana slide into utter bankruptcy, hyperinflation, and an utterly desperate socioeconomic crisis in the face of
cocoa prices ten times as high as those in the final Nkrumah
phase. In the last years of the Acheampong regime, corrupt
diversion of cocoa revenues occurred on a scale that wholly
eclipsed CPP blemishes.[153]

GUINEA: THE RESTLESS SOCIALISM OF SÉKOU TOURÉ

In Guinea, a two-decade venture in socialism was brought to a
close in 1978, when the perennial leader Sékou Touré quietly
veered toward economic liberalization.[154] These twenty years
were marked by volatile shifts in doctrinal stress, from declaration of class war to periods of subdued ideology. Throughout, the
supreme arbiter of both ideology and politics has been Touré
himself; the often whimsical and sudden shifts in public rhetoric
reflected the moods of the president rather than any changing
balance of contending philosophical currents. Yet beneath these
mercurial oscillations in official discourse the major patterns of
development policy remained relatively stable.

The genesis of Touré's ideological perspective was markedly
different from that of the other leaders we have examined. He
completed only primary school, and his further learning was au-

todidactic; in subsequent years, he was always suspicious of university-trained intellectuals. His socialism was learned in the union ranks, initially the Stalinist Communism of the French *Confédération Générale des Travailleurs* (CGT). After 1948, he began to veer toward a worker-centered position, and was primarily concerned with union matters. In the 1950s, when he shifted his action to the party's political realm, his discourse embraced radical populist nationalist themes. Rivière offers a resume of Touré's political thought:

... the final statement of this ideology was above all the brainchild of the Guinean leader who had been trained in three schools of thought—those of Africa, the West, and Marxist socialism. The basic aim of Sékou Touré's socialism or noncapitalist approach (for it was not until 1962 that the term "socialist path" was used), is to alter the relationship between human beings. This is to be done by decolonizing their viewpoints and attitudes, and by creating a new man freed from a system of capitalistic exploitation and participating with all his strength in the development of his nation. Here nationalism transcends socialism, just as support for the regime has priority over promotion of the revolution. . . . Nor was there any question of the class struggle until 1967, for in a newly independent country the contrasts between social classes should not be artificially aggravated. Furthermore, it was assumed that such differences would disappear in a revolutionary and democratic state through the action taken by a single party—the party for all the people. . . . [155]

The ebb and flow of socialist intensity in Touré's positions correlated with another central characteristic of the regime: the psychosis of the permanent plot. Major discoveries of real or imaginary conspiracies were usually accompanied by an escalation in ideological tone, differentiating the regime from the ever-reborn fifth column of ideological criminals—deviationists and counterrevolutionaries. This was true in 1964, when a wave of purges of would-be compradore elements occurred; in 1967, when class struggle was declared in the wake of a plot discovery; in 1970, following upon the very real Conakry incursion by

Portuguese mercenaries joined by Guinean dissidents; and in 1976, following the "Fulani plot." A leftward ideological lurch occurred on each of these occasions; as its energies became expended and the purported conspirators were pilloried and punished (often killed), the rhetorical temperature gradually lowered.[156]

When Guinea was suddenly granted independence—and suffered the fury of de Gaulle's vindictive indignation at its having asked for sovereignty—there was an initial period of euphoria. There could be no doubt about the overwhelming popular support enjoyed by Touré and the *Parti Démocratique de Guinée* (PDG). The mobilization of a people seemed to hold the promise of a revolutionary conquest of poverty. The will, the momentum, the resources all seemed to be present. Guinea at that time was— after Senegal and the Ivory Coast—the most prosperous of French sub-Saharan territories and had a more impressive resource base than any other: two-thirds of the world reserves of bauxite; iron ore, diamonds, silver, among other minerals. The country was also endowed with promising hydroelectric potential and had good prospects for commercial agriculture. A charismatic leader disposed to a socialist orientation; a people united in anticolonial intoxication; a rupture with international capitalism, imposed by the Gaullist determination to punish its wayward colony and by the initial reluctance of other Western powers to step in: all this appeared to open revolutionary vistas rarely seen.

A socialist strategy was swiftly fashioned. The initial phase, 1958–60, was seen as a period for consolidating the independence; 1960–63 was to see the implementation of a three-year plan that would lay the groundwork for socialist construction, to be followed by a seven-year plan that would propel Guinea into a stage of self-sustaining development. In an atmosphere of hope and excitement, overseas socialist advisers, most notably French Marxist Charles Bettelheim, were summoned to aid in the preparation of the three-year plan. However, economic implementation began to unravel before a real beginning had been made on the three-year plan, and the seven-year plan was little more than a shopping list of projects, only a few of which ever saw the light of day. By the 1970s, it was clear that the socialist sector was at an impasse, and the ransom of socialism was a demeaning dependence of the state upon the neocolonial bauxite enclave.

The basic socialist strategy proposed by Bettelheim included the assertion of state control over trade, currency, credit, and prices; expansion of state enterprises; nationalization of power, gas, and water distribution; and the promotion of comprehensive cooperatives to socialize the rural sector. The major thrust of socialism was dictated by the nature of the colonial economy, which was still at a mercantile stage. The most visibly powerful and prosperous French businesses were the import-export trading houses. The foreign private sector—outside of mining—was removed not by nationalization (excepting the utilities) but by strangulation.

In the mercantile field, the first major move was the creation of the *Comptoir Guinéen du Commerce Exterieur* (CGCE) in January 1959; this was given an initial monopoly on trade with Communist states and an import monopoly on such basic items as rice, sugar, flour, cement, beer, and matches. However, immediate problems of disorganization made the CGCE dependent on the still-surviving foreign banks and trading companies, who had little interest in assuring the success of this experiment. To break French financial control, Guinea launched its own currency in March 1960, which lacked convertability. French mercantile establishments, unable to repatriate their profits, went into hibernation, further aggravating the crisis of the CGCE.

To fill the void created by the virtual cessation of French trading firm activity, a domestic parallel to the CGCE, the *Comptoir Guinéen de Commerce Interieur* (CGCI), was launched in May 1960. Its sweeping mandate was to carry out all sales operations, represent overseas concerns, undertake market studies, collect and store export commodities; provide repair and maintenance services for diverse equipment; fix merchandise prices. The CGCI wholly lacked the skills and resources to fulfill its mission, and commercial dislocation intensified. Mercantile paralysis was averted only by quietly permitting Guinean private traders to step into the breach. A nominally public but in practice private trading sector necessarily required an informal interpenetration of public servant and private merchant—leading in turn to the 1964 campaign against the nascent "compradore bourgeoisie" in the public sector, and a further extension of state cotrol over the trading sector. The numerous Guinean merchants whose assets were confiscated at this time formed the first wave of what was to become a major exodus of Guineans from all walks of life. In 1961, the two state trading conglomerates were broken down into seventeen specialized organizations, but there was no alteration of the multiple difficulties that paralyzed their operations. A brief liberalization in 1963 was followed by draconian new controls on the commercial sector in 1964. From this time forward, the tension between the socialist-inspired formal regulation and the incapacity of the state sector to perform marketing services fostered a twilight trading system that had both high risks and lucrative profits. To achieve commercial success one was required to evade legal requirements: smuggling, diverse black market operations, import license traffic, and kindred activities became the heart of the mercantile economy. For those willing to take the risks and able to secure protectors and accomplices in the state apparatus such trade was extremely remunerative. It was also uncertain and perilous; the risk of being denounced as a counterrevolutionary was constant.

In the manufacturing sector, a few private firms lingered, no doubt in the hope that a change of regime would transform the climate; by 1966, these employed only 1,719 workers.[157] By 1971, most of them had closed their doors. At this time, the entire private sector included only 41 commercial enterprises, 439 retail stores, and 779 specialized traders.[158] A small state-owned manufacturing sector was created in the 1960s (printing press, cigarettes and matches, cannery, sawmill, textile plant, meat packing plant, vegetable oil mill). Of these undertakings, only the Chinese-built cigarette and match complex operated profitably and well. The others are all textbook cases of failed projects (shortages of needed inputs, poor markets for output, unsuitable machinery) and operate at a small fraction of capacity. Altogether, this sector constituted 2.6 percent of GNP in 1968.[159]

The cornerstones of socialist construction in the countryside, in the first years, were the "human investment" campaign and the promotion of production cooperatives. The former, which sought to capitalize on the mass fervor of the independence period to mobilize communities for voluntary public works projects, worked impressively in 1959, fitfully in 1960, and then not at all. Some 2,200 buildings were completed by "human investment" volunteers in 1959–60, mainly schools and mosques.[160] The *Cooperatives Agricoles de Production* (CAP) at their peak in 1962 had 60,000 nominal members in 559 units; however, a quarter of these were inactive. The three-year plan called for 30,000 hectares of collectively tilled fields, but in 1962 the number of hectares actually under cultivation was only 10,000, and by 1964 it had dropped to 2,200. Most of the plots were poorly maintained and reluctantly cultivated, and their yields were well below those of family fields.[161]

When the CAP failed, Touré unveiled a new set of cooperatives in 1965; by 1972, these had failed in their turn. Derman, one of the rare scholars to undertake rural fieldwork in Guinea after the early 1960s, found that the cooperatives he observed about 1970 in Fouta Djallon consisted of a cotton field planted with seeds distributed by the government and cultivated by villagers, who were expected to contribute voluntary labor in the fields; they naturally did as little as possible. Cooperative facilities were also offered to buy tomatoes, mangoes, and oranges; in reality, these were simply forced deliveries to the state at prices below the market level. The peasants tended to view them as organs of forced labor for the personal enrichment of state officials.[162]

In 1974, Touré declared yet another agrarian revolution and prescribed a new set of cooperatives. The official newspaper *Horoya* commented: "Analyzing the causes of the poor functioning and extinction of previous cooperative, the Comrade Strategist Ahmed Sekou Touré remarked that their permanent flaw had been to harbor capitalist conceptions, and seek only individual gain. The cooperative is thus not viewed as the common property of the collectivity in which, on an equal basis, each has a right to participate."[163] Derman adds, "Thus, the PDG judges past attempts at the formation of rural cooperatives as failures because they were based not on socialist conceptions but capitalist ones. . . . To explain the failure of the past on the incorrect ideas of the population without asking where they got them, why they maintained them, and what will lead them to change those ideas, is inadequate."[164]

By 1978, Touré himself appears to have concluded that the socialist pathway had failed; such a conclusion is difficult to dispute. The anemic state manufacturing sector barely limped along, and private manufacturing had virtually disappeared. Output of all export commodities, except bauxite-alumina and pineapples, which were produced in the foreign enclave, steadily dwindled, with iron ore, gold, and diamonds disappearing from the export figures altogether (remaining diamond production reportedly being delivered directly to the presidency).[165] Policies undertaken to smash the bonds of neocolonial and capitalist dependency had paradoxically reinforced it: the share of bauxite and alumina in exports rose from 46.8 percent in 1964 to 70.7 percent in 1972; Swiss-produced pineapples were an additional 10 percent.

Faced with constant and growing revenue and exchange deficits, the Guinean state could survive only by bartering its rich natural resources to foreign operators. A series of mining concessions was made to foreign partners for bauxite and alumina productions: Fria (Olin Mathieson, Péchiney-Ugine); Kindia (USSR); Tougué-Dabola (Alu-Suisse and Energoprojekt of Yugoslavia); Boké (ALCAN, Alcoa, Harvey Aluminum, Péchiney-Ugine, Aluminim-Werke, Montecatini-Edison). Some observers regard a number of these arrangements as being quite unfavorable to Guinea, a reflection of the weakness of Guinea's bargaining position. For example, Fria (now Friguia) pays Guinea only its shareholder entitlement of foreign exchange earned (65 percent) and retains the rest.[166] The Soviet bauxite deal valued the exported production at little more than a third of the world market price, and these revenues were entirely used to repay an 8,300 million ruble Soviet debt (including the 83 million ruble loan that financed the bauxite project).[167] The Swiss-based combine that produces and exports pineapples, the *Compagnie de Financement du Commerce Extérieur* (COFICOMEX), was granted a twenty-five-year exclusive concession in 1967, enabling it to retain from export sales debt repayment to the Guinea government and its import needs.[168] A deal for iron ore extraction was signed with a Japanese combine in 1973.

Overall, the agricultural picture is bleak. Of the commercial crops, only pineapple production has increased. A country that could easily produce a food surplus has spent 20 percent to 40 percent of its import outlays on food supplies, receiving in addition substantial PL480 (United States farm surplus) shipments in the 1960s. As but one example, output of paddy rice—the main food staple—fell from 360,000 tons in 1964 to 200,000 in 1972.

Although Touré retained some of his personal popularity, and the PDG, despite the authoritarianism inherent in its democratic centralism, still had an effective country-wide presence, by 1960 a harsh and oppressive dimension to the exercise of power became visible. In the first "plot" discoveries, ten persons died after enduring torture. Each new "conspiracy" revelation was followed by a wave of political arrests. In February 1971, some ninety-one death sentences were passed on those accused of collaborating with the Portuguese incursion; the 1976 "Fulani plot" led to the death in prison of former OAU General Secretary Diallo Telli. Boiro prison near Conakry acquired a sinister reputation for its torture chambers.[169]

Economic distress and political repression produced a large-scale exodus at all levels of the social hierarchy: intellectuals to escape the climate of fear and suspicion, merchants to elude the uncertainties of commerce in a socialist environment, peasants to find economic refuge. Nearly a fifth of the population emigrated to neighboring countries, especially Ivory Coast. Only Guinea, among the populist socialist regimes, provoked such a flight. A Guinean historian, Lansine Kaba, provides an apt epitaph to two decades of the revolutionary socialist state: "The PDG, in fact, has not liberated the Guineans from tyranny and poverty, despite 20 years of rule—and despite President Touré's famous saying to General de Gaulle in 1958 that 'we prefer freedom in poverty to opulence in servitude.'"[170]

Epitaph indeed: at the moment these lines were being written, as the second decade of the Guinean revolution closed, Touré was—*sotto voce*—pronouncing a requiem to socialism. The fateful blow came from a wholly unsuspected quarter: the women, once the ardent militants of the Guinean revolution. The shots that were fired in Conakry on 27–28 August 1977—and the several dozen market women martyrs they created—proved in time to be the death knell for socialism itself as it had been known since 1958.

The women's revolution was provoked by one of the salvos fired by Touré at the everlasting dragon of petty capitalism. All village markets were ordered closed; the local cooperative store, operated by local party and state functionaries, was accorded a total monopoly of local trade, and all farmers were required to deliver all their crops to them. Women, who played a crucial role in both rural and urban markets, were particularly affected by this measure. Protest demonstrations by market women began in small centers, then—as news of them filtered through the remarkably efficient informal communication network—spread to provincial towns, and finally to Conakry itself. Accumulated resentments over shortages, inflation, and generally declining well-being spilled over into volatile protests, which included sackings of state buildings and police stations. Equivalent protests by men would doubtless have been repressed with whatever level of brutality was required, but it was much harder for security forces to fire on women.

The crescendo of protest peaked in Conakry on 27–28 August with a march of many thousands of women on the presidential palace. The magnificent oratorial talents of Touré, which had won him mass adulation so many times before, were no match on this occasion for the anger of the demonstrators. The order was given to fire on the women; reportedly, a number of Guinean troops who refused to obey were themselves executed, and the Cuban palace guard had to intervene to disperse the protestors.

The psychological impact of this remarkable women's revolution was profound. While the market women were driven from the presidential palace, news of these dramatic events—while little known abroad—swiftly spread to all corners of Guinea. At first the party organ, Horoya, thundered that these episodes were but one more battle in the "historical struggle between revolution and counterrevolution" and Touré himself reacted by scornfully stigmatizing the marchers as merely the "tail of the Fifth Column." But the accumulated frustrations dramatized by these events were not so easily dismissed. Not long after, the offending decree was quietly withdrawn, and by April 1978 Touré was in Monrovia as smiling participant in a "Summit of Reconciliation" with his fellow heads of state from Liberia, Ivory Coast, Senegal, Gambia, and Togo.[171] Touré, in popular parlance the "great elephant," was now lumbering down a different pathway.

MALI: BUILDING SOCIALISM WITHOUT RESOURCES

The Mali case is similar to that of Guinea, with the important exception that this landlocked state lacks the rich resource potential of Guinea.[172] The Malian political elite who chose the socialist option were intellectuals rather than trade union leaders, but their perspectives were quite comparable in the initial phase. The immediate steps taken pursuant to the socialist option were closely parallel: state control of import-export trade, creation of a few public sector industries, comprehensive planning, a national currency outside the franc zone, a rural strategy based on production cooperatives as the *summum bonum*. While the rural penetration of the *Union Soudanaise* (US) was less than that of the PDG, in style and structure they were much alike. Colonial capitalism, as in Guinea, was above all associated with the French trading houses; economic development was very slight. And it did not improve during the socialist years.

There were, of course, some differences. There was no multinational mineral enclave offering financial succor to a disappointing socialist sector. Modibo Keita had less personal ascendancy than Touré; the socialist option was an initial consensus of the political leadership, with a strongly ideological core supplied by Seidou Badian Kouyate, Madeira Keita, and Ousmane Ba. The experiment did not last nearly as long: while the post-Keita regime from 1968 pursued only an ambivalent and partial retreat from the more rigorous ideological path chosen in 1960, nonetheless the demise of the first regime clearly marked the end of an era. More clearly than in Guinea, the socialist experiment pitted a state class of bureaucrats and politicians, who provided its impetus and were its sole beneficiaries, against a traditional mercantile class, in opposition from 1962 on, and a peasantry that initially greeted political liberation with enthusiasm but soon became disaffected, retreating into economic exit and political dissimulation.

As in Guinea, a mood of euphoria and expectancy attended the initial commitment to the socialist orientation. In September 1960 the Congress of the ruling party unanimously endorsed this choice. The temper of the times is well expressed by Kouyate's defense of the socialist strategy:

The underdeveloped countries cannot follow the same road as the European countries in the matter of the process of their economic development, and that is for evident reasons: slowness of capital formation, subordination of the general interest, and the collective well-being to profits realized by individuals. . . . Therefore, the only path permitting Mali to develop rapidly and harmoniously would be that of the socialist economy characterized by planning and the decisive role of the state in the economic life.[173]

Comprehensive planning was the crucial motor for the socialist state; French Marxist Bettelheim was brought in here as well, and the planning team that prepared the five-year plan that would place Mali on the socialist path was directed by Samir Amin, who subsequently contributed much to the literature on African dependency.

By the time of the Keita overthrow, virtually everyone agreed that the plan, and the strategy to which it was linked, had failed. The postcoup leaders offered a possibly interested resume:

The First Five-Year Plan . . . has resulted in an unmitigated failure, despite some commendable realizations in the industrial sector and some spectacular realizations in the field of infrastructure. . . . The inefficiency of the productive sector, the low level at which modern enterprises have been operating, and the absence of a taxation system adapted to the rural world have both prevented the realization of an export output sufficient to cover imports and of a surplus revenue that would have allowed to cover the ever-increasing recurrent administrative costs. Consequently, a point of equilibrium could be reached only by resorting to an inflationary currency circulation and by external indebtedness.[174]

By 1965, Amin, the principal architect of the plan, had all but abandoned hope for its success. While he continued to insist that the 11 percent growth rate, the high level of external aid neces-

sary to finance the plan, and public corporation sur;
were presumed to generate domestic state capital were
tially realistic assumptions, he bemoaned the multiple
the Malian state:

If, instead of bringing to the capital budget the billions fc
public enterprises must have their deficits covered by th ˸p˸˸˸
budget, the state sector, rather than being an engine of development,
will become in fact a brake on economic development. . . .

The gap between the Plan and its implementation has become so
great that one may wonder whether there really exists any effective
planning in Mali. . . .

The fact that traditional agriculture has yet to take off (because state
and political cadres proved unable to mobilize and motivate the peasantry) is in the last analysis the true cause of Mali's difficulties, which
are obviously aggravated by the disorderly and excessively rapid growth
in current administrative expenditures.[175]

Whether the failure of the plan is attributed to the incompetence of Malian cadres, as Amin argues, or to the shortcomings
in the document itself, it does stand out in retrospect for its visionary qualities. Of the $256 million of planned investment,
over half was to come from foreign aid, with Western and Eastern
donors joining hands. Some $86.4 million was to come from
public corporation profits (in the event, there was a net loss of
$15 million), with the state trading conglomerate Société ma-
lienne d'Importation et d'Exportation (SOMIEX) to contribute
the lion's share; it was scheduled, by 1964, to generate profits
equal to one-third of GDP.[176]

SOMIEX was granted a monopoly of the peanut trade as well
as of eleven other basic items, including sugar, salt, and tea. Although it did turn an annual profit of $2–3 million during the
Keita years and rapidly increase its share of recorded commerce
from 26.5 percent in 1961 to nearly 90 percent by 1967, it did not
charge lower prices than private traders and its quality of service
was poorer.[177]

The foreign trading houses quietly curtailed their activities
and withdrew in the face of state trading operations, but the po-

tent traditional trading sector chose to confront them. The Malian merchant class was no mean adversary. Meillassoux describes them: "All together, these merchants form a kind of native bourgeoisie of African stock and culture. They work in an almost exclusively African milieu, providing an African market with African goods. They dress in a traditional manner, often sumptuously. Their cultural model is not European, but Arabian." [178] They have long dominated the kola and cattle trade and more recently have moved into cloths and transport. Their hostility to the new order became open when the Mali franc was created in 1962; subsequently their considerable commercial talents were deployed in smuggling and other illicit operations. The market for their services was enhanced on the one hand by the falling real prices decreed by the state for rural produce and on the other by the sporadic shortages and operating flaws in SOMIEX.

Their class antagonist was the bureaucratic bourgeoisie, who were entrenched in the state sector. In the words of one Marxist analyst:

Upon attainment of independence, the first task of the newly-installed bureaucratic class was therefore to create an extensive public sector so as to economically anchor its politically dominant position, basing its power on collective, rather than private ownership of the means of production. . . .

Thus this so-called "socialism" appeared more as a kind of "étatisme" characterized by a deliberate proliferation of jobs for incoming recruits to the dominant group.[179]

In Mali, some 95 percent of the population was rural; there were only very limited prospects for an industrial strategy, and agricultural development was crucial. Agrarian stagnation was indeed, as Amin noted, crucial to the failure of the plan. It can be explained in several ways.

One evident misallocation was the attribution of half the plan's agricultural investment to the *Office du Niger*, which has drained state resources for fifty years with little visible benefit. This choice cannot be blamed on socialism; profitability for the

Office du Niger for half a century has been a will-o'-the-wisp lying just beyond an ever-receding horizon. Its bureaucracy, a potent interest group, has demonstrated nimble dexterity in garbing its resource claims in the dominant ideology of the moment, whether it be colonial capitalism or populist socialism. From its inception in 1928 until 1959 it consumed 48 percent of state investment; though claims of an irrigable potential of 1.2 million hectares had been made, by the 1950s only about 20,000 were used, and fewer than 10,000 farmers were involved at the end of the colonial era. Reconceptualized by its bureaucracy as a spearhead of socialism, during the plan period the *Office du Niger* was busy opening irrigated land at $1,100 per acre to obtain $54–80 of crops. Meanwhile, its new socialist director, Samba Lamine Traore, reiterated the arguments of his French predecessors that only the last 10 percent of investment was needed to amortize the 90 percent already placed in this sinkhole; the scheme, it was now claimed, offered a decisive opportunity to demonstrate the superiority of collective cultivation. The beneficiaries of the large sums of public capital poured into the *Office du Niger* were its own bureaucracy and its foreign suppliers.[180]

Socialization of the peasant sector was to occur through obligatory creation in each village of a "precooperative." This involved collecting a $2.40 entry fee from the skeptical new members, which was never seen again. The initial momentum of the party, joined to the inherited state structures, made it possible to achieve formal compliance. Each family was to cultivate one hectare of a collective field in addition to their own plot. In 1964–65 Jones found that the cooperatives were at least nominally present, and village heads had learned to express official enthusiasm for the scheme when visitors passed. In reality, as little time as possible was allocated to the collective field. The actual surface thus cultivated was no more than 5 percent of the official goal of 350–400,000 hectares, and its yields were less than a third of those of family plots. As evidence mounted that neither the cooperatives nor the collective fields were taking root, party leaders excoriated the peasants for their failure to comprehend the benefits accruing from the agrarian revolution. In a rural development seminar in May 1968 party leaders noted with regret that

> most cadres and militants consider the collective field to be a simple demonstration plot. . . .
> It must now be clear for all that the collective field is the kernel of the large, polyvalent collective farm that we want to achieve. It must be a model field needing to be extended progressively at the expense of the individual fields. . . .[181]

What the peasants did perceive was that their real income was declining; the net effect of state agricultural policy "was to drastically worsen the rural areas' terms of trade with their trading partners, whether that meant official Mali or abroad." Prices were held constant, while the consumer price index rose by 50 percent; most goods were simply not available in the countryside.[182] The result was a partial disengagement of the peasant from the state trading network.

The dreams of 1960 died slowly; as late as 1964, Modibo Keita could still assert:

> In two years at most, the Mali Republic will be essentially self-sufficient in consumers' goods, and will thenceforth have to import only investment goods. If the Malian experiment succeeds, I am convinced that all other African states . . . will be obliged to take our course if they wish to avoid the subversions, revolutions and coups d'etat they are experiencing now. A hungry people living in misery which sees that its leaders live in insulting opulence will have to rise up, regardless of the security and repressive measures instituted. That's what all African states will find out if they don't try to correct their methods of economic development.[183]

It was Mali itself that experienced a change of regime in 1968, although the postcoup leaders have yet to define a clear-cut development strategy. A heavy debt (estimated at about one-third of GDP), a deteriorated currency, a burdensome state payroll (87 percent of registered employment), a complex of state enterprises of which only a few broke even, peasant lassitude, and

merchant hostility: the Keita era had little to offer by way of off-
setting achievement. For many, its demise ended the first wave of
socialist experiments in West Africa.

FINAL REFLECTIONS

Radical populist socialism, then, has a quite mixed record. The
balance sheet on Tanzania, Algeria, and Guinea-Bissau, while
ambiguous, is more favorable than that for Ghana, Guinea, and
Mali. Wherein lies the difference? I suggest that the answer lies
in the greater competency with which the strategy was pursued.
Algeria had a stronger state and a better manned administration;
the same could be said of Nasser's Egypt, whose socialist phase
delivered some tangible benefits. Algeria also enjoyed a far more
favorable revenue situation than did the others. In the cases of
Tanzania and Guinea-Bissau (at least until November 1980), the
quality of leadership stands out: miscalculations (the 1973–75
ujamaa campaign) were quickly recognized, and there was a
willingness to contemplate remedial measures. Of the six cases,
the a priori dimension of ideological preference was more marked
in Guinea and Mali, reflecting the more systematic socialist models that guided the initial planners—this in turn was traceable in
part to the more explicit Marxist content of their thought and
also to the mood of visionary optimism that attended decolonization throughout Africa.

The particular liabilities of the populist socialist pathway
were not clearly recognized two decades ago, while the infirmities of the capitalist alternative were much more apparent.
The most dangerous of the pitfalls were linked to the nature of
the postcolonial state: its weaknesses, externally and internally,
and its own role as vector of class formation. Multinational capital, highly suspicious of populist socialism in the early 1960s,
used the leverage provided by economic dislocation to drive hard
bargains in Ghana (Volta Dam) and Guinea (bauxite schemes).

of external capital saddled the state with
ects through the supplier-finance route, es-
old war considerations exerted a strong pull
astern aid, with the populist socialist states
en as a critical battleground. The public sector industrial projects promoted by the Soviet bloc frequently proved naive in conception and poor in execution. To these external handicaps,
which particularly afflicted Ghana, Guinea, and Mali, were
added the internal shortcomings of the state in imposing economic discipline on public sector enterprises. These operated
under enormous social pressures to enlarge their rosters of employed personnel, but with little effective accountability in the
performance of their assigned services, especially those in the
trade and marketing sphere. Finally, the ideological leadership
failed to ponder the class nature of the state itself and the latent
conflict of interest between the state and the rural population, indigenous commercial groups, and others not part of the nascent
politico-bureaucratic bourgeoisie. Thus it was that policies philosophically conceived to bring material abundance and social
liberation to the humbler strata of the citizenry could in practice
degenerate into class aggrandizement of the state bourgeoisie;
this was particularly marked in Ghana, Guinea, and Mali.

Certainly disparities in the resource base, both within this
set of states and between them and the other groups, are of considerable importance in explaining the divergence of outcome.
The oil and gas revenues open up for Algeria a range of policy
possibilities that is simply not open to Mali or Guinea-Bissau.
It is worth noting that, according to World Bank data, Mali and
its equally landlocked and impoverished but market-economy
neighbor, Upper Volta, have almost identical real per capita
growth rates since 1960 (0.9 percent for Mali, 0.6 percent for Upper Volta).[184] Though its venture in populist socialism in the
Keita years did not succeed, the question may be legitimately
raised whether any policy orientation would have fared better.

I would not, however, conclude that these experiences demonstrate the unviability of a populist socialist strategy. The positive elements in the Tanzania, Algeria, and Guinea-Bissau cases preclude such a trenchant judgment. The lessons of the first wave of socialist experience in Africa have been carefully weighed, and an earnest effort is visible in both theory and practice to retain the egalitarian vision of socialism while averting its possible pitfalls.

4

The African Capitalist State

CAPITALISM: PRAGMATISM OR IDEOLOGY?

The capitalist pathway in Africa has numerous followers but few partisans. Roughly half the fifty-one African states in reality pursue a development policy primarily premised upon the modified version of the market economy that characterizes the late-twentieth-century capitalist state. Yet only a handful proclaim their devotion to an economy that is centered on the private sector. The number of exemplary states is even smaller; I believe it reduces essentially to three: Ivory Coast, Kenya, and Nigeria. This chapter will focus upon their experience.

A few words of commentary are in order on the peculiar reluctance of political leaders to espouse openly the market economy. To begin with, those who eschew socialism usually describe their decision as a rejection of ideology. Socialism is portrayed as a set of a priori, abstract principles that lead to policy deduction that is out of kilter with realities. The nonsocialist avenue, by contrast, is the road of pragmatism, of the application of practical reasoning to the empirical selection of appropriate policies. The theses of socialism are ideology; their antithesis, the market economy, is anti-ideology.

By way of illustration, I should like to recount a debate I attended in 1972 between Brigadier C. O. Rotimi, then military governor of the Western State in Nigeria, and Ibadan University

students. Facing a packed auditorium, Brigadier Rotimi first offered a quite academic discourse on the role of the military in
developing countries; he then opened the floor to questions. One
audacious student queried the brigadier as to the federal military
government's interest in exploring socialist alternatives. Rotimi
responded with a disarming chuckle that the business of the military government was merely to "clean up the mess" and to at-
tend to practical problems; students could devote deep study to
ideological questions and be prepared to provide guidance to the
country when the eventual return to civilian rule occurred. For
the military rulers, policy choice was common sense plus clean-
liness. Yet their policy was more than a random set of practical
homilies; it was a highly nationalist version of capitalism.

The socialist alternatives the students were invited to study
generally do include a more specific vision of the future than
does the market-economy perspective. Implicit in these blueprints are particular guidelines for fulfillment of the vision. This
sense of a charter for the future no doubt contributes to the apparent contrast of *ideology* and *pragmatism*. The capitalist pathway, in comparison, lays claim to a method of economic policy
management whose presumed efficiency will lead to beneficial
but unspecified results.

Yet I believe that *ideology* versus *anti-ideology* is a false
antinomy. Policy choice for market-economy states does derive
from an interrelated set of premises that collectively represent a
paradigm and are derived from neoclassical economics, as modified by the Western school of development economics. If an ideology is understood as a system of beliefs that serve as a standard
of evaluation and a guide to action, then the capitalist pathway is
much more than formless pragmatism; it constitutes an ideology
in its own right. What then are these policy premises?

THE CHARACTERISTICS OF THE AFRICAN CAPITALIST STATE

The bedrock postulate, to begin with, is that a high value must be attached to the market as an allocator of resources. As applied in Africa, this by no means implies untrammeled operation of an unregulated market. State intervention is pervasive, in ways we will delineate. But a significant place is reserved for private markets, and a positive valuation of their developmental role persists.

Second, capital is viewed as the crucial factor of production, and important spheres are reserved for the private sector. In fact, the state sector is invariably quite large, but no intrinsic merit is believed to inhere in public enterprise. Nationalism intervenes in both the socialist and capitalist states to render ambiguous the value of foreign capital, but no such doubts exist as to the positive social and economic functions of indigenous capital. The benign view toward private property has important implications for both urban and rural land patterns; in the agricultural sector, while state regulation of marketing in the export sector is invariably large, petty rural capitalism is encouraged.

Third, the paradigm implies an open economy. This does not mean unrestricted movement of foreign capital, in all circumstances, but it does postulate trade relationships as beneficial. A strong exchange relationship with the industrial economies is a presumed corollary of development; relatively little is heard of the concept of "self-reliance" and nothing at all of the more visionary goal adumbrated in some scientific socialist circles of "disengagement" from the international capitalist economy.

Fourth, while nearly all African capitalist states are at least nominally nonaligned, in the economic sphere predominantly Western relationships are viewed as perfectly natural. Force of circumstance, as we have seen, imposes similar patterns on both populist and Afro-Marxist socialist states; however, the market-economy states have no sense of being swept reluctantly into undesired relationships. For training and technology, in the whole gamut of aid linkages Western partners have quiet preference.

The premise of equality factors into the capitalist pathway model in a quite different way. The distinction between capitalist and socialist states lies not in an egalitarian thrust exclusive to the populist or the Afro-Marxist. As Coleman has eloquently argued, "egalitarianism pervades all aspects of modern political life and culture and all forms of modern political ideology."[1] The contrast rather lies in the kinds and degrees of inequality that are ideologically tolerable, within the broader framework of equality as an acknowledged ideal goal. Provided that the entrepreneurs are indigenous, little opprobrium attaches to accumulation of wealth, above all if it results from autonomous mercantile or industrial activity. In the rural sector, the successful petty capitalist farmer is showered with government blessings and admired for his "modernity" rather than castigated as a "kulak." Equality, thus viewed, is above all to be applied at the level of opportunity, and not necessarily in returns. Thus we find no discernible difference in the priority accorded to educational expenditures; all ideological trails lead to massive expansion of the formal educational system.

The type of political system deducible from the capitalist-oriented development paradigm is ambiguous. At a general level, it has been argued that constitutional democratic regimes arise only in market economies; for example, Lindblom suggests that

However poorly the market is harnessed to democratic purposes, only within market-oriented systems does political democracy arise [emphasis in original]. Not all market-oriented systems are democratic, but every democratic system is also a market-oriented system. Apparently, for reasons that are not wholly understood, political democracy has been unable to exist except when coupled with the market. An extraordinary proposition, it has so far held without exception.[2]

However, even if this observation of historical fact is accepted, it does not follow that the market-economy preference inexorably dictates the liberal democratic state, either as philosophical postulate or practical reality. Indeed, if we combine the theses of Huntington and O'Donnell, we find the contrary logic: in the African circumstance, the market economy is likely to require an authoritarian state. For Huntington, the general recourse to authoritarian formulas, military or other, derives from the "praetorian" character of many developing societies: "the general politicization of social forces and institutions" that simply overwhelm the organized political and constitutional mechanisms for incorporating them into a political process.[3] O'Donnell pursues a parallel argument further to maintain that, beyond a low level of development, the political mobilization of what he terms the "popular sectors" will necessarily outstrip the capacity of constitutional democratic states to respond to their pressures within a capitalist framework; in these circumstances, both indigenous middle classes and foreign capital will discover that their security can be preserved only by the creation of a bureaucratic-authoritarian state.[4]

Yet another perspective emerges from consideration of the divergent origins of Western and African states. The constitutional democratic state and private market economies grew in a symbiotic relationship in the West, through a dialectic of the broadening and deepening role of the modern state, on the one hand, and the parallel struggles to preserve individual liberty and protect private property on the other. As the state grew, constitutionalism imposed constraints and limits upon its operation.

With a handful of arguable exceptions, the contemporary African state originates essentially in colonial conquest. The building of the state apparatus grew out of the imperatives of alien control and dominion. The colonial state had thus in its genesis and evolution a vocation of domination; the institutions that developed to accomplish this domination comprised the quintessential bureaucratic state, staffed by a foreign mandarinate.[5] Democratic institutions were hastily concocted and uneasily grafted to the enduring authoritarian substructures of the colonial state to permit the colonial occupant to "withdraw with honor." Thus the mercantilist capitalism of the colonial state had no relationship at all with liberal democracy.

Other characteristics distinguish the model African capitalist state from the model Western state. The African capitalist state achieved sovereignty at a time when all modern polities were committed to the welfare state. The Western capitalist state had as nineteenth-century incubus a phase in liberal thought that viewed the state as a veritable nightwatchman. While such a view has come to be eclipsed by the rapid development of the welfare state, especially after World War II, its legacy survives as a philosophical undercurrent that has no real parallel in Africa. Thus a heavy commitment of the state to the creation of social infrastructure is a postulate that characterizes the African market-economy states (as well as those that have chosen the other pathways).

Further, nationalism was and is a common theme of both African capitalist and socialist states. The commitment to anticolonial nationalism preceded both socialism and capitalism; in the market-economy states it never became coupled to socialism. There are, of course, important differences in degree: nationalism in Ivory Coast, particularly with respect to the former metropole, is vastly less assertive than in Nigeria in the 1970s.

In addition, the crucial concept of "developmentalism" intervenes. All African states share a belief that they are, relative to the yardstick of abundance provided by the economically advanced states (socialist as well as capitalist), less developed. This perception of a poverty lag was not present in the emergence of the liberal democratic market state in the West. Important policy consequences flow from this perception. "Growth" is an imperative, and no one believes that it can be left to the beneficent workings of the invisible hand. State intervention and leadership are deemed critical by African capitalists as well as socialists. Only the content and orientation of this intervention are at issue.

All of this adds up to a capitalist orientation deeply tinged with statism. Herein the colonial state—whose congenital paternalism grew apace with its enlarging capacities—and the postcolonial state—developmentalist and welfarist—commingle. The scale of the social overhead in itself guarantees a quite large state. To it is added an invariably hefty public sector in the productive sphere: export marketing; utilities; large-scale projects for which domestic capital is insufficient and foreign capital inexistent; partnerships with multinational capital, possibly as interim surrogate for the indigenous capitalist class. This state sector was already well developed under mercantile colonial capitalism and has developed momentum since that time, without benefit of socialist prescription. However, its tutelary intent for a portion of the parastatal sector demarcates the capitalist states from those of socialist vocation. No doctrinal value is attached to the state sector, as it is in the socialist desire to control the "commanding heights" of the economy.

Schatz provides a recapitulation of these trends in modeling the African market-economy state as "nurture capitalism." Though his paradigm derives from the Nigerian experience, it could be more broadly applied. The defining characteristics of nurture capitalism are four:

1. Private enterprise is expected to provide the basic developmental thrust in the directly productive sector
2. For this to occur with the anticipated vigor, a congenial environment is assured for all capital, domestic and foreign
3. At the same time, an awareness, from a nationalist perspective, of the risks of total foreign domination of the economy dictates strenuous promotion of indigenous capital
4. The contradiction implicit in 2 and 3 triggers sharp and continuous conflict between multinational and national capital[6]

The phrase *nurture capitalism* is apt; it captures some crucial aspects of the African market-economy orientation: the close relationship between indigenous capital and the fostering state, the ambivalent nexus with foreign capital. Like socialist forms in

Africa, African capitalism has evident resemblances to the parent species, but also particular adaptations to its adopted environment.

IVORY COAST: THE "MIRACLE" DISSECTED

Ivory Coast is by some distance the most influential exemplary state on the African capitalist pathway; I turn first to this beacon of free enterprise.[7] Despite the early postwar tactical alliance with the French Communist Party by veteran *Parti Démocratique du Cote d'Ivoire* (PDCI) leader Félix Houphouët-Boigny, from the early 1950s the Ivory Coast leadership has been resolutely committed to capitalism. The espousal of the market economy has been open and forthright; it was never camouflaged, as in Kenya, beneath a gloss of "African socialism." The bluntness, even acerbity, of the Ivorian refusal to align with the early wave of African socialism, at least verbally, at a time when these diffuse doctrines enjoyed general vogue made Ivory Coast a test case. More than an option, the Houphouët-Boigny strategy was stated as a challenge to the socialists. Thereafter, the remarkable statistics generated by the Ivorian economy compelled examination. Acclaimed by some as a miraculous showcase for capitalism, decried by others as a cancerous neocolonial excrescence, Ivory Coast could be adulated or detested but not ignored.

The raw statistics are phenomenal and in their aggregate form not in dispute between admirers and detractors; the debate rages around their meaning and implications. Over the last three decades, annual growth rates have averaged 7–8 percent. According to World Bank figures, the real per capita growth in the 1960–76 period averaged 3.3 percent annually. This brought per capita income up to $650 per capita by 1976 (or $798 per capita in 1975, according to the United Nations *Yearbook of National Accounts Statistics*). This remarkably high per capita increase over time was achieved in the face of the most rapid rate of population growth in Africa: 4.4 percent over the same period. This population dynamic was in itself a testimonial to the Ivorian performance: it reflected not simply Ivorian fertility rates but a massive inflow of population from neighboring countries such as poverty stricken Upper Volta and economically derelict Guinea. Over a quarter of the Ivorian population is of foreign origin. Although several African states showed higher per capita growth rates during this period, they were beneficiaries either of the petroleum bonanza (Libya, Nigeria, Gabon) or of mineral-based increases (Togo, Mauritania, Tunisia) or they were microeconomies dependent on peculiar extraversion (Lesotho, Swaziland, Seychelles, Djibouti).[8]

Most important of all, Ivorian growth was largely based upon the agricultural sector. Except for modest amounts of oil now coming into production, the country has no important mineral assets yet discovered. Beginning with a monocultural coffee base in the 1950s, the agricultural sector has been rapidly extended and diversified: cocoa, palm oil, pineapples, cotton, and sugar now are also important crops. While some of these have been developed on plantations (especially oil palms), much of the agrarian dynamic has come from individual Ivorian planters. Agricultural expansion axiomatically involves large numbers of people, both in the production and the rewards; an oil industry, for example, employs only a handful, though its benefits may be spread through social overhead investment in such amenities as schools and health facilities.

The swelling revenues from agricultural exports have also been used to create a modest industrial base. Industrial growth rates of up to 15 percent have been recorded in recent years. Although the Ivorian external debt has grown substantially in recent years (from $388 million in 1969 to $1.536 billion, including undisbursed, in 1975), in 1978 there was a healthy $478 million external trade surplus. There is no reason to challenge the conclusions of a recent World Bank study of the Ivorian economy: "Few countries, developed or developing, can match the economic growth record of the Ivory Coast. Its annual growth rate in real terms of over 7 percent during the past twenty-five years is unique on the African continent."[9]

One recent critic of the Ivorian path summed up the essence of the strategy in four points:

1. Cooperation with France in all fields
2. An evolutionary pathway, and rejection of class struggle ideologies, on the grounds that classes do not exist in Ivory Coast
3. An unrestricted reliance on foreign and local private initiative
4. An Ivorian-centered policy, and marked reticence toward the formation of larger African entities[10]

This portrait may be completed by noting the strong statist thrust of Ivorian policy. Planning has played an important part in Ivorian policy: for example, in the promotion of such major regional development projects as the San Pedro port to open the isolated southwest and sundry sugar and cotton schemes for the north. Oil palm development has been spearheaded by the parastatal SODEPALM, which has introduced new high-yielding varieties, mainly on plantation tracts under primarily French management. A large and proliferating set of parastatal enterprises has emerged. By the early 1970s, some 60 percent of total investment came from the public sector, up from 40 percent in the early years of independence.[11]

President Houphouët-Boigny has offered the following capsule resume of the regime's ideological perspective on development strategy: "We are not socialists, in that we do not believe in giving priority to the distribution of wealth but wish to encourage the creation and multiplication of wealth first of all. Our major concern is with the human aspect of growth. Our system cannot be described as liberalism either, but it can be likened to a planned economy. We are following a policy of State capitalism."[12] Otherwise put, the economic liberalism that undergirds Ivorian policy is permeated with statism. While nationalism is by no means absent, it is tempered by a willingness to accept a high degree of foreign—especially French—participation in the

TABLE 4.1. Acreage of African Coffee and Cocoa Plantations

Year	Cocoa	(000 hectares) Coffee	Total
1946	115	158	273
1950	153	158	311
1956	222	318	540
1960	240	525	765
1974	920	1,235	2,155

SOURCES: Bonnie Campbell, "Ivory Coast," in West African States: Failure and Promise, ed. John Dunn (Cambridge: Cambridge University Press, 1978), p. 72; for 1974 Bastiaan A. den Tuinder, Ivory Coast: The Challenge of Success (Baltimore: Johns Hopkins University Press, 1978), pp. 39–40.

economy, both as a source of capital and of managerial personnel. Export agriculture is the central pillar of the entire structure.

The point of departure for the Ivory Coast political economy was the rapid emergence in the 1940s and 1950s of an African planter class, rooted initially in coffee production. The greater efficiency of the African petty capitalist farm—at first family-based—permitted this sector to swiftly eclipse European planters, who dominated the small prewar economy. Though in 1942 European operators produced 55 percent of the coffee, a decade later—despite multiple discriminatory measures in their favor—European planters accounted for only 6 percent of coffee exports.[13] By 1974, there were some 350,000 coffee plantations covering 1,235,000 hectares and 225,000 cocoa plantations covering 920,000 hectares.

After independence a number of these estates (such as the presidential plantations) became large, but the bulk of the holdings were of only a few hectares. In the middle 1960s, Amin estimated that only 10,000 of the coffee and cocoa planters (who numbered nearly 500,000 by 1976) earned more than $1000 per year; only a few hundred had large plantations in the 50–100 hectare range and employing a dozen workers or more.[14] By the 1960s, this burgeoning rural petty capitalism was employing large numbers of wage laborers, of whom over half were non-

Ivorians (and those that were Ivorians were overwhelmingly migrants from the impoverished northern regions). There were nearly 700,000 foreign African laborers in the rural sector by the 1970s.

This relatively prosperous planter class formed the core of the nationalist movement in the 1950s; the dominant Ivorian political movement, the PDCI, grew out of an association of African planters, the *Syndicat Agricole Africain*. The dramatic contrast between the Ghanaian and Ivorian development strategies may be partly understood in terms of the different social bases of the PDCI and CPP leadership: in Ghana, Nkrumah, as we have seen, was implacably hostile to petty cocoa capitalism, while in Ivory Coast the central thrust of policy rested upon the "planter bourgeoisie." [15]

After independence, agricultural diversification was promoted. New crops were developed under the direction of parastatal agencies: SODEPALM (oil palm), SOCATCI (rubber), SODESUCRE (sugar), CIDT (cotton), SODEFEL (fruits and vegetables), among others. Though provision was made for outgrowers, large plantation tracts provided the main basis for production, especially for products like oil palm, rubber, coconuts, bananas, sugar, and pineapples. While in the 1950s coffee and cocoa overwhelmingly dominated the agrarian sector, by 1975 other crops (especially palm oil, cotton, and pineapples) accounted for 25 percent of total output. There was also progress in food production, although more than $100 million in food imports were required by the late 1970s. From 1965 to 1975, a rural populace that increased by 27 percent grew 42 percent more food; per capita urban food imports decreased from 200 kilograms to 115 kilograms during this decade. [16]

Another important component of the rural economy has been the logging industry, which rapidly expanded with the opening of Abidjan harbor in 1950 and San Pedro in 1972, plus the rapid extension of an all-weather road network in the southern forest zone. This sector, dominated by capital-intensive foreign ventures, has accounted for 7 percent of GDP in recent years, or 20 percent of exports. While it employs large numbers of workers (20 percent of the industrial labor force), its opponents point to both the foreign domination and the creaming of the forests for high value species. Areas of dense forest declined from 9.8 million hectares in 1956 to 5.5 million in 1973; though most of this occurred through agricultural clearing rather than logging operations, little has been replanted.[17]

Despite the predominant role of the coffee–cocoa planter class in the PDCI, levels of taxation have been quite high, as table 4.3 demonstrates. Farmers have retained only about 50 percent of the export value of both coffee and cocoa; particularly for cocoa, where there is very little value added through processing after the beans leave the farm gate, this is a very high figure and nearly approximates the fiscal burden imposed upon Ghanaian cocoa planters.[18] A World Bank study revealed that Ivory Coast export taxation on the timber industry was the highest in West Africa, averaging 20 percent of f.o.b. value from 1965 to 1974, compared with 11 percent for Cameroon and 6 percent for Ghana.[19]

Industrialization has made reasonable headway in recent years, with expansion of manufacturing value added averaging 15 percent. From 1960 to 1974, the share of manufacturing in GDP rose from 4 percent to 12.3 percent. Industry falls into two basic categories: (1) processing of agricultural raw materials (sawmills, palm oil refineries, textile plants, soluble coffee, pineapple canneries, and the like), and (2) import substitution plants (metal products, fertilizers, footwear, machinery). The agroindustries accounted for 55 percent of the total in 1974. Industry is heavily concentrated in Abidjan, with about two-thirds of the total. As table 4.4 demonstrates, there is a very heavy reliance on European personnel for management of these enterprises; they earn an average of two to three times the salaries they might gain in Europe. Admirers of the Ivorian achievement point to the steady growth of this sector, which Western advisers believed to

TABLE 4.2. Production of Major Agricultural Commodities, Ivory Coast

					(000 tons)					
Commodity	1900	1920	1940	1945	1950	1955	1960	1965	1970	1975
Logs	13			10	106	169	839	1,955	2,511	2,372
Coffee		46	23	38	54	85	148	186	195	255
Cocoa		1	45	27	62	75	63	126	143	169
Bananas							73	128	141	136
Pineapples (fresh)							3	5	17	70
Rubber								3	11	15
Cotton (lint)								2	12	12
Palm oil									12	114

SOURCE: Bastiaan A. den Tuinder, Ivory Coast: The Challenge of Success (Baltimore: Johns Hopkins University Press, 1978), pp. 15, 342.

TABLE 4.3. Distribution of Export Earnings from Cocoa and Coffee, Ivory Coast (in percent)

	1965–66		1974–75		Average 1965/66–1974/75	
Recipient	Cocoa	Coffee	Cocoa	Coffee	Cocoa	Coffee
Farmers	80	50	53	65	50	54
Traders, transporters	36	17	10	15	12	15
Government (export tax)	33	15	13	19	22	16
Stabilization fund	−49	18	24	1	16	15
Public sector*	−16	33	37	20	38	31

*Export tax plus stabilization fund
SOURCE: Bastiaan A. den Tuinder, Ivory Coast: The Challenge of Success (Baltimore: Johns Hopkins University Press, 1978), p. 81.

have poor prospects in 1960. The numerous critics of the Ivorian model point to the neocolonial mode of industrial development. Not only is the great majority of managerial personnel French (who draw munificent salaries and repatriate much of their earnings), but the capital itself is mainly foreign: over two-thirds of manufacturing equity, excluding wood products (also foreign dominated), in 1975, with the state holding about three-fourths of the balance.[20] More recently, to counter the claims of neocolonial subservience, the Ivorian share in industrial equity had risen to 54.6 percent by late 1977; this has been largely in the form of state capitalism, as only 6.64 percent of the total was held by private Ivorian capitalists.[21] In contrast to Kenya and Nigeria, Ivory Coast has made little real effort to foster national capitalists in the industrial sector. Herein lies the very kernel of the Ivorian debate: is the undisputed quantitative success worth the ransom of neocolonialism?

The critique of the Ivory Coast model holds that this neocolonial pattern necessarily engenders very large and growing inequalities; the benefits of the economic "miracle" are reserved for the external estate, the planter bourgeoisie who formed the first political generation, and a new class of politico-bureaucratic personnel, who directly or indirectly siphon into privatized channels the surplus extracted by state capitalism. The flavor of these arguments is expressed by Campbell:

The planter-politician group who have become the country's ruling class have thus met with considerable success in perpetuating the past pattern of accumulation and distribution of surplus between their foreign partners and themselves. They have succeeded at the same time in transmitting their past scale of privileges and their effective hold on national income. Especially striking is the sheer effectiveness with which political monopoly was established and has been perpetuated. . . .

. . . it was the *bourgeoisie de planteurs* which were to determine the class character of the Ivorian state. . . . But their success has imposed heavy costs on the rest of the Ivorian population. Economically, it has meant a steady outward flow of profits on foreign investments and of surplus exported through the highly unequal terms of market ex-

TABLE 4.4. Survey of Wage Earners in the Industrial Sector, 1968, Ivory Coast

Category of personnel	Total	Ivorian	Other African	European
Managerial	503	20	4	479
Professional-technical	792	31	13	748
Supervisory technical	1,659	435	157	1,067
Other supervisory	1,233	581	230	422
Subordinate	2,818	1,759	1,018	41
Skilled workers	5,668	3,769	1,831	68
Semiskilled workers	15,638	9,989	5,647	2
Unskilled workers	15,751	6,230	9,515	6

SOURCE: Bonnie Campbell, "Ivory Coast," in *West African States: Failure and Promise*, ed. John Dunn (Cambridge: Cambridge University Press, 1978), p. 107.

change. Politically, it has meant sharp restrictions on political freedom and on popular participation in public affairs. . . .

The external constraints implied by the present pattern of growth and the internal inequalities which it will necessarily continue to imply will compel the state to become increasingly centralized and authoritarian. . . . In this regard it will be increasingly necessary for the state to intervene to mask, control, marginalize or suppress the opposition which is certain to arise.[22]

The tree of neocolonialism that shades Ivory Coast thus bears the bitter fruits of dependency, inequality, and oppression. Has growth in Ivory Coast been the Faustian pact that Campbell suggests? Has it simply been, as Amin has argued, "growth without development"? Or, worse yet, the "development of underdevelopment," as Andre Gunder Frank and his followers would argue?

In terms of dependency, it is true that self-reliance has never figured prominently among Ivorian ideological values. The very choice of an export-centered growth strategy necessarily—if it works—brings ever-tightening bonds to the international economy. The place of foreign trade in the total economy has increased: from 60 percent in the 1960s to 75 percent more recently.[23] The number of French residents in the country has risen from 10,000 at independence to about 50,000 today. Foreign capital, and more recently heavy public and private external borrowing, has financed Ivorian growth.

At the same time, within the asymmetrical frame of a small and relatively poor country's linkages with the international economy, it would be misleading to conclude that the country descends ever deeper into the maelstrom of bondage. Contrary to the mechanistic assumptions of the more doctrinaire dependency theorists, the weaker partner has choices available to optimize its returns. Precisely because Ivory Coast has had stable and above all competent leadership, some aspects of dependency have been mitigated. There has been a diversification of both trading and investment partners; for example, 65 percent of Ivorian imports came from France in 1960, and only 39 percent in 1975.[24] The greater strength of the Ivorian economy places the country in a much stronger position than, say, Guinea in bargaining with foreign capital and creditors. To assume that these advantages are willfully set aside in order to confer windfall benefits upon the external partner requires one to believe that the judgment of the leadership is blinkered by some combination of venality, naivete, and stupidity.

However, there is incontestably a strong element of dependence implicit in the strategy. Stryker describes the dilemma: ". . . dependency is largely the obverse of growth—they *reinforce* one another. Rather than blocking growth, dependencies have underwritten it and spurred it in Ivory Coast. The trade-off is visible and severe: very real economic progress at the price of very real sectoral, financial, and social imbalances."[25]

Inequality is certainly present in complex forms in Ivory Coast. Its dimensions include multiple polarities: foreign estate/Ivorians; politico-bureaucratic elite/mass; Abidjan/hinterland; south/north; Ivorian/immigrant African. The sumptuous skyscrapers of Abidjan and the elegant air-conditioned bungalows in Cocody, in the face of a $640 per capita GDP, are ample demonstration that some people do exceedingly well out of the Ivory Coast miracle.

The 50,000-strong external estate clearly is a prime benefiary. Not all French residents draw plutocratic stipends; there are teachers and secretaries as well as financial advisers and managers. However, those at the top are very costly—as I noted earlier, they earn two to three times their European salary—and their remittances are equivalent to about 10 percent of total export commodity earnings (or, in 1975, about $100,000,000). Europeans in 1971 constituted 6.8 percent of the enumerated urban wage and salary earning work force, but received 32.2 percent of the total wage bill.[26] Ivorian authorities are not oblivious to this dimension of inequality and have been pursuing an Ivorianization policy with reasonable vigor. By 1974, the fraction of Ivorian supervisors and managerial personnel had risen from the minuscule proportions documented in table 4.4 to 28 percent. A (problematic) goal of 60 percent was to have been achieved by 1979.[27]

The disparities between Abidjan and the hinterland and north and south are deeply rooted in economic geography and are unlikely to abate. The high concentration of industry in the capital is induced by the concentration of both the potential markets for many products and the numerous external economies in this location. The north–south disparity is grounded in the differential cash crop potential of the savanna and forest regions. Nobel Prize–winning economist Arthur Lewis noted long ago that in West Africa the forest regions generated five times more per capita income than the savanna.[28] Cotton takes several times as much labor per hectare as does coffee or cocoa, and its return is considerably less.

At the very bottom of the scale are the million immigrant African laborers, who provide the bulk of the agrarian wage force. Government efforts to equalize income tend to focus on citizens; the availability of this pool of very low-wage foreign labor has no doubt been a significant factor in the formation of a rural surplus. Remarkably, these workers do succeed in saving enough from their meager earnings to remit home about $50 million annually. A growing number have found their way into the urban sector and more direct competition with Ivorians for desirable jobs; others, especially among the economic refugees from Mali and Guinea, had mercantile skills for which Ivorian capitalism provided an outlet and have prospered. Curiously, the most visible inequality-born social tensions focus upon the more successful of the immigrant Africans; Campbell, in her critique of the Ivory Coast pathway, laments that ". . . hostility towards strangers has been largely, although by no means exclusively, directed toward non-Ivorian Africans rather than the more fundamental and deeper cause of inequality, the European community." [29]

While inequality is clear and present, there are significant mitigating facts. Worker wages in Ivory Coast (outside the immigrant-dominated rural sector) are not particularly low by international standards. In 1972, with the official legal minimum wage in Ivory Coast indexed at 100, the Zaire figure was 93, Senegal 87, and Togo and Cameroon 67. In 1973, the average monthly wage in Taiwan was 4–5,000 CFAF (roughly 225=$1) and 10,000 CFAF in Singapore, compared to 20,700 CFAF in Ivory Coast in 1974. Chenery in his 1970 calculations for overall patterns of income inequality had placed Ivory Coast in the "high inequality" category; den Tuinder, recalculating the information for 1973–74, put it in the virtuous set of low inequality countries, an intriguingly disparate set of high social justice performers including such states as Sri Lanka, Thailand, Taiwan, Yugoslavia, Japan, Hungary, Canada, and the United States. [30] Den Tuinder found that, whereas the lowest 40 percent received 10.8 percent of the total and the top 20 percent some 57.1 percent in 1970, in 1973–74 the bottom category increased their haul to 19.7 percent, while the top bracket share diminished to 51.6 percent. [31]

Finally, we come to the questions of human dignity and participation. The regime is mildly authoritarian, but the number of persons incarcerated for political reasons in the past two decades is small, certainly no larger than in the most open and participative of the socialist exemplary states, Tanzania. There is no common measure with the extensive application of the Preventive Detention Act under the Nkrumah regime or the periodic capricious repression in Guinea. One useful measure is the extremely small security force, which numbered only 4,950 in 1978. There has been no necessity to contain the "popular sectors," as in the capitalist bureaucratic-authoritarian state in the southern cone of Latin America analyzed by O'Donnell. Intellectuals enjoy some scope, although certainly not unrestricted opportunities to mobilize opposition.

Opportunities for participation are certainly modest. The PDCI is not to be confused with an instrument of mass mobilization. However, Houphouët-Boigny did introduce competitive single-party elections in 1981 similar to those in Tanzania and Kenya. Some 650 candidates ran for 147 seats; 120 of the winners were newcomers. The "opening" provided by this opportunity for competitive elections is undoubtedly of some significance, though the turnout was low. Overall, there can be little doubt that Houphouët-Boigny and his regime enjoy at least moderate legitimacy. Few Ghanaians or Guineans at present would dispute the fact that Houphouët-Boigny has decisively won the famous West African wager of 1957.

And yet the wager is not necessarily won for all time. The political legitimacy of the PDCI regime and its capitalist strategy is closely tied to the image of "success." The tensions of inequality remain latent only so long as the effectiveness of its pathway remains demonstrated. Should the "miracle" become tarnished, the political tranquility could erode. At the end of the 1970s, the glitter was indeed somewhat dulled. The external debt reached the dangerous level of $3.5 billion. For the first time, some huge investments—particularly the northern sugar projects (over $1 billion)—threatened to turn out badly.[32] Imminent production from newly discovered offshore oil wells might provide the antidote. At the same time, the "miracle" would then for the first time become tributary to geologic good fortune.

KENYA: FROM SETTLER COLONIALISM TO AFRICAN CAPITALISM

Like Molière's Monsieur Jourdain, who recognized only belatedly that he had been speaking prose all his life, Kenya, the second exemplar of the capitalist pathway, arrived by degrees at a conscious realization of its own options. In the initial years, something remarkably similar to nurture capitalism was energetically presented as African socialism. The labors of the first post-independence five-year plan were preceded by the adoption of an official doctrinal pronouncement on "African socialism" that was duly debated by the cabinet and formally adopted by Parliament.[33] While the document argues the compatibility of the African socialist creed then extant with the market economy, it seems too cynical to suppose that its adoption—and the rhetorical importance attributed to it—was a mere exercise in self-deception. The idea of socialism, ill-defined and formless as it was, held real value for much of the political class at that time. Even today, the phrase occasionally recurs as a passing incantation, though by the 1970s the political elite had become sure of itself and confident in the capitalist strategy that had been pursued.[34]

In this initial ideological statement, African socialism was clearly differentiated from scientific socialism, as well as from classical capitalism. "As predictive models of what would happen to factory system societies, both Marxian socialism and *laissez faire* capitalism have been failures. The economic systems in actual use throughout the world today bear little resemblance to either model."[35] Therefore, pragmatism was de rigueur: "African Socialism must be flexible because the problems it will confront and the incomes and the desires of the people will change over time, often quickly and substantially."[36] Nationalization was specifically eschewed; because of the necessity for compensation, the costs far outweighed the gains. A toothless form of socialism, no doubt: but one must recollect that at that time Tanzanian socialism was equally diffuse. Only with the Arusha Declaration and policies flowing from it did Kenya and Tanzania become clearly contrasting development experiences. Leys, in his provocative critique of Kenyan capitalism, notes that it was only by the end of the 1960s that "a quite elaborate version of the private-enterprise creed, adapted to Kenyan circumstances, had been diffused throughout the higher bureaucracy, and among senior KANU politicians."[37] This subtle metamorphosis, by which the golden moth of Kenyan capitalism emerged from the chrysalis of African socialism, is well reflected in a speech given in 1967 by a leading Kenyan parastatal official to a manufacturing association conclave:

> We . . . believe in free enterprise. This is a system of social, economic and political arrangements designed to solve the basic economic problem with greatest efficiency.
>   I am convinced that unless the African who forms more than 95% of Kenya's population feels that he is part and parcel of our industrial and commercial economy, just as he has begun to feel in the agricultural sector of our economy, it could be difficult to create a stable economy. . . . It is vital that our industry be identified as truly local by the ordinary man in the street. . . . Those who value the free enterprise system have at times to make great sacrifices for its preservation. African Socialism does not conflict with the free enterprise system but it does require that property be used in the mutual interest of society and its members. . . .[38]

A key to understanding both nationalism and capitalism in Kenya is the central role played by the Kikuyu in leading the opposition to colonial rule and enjoying a predominant (if not hegemonic) role in the postindependence years until the death of Mzee Jomo Kenyatta in 1979. The particular sequences of colonial capitalism in Kenya fostered among Kikuyu intensely held mobility aspirations that were frustrated by the blockages of the settler-dominated colonial state. While the disabilities of the colonial system bore to varying degrees upon all ethnic communities in Kenya, nowhere was the confrontation between awakening aspirations and colonial mechanisms of social closure more bitter than in Kikuyuland.[39]

From the outset, the settler-centered capitalism impinged particularly upon the Kikuyu. They lost less land in the spoliation that created the "white highlands" than did the neighboring Masai, but their higher population density and sedentary agricultural economy made the impact higher. Further, the ample estates provided to settlers at nominal cost could be exploited profitably in the early colonial years only if a bountiful supply of low-wage African labor were available. This burden fell essentially upon Kikuyu shoulders; until the 1920s, the labor supply was assured by diverse coercive measures such as impressment and taxation. Subsequently, a growing scarcity of land in Kikuyuland forced increasing numbers of young Kikuyu into the estate labor force.

While smoldering resentments were fanned by the land question, the Kikuyu countryside was penetrated by an extensive mission educational system. Also, the major urban center of the colony, Nairobi, was situated in the midst of Kikuyuland.[40] Various other explanations have been adduced for the thrusting dynamic of Kikuyu society: high order of achievement motivation in the culture, kinship structure pushing some young out to form new settlements; land tenure system approximating individualized holdings, for example. Beyond dispute is the early and keen aspiration for the material benefits of modernization. The Kikuyu played the crucial role in the early nationalist associations: the Kikuyu Central Association (1924), the Kenya African Union (1944), and the forest insurgency in the 1950s misleadingly labeled "Mau Mau" by the British.

The character of the Mau Mau uprising provided for some time a radical aura to Kenyan nationalism. Even though the forest fighters articulated no clear ideology beyond the use of such symbolic titles as "General China" and "General Russia," the very violence of its challenge to colonial rule made it a fearsome force. Its recruits were drawn from the most impoverished elements in Kikuyu society: landless squatters on white farms, urban lumpenproletariat in Nairobi. The oathing rituals by which the social discipline of the forest fighters was maintained facilitated its portrayal by colonial authorities as an "atavistic" and "barbarian" movement and legitimated in European eyes the merciless repressive campaign that decimated the forest bands from 1952 to 1956. But Mau Mau in reality was not only the spearhead of nationalism, but also a social revolutionary movement that came into increasing conflict not only with the colonial security forces but also the affluent, educated, and well-placed Kikuyu.

From the ranks of the latter was drawn the Kikuyu leadership of the Kenya African National Union (KANU), destined to become the dominant party. The shadow of Mau Mau still rested upon the KANU leadership, in particular upon its most prestigious leader, Kenyatta—a "leader of darkness and death" to many Europeans. When Britain in 1960 conceded the principle of African rule in Kenya, panic seized the immigrant communities; capital flight reached £1 million monthly, and symptoms of economic stagnation multiplied.[41] The emergent Kenya leadership recognized the need of reassuring capital; during the emergency days, the colonial administration had come to accept the necessity of opening the doors of individual economic opportunity to Kenya Africans, in particular Kikuyu. The confluence of these two imperatives—mobility opportunities for Africans and preservation of confidence in private capital—provided the genetic material for Kenyan capitalism.

The first and in retrospect perhaps the decisive step was taken in 1955 with the adoption of the Swynnerton Plan. The forest insurgency made politically necessary some accommodation of land hunger in Kikuyuland. The option exercised was full consolidation and individual registration of African land in the

Kikuyu areas; this reform was to become in later years the model for land policy throughout the country. It was fully recognized that the plan meant dramatic new opportunities for successful farmers and landlessness for the others: "In the past Government policy has been to maintain the tribal system of tenure so that all the people have had bits of land and to prevent the African from borrowing money against the security of his land. . . . In the future . . . Government policy will be reversed and able, energetic or rich Africans will be able to acquire more land and bad or poor farmers less, creating a landed and a landless class. This is a normal step in the evolution of a country."[42] The land registration, linked to an end to restrictions on African entry into coffee cultivation and access to rural credit, was a powerful stimulus to petty rural capitalism in Kikuyuland.

However, as the prospect of independence became tangible, it was clear that African access to at least a portion of the seven million acres held by Europeans was crucial. But how gain it? On what terms? As African political leaders began to view themselves as inheritors of the political kingdom, they quickly grasped the importance to the state of maintaining existing levels of saleable surplus from the white farms; both export revenues and state fiscal returns depended upon it. Thus a simple seizure of the land and its total subdivision into peasant smallholdings freely distributed to the landless was excluded as a strategy, even though the vocal militant wing of KANU and the former forest fighters called for just such a solution. First, this would transfer the entire burden of compensation to the state—which could either sever its access to external capital markets by simple confiscation or burden itself with a crushing debt by taking on the full liability. Second, transformation of the large capitalized units into peasant smallholdings would mean lower total output, more local consumption, and therefore a greatly reduced surplus whose extracted value would partially accrue to the state.

Yet another more private-regarding motivation is suggested by Leys. If land was simply distributed, it would inevitably go primarily to the ethnic community in whose territory it was situated. Kikuyu would thus be shut out of the Rift Valley and limited to recovery of their own lands. Leys quotes the observations of a former squatter who had his eyes on Rift Valley land:

> I knew there were these two possibilities—one that the Rift Valley would be divided free amongst all the tribes, and two, that it would have to be bought. . . . Eventually I thought I would try and find out what the leaders of the Kikuyu people thought. . . .
>
> After talking to some more Kikuyu leaders, I began to see the issue more clearly. The Kikuyu were beginning to think that if the Rift Valley was to be divided among the tribes, they would have very little claim. The Masai would get whole stretches of it to the west of Kijabe, and the various Kalenjin groups would claim much of the rest. The leaders could see that it would be better politics to settle all the major disputes about political matters first; and then eventually open the Rift Valley to all who could affort to buy it.[43]

Thus the land was to be sold. Private capital was to be reassured by payments at full market price, calculated on the relatively high 1959 values. "The Government of an independent Kenya," declared Kenyatta in one of his first statements after being released from detention in 1961, "will not be a gangster Government."[44] Land pressure was to be relieved by converting a segment of these lands into "high density" settlements, or small peasant holdings of a few acres. At the same time, the door of opportunity was opened to somewhat larger operators in "low density" settlements of roughly 15–30-acre holdings. These two patterns, in which the state played a crucial intermediary role as custodian of land transfer and financier, were the most dramatic aspects of land policy; they were known as the "settlement schemes." After independence, a further pattern of direct sale of large farms to African buyers gathered force; the sales were frequently facilitated by concessionary finance through parastatal agencies. Finally, a substantial fraction of the ranch and plantation land remained in white hands.

The land transfer component of decolonization had critical psychological functions. The seven million settler-held acres were the pivotal grievance of anticolonial nationalism; no majority rule formula could be viable unless there was visible movement toward dismantling this sector. The settlement schemes were the symbolic stage on which was enacted the wrenching adjustment from settler dominion to African state. While attention was riveted upon the changing roles of the actors, the market-economy setting remained unchanged.

At first, the settlement schemes were of modest scope and low density concept; the first version, launched in 1961, was intended to serve 1,800 "yeoman" farmers on plots capable of generating £250 of annual net income, and 6,000 "peasant" farmers on holdings with a £100 revenue potential. This scheme quickly proved too small in numbers affected and too exclusive, and by 1962 another category of "smallholdings" targeted at £25–40 earnings was established. The "yeoman" category was dropped; the "peasant" category was redesignated as "low density" and the smallholder "high density." The entire program became known as the "million-acre scheme"; to it was added, in 1965, a squatter settlement program aimed at people who occupied lands on the periphery of white farms, whose presence had been tolerated by the settler farmers in return for their labor. After a decade of implementation, by 1971 the settlement schemes had transferred ownership to 5,000 "low density" farming families, 29,000 "high density" smallholders, and 18,000 squatters. In total, 1.5 million acres (21 percent of the former white highlands) were transferred under the settlement schemes, covering roughly 500,000 persons (counting families). The total cost of the million-acre scheme had been about £29 million, of which £10 million was covered by British grants and £14 million by external borrowing. There was some drop in marketed output; Leys estimates that cash sales from the settlement farms in 1969–70 were about £2.5 million, compared to £4.5–5 million sold under European management.[45]

The prime beneficiaries of the settlement schemes were the former European owners, who were able to extricate their capital (and capital gains) through a market sustained by state action. The 500,000 Africans who drew their livelihoods from these lands were generally net gainers as well, though many had difficulty in meeting debt payment obligations incurred in obtaining the land; by 1970 some 44 percent of the debt was in arrears. The political effect was beyond doubt tranquilizing; even the critics of the Kenya path concede that settlement "reduced the political risks by reducing land hunger in the short run."[46] The land policy was also effective symbolic political theater; Africans had cracked the hitherto impenetrable sanctuary of the white highlands, while domestic and external private sector interests were reassured by the market-centered principles that had guided the operation.[47] There was a modest economic cost to the state, both in somewhat reduced cash output (with its fiscal and foreign exchange effects) and external debt burden incurred; as one external mission studying the agricultural sector in the mid-1960s suggested, "Kenya was agreeing to reduce her future national income in order to facilitate a smooth social transition."[48]

Meanwhile, another important change in the rural economy was gaining momentum: European farms were being purchased privately as intact units by members of the newly prosperous African (especially Kikuyu) political, administrative, and business elite. About 1.6 million areas of European farmland passed into African hands by this means, for an estimated £20 million. The new proprietors were by no means all politicians or businessmen; a number of the sales were to diverse partnerships or cooperatives. Perhaps a third of the purchase price came from public loans. Many of these farms soon encountered severe difficulties: the debts incurred in purchase left the owners unable to raise operating capital; the partnerships lacked the social cohesion to sustain production discipline; there was a lack of experience in the management of large, highly capitalized units. Output frequently dropped to a third or less of former production.[49]

Finally, a sizable European farming sector remained in the roughly four million acres of the old white highlands that had been devoted to coffee, tea, or sisal estates, or extensive ranches. The 1970–74 Development Plan anticipated that only a small fraction of these holdings would pass into African hands. Increasingly, the large farm sector saw common interests crossing racial lines. The number of really big units was limited—according to the World Bank report of 1975, some 3,000 to 3,200 farms over twenty hectares in the high or medium potential areas.[50] But their contribution to total output of the highest value crops, such as tea and coffee, was substantial.

Leys summarizes the new rural economy:

the boundaries between the old "large-farm" sector and the "African land units", the one expatriate and capitalist, the other African and— at least till the 1950s—not only "peasant" but "poor-peasant", were swiftly obliterated. In their place arose a new rural structure, predominantly occupied by Africans, with the foreign-owned plantations and ranches still operating, much less visibly, though still more profitably, on the side-lines. It contained a system of gradations of acreage, capitalization, access to credit and knowhow and political protection which cut across the distinction between the former white highlands and the rest of the country. . . . At the top were some very large-scale individual landowners, some of them with farms purchased from Europeans, others with several hundred acres—not necessarily in one "parcel"—in the former reserves. These men were linked professionally, socially and economically to the foreign capitalist enclave. . . . Their farms were mostly run by salaried managers, in some cases by Europeans. At the bottom of the scale were the "peasant" masses, mostly now with freehold land titles, though with little access to capital, extension services, or other inputs, and—especially among the Kikuyu—a growing minority of landless labourers and squatters.[51]

As the new structures became consolidated and the issue of racial allocation faded, government policy became more firmly wedded to the central goal of productivity, to be promoted through market mechanisms. Registered, individual land title became the predominant pattern: it was virtually complete in Kikuyuland and adjacent areas and spreading fact in most of the cultivated lands. Still, in 1970, some 73 percent of the total land area remained in customary tenure—though most of this was

sparsely populated scrub or semidesert land with pastoral populations.[52] The commitment to rural capitalism did not preclude
modest encouragement of a marketing cooperative sector; while
its performance was mixed, on balance the Kenya cooperatives
functioned more effectively than their Tanzanian counterparts.[53]

In terms of growth, there can be little dispute about the success of this productivity-centered strategy. Commercial agriculture has made steady real gains ranging from 2 percent to 10 percent, as table 4.5 indicates. Further—in sharp contrast to many
African states—Kenya has remained self-sufficient in food production during most years and provided urban consumers with
their foodstuff staples at substantially lower costs than in neighboring states (until the 1979–80 maize crisis).[54] Major innova-
tions have been achieved—for example, the introduction of
hybrid maize to small farmers; the smallholder end of the farming spectrum has become much more involved in cash agriculture. Agriculture remains crucial to the overall economy, run-
ning about 35–40 percent of GDP and 70 percent of export
earnings. Its relatively robust health has provided much of the
momentum for the economy as a whole.

Critics of the Kenya pathway point to the price paid in widening inequalities. Powerful evidence is available to buttress this
claim. The 1972 ILO report on employment and incomes recorded, as the top end, some 476 farms exceeding 1,000 hectares
and 15 over 20,000 hectares, covering nearly two million hectares in all. At the bottom, roughly 17 percent of peasant house-
holds were entirely landless.[55] The government has shown little
inclination to curb this trend, which could be accomplished
through such measures as a land tax on large holdings or ceilings
on farm size. Though nominal income tax rates on high incomes
are theoretically heavy, there are numerous exceptions, and
widespread evasion is practiced by the self-employed (as, for example, large farmers).[56]

On the other hand, there are some aspects of policy that do
mitigate the inequality-generating dynamic of the capitalist-

TABLE 4.5. Average Annual Production Increases. Major Kenya
           Marketed Crops, 1962–71

Crop	Annual average % change
Coffee	3.3
Tea	11.5
Sisal	−4.9
Wattle bark	−6.9
Cotton	9.0
Sugarcane	18.5
Cashew nuts	4.3
Pulses	−2.1
Maize	7.6
Rice (paddy)	10.5
Wheat	9.9
Pineapples	34.0

SOURCE: John Burrows et al., *Kenya Into the Second Decade* (Baltimore: Johns
Hopkins University Press, 1975), p. 449.

based strategy. The tax burden imposed upon the countryside
through export taxes, marketing board policy, and price setting is
quite low. In the 1960s, export taxes—imposed only on coffee
and sisal—amounted to less than 2 percent of all government
revenues and averaged only £1 million altogether. These taxes
were eliminated altogether in 1973.[57] Marketing boards were
never used as mechanisms for surplus generation through "price
stabilization" schemes, as in Uganda, Ghana, Ivory Coast and
Nigeria. This is to be compared with the Ghana and Ivory Coast
patterns, where a third or more of the crop value was retained by
the state. Export crops and marketing board commodities were
produced on settler farms in colonial days; the white farmers
were vigilant and effective defenders of their interest and would
never have permitted the kind of indirect fiscal burden transferred to the farmer where African peasants were the export producers. The low taxation of the rural sector obviously confers
greatest benefits to the large export crop farmers. However, for
crops such as coffee, the number of smallholder producers is

very large. While Kenya, like virtually all countries, has held down foodstuff prices in the interest of urban consumers, in real terms Kenya prices have for most of the postindependence period been more favorable than those of either Uganda or Tanzania—as is conclusively demonstrated by the continuous pattern of leakage of Ugandan and Tanzanian farm produce into Kenya marketing channels.

Further, the Kenya administration has been effective in delivering services and amenities to the rural sector. In 1971, Kenya spent 26.9 percent of its budget on education, one of the highest rates in the developing world.[58] Dispensaries have been made free, and the local road net greatly extended. While real comparison is elusive, most students of comparative bureaucracy agree that Kenya has a relatively competent administration. Bienen builds upon this attribute to develop the intriguing argument that the regional administration constitutes the prime agency for political participation because it is the major contact point between state and citizenry, it is charged with explicit social and economic transformation tasks, and it is instructed to serve as channel for local grievances and demands.[59]

The many studies of rural Kenya and its governance, while in a number of cases critical of the capitalist path, cumulatively convey a sense of relative effectiveness.[60] Indeed, one has argued that Kenya has the most comprehensive program for rural growth in all of Africa.[61] There are also substantial survey data supporting the view that postindependence policy has generated substantial optimism among the citizenry about their personal future.[62]

The other sectors of the Kenya economy have prospered as well; manufacturing has grown at a buoyant rate, despite the loss of anticipated regional markets through the decline and fall of the East African Community and the frequently conflicted relationships with most of its neighbors. The growing Western confidence in Kenya as a stable and exemplary capitalist state brought substantial inflows of foreign capital. In commerce and industry,

Leys argues, the 50 percent increase in production and 100 percent rise in annual investment rate was almost wholly tributary to foreign capital—at first transferred from the agricultural sphere, then increasingly flowing from a new wave of multinational entrants.[63]

The effort to secure an African share in this proliferating new external estate came through several channels: state controls, Africanization of management, and African participation in ownership. The control approach, exercised through taxation, exchange control, and interministerial monitoring, at first had little effect. The state was ill-equipped to match corporate ingenuity in the artful deflection or evasion of controls, though its capacities increased over time. Africanization of staff had more policy bite: companies were forced to demonstrate that qualified locals were not available for managerial positions; indeed, they soon perceived the advantages inherent in the protective support that was provided by local staff who were adequately socialized into corporate fidelity and suitably affiliated to local networks of influence. By 1971, one survey found that 23 percent of managerial positions in American firms in Kenya were localized, while another found that 43 percent of the executive posts in a sample of fifty-two companies were held by Kenyans (a far higher figure than for Ivory Coast).[64] The Africanization trend continued strong through the 1970s.

Many foreign corporations found it expedient, indeed indispensable, to include Kenyans as directors of the Kenyan subsidiary. The speed of this trend is demonstrated by surveys of the "top fifty" corporate directors in 1968 and 1974; in the first year, 82 percent were foreign, while in 1974 the same percentage were Kenyan citizens, though half of these were European. Asians, citizen and noncitizen, were suffering eclipse. By 1974, Kenyan Africans chaired the boards of directors of such important conglomerates as Lonrho-Kenya and Mackenzie Dalgety.[65]

Beyond winning a beachhead in the external capital sector, the new Kenyan business class received active support from the nurture capitalist state. Kenya, however, faced one delicate obstacle in its nurturant role that did not confront Nigeria: assuring that the blessings of capitalist opportunity underwritten by the state went to Africans. The citizenship criterion alone would leave many Asians, as well as some Europeans, eligible for support. While Kenya was prepared to tolerate non-African enterprise, it had no intention of supporting it. On the contrary, the object of nurture capitalism was to gradually enlarge the sphere of economic activity dominated by African business. The banking system, in which the state acquired a major role in the 1970s, was used to purvey credit to Kenyan capitalists. Kenyan-owned firms have been provided with preferential state contracts and purchases and are otherwise supported. Nonresident firms were permitted to borrow locally only 20 percent of investment costs, while local firms could obtain 60 percent. Various state credit agencies have provided African merchants the wherewithal to buy out Asian trading firms. The Trades Licensing Act, first passed in 1967, has been employed aggressively to circumscribe the noncitizen mercantile sector; by 1975, it was being invoked against citizen Asian enterprises as well (sixty-nine such firms received quit notices that year).[66] The African business class, wholly restricted to peripheral commercial activities under colonial rule, had rapidly become an important social as well as economic force in the postindependence years. While its first expansion was concentrated in such sectors as retail trade, road haulage, and small-scale contracting, where access was relatively easy, increasingly its domain spread into the productive sector.

The overall performance of the Kenyan economy, then, was impressive. A capitalist strategy, suffused with nationalism, did bring broad-based growth whose benefits were felt by a large fraction of the populace. At the same time, the gains were certainly disproportionately tilted toward the narrow strata of top political, administrative, and mercantile figures at the summit of Kenyan society and to the foreign estate, whose expansive consumption patterns fixed the expectations of their Kenyan count-

TABLE 4.6. Annual Average Growth Rates Compared, Kenya and Tanzania

	1964–67	1968–72	1973–74	1975–76	1977
Manufacturing					
Kenya	7.6	9.3	9.3	7.6	15.0
Tanzania	6.8	4.0	2.0	3.3	5.4
Commercial agriculture					
Kenya	5.2	6.7	2.4	3.5	10.0
Tanzania	4.1	2.7	1.8	3.2	5.6
GDP, constant price					
Kenya	6.8	6.8	5.3	3.2	7.3
Tanzania	6.4	4.6	3.5	4.4	5.9

SOURCE: Joel D. Barkan, "Comparing Politics and Public Policy in Kenya and Tanzania," in *Politics and Public Policy*, ed. Joel D. Barkan and John J. Okumu (New York: Praeger Publishers, 1979), pp. 16–17.

erparts. At the nether ends of society, the growing landless rural population, especially in the densely populated Central Province (approximately Kikuyuland), and the paradox of stagnant or declining private sector employment in the face of swift expansion cast ominous shadows upon the future. Their darkness alarmed admirer and critic alike.[67]

The buoyant growth rate, crucial to the legitimacy of the Kenyan pathway, was threatened by the end of the 1970s on several fronts. One secret of success was the very low level of defense outlay. The deepening crisis in the Horn, which reinforced the Kenyan conviction that it was surrounded by hostile states, led to a major program of arms purchases in 1979. Rapidly rising energy consumption and oil costs hit hard. In 1980, major maize shortages afflicted urban consumers, illuminating the vulnerability of the economy to shortfalls in marketed cereal output. The growth rate fell to 3.1 percent in 1979 and 1979–83 projections have been revised downward to 5.4 percent. Economic Planning and Development Minister Zachary Onyonhra has warned that growth could be as low as 2.5 percent.

The capitalist order fashioned in Kenya was not heavily repressive, though by various devices those who actively challenged it were isolated or excluded. Such was the fate of the long-time leading opposition figure, Oginga Odinga, whose public populist socialism coexisted with his private mercantile success.[68] After 1969, with the banning of the Kenya Peoples' Union (KPU), Kenya became, like most other African countries, a one-party state. Some leeway, however, was given to backbenchers in the parliamentary context; its limits were demonstrated by the murder of radical populist MP J. M. Kariuki in 1975 and the subsequent detention of several other particularly outspoken parliamentarians.

Yet, despite these shortcomings and the disabilities of dependency so powerfully argued in the Leys indictment of neocolonialism in Kenya, obituaries for Kenyan capitalism are premature. The resiliency of the regime was persuasively demonstrated in the smoothness of the transition following the death of Kenyatta. Notwithstanding the innumerable Jeremiahs who forecast the dissolution of the state, Kenyan capitalism acquired reborn legitimacy by both the process and outcome of succession. Many applauded the removal from power of the innermost caste—the Kiambu Kikuyu combine, which gravitated about the Kenyatta "royal family" and was associated with a number of the more unsavory transactions incarnating what a Tory premier once called the "unacceptable face of capitalism."[69] The political decompression that ensued under the new president, Daniel arap Moi, epitomized by the release from prison of writer James Ngugi, won a reprieve from the intensifying criticism of the intelligentsia.[70] The elections in 1979, modeled on the TANU pattern of competition within the regime party, yielded results analogous to those in Tanzania: the spectacular defeat of nearly half the incumbents, including leading ministers (seven of twenty-two minister-candidates) and the KANU party secretary. The degree of turnover brought renewed legitimacy, while also revealing the undercurrents of discontent. None of these positive developments in the political sphere obliterates the shadows on the future. They do, however, call into question the apocalyptic forecasts.

NIGERIA: NATIONALISM, NURTURE CAPITALISM, AND PETROLEUM

Nigeria, our third major instance of the capitalist pathway, has a flavor all its own.[71] More national, more nationalist, more Nigerian: the vibrant qualities of indigenous capitalism immediately strike the most casual visitor to the country. The roadway traversing the densely settled lands between the two largest cities, Lagos and Ibadan, is an almost continuous strip of mostly petty Nigerian enterprises—capitalism run riot. Nigeria has gone far further than Ivory Coast or Kenya in promoting local ownership, beginning with oil, in which by 1979 the Nigerian National Petroleum Corporation (NNPC) held 60 percent equity. At the same time, in the 1970s the national economy resembled an inverted pyramid, teetering precariously on a hydrocarbon pinnacle that produced over 90 percent of exchange earnings and state revenues but employed no more than 20,000 persons. Despite Nigerian majority public equity, this sector depended very heavily on the giant international oil companies for exploration and production technology. The base of the pyramid was the ailing and stagnant agricultural sector, which nonetheless must provide a livelihood to 70 percent of the population. Nigerian nurture capitalism found the state offering active shelter and nourishment not only to indigenous entrepreneurs but also to a state class of politicians and officials who converted public power into private enterprise. The compenetration of the political and economic realms, while quite widespread in contemporary Africa, was nowhere more pronounced than in Nigeria; in the lapidary phrase of one critic, "The ethics of business penetrated politics, the ethics of politics penetrated business; the ethics of the gangster penetrated both." [72]

The emergence of a capitalist option in Nigeria crystallized by degrees. By the 1970s, the commitment had become quite robust and was shared by most sectors of the political elite. In the early 1960s, however, with African socialism at the height of its prestige, the First Republic parties for a time clothed their policy pronouncements in socialist phraseology: the National Convention of Nigerian Citizens (NCNC) in 1962 declared for "pragmatic African socialism," while Chief Obafemi Awolowo's Action Group (AG) laid claim to a more virile democratic socialism. Even the Northern Peoples' Congress (NPC) made passing reference to the doctrine. With the possible exception of the untested Awolowo doctrine, *pragmatism* rather than *socialism* was the operational term. In the words of one commentator, the socialism of the First Republic platforms was "the right of everyone to own his own business." [73] During the years of military rule, socialism disappeared entirely from public discourse, and capitalism became more nationalist in tone, epitomized by the 1972 "indigenization decrees" requiring Nigerian ownership of a wide swath of the economy. The institutionalization of a market-economy perspective in the public consciousness received dramatic confirmation in the 1979 electoral campaign. While the Peoples' Redemption Party (PRP) of Aminu Kano and, to a lesser extent, the Unity Party of Nigeria (UPN) of Awolowo sought to project a somewhat more radical image, there were no full-throated calls for socialization.

The radical impulse has occasionally surfaced in Nigerian politics, but generally without clearly defined ideological goals. In the late 1940s, the Zikist movement briefly articulated a militantly anti-imperial perspective. In the words of the movement's founder:

Zikism is irredentism. It is a God-sanctioned plan. It is a rejuvenated universal philosophy; it is not jingoism; it is not racialism; it is not anarchism; it is not monistic; it is not sarcastic; it is not apologetic; it is faith in life, a creative impulse. . . . Zikism . . . must mean "the redemption of Africa from social wreckage, political servitude and economic impotency". . . . Africa is then to be saved from ideological confusion, psychological immaturity, spiritual complacency, and mental stagnation."[74]

These words were echoed in the flamboyant but vacuous radical lexicon of the leader of the Ibo majors' coup of January 1966, C. K. Nzeogwu. The general strike in 1963, the Tiv rebellion of 1964, the Yoruba peasant unrest from 1965 to 1968 that peaked in the violent *Agbekoya* tax revolt of 1968 all had strong populist undercurrents.[75]

However, none of this coalesced into a significant constituency for socialist ideas. Several possible explanations suggest themselves. The Nigerian business class was larger and more deeply rooted than in any other of the cases we have examined. A number of the most prominent politicians had pursued successful business careers before bidding for political leadership: Awolowo, Nnamdi Azikiwe, and Waziri Ibrahim are conspicuous examples. The strong impact in First Republic years of a northern political elite with close ties to the traditional ruling class played its part; these leaders were deeply suspicious of radical ideas of any sort, which they viewed as carriers of equally abhorrent southern domination or of the dissolution of extant northern social hierarchies. The saturation of the political realm with ethnic metaphors defining social conflict as essentially a division of the "national cake" among regional competitors likewise served to inhibit the emergence of sharply defined ideological alternatives.

The most central fact of the postindependence Nigerian political economy has been the total transformation from agricultural exporter to major oil producer. The colonial economy had rested upon a small number of export commodities: palm oil, cocoa, groundnuts, rubber, and cotton. Tin and coal mines made a small contribution, while the large population and significant urban sector sustained a moderately vigorous domestic trade in such items as kola, cattle, staple foods, edible oils, and

TABLE 4.7. Percentage Composition of Nigerian Exports

Commodity	1946	1954	1964	1976	1978
Cocoa	15.9	26.8	19.1	6.0	4.9
Palm kernels	17.5	15.6	10.0	1.3	0.5
Palm oil	8.6	9.2	5.1	0	0
Groundnuts	23.9	20.4	16.5	2.9	0
Groundnut oil	0.5	2.6	3.5	1.1	0
Tin ore	12.0	3.5	6.0	0.7	0.1
Timber	1.6	2.4	3.8	0.7	0
Cotton	2.3	5.0	2.9	0.2	0.1
Rubber	5.9	2.0	5.2	0.9	0.2
Oil			15.2	85.7	94.1
Other	11.8	12.5	12.7	0.5	0.1

SOURCES: Gerald K. Helleiner, *Peasant Agriculture, Government, and Economic Growth in Nigeria* (Homewood, Ill.: Richard D. Irwin, 1966), p. 30; Federal Republic of Nigeria, *Economic and Statistical Review 1977* (Lagos: Federal Ministry of Information, 1978).

beverages. However, the GDP per capita was no more than $100, and Nigeria ranked near the bottom in aggregate measures of prosperity.

Exploration for oil dates from 1937, but the first exploitable strike did not occur until 1957. The first export was in 1958, but the year prior to independence state revenues from oil were less than $3 million. By 1965, oil was the most important export, although on the eve of the civil war, with 600,000 barrels daily output, petroleum was worth only $213 million. The civil war interrupted the oil bonanza, as onshore production had to be suspended. From 1970 on, output rose swiftly, reaching a plateau oscillating about 2 million barrels daily in the late 1970s. The fillip provided by the 1973 oil price rise sent state revenues and exchange earnings soaring. From 1971/72 to 1975/76, oil revenues for the state rose from $860 million to $6.9 billion, or 87 percent of the total. That same year, oil yielded 93 percent of export earnings. By 1980, well over 90 percent of both revenue and exchange came from petroleum; sales might well pass $20 billion.[76]

This extraordinary rise in government revenues permitted a truly phenomenal expansion in the scope of state activity. The governmental apparatus in colonial Nigeria had been of modest dimensions; state outlays rose from £2.9 million in 1913 to a mere £7.4 million in 1937. This figure doubled to £14.1 million in 1946, then expanded nearly fivefold to £60.7 million in 1954. By 1966, it reached £214 million, then swelled to £2.7 billion a decade later.[77] From 1950 to 1962, state expenditures rose five times faster than GDP. This fiscal gusher permitted easy financing for the civil war and expansion of the armed forces from 10,000 in 1966 to 250,000 in 1970 (shrunk to 160,000 by 1979); the remarkable drive for universal primary education by 1976 became conceivable, though the goal was not quite realized. The fiscal hegemony of the federal treasury, which collected these levies, was also assured.

The rapid oil expansion, of course, was quite independent of either ideology or policy on the Nigerian side. As a World Bank report laconically observed, "petroleum represents a typical enclave industry whose contribution to the economy is limited largely to its contribution to government revenues and foreign exchange earnings."[78] In 1965, the petroleum industry employed only 17,178,[79] a figure that has not substantially increased. During the early phase of oil development, the newly independent Nigerian government had few trump cards in bargaining with the oil companies and made little use of what leverage it did have. During the civil war, the distractions of national survival diverted all energies to eliminating the secession. From 1970 on, however, a determined effort was made to enforce a more generous share of the returns for the host country. In 1970, some 60 percent of the value added accrued to the oil companies. New agreements negotiated that year lowered the fraction retained by the investers to 43 percent the following year and to 30 percent

TABLE 4.8. Contributions of Petroleum Sector to the Nigerian
          Economy

		(N£ 000,000)		
	1964	1966	1970	1971
Gross proceeds	33	101	265	508
Value added (factor costs)	15	76	208	450
Wages and salaries	2	3	4	6
Government income	11	16	81	248
Investment income	1	57	123	196
Value added as % of GDP	1%	5%	9%	17%
Net foreign exchange earnings	25	43	132	293

SOURCE: Wouter Tims, *Nigeria: Options for Long-Term Development* (Baltimore:
Johns Hopkins University Press, 1974), p. 72.

by the mid-1970s. In 1971, the Nigerian National Oil Corporation
was established, through which the state began to acquire equity
in the oil operations; in 1976 it was reorganized and merged with
the oil ministry as the Nigerian National Petroleum Company
(NNPC). By 1979, NNPC equity in oil production was raised to 60
percent.[80] However, as table 4.9 shows, profits for the oil companies remained very high in the mid-1970s.

The self-assertiveness Nigeria displayed toward the oil companies in the 1970s reflected the altered psychology of Nigerian nationalism. The Western-leaning and low-keyed orientation of First Republic diplomacy was, in Nigerian eyes, poorly
rewarded in the civil war crisis, when the Soviet Union proved
to be the most reliable source of arms supply and external support. The Federal triumph in 1970 and the new vistas opened
by swelling oil revenues engendered a new mood of self-
confidence. In turn, this brought a determination to demand
more forcefully Nigeria's full share in resource exploitation.
Symptomatic of this new thrust was the decision in 1971 to join
OPEC, which not long afterward named a Nigerian as general
secretary. While Nigeria did not pioneer the formula for partial
nationalization of the petroleum equity, Lagos in the 1970s was
tough and determined in its dealings with the companies. The

TABLE 4.9. Earnings on United States Direct Private
            Investment Abroad

| | ($ millions) | |
	1975	1976
Total, all areas	16,434	18,843
% of investment	13.2	13.7
Africa, total	651	794
% of investment	16.3	17.8
South Africa	139	202
% of investment	8.8	12.1
Liberia	53	45
% of investment	15.9	12.9
Nigeria*	284	192
% of investment	53.1	56.3

*The great majority of American direct investment in Nigeria was in the pe-
troleum sector.
SOURCE: Gordon Bertolin, "U.S. Economic Interests in Africa: Investment, Trade
and Raw Materials," in *Africa and the United States*, ed. Jennifer Seymour Whitaker (New York: New York University Press, 1978), p. 27. Reprinted by permission.

companies in turn brought into the fray their key leverage: technological control, exercised through slowdowns in exploration
and new-field development, a strategy pursued for some time in
the late 1970s. First Republic Nigeria had been an acquiescent
junior partner of the oil companies; the Nigeria of the 1970s was
an exigent collaborator-adversary.

Although oil has profoundly transformed the revenue base
for development choice in Nigeria, much of the basic shape of
policy has remained fairly consistent. Social overhead has always enjoyed a priority claim, especially in the educational field;
this partly reflects the relative openness of the political system,
even during the phase of military rule. Pressure for amenities is
intense—first unleashed by the political platforms of the First
Republic, then reignited by the "rich country" psychosis of the
oil bonanza. As one observer noted, the Obasanjo government
was able "deliberately and publicly to underestimate Nigeria's
growing oil revenue,"[81] but it could not conceal it altogether. In-

dustrial development, especially in the spheres of consumer goods and import substitution articles, has been a constant aim. Great pressures for urban jobs made the creation of employment imperative. Beyond this consideration lay the more diffuse equation of industrialization and modernization. Finally, agriculture received little attention. The agrarian based economy connoted colonial poverty. Through the 1960s, until the oil revenues gained full momentum, the role seen for agriculture was to generate surplus for development in other fields, extracted through fiscal and pricing mechanisms.

Some changes in emphasis were discernible during the 1970s, as nationalism weighed more heavily in the policy equation. There was much more stress on Nigerian capital in the industrial and commercial spheres. The role of technology in dependency was more clearly perceived, and high priority was accorded to equipping the country with technical cadres. The damage done to agriculture by extractive state policies became visible, as production of most export commodities shrank and costly food imports ate into foreign exchange reserves. The rural sector no longer made a significant contribution to development finance. Incentives to the farming community became for the first time a conscious concern.

The industrial and mercantile fields were the major arena for the uneasy and often conflicted relationship between domestic and foreign capital groups. These tensions, which first became visible about 1949, have been a recurrent theme in the political economy since that time.

Schatz, in his study of Nigerian capitalism, dates the first real Nigerian pressures for expanded opportunities for indigenous entrepreneurs from 1949. Constitutional changes opened new avenues for Nigerian political participation, which created a vehicle for indigenous capital claims. One sign of changing times was that the Public Works Department abandoned its monopoly of state construction in 1950, opening up what was to prove a lucrative avenue of privately contracted building that gave a start to many Nigerian entrepreneurs (as well as to some foreign contractors). The scale of capital generation opportunities in this sphere is suggested by Kilby's finding that construction costs from 1950 to 1963 rose 285 percent, while overall prices increased only 36 percent.[82] At the same time, the major colonial mercantile conglomerates, such as UAC, John Holt & Co., and A. G. Levantis, were redeploying their Nigerian holdings into small industrial ventures: beer, plastics, canning, enamelware, beverages, and the like.

In the 1950s, as Nigerian political parties gained control first of regional governments, then of the federal institutions, an ambivalent view toward national capitalism became apparent. Even though many of the first generation of leaders were drawn from an emergent national capitalist class, there was a growing awareness of the limits of the skills and capacity among indigenous entrepreneurs. With "pragmatic socialism" beginning to enter political discourse by the late 1950s, the public corporation for a time enjoyed favor as an alternative to the Hobson's choice between an inadequate Nigerian capitalism and an undesirable foreign capitalism. In this phase, which Schatz dubs "nationalist nurture-capitalism with state-capitalist and welfare tendencies,"[83] a parastatal sector took form, building upon the marketing board nucleus that dated from World War II. However, by the early 1960s serious flaws were evident in the public sector; virtually none of the state enterprises proved profitable and few "could be called successful by any economic standard."[84] An unacknowledged shift took place back to reliance upon foreign investment, partially mitigated by pressure for Nigerianization of cadres and the sale of some shares at low prices to the state and private Nigerians.

From 1970 on, the renewed self-assertion of Nigerian nationalism swung the pendulum back toward national capitalism. The Second National Development Plan in 1970 stressed economic independence as a central policy goal: "A truly independent nation cannot allow its objectives and priorities to be

distorted or frustrated by the manipulations of powerful foreign investors." Indigenous ownership was one potent weapon
against dependency that would "maximize local retention of
profit, increase the net industrial contribution to the national
economy and avoid explosive socio-political consequences." At
the same time, the state had an important role to play as trustee
for national capitalism; it was "vital . . . for Government to acquire and control on behalf of Nigerian society, the greater proportion of the productive assets of the country." [85]

One major instrument for accomplishing these goals was the
Indigenization Decree of February 1972. This legislation defined
two major categories of economic activity in which foreign interests would be required to wholly or partially withdraw through
sale of equity to Nigerian buyers. Some twenty-six categories of
business (Schedule I) had to be entirely turned over to Nigerian
purchasers; these included mainly small industry, services, and
retail trade, spheres in which foreign capital was in good part
Levantine. A second set of twenty-seven larger types of economic ventures, characterized by larger scale and greater organizational or technological complexity, were required to offer 40
percent equity to Nigerians. These measures, while extensive in
their impact, generally exempted the largest foreign investments,
in fields such as tires, carpets, textiles, blankets, and vehicle assembly. Less than half the manufacturing value added in 1972
was in enterprises covered by the Indigenization Decree. In addition, Nigerian participation in these spheres was already extensive; Schatz estimates that by 1967 Nigerians already held 56 percent of total equity in the Schedule I sector and 32.4 percent of
Schedule II enterprises.[86] In 1976, a further Indigenization Decree imposed a 60 percent Nigerian ownership for an important
new array of enterprises, including banks, trading companies,
and more industries.

Whatever its limitations, the Indigenization Decree did bring
about a large-scale transfer of assets. The willing buyer–willing
seller concept of the scheme, sanctioned by a 1974 deadline for

compliance (in practice extended for a number of firms), prevented potential compensation claims. Some state governments, as trustees for national capitalism, acquired significant holdings; the state as well, in its nurture role, provided generous credit arrangements to enable Nigerian investors to exploit this newly opened commercial frontier. At the same time, windfall gains were provided for a number of well-connected Nigerian entrepreneurs; the average share price of thirteen publicly held manufacturing firms hit by indigenization rose 50.7 percent over the transfer price set by the state, while for eight commercial companies and a set of service companies the appreciation in the wake of equity transfer was 29.6 percent and 33.9 percent respectively. In addition, dividend rates of 50 percent were common in the postindigenization period. Beyond these dazzling gains, a number of Nigerians earned lucrative rewards for cooperating in asset-transfer arrangements favorable to the foreign firms.[87] Not only was it the politically connected business class that captured the principal benefits of these measures, but there also was a marked regional concentration of the windfall. The greatest number of the enterprises concerned were located in Lagos and the former Western Region; in 1964, some 62 percent of foreign- and state-owned industry was situated in these areas.[88]

Construction contracting was another vital sphere for promotion of national capitalism. Nigerian contractors enjoyed a 5 percent preference on all bids, even though their reputation was not very good. Public construction projects were a particularly dynamic engine of corruption; most in fact were not bid but negotiated, a practice that permitted the state representatives to share in the proceeds. Ironically, in not a few cases the Nigerian contractor would then subcontract the actual work to a foreign firm.[89] The Universal Primary Education scheme, with the $1 billion of new school construction it implied, offered fertile pastures for the contractor class.

However, the solidity of Nigerian capitalism remains uncer-

tain. Its heavy dependence on state nurture has tended to channel it into spheres such as contracting, where political favor can
bring high returns. Commerce, with its prospects of quick turnover and return, tends to be more attractive than manufacturing.
For large industrial ventures, foreign capital continues to pre-
dominate; the vigor, versatility, and dynamism of the individual
Nigerian entrepreneur is not easily molded into corporate institutional form. The manufacturing sector expanded fairly rapidly in the aggregate; during the first dozen years of independence its annual growth rate was 11 percent.[90] While many in
Nigeria have a quite ebullient outlook on the prospects for national capitalism in foreign partnership—for example, the authors of the Third Plan in the early 1970s—others paint the future in more somber hues. For example, one Marxist critic of
Nigerian development concluded that

Profit-making continues to depend on collaboration with foreign firms
and on the favour of the state. The state continues to control access to
money, contracts and commercial opportunities. Politics is a struggle for
the control of these resources. But these resources are also means by
which politics is carried out. . . . Politics is assumed to be a business of
reconciling divergent interests, pursued by competing elites. Questions
of foreign domination, class power and state policy are ignored or
evaded. Bourgeois domination, the purpose and foundation of such politics, is taken for granted.[91]

In a more nuanced vein, both Schatz and Kilby see many obstacles ahead in the further evolution of nurture capitalism.

The major casualty of Nigerian development policy has been
agriculture. After independence production for most commercial
crops declined, and growing amounts of food imports were required. The only redeeming feature in the dismal catalogue of
agrarian failure was a general recognition by the mid-1970s of the
calamitous state of Nigerian agriculture.

Colonial agricultural policy in Nigeria, in keeping with the
general pattern in Africa, was a tale of export commodities. Palm
oil from wild trees became the first significant export in the nine-

TABLE 4.10. Sectoral Growth Rates, Nigeria

Sector	$ share, 1958/59	$ share, 1970/71	Average annual growth, in real terms			
			1950–57	1958/59–1962/63	1962/63–1966/67	1966/67–1970/71
GDP	100.0	100.0	4.1	6.4	5.5	5.5
Agriculture	68.4	50.0	2.9	4.6	2.0	0.8
Mining and oil*	0.8	11.6	3.1	27.0	44.0	26.5
Manufacturing	4.4	8.8	5.6	13.9	10.5	9.7
Power, transport, communication	7.3	8.3	15.1	12.1	5.5	3.8
Services	19.1	22.1	3.4	6.8	7.0	6.2

*The oil contribution to GDP appears relatively low because such a large fraction of the value in these years accrued directly to foreign owners.

SOURCE: Wouter Tims, *Nigeria: Options for Long-Term Development* (Baltimore: Johns Hopkins University Press, 1974), pp. 12–13.

teenth century, after the demise of the slave trade; for some time, Nigeria was the world's leading source of this commodity. Cocoa plantations emerged in the Western Region early in the twentieth century; Nigeria took second place to Ghana in this crop. When the Nigerian railway reached Kano in 1912, there was a swift expansion of groundnut cultivation; for several decades, Nigeria was the world's leading peanut exporter, accounting for 40 percent of the world trade in 1958.[92] More recently, especially after World War II, rubber in the midwest and cotton in the north became significant crops. Directly or indirectly, the state apparatus was essentially financed by levies upon the agricultural sector.

The oil palm was the first pillar of the Nigerian colonial economy; before World War I palm oil averaged 82 percent of export earnings.[93] Nigerian palm oil, an Eastern Region peasant enterprise, provided much of the supply for the Lever Port Sunlight soap factories during these years. Over time, however, the palm oil industry stagnated. From 1939 to 1954, the average contribution to export earnings was 34 percent of the total, and 22 percent in 1955–65. For a brief period in the first postwar decade a sharp rise in peasant earnings led to increased planting and more extensive harvesting of wild trees. From 1955 on, returns to producers went into steady decline, partly because of unfavorable world market trends but also because of higher relative levels of fiscal extraction from this sector. Taxation had always been relatively high; it is estimated that in 1931 the local head tax captured 19.9 percent of palm oil earnings in the east.[94] However, the creation of the state marketing boards during World War II sharply increased levels of effective taxation; Bauer estimates that over 50 percent of the net producer profit from palm oil was extracted through the state pricing formula.[95] This was not at first perceived by the peasant, whose own real returns did rise from 1945 to 1955. However, from 1955 the price steadily fell, until by the early 1960s the returns were below the depression levels.[96] Production for the domestic cooking oil market, which escaped much of this taxation, became relatively more attractive. The Lagos price index for edible oils went up from 100 to 138, and in Enugu increased from 100 to 154 from 1959 to 1962, while the export price was declining.[97]

The final blow to the export side of the industry came in the 1960s and 1970s. Vastly more productive plantation oil palms were established in Ivory Coast and Malaysia. By the 1970s, Nigeria had ceased to be a significant exporter.

The cocoa sector followed a somewhat similar trajectory. The first cocoa farms date from the 1880s, but production levels became significant only in the early decades of this century. As in Ghana, the spread of the crop—confined to an area 200 miles wide and 50 miles deep in Yoruba country—came mainly through African initiative; the colonial administration at first wanted Yoruba farmers to grow cotton, a plan which the farmers strenuously resisted.

The dynamic era of cocoa expansion was from 1910 to 1940; the period of rapid price increases in the first postwar years then stimulated new plantings, which produced a new surge of output in the early 1960s. Thereafter, a series of unfavorable factors led to stagnation. Effective taxation rates, through export tax and marketing board pricing, averaged 39.4 percent of the total value from 1947/48 to 1953/54, and 26.1 percent from 1954/55 to 1961/62. The Western Region Marketing Board withheld some £14.3 million from producers (mainly cocoa) from 1954 to 1961, little of which found its way back into the rural social infrastructure.[98] Universal primary education diminished the supply of family labor, school fee payments transferred rural savings from cocoa to education, and rising wage costs made the hiring of additional labor difficult.[99] Overall, cocoa exports averaged about 100,000 tons in the 1940s, then rose to an all-time peak of 323,000 tons in 1970/71 before entering a phase of steady decline to a mere 160,000 tons in 1976/77.[100]

Groundnuts, the third major crop, were the major cash com-

modity for the Northern Region. Significant exports began when
the rail line to Kano was completed in 1912; they reached 50,000
tons in 1916, 245,000 by 1934, and 614,000 in 1963. At the peak,
some two million acres were in peanut cultivation. In the 1950s
and 1960s, marketing board taxation of groundnuts was much
less than for palm oil or cocoa, for reasons which are not clear;
for the 1954–61 period, the average fiscal levies on peanuts averaged 14.9 percent.[101] A substantial fraction—roughly 30 percent—
was consumed on the local market.

Groundnuts first ran into difficulty during the civil war,
when the Kano–Port Harcourt rail line was cut off, hampering
marketing operations. The drought years in the Sahel, seen initially as a temporary setback, were devastating. But exports—
which were still 500,000 tons in 1970—remained virtually nil
even when the rains returned in 1975. This sea change in northern peasant agriculture remains imperfectly understood, though
most observers believe that farmers have found food crop cultivation more profitable.

The trends for the other export crops, rubber and cotton, are
not less discouraging. A spurt of rubber output, centered in the
Edo zones of Bendel state in the 1950s, was spurred by a period
of attractive prices. Since independence, production has stagnated in the vicinity of 60,000 tons. Latex processing, which is
based on peasant improvisation, yields rubber sheets of modest
quality.[102] Cotton, a northern crop, expanded rapidly after World
War II, supplying a growing textile industry as well as some exports (27,500 tons of lint in 1970). In the 1970s, the stagnation
afflicting the entire traditional export farm sector hit cotton as
well.

Public agricultural investment during the first decade of independence was directed to singularly unsuccessful schemes.
Plantations were promoted for cocoa, rubber, and especially oil
palm. Careful cost calculations for the latter showed that production costs were twice as high as those of the peasant producers,

TABLE 4.11. Export Production Trends, Major Crops, Nigeria

Crop	(000 tons exported)					
	1950	1957	1962	1967	1973	1977
Cocoa	99.9	117.1	195.0	244.0	213.8	199.8
Groundnuts	311.0	302.0	530.0	540.0	198.7	1.2
Palm kernels	416.0	406.0	362.0	162.0	137.6	225.2
Palm oil	173.0	166.0	118.0	16.0	0.0	0.0
Rubber	13.6	40.0	59.6	47.9	49.4	30.4
Cotton (lint)	12.6	25.2	23.2	33.0	8.3	11.4

NOTE: The rapid growth of urban markets as well as more advantageous prices for domestic sales diverted both groundnuts and palm oil to the local market; the drop in production is not as great as the drop in exports. Similarly, the opening of new textile factories in the 1960s partly explains the drop in cotton exports.

SOURCES: Jerome C. Wells, *Agricultural Policy and Economic Growth in Nigeria 1962–1968* (Ibadan: Oxford University Press, 1974), pp. 62–63; Federal Republic of Nigeria, *Economic and Statistical Review 1977* (Lagos: Federal Ministry of Information, 1978).

with no equivalent rise in revenues. By the time of the civil war, all the state oil palm plantations were in deficit. The state oil mills did little better. A costly settlement scheme in the Western Region, inspired by the Israeli *moshav* (a form of communal farm), was a painful fiasco. About 1,500 school-leavers were established on cleared land at a cost of £4,000 per person; they produced yields far below those of neighboring peasant farms. The state persevered in these ventures long after their failure was apparent, a perverse determination that consumed much of the available resources for agricultural programs. Wells attributes it to administrative inflexibility and long delays in absorbing policy feedback.[103]

By the 1970s, there was no longer any doubt that agricultural policy was a disaster area. As in Tanzania, the state had underestimated the peasant option of exit; over time, the younger generation would migrate to town, and the older one would redeploy its efforts toward local consumption and domestic food

TABLE 4.12. Trends in Real Wages and Producer Prices,
1948–64, Southern Nigeria

| | (Index: 1948 = 100) | | | | | |
| | Western | | Eastern | | Northern | |
Category	1948	1964	1948	1964	1948	1964
Cocoa price	100	119				
Rubber price	100	130				
Palm oil price			100	58		
Palm kernel price	100	90	100	65		
Groundnut price					100	154
Cotton price					100	224
Unskilled wage	100	309	100	221	100	287
Semiskilled wage	100	319	100	229	100	334
Skilled wage	100	155	100	111	100	180

SOURCE: Gerald K. Helleiner, *Peasant Agriculture, Government, and Economic
Growth in Nigeria* (Homewood, Ill.: Richard D. Irwin, 1966), p. 38.

crops whose marketing circuits escaped the state fiscal arm.
Table 4.11 illustrates the unfavorable trends in relative urban and
rural welfare. The nature of national needs had also dramatically
changed; the provision of food for the burgeoning urban areas,
which reduced exchange-draining imports, became a more urgent need than promotion of the classical export crops. Yet this
was a sphere in which the state agricultural policy apparatus had
no accumulated experience at all; its modest efforts historically
had always been directed at the export crops. There was clear
public recognition of the nature of the problem and of the need
for action through higher prices and the elimination of agricultural export taxation. What remains to be demonstrated is
whether the state has the capacity to reverse the losses of the last
two decades.

   To what extent can we relate the manifest failure of agricultural policy to the developmental ideology espoused? Apparently, the concept of nurture capitalism applied mainly to the urban mercantile and industrial sectors. In contrast to both Kenya
and Ivory Coast, in Nigeria the political class has neither germi-

nated from a rural bourgeoisie nor sought agricultural outlets for its capital. Petty rural peasant capitalism received remarkably little encouragement from the state; on the contrary, it was heavily taxed and encumbered with generally unfavorable state pricing policies. Granted that the diffuse sense that "modernization" was essentially an industrial process permeated major resource allocation choices, particularly in the 1960s; and that southern Nigerian politicians at first believed that agrarian surplus would finance a development that would ultimately bring a better life to all; nevertheless, errors in farm policy appear to be less a result of the ideological preference of the state elite than of the low priority accorded it. The paternalistic superstructure of state market intervention in the export sphere was maintained. To this were added some ill-fated state ventures, such as the plantations, oil mills, and settlements. This statism drew no philosophic inspiration from "pragmatic socialism," but did reflect firmly rooted administrative habits bequeathed by the colonial regime.

The overall impact of Nigerian capitalism has probably been to increase inequality, although rigorous measurement has yet to be made.[104] Certainly the rural sector has failed to enjoy income gains remotely proportionate to the increases in per capita GDP produced by the oil bonanza.[105] Urban workers have perhaps come closer than farmers to holding their own, with periodic large wage awards. However, these affect only those holding jobs and do not benefit the very large number of urban poor who are locked into the informal sector and unemployment.[106] Exceptional opportunities have been open for wealth accumulation by the political class and those linked to them by affinities of kinship or clientage. The scale of corruption in Nigeria suffuses perceptions of inequality with distrust and cynicism; in 1965 a survey of African students in Ethiopia, Uganda, Zaire, Senegal, and Nigeria found Nigerians not only relatively the most distrustful of politicians, but displaying an astonishing level of absolute cynicism. Some 83 percent believed that politicians as a class were never honest.[107] Periodic colossal scandals sustained this presumption of peculation; students were not alone in immediately believing 1980 newspaper reports—later disproved—of a $4 billion embezzlement in the NNPC. The saving grace of the political system has been that, for the most part, successive heads of state or government have been exempted from the perception that high office is a license for pelf-seeking.[108] There has been no Nigerian Acheampong or Mobutu.

The most redeeming features of the Nigerian polity have been its fine performance in the field of human rights and the openness that has characterized political life, even during the long period of military rule. Despite the high degree of politization of ethnic cleavage, decanting into civil war, the number of politically inspired incarcerations has been limited and confined mainly to the First Republic era (the political trials of Anthony Enaharo and Awolowo).[109] The post–civil war reincorporation of the secessionist areas was accomplished with real magnanimity. Few military regimes have tolerated so wide a scope of open public debate. After careful and searching self-study, a new constitution was adopted in 1979, founded upon the social realities of the country and its painful earlier experiences. The new democratic order is evidently supported by a widely shared public commitment to civil liberties and political rights, which would make unthinkable the neo-Leninist political apparatus erected by the Afro-Marxist states.

Thus the nationalist nurture capitalist state that became consolidated in the 1970s demonstrated real resiliency. The swelling petroleum revenues offered a leeway in policy choice and even margin for error, which poverty denies to most African states. Yet this singular dependence upon a finite resource is also the greatest peril. The political economy is not securely rooted in a self-sustaining dynamic of development. Nigeria without its oil revenues would be in desperate circumstances; were the deep social fissures subjected to the pressures generated by intense scarcity, the most fearful and dangerous tensions would appear likely.

THE CAPITALIST PATHWAY: RANSOM OF GROWTH

The capitalist pathway in Africa has led to some undeniable successes. Ivory Coast has demonstrated that in terms of sheer growth the export-based, "associated-dependent" strategy can yield impressive results. At the same time, there are trade-offs. In the Ivory Coast instance, a client relationship with the former metropole and very high rewards to a proliferating European population have been the ransom. In Kenya as well, a predominant role for foreign capital has been the price of growth; if economic autonomy and self-reliance are accepted as valid national goals, a sacrifice has clearly been made. Rapid enrichment was made possible as well for a rather narrow political inner circle in the Kenyatta years. Nigeria has been the most nationalist of the three in its nurture capitalism strategy; at the same time, its growth performance—outside the crucial oil sector—has been the least impressive of the three, particularly in the agricultural field.

There are some differences in the social texture of African capitalism in these three states. A planter bourgeoisie in Ivory Coast formed the initial core of the political class; rural Ivorian capitalism has received more state support than has national enterprise in the industrial or service sectors, where the foreign senior partner shares the stage with Ivorian parastatals. In this respect, the Nigerian nurture capitalism model is only partly applicable. In Kenya, an African capitalist class has taken rapid form both in commercial farming and in the mercantile, service, and even manufacturing sectors. State support has been critical to African capitalist expansion. In Nigeria, nurture capitalism has not extended to the rural sector; the business substructure of the political bourgeoisie lies, above all, in mercantile ventures and public contracting.

Though inequality is pronounced in all three cases, there are some mitigating factors. All three countries have invested heavily in social infrastructure, above all schools, with Nigeria standing out in this respect. The effectiveness of Ivory Coast and Kenya (but not Nigeria) in promoting rural growth has brought benefits to important segments of the rural populace—leaving behind notably the migrant (mainly non-Ivorian) workers in Ivory Coast and the growing numbers of landless peasants in Kenya. Kenya, in contrast to Ivory Coast (and Nigeria until the mid-1970s), has maintained very low levels of taxation of the farming community, a significant and underrecognized factor in rural well-being.

All three states are hostage to continued high growth, in order to sustain the political legitimacy of their ventures in African capitalism. In the cases of Ivory Coast and Kenya, the "success" image—and positive comparison with less prosperous neighboring states—is a crucial justification for the options pursued. In Nigeria, the exceptionally high state revenues deriving from petroleum make possible significant outlays to the states and local administrations for amenities, a policy that affords the state greater legitimacy. There is little leeway for major policy miscalculations, such as the billion dollar sugar scheme in Ivory Coast undertaken in 1974, which faces bleak prospects for profitability in the short term. Sudden misadventures, such as the perceived need for major weapons purchases in Kenya in 1979 or maize shortfalls, threaten not only plan goals but the viability of the regime's chosen pathway. I would suggest that the political acceptability of the African capitalist pathway rests not upon a widespread philosophical preference among the populace for the liberal market economy, as is the case for a number of Western countries, but on a more contingent consent grounded in the effectiveness of a regime's performance.

For different reasons, the economic outcomes in the first two decades in these three states have been sufficiently favorable to allow some degree of openness and access to persist in the political realm, most notably in Nigeria. In all three instances African capitalism has been constructed without recourse to the Huntington-O'Donnell authoritarian containment state. Were these regimes to feel the repercussions of perceived failure, rather than be spurred by what the World Bank termed the "challenge of success" in Ivory Coast, the preservation of capitalism with minimal coercion might become problematic.

THE PITFALLS OF AFRICAN CAPITALISM: GABON AND ZAIRE

There are some perils in the capitalist option that are less clearly visible in the three states we have considered at length than in some others. One is the unadulterated enclave economy model, exemplified by Gabon. During the colonial period, this sparsely populated territory subsisted mainly on a logging industry, already in decline when independence came in 1970. However, in the 1960s a foreign-operated mineral economy quickly transformed the country into an extraverted polity with a revenue-rich state and an impoverished peasantry. Oil production began in 1957 and a decade later had reached 3,477,000 tons per year, an enormous amount for a country with fewer than a million inhabitants. Manganese ore, exported via Congo-Brazzaville, came into production in 1962 and by 1972 totaled 1,836,000 tons annually. Uranium concentrate exports began in 1961. These three commodities produced an apparently spectacular growth rate of 14.5 percent per year from 1970 to 1976, and a per capita income in 1976 of $3,780, second only to Libya in Africa.[110]

Yet, examined more closely, these figures are less heartening. Only a handful of Gabonese were employed in producing this wealth: no more than 1,000 in the oil wells, 1,100 in the uranium mines. The manganese mining combine, COMILOG, after twenty years of operation had only 50 Gabonese managerial cadres among its 3,500 total work force.[111] Indeed, the visitor to Libreville is struck by how little in this sumptuous array of new skyscrapers is really Gabonese, except for the state apparatus itself. Not only are the European technical personnel numerous in all walks of life, but many skilled positions are occupied by other Africans: Togolese and Beninians in particular. Much of the mercantile sector is also non-Gabonese: up-country rural trade in the north is organized mainly by Bamileke merchants from Cameroon, and Malian and Senegalese traders occupy many of the stalls at the marketplace. At the hotels, many of the waiters and domestics are Equatorial Guinean refugees. While the mineral economy booms, the rural economy stagnates; there has been no significant development of any cash crop since independence. State revenues have dilated remarkably, increasing tenfold from 1960 to 1973; a fraction of these was converted into amenities outlays, which have helped maintain social peace and dissipate any potential opposition movement. In 1970, Gabon state expenditures were two and one half times those of Togo, though the population was little more than a quarter as large.[112] However, much of the public investment has been lavished on Libreville; outlays for the 1977 OAU summit conference were so exorbitant that even Gabon's mineral cornucopia did not prevent a momentary debt crisis and immersion in one of the IMF's legendary cold showers of an austerity program. It is hard to discern in this hyperextraverted polity an exemplary model of successful development.

Zaire is a rather different specimen of the perverted capitalist state.[113] The litany of the social, political, and economic distress in that tormented land is now familiar to most obervers and need not be recited in detail. A country endowed with vast natural resources, Zaire in 1970 appeared to be on the verge of a rendezvous with abundance; a breathtaking set of objectives was targeted for 1980. By the end of the decade, however, the encounter was with despair: real wages no more than 10 percent of their 1960 level for those urban workers who held jobs; massive deterioration of rural well-being and crisis so profound that only the most resolutely sanguine could see any hope of early recovery. How did a capitalist pathway that brought reasonable prosperity to Ivory Coast and Kenya yield such catastrophic results in Zaire, which had vastly greater resource potential than the other two countries?

After an aborted decolonization from 1960 to 1965, Zaire experienced five difficult years, dominated by sheer political survival. The state lost control of its key resource zone of Shaba for half this period, was torn by a wave of rural uprisings in 1964–65, and was heavily penetrated by external influences, both through the United Nations and sundry major powers, with Western influence predominating. The image of generalized disorder and chaos (albeit exaggerated) that prevailed both within and without the country served to legitimate the seizure of power by the military high command, led by General Mobutu Sese Seko (then Joseph Désiré), on 24 November 1965.

The new regime of Mobutu initially enjoyed substantial success. The zones of rebellion atrophied, and central control was reasserted throughout the country. The bureaucratic-authoritarian legacy of the colonial state facilitated the resurrection of an apparently monolithic polity that by the late 1960s enjoyed unchallenged authority, considerable legitimacy at home, and acceptance in Africa and the world. During the First Republic, the state budget, little more than an open-ended register of uncontrolled disbursements, had produced escalating inflation; the Mobutu regime regained reasonable control over its financial arteries. In 1967, a well-conducted stabilization program under IMF auspices virtually ended inflation for several years. Foreign exchange reserves began to accumulate, and investment—which had virtually ceased in the uncertain First Republic years—again became possible. By 1970, the regime was able to boast that its currency, the zaire, was used as an international reserve money by the IMF.

During the first five years of Mobutu's reign, a strategy that bore some distant similarity to the Nigerian "nurture capitalism" model gradually emerged for defining relationships with external capital. The ideological underpinning for the Mobutu design was termed "authentic Zairian nationalism" (subsequently "authenticity," and finally, the personalist creed of "Mobutism"). This platform, which was strenuously nationalist, disclaimed other philosophical derivation; as Mobutu frequently asserted, the regime was "neither left, nor right, nor even in the center." An ill-defined radical nationalism was postulated as an alternative to both socialism and capitalism. In reality, this ideological pragmatism translated into a threefold relationship with capital:

1. A reserved and even hostile attitude toward colonial capital, founded on the conviction that it was historically linked with imperial exploitation and that much of it had been internally generated by the very high profit rates in the postwar era; continued economic hegemony by colonial capital was an unacceptable affront to authentic Zairian nationalism

2. A friendly and receptive orientation toward new foreign capital, with a strong desire for diversification of external economic partners

3. A determination that the Zairian politico-commercial elite should have the opportunity for participation in capital enterprise; as this group possessed no capital, it had to be obtained from the state, either openly or more frequently illicitly through rents extracted from the exercise of power or intermediary services provided to abet the entry of foreign capital (in more cynical terms, corruption)[114]

Pursuant to these goals, the regime moved quickly to assert control over colonial capital; indeed, its aggressiveness won important internal legitimacy in intellectual circles, thereby facilitating the consolidation of its power. The key event in the contest with colonial capital was the nationalization of the mining giant, the *Union Minière du Haut-Katanga* (UMHK), a subsidiary of the powerful Belgian conglomerate *Société Général de Belgique* (SGB). UMHK was nationalized in January 1967; however, in the end, Belgian capital secured a generous compensation package for UMHK and a lucrative management contract (which absorbed most of the UMHK European cadres) for a sister subsidiary of the SGB. But to all appearances this capital Goliath had been wrestled to the ground by the audacious Zairian state.

Meanwhile, the effective financial stabilization program and the apparent political solidity of the Mobutu regime attracted growing interest on the part of international capital. A relatively generous investment code was adopted in 1969; undertaking a series of pilgrimages to foreign capitals, Mobutu displayed the glittering geological reports and multiplied his assurances that, however firm the regime might be with colonial capital, new foreign capital was an entirely different category assured of iron-clad guarantees. He was not alone in appealing for investment in Zaire; the American diplomatic establishment wooed United States investors as ardently as did the Zairian leadership. As a veritable Klondike mood developed, most Western embassies provided eager support for their respective corporate bidders for participation in what many believed would be a Zairian decade of spectacular growth. Meanwhile, major international banks, flush with Eurodollars and faced with contracting lending markets in the industrial world, found Zaire—then seen as politically stable and resource rich—an exceedingly attractive target for loan capital. Private as well as public foreign credit was readily available, with too few questions asked as to the viability of the projects that the loans were intended to underwrite.[115]

More closely examined, the bullish reports of a massive influx of new foreign capital into Zaire had disconcerting features. The most knowledgeable foreign scholar specializing in Zairian development, Benoit Verhaegen, labels the process, in a searing critique, "technological imperialism." The capital flow, rather than constituting long-term equity investment, was primarily in the form of loans, contracted services, and sales of technology. This form of capital deployment was attractive because "it produces an immediate profit safe from political and economic risks," and is "profit taken at the time of sale, before production and independently of profitability."[116]

A characteristic example is the $200 million Maluku steel mill near Kinshasa. From the moment of his accession to power

Mobutu was committed to this project. There was no lack of foreign contractors eager to build the plant, but no external capital
that wanted any part of ownership. Foreign consulting firms produced glowing feasibility studies, arguing the centrality of steel
products in an industrial economy and pointing to the inexpen-
sive power source of the Inga dam, plus huge iron ore deposits
near Banalia and Umbundu in the far interior. Foreign firms sold
their services as turnkey contractors; the Zairian state bore the
entire risk of the enterprise, with borrowed capital. One could
well understand the reticence of foreign capital on equity involvement in this scheme. Enormous infrastructural investment
would be necessary before domestic iron ore would be available.
In the meantime, the mill had to operate entirely with imported
scrap, which was both unattractive in operating costs and susceptible to the very real risk—which soon materialized—of foreign exchange shortages that would make impossible the importation of adequate supply. The Maluku mill has operated fitfully,
always at a small fraction of capacity and at high cost. There is
little prospect that it will amortize the capital committed by the
state in the foreseeable future.

An even more dramatic example is the interrelated giant
projects of the second phase of the Inga dam, in lower Zaire, and
the 1,100-mile Inga–Shaba direct current power transmission
line, transporting Inga power to the Shaba mining areas. Inga II,
estimated at $300 million, would not have had assured custom-
ers for its 1,200 megawatts of generating capacity without the
power line; indeed, as Inga–Shaba will now not be completed
until 1983, little of the Inga II power is used, though the capital
reimbursement charges on the foreign loans that paid the overseas contractors must be met. When Inga–Shaba was first mooted
at the beginning of the 1970s, it was advertised as a $250 million
project. Several overruns later, it is now projected for $680 mil-
lion. The testimony of representatives of the Export–Import Bank
before a Senate committee reviewing the most recent overrun financing in 1979 was revealing: "There is no question that for

some years the state is going to have to underwrite some of the cost of Inga power for Gecumines. If you include everything in power cost, including the operating cost, the amortization, everything else, we figure over the Inga-Shaba line might [sic] cost as much as 70 to 80 mills, or 15 to 16 cents for copper. That is ridiculously high."[117] By way of comparison, VALCO, the Kaiser-Reynolds aluminum smelter in Ghana, paid Ghana 4.75 mills for power in 1980.[118] In effect, the Inga–Shaba power line will not be able to generate revenues sufficient to repay the huge debts incurred in its financing. To be sure, the foreign lenders will insist on eventual repayment; it is Zairian society who will pay the penalty charges for this colossally ill-conceived project that was so eagerly fostered by foreign contractors and their diplomatic promoters.

Several unhappy circumstances converged to bring about this calamity. For the regime, the project had superficial political attractiveness because it would bind the restive and rich Shaba mineral zone to distant Kinshasa through these new high-tension lines of dependency: a flick of the switch in the capital and Shaba closes down. The reverse of this reasoning, the great vulnerability of the line (which passes through long stretches of particularly disaffected populace) to sabotage, was given little consideration. To this must be added the opportunities for high-placed state personnel for private gain in contract awards of this magnitude. The contractors, as Verhaegen notes, have no interest in the profitability of the scheme; the terms of the contract are their sole preoccupation. A venture so vast inevitably attracts rival bidders from several countries; the respective embassies are ineluctably drawn into the contest in promoting the cause of their fellow nationals. In this dangerous dialectic, the unrepresented interest is the long-term well-being of Zairian society, and for that matter of the state itself.

The direct investment that did occur during the early 1970s brought little benefit to Zaire. The cluster of small plants, mainly in the Kinshasa area, was hard-hit by the crisis. The Gulf offshore oil concession, which began operation in 1975, permitted the company to retain 90 percent of the profits for the first five years of exploitation in order to recover its capital; as the oil pool in question is not very large, this exceedingly generous provision meant that Zaire derived little benefit from its entry into the ranks of petroleum producers during its hours of agony in the late 1970s.[119] The most important direct investment, the *Société Minière du Tenge-Fungurume*,[120] gained access to an exceptionally rich set of copper deposits in 1970. After $250 million was sunk into the project, it was mothballed in 1976 before reaching real production because of the poor prospects for copper prices.

The cumulative impact of the loan-contract-technology sale pattern that predominated in the Zairian connection to external capital was disastrous. The fall in the copper price in 1974, linked to the domestic economic dislocations noted below, brought about the virtual bankruptcy of the state in 1975. Since then, a series of debt reschedulings and improvisations have averted formal default, but the future of Zaire is mortgaged for many years. The external debt by 1980 exceeded $6 billion, well in excess of the GDP, and arears totaled $1.1 billion at the end of 1979.[121]

The promotion of national capitalism was equally damaging. This developed only gradually in the first years of the regime, largely through the profitable opportunities offered to politically connected Zairians to serve as directors of the parastatal enterprises that succeeded some of the colonial corporations. More generally, the translation of political power into allied private enterprise and the constitution of personal fortunes by illicit means began to be widely visible by about 1970.

But the massive thrust came on 30 November 1973, when President Mobutu announced a sweeping set of measures that were justified as a giant step toward economic independence. "Plantations, ranches, and commerce" were to be completely Zairianized, although there was no initial definition of the scope of these concepts. In contrast to the 1972 Nigerian indigenization decrees, which may have served as partial stimulus, little thought had been given to implementation. The measures, clearly inspired both by the undoubted nationalism of the regime and the desire to permit the politico-mercantile ruling class to become national capitalists as well, were conceived by Mobutu alone. Through the successive improvisations that ensued, three facts became clear. First, the businesses covered by the measure, which cut a huge swath through the economy, were to be distributed as patrimonial benefice to the political class, beginning with the president himself, who constituted an imposing agrarian empire, *Cultures et Elévages du Zaire* (CELZA), from expropriated plantations. Second, there was no real provision for compensation, either by the Zairian beneficiaries or by the state. Third, many of the Zairianized businesses were clearly headed for swift bankruptcy, either because the Zairian acquirers simply stripped their assets and abandoned them or because they lacked the business experience, commercial contacts, and access to capital resources to sustain them. There was, in short order, a serious dislocation of the commercial and plantation sectors of the economy and a wave of popular resentment at the sordid nature of this class action by the political bourgeoisie. To add insult to injury, the copper price break occurred in April 1974, when the negative consequences of these measures were just beginning to make themselves felt.

Faced with the manifest failure of this adventure, Mobutu chose to force the pace. On 30 December 1974, the president announced an even more sweeping set of measures, billed as the "radicalization of the Zairian revolution." The larger of the businesses were to be placed in the hands of the state, whose domain was further enlarged by the expropriation of a further set of enterprises that encompassed much of what remained of the colonial capitalist sector. The political class entered the scene on this occasion as nominated "delegates-general" to manage the newly parastatalized undertakings. The new measures were accompanied by ferociously radical rhetoric; Mobutu "declared war" on the bourgeoisie. Peace soon returned on the class war front; the principal consequence of the radicalization measures was to project the fiasco of the 30 November program upon a larger canvas.[122]

The economic crisis Zaire faced by late 1975 greatly increased the leverage of external capital interests affected by the Zairianization program, as well as Western governments. Among the conditions for the series of last-minute reprieves granted Zaire from full default was abandonment of the "radicalized revolution." Some of the beneficiaries were able to keep their newly acquired properties; indeed, a few had managed them well. But most were forced to surrender them to any former owners who were disposed to return to the country. By this time, the Mobutu regime itself was at bay, hounded by its creditors, reviled by much of its populace, diplomatically isolated on the African scene by its ill-judged Angolan adventure in partnership with the United States and South Africa, convulsed by hyperinflation and a rapid decline in mass well-being.

To a number of observers the Zaire case is a clear example of the inevitable contradictions of capitalism and of the bankruptcy of the Western economic system in its third-world relations.[123] In its extreme form, implying conspiratorial intent on the part of international capitalism to enserf Zaire, this argument may fall prey to what one writer termed an "anthropomorphic tendency to ascribe cunning and foresight to large abstractions such as world imperialism or late capitalism."[124] Indeed, the perversely interventionist policies of the Mobutist state could, from a different point of view, be charged with denying capitalism its essential regulative mechanism of the market. A *Wall Street Journal* reporter in 1980 made the engaging argument that the Afro-Marxist capital of Brazzaville, across the river from Kinshasa, operated like a market economy while the economic atmosphere in Zaire felt more like the stereotypical East European Marxist-Leninist model.[125] Or, put another way, it might be suggested that the peculiar configuration of power and perspective in Mobutist

Zaire led all participants in capital transactions—bankers and foreign purveyors of goods, construction services, management skills, and technology, on the one hand, and the dominant political personnel of the state apparatus, on the other—to ensure that profits accrued at the point of the exchange, with the costs and risks transferred to Zairian society by way of mortgage against the future. This phenomenon occurred not through imperial machinations but rather through the situational calculations of actors who all shared a lack of confidence in the long-run stability of the Zairian polity. No one, in the early 1970s, even dimly foresaw the dimensions of the tragedy that lay ahead; indeed, many truly believed they were doing the lord's work, laying the groundwork for the development of the natural riches of the country.

There is yet another aspect that merits reflection. In a forthright speech in November 1977, Mobutu denounced what he termed the "mal zairois," a corrosive venality that had penetrated the entire fabric of the state. The implausible scope and diversity of corruption in Zairian public life has been extensively documented. Gould devotes an entire book to catalogue its variant forms.[126] The archbishop of Lubumbashi inventoried its evils in 1976 in an anguished pastoral letter.[127] One may suggest that the *enrichissez-vous* private ethic, which is the propelling force for capitalism, if unrestrained by a public-regarding ethic within the state domain itself, carries the risk of a cancerous perversion of the polity. A Zairian scholar, Mwabila Malela, in a thoughtful commentary on the radicalization measures, suggested that in the Western world the potential for abuse in capitalism was circumscribed by the Judeo-Christian ethic of the society at large.[128] In China, he continued, the seeds of Stalinist despotism embedded in Communism are restrained by the persistence of the Confucian ethic. Zaire, in contrast, was seeking to chart a course without a societal ethic; one urgently needed to be rediscovered within the cultural heritage of the country, whatever its future course might be.

There are thus important hazards in the capitalist option that go beyond the growth versus equality and dependency versus self-reliance trade-offs visible in the Ivory Coast and Kenya cases. It is probably true that no Afro-Marxist or populist socialist state has experienced corruption on a Zairian (or even Nigerian) scale; the doctrines of egalitarianism that are so central to these ideologies appear to inhibit extreme venality. At the same time, the much greater probity of the state in Ivory Coast and Kenya argues that this form of perversion is not an ineluctable concomitant of the capitalist path in Africa.

5

African Ideological Preference and Great Power Relations

> As the class struggle intensifies, ideological demarcation in the independent African states deepens. Right-wing political forces often gravitate towards pro-imperialist positions, while the Left forces come closer to scientific socialism. The spread and entrenchment of the socialist world outlook in Africa undoubtedly mark the beginning of a new, higher stage in the development of the African revolution.
>
> Anatoly Gromyko, 1979[1]

IDEOLOGY AND THE EXTERNAL ARENA

We now shift our scrutiny to the international implications of the ideology–policy nexus in African development. A simple view might expect that those global titans, international communism, led by the Soviet Union, and the world capitalist system, orchestrated by the United States, would each project upon Africa its own opposite visions of the realms of light and darkness. By this logic, the Soviet Union might be expected to provide strong backing for the Afro-Marxist states, while the United States would lavish its affections upon the African capitalist exemplars. At the African end, one might anticipate a reciprocal set of affinities: the scientific socialists should find their natural partnership with the camp of socialism, while Afro-capitalists would find shelter within the constellation of Western political economies. The populist socialist regimes could be expected to oscillate between these poles, perhaps shading their preferences toward the socialist end, in view of their anticapitalist impulses.

In truth, few observers will be surprised that empirical reality diverges rather widely from this schematic view. While the natural affinities created by a commonality of world view are by no means inconsequential, they are crosscut by a number of other determinants of great power and African state international behavior. Reason of state considerations and globally defined geopolitical interests have frequently dictated great power policies in Africa that are at variance with apparent ideological logic. From the African perspective, the practical necessities of economic requirements, as well as overriding nationalist preoccupations, constantly skew external alignments.

What then are the relationships between ideological preference and external ties? In this chapter I shall explore the empirical record of two decades of African international relations in order to locate the key vectors. I shall focus in particular upon those interactions between Africa and the major powers that incarnate the respective realms of communism and capitalism, the Soviet Union and the United States. On the African side, particular but not exclusive stress will be given to the exemplar states considered in the earlier chapters. As a basis for appraising the influence of ideological perspective in conditioning relationships, I shall scrutinize several spheres of interaction: political, military-strategic, economic aid, trade patterns. This inventory of the actual interactions will then permit a more discriminating statement of the ideology–alignment overlap.

PHASES AND THEMES IN SOVIET AND AMERICAN POLICY

Until the 1950s, Africa was an inconsequential diplomatic field for both the Soviet Union and the United States. The approach of independence—and crises such as the Congo affair—extended the terrain of the cold war to Africa, and both powers defined much more activist African policies. The disappointments of independence, the kaleidoscope of coups, and the evanescent character of affinities and orientations led to a parallel diminution of interest on the part of both powers by the middle 1960s. Then, a decade later, two almost simultaneous events, the Portuguese coup of April 1974 and the first army mutinies initiating the creeping coup in Ethiopia, utterly transformed apparently stable patterns in the Horn and southern Africa. A resurgent interest in African affairs was visible in both Washington and Moscow, and each developed a somewhat altered policy perspective. Thus, while I shall focus on relationships over time, it is well to recall that there have been several discrete periods. Particularly intriguing is the parallelism of American and Soviet relations with Africa; each traversed phases of initial disinterest, then sudden activism, followed by receding concern, then brusquely reawakened engagement. By way of prologue, these stages are recapitulated in table 5.1.[2]

However significant the nuances that demarcate one phase from another, there are also overarching themes that span the entire period for both global powers. Table 5.2 suggests a summary overview of the persistent dimensions of Soviet and American policy. Juxtaposed is a corresponding list of policy perspectives that can be said to reflect the mainstream concerns of African diplomacy.

To explore the international dimension, I shall first consider Soviet and American perceptions of African ideological discourse. I shall then examine in succession Soviet and American political, military, and economic (aid, trade, investment) relationships with Africa as functions of African ideological preference. The canvas is then reversed to permit an exploration of the impact of ideology on African choices of great power partnership.

TABLE 5.1. Stages in Soviet and American Relationships with Africa

Period	Soviet policy	American policy
1950s	Stalinism; hostility to African nationalists as "national bourgeoisie" likely to ally with imperialism	Eisenhower and Dulles; paternalistic, NATO-centered posture; support for European allies in "moderate" decolonization
Early 1960s	Khrushchev; backing for "national democracies" led by "revolutionary democrats" seeking "noncapitalist path" to socialism	Kennedy and New Frontier, high hopes for "showcase" states with liberal image; developmentalist orientation
Late 1960s	Brezhnev; disillusionment with "national democracies"; stress on state interests, state-to-state relationships	Johnson; interest in Africa fades before Vietnam preoccupation; steady erosion of aid
Early 1970s	Same as late 1960s	Nixon and Kissinger; "tilt to the whites" in southern Africa; private investment and loans to replace aid
Late 1970s	Renewed interest in southern African liberation; Angola, Ethiopian commitments; satisfaction at spread of "socialist orientation"	Carter and Young; active effort for Zimbabwe-Namibia settlements; seek collaboration with OAU influentials

TABLE 5.2. American, Soviet, and African Foreign Policy Themes

United States	Soviet Union	Africa
Supporting "moderate" regimes	Diplomatic presence	Liberation of southern Africa
Opposing Soviet bloc influence	Counterimperial	Nonalignment
Modest levels of economic aid	Counter-Chinese	African dignity, opposition to racism
Encourage Western investment	Back liberation movements	
"Peaceful change" in southern Africa	Active military supply	Inter-African concert
Sporadic military/strategic interest	Modest aid focused on public sector	Economic independence, development
Access to resources	Favor noncapitalist development; littoral military facilities	New International Economic Order

SOVIET AND AMERICAN IMAGES OF AFRICAN IDEOLOGY

How, then, is the changing nature of ideological discourse viewed by the Soviet Union? As the Stalinist anathema toward third-world "national bourgeois" leaders softened, Soviet analysts began to take an interest in the radical regimes of the independence era. By 1960, a new theory of "national democracy" was unveiled that took cognizance of third-world situations where radical anti-imperialist, though not Marxist-Leninist, leadership seized power. While "national democracies" were ruled by bourgeois elements and lacked a proletarian social base, they were not tied to capitalism or imperialism; even better, they were hostile to domestic capitalism and international imperialism. "Revolutionary democrats" who led these states could, with adequate support from the increasingly powerful camp of socialism, create the conditions for the eventual construction of socialism while bypassing the capitalist stage. In Africa, the concept came to apply to Ghana (1961–66), Guinea, Mali, Algeria, and Egypt. However, the premature demise of several "revolutionary democrats" (Nkrumah, Ben Bella, Keita) and the economic misadventures they encountered momentarily discredited the national democracy concept in the late 1960s.

In the 1970s, the concept of the noncapitalist pathway was revived as the emergence of the Afro-Marxist state attracted Soviet interest. This option could be chosen by progressive elements of the petty bourgeoisie, which, according to Ulianovsky, "has grown, as a rule, faster than the ranks of the proletariat. In its majority it lacks the basic sources of accumulating capital, it is patriotically minded and it is a motive force of the anti-imperialist struggle. Together with the peasantry and the semi-proletariat, this section is the main force from which revolutionary democracy springs and by which it is supported."[3] The weakness of the proletariat devolves a special mandate of transitional leadership upon this noncapitalist petty bourgeoisie of intellectuals and military officers. The relative weakness of the domestic bourgeoisie provides a zone of autonomy for the state, "which has an extensive area for economic manoeuvre."[4] A noncapitalist pathway is not to be confused with socialism; even those countries that officially endorse Marxism-Leninism as state doctrine are not Communist, in the Soviet view. This is rather a transitional stage, preparing the ground for eventual construction of socialism; "it is impossible to build a socialist society in countries with age-old backwardness in the shortest period of time."[5] Rather, writes another analyst, noncapitalist development "leads to transitional conditions in all major spheres of social life, which, when the anti-imperialist and democratic problems are solved consistently, will be invariably directed against capitalism and will open up the way for a socialist revolution."[6]

By the late 1970s, Soviet analysts took due note of the appearance of the Afro-Marxist state. Revolutionary democracy is now portrayed as having emerged in two stages. "Revolutionary democratic thought in Africa," writes Kosukhin; "stemmed from the national liberation movement, from the search for a way of development undertaken by the countries which freed themselves from colonialism. It was the result of the active influence of the broad masses . . . who reject capitalism and regard it as being connected with colonialism in all its forms, old and new."[7] Revolutionary democratic ideology then went into "temporary retreat" in the late 1960s, but was resurgent in a second stage "characterised by an acceleration of the progressive evolution of the ideology, and by the emergence of new states whose leaders are convinced of the need to endorse the socialist alternative. At this stage revolutionary democracy comes closer to scientific socialism, and in a number of countries Marxism-Leninism is officially proclaimed the ideological basis of the party and the state."[8]

However, Soviet analysis is careful not to accept at face value a regime's self-designation as Marxist-Leninist. Although

Gromyko notes that five countries have opted for scientific socialism (Angola, Mozambique, Benin, Congo, and Ethiopia; Somalia, Madagascar, and São Tomé are omitted from the list), he adds in the same breath that "in these and some other countries, despite numerous difficulties, revolutionary democracy is coming closer and closer to the ideology of Marxism-Leninism."[9] Thus an official declaration by a regime for Marxist-Leninist doctrine suffices to establish its proximity to the portals of scientific socialism but does not force entry. Even more striking, Soviet analysis does not sharply distinguish the Afro-Marxist state from some of the populist socialist states; the crucial category is that of "socialist-oriented countries," which in addition to those listed above includes Algeria, Guinea, Tanzania, and, some say, Libya.

Furthermore, there is a marked sense of the vagaries and volatility of "revolutionary democracy." According to Kosukhin,

inside the revolutionary-democratic movement there is a trend whose representatives (owing to petty-bourgeois, religious-nationalist and other deep-rooted beliefs, to imperialist pressure and other factors) show inconsistency, vacillations in regard to scientific socialism, to worldwide experience in socialist construction. Some factions of revolutionary democracy do not go beyond the framework of petty-bourgeois relations in their socio-economic reforms.

. . . the wavering of some revolutionary-democratic leaders leads to their slipping into Right nationalist and even chauvinist positions. In such cases we see a political degeneration of revolutionary democrats who have actually become bourgeois nationalists and no longer express the interests of broad sections of the radical petty bourgeoisie and the working masses. . . .[10]

To combat these contradictions, revolutionary democracy must urgently create vanguard, Leninist parties. This process has occurred only in the recent, second stage of revolutionary democracy. Through openly embracing Marxism-Leninism and "democratic centralism" as its operating mode, the ruling party, in Kosukhin's words, "is marked by a greater degree of class distinctiveness, by the ideological unity of its steering core; the views of the Left Marxist wing of revolutionary democracy thus take deeper roots in the party."[11] At the same time, Kosukhin warns, "by their social composition they are to a considerable extent parties of the revolutionary intelligentsia. The traditionally tribal and petty-bourgeois illusions of the working class, the peasantry and in no small measure the intelligentsia make it difficult for these parties to become a veritable revolutionary proletarian force. . . ."[12]

States of "socialist orientation" face both the vagaries of the social content of ruling socialist parties and the evanescence of power in Africa. Not only may "revolutionary democrat" incumbents stray from their path, but they are subject to sudden overthrow. An authoritative East German commentary states this point:

because of the weaker social base, the inconsistencies . . . in the thinking and behavior of predominantly petty bourgeois-peasant forces of leadership, the lack of experience and cadres, and not least of all on account of the strong economic positions and the ideological influence over which imperialism continues to dispose in these countries, the development of the countries with a socialist orientation is by no means irreversible. Changes—conceivably of a precipitous nature—are possible.[13]

Thus, in sum, the spread of a socialist orientation is a powerfully positive trend. Credence is given some, but not all, of the Afro-Marxist states for their efforts to approximate Marxist-Leninist ideology and political structure. However, none of these states is Communist, and all contain contradictions that render them susceptible to "changes of a precipitous nature."

The perils of the precipitous change have likewise haunted American policy, though evidently with a different perspective on which convulsions were most distasteful. As premise of departure, there has been an anxious concern over ideologies that appear proximate to Soviet Communism. The United States role in Africa first achieved significance during the most intense period of the cold war, and both the Dulles and Rusk variants of

African diplomacy were pervaded by an evangelical determination to confront international communism on every battlefield. Although this passion greatly diminished over time, the underlying counter-Soviet theme in American policy has influenced perceptions of African ideology. Indeed, in the late 1970s much policy debate hinged upon what priority should be accorded to counter-Soviet considerations. A school of "globalists," incarnated by Carter National Security Adviser Zbigniew Brzezinski and erstwhile Secretary of State Henry Kissinger, tended to situate most world events within the context of the overall world encounter of West and East; regional developments were seen as theaters of struggle whose outcomes require interpretation within a broader frame. Kissinger, from this perspective, viewed the rise of Afro-Marxism with dismay. "Regionalists," on the other hand, view African developments as primarily shaped by indigenous forces and factors. They stress the specificity of particular situations and the essentially African and nationalist character of the diverse strands of socialist thought in Africa. Former United Nations Ambassador Andrew Young, his successor Donald McHenry, and ex-Assistant Secretary of State for African Affairs Richard Moose were consistent regionalists.[14] In practice, policy perspective and ideological assessments have been the uneasy product of the oscillating strength of these two perspectives, buffeted by the unfolding dynamic of events.

There is no precise analogy to the "national democracy" debate in American official perspectives on African ideologies. At any given point in time, there has been a diversity of views on the significance of ideology in Africa and the meanings to be attached to it. The value attached to the "pragmatic" cast of mind, lightly tinged with cynicism concerning political rhetoric, induces an initial skepticism toward ideological categorization of regimes and leaders. These caveats notwithstanding, there are some observations that can be made concerning perceptions of ideological pathways by the United States policy community.

The first wave of populist socialist regimes aroused much

greater apprehensions by their Soviet affinities than they did by actually pursuing internal policies in the name of socialism. Secretary of State Christian Herter publicly complained in September 1960 that Ghana was moving toward the Soviet bloc largely because of Nkrumah's external policies; there was no comparable murmur of disapproval in 1961 in the wake of Nkrumah's socialist measures. The difficult and often poor relations with Nasser's Egypt and Algeria as well had little to do with internal land reforms or nationalizations, but rather focused upon the radical anti-imperialism of their foreign policies and—especially in the Nasser case—the intimacy of the Soviet military connection. Conversely, when socialist Guinea came into momentary conflict with the Soviet Union, a major aid program was swiftly mounted, undeterred by the Bettelheim-designed development plan. The relatively large amounts of aid supplied over the years to populist socialist Tanzania is another case in point. Socialist or not, Tanzania evoked admiration within a significant segment of the policy community; the benign malady of Tanzaphilia was by no means exclusive to academe.

African socialism in the early 1960s contained little doctrine that was hostile to the premises of the market economy. Indeed, an American liberal economist participated in the drafting of the authoritative Kenyan doctrine relating "African Socialism" to planning and policy choice. Further, socialist regimes of diverse hues were quite receptive to major American capital involvement in natural resource projects: Nkrumah signed the Volta River deal with Kaiser after the April 1961 Dawn Broadcast; Olin Mathiesen and Harvey Aluminum were generally unscathed in the socialist oscillations of Sékou Touré; Gulf Oil collaborated amicably with the Marxist-Leninist regime in Angola, which remained unrecognized by the United States government.

This is not to say that the socialist option encounters no skeptical commentary. The most mordant assault upon the wisdom of the socialist strategy has come from Elliot Berg, who castigated the West African version of socialism as the application of the wrong idea at the wrong time in the wrong place.[15] The imposing economic growth of Kenya and Ivory Coast (though not of course the calamity of capitalist Zaire) were often advanced as solid evidence of the superior performance of the market-based economy.

In 1975, when the Afro-Marxist option appeared to be surging through the continent, there was a moment of anxious concern, particularly in the geopolitical camp. Kissinger solemnly warned of the grave dangers of a cancerous spread of Marxism in the third world, though the malignancy perceived had more to do with Western interests than with a conviction that such regimes inevitably must fail internally.

The wave of Marxist-Leninist conversions then subsided, as did the hegemony of the globalist perspective. By 1979, Undersecretary of State David Newsom, called upon to testify before the House Foreign Affairs Africa Subcommittee on "communism in Africa," was careful to downplay the significance of Afro-Marxism:

When we speak of Communism in Africa, we are speaking almost exclusively of the role of the Soviet Union, the Eastern European countries under Soviet domination, Cuba, and, to a much lesser extent, China.

A few African governments—Mozambique, Angola, Benin, Congo, Ethiopia—describe their policies or ruling parties as Marxist-Leninist or scientific socialist but their policies are mixed and do not follow any rigid Soviet model. Even in Ethiopia there is evidence of a resistance on the part of the leadership to the total adoption of the Marxist-Leninist pattern of internal policies and organization.[16]

THE POLITICAL CONNECTION

Have political relationships followed ideological lines? To some extent they clearly have. With the exceptions of Somalia since the 1977 rupture and Madagascar, the Soviets have a large and active political presence in the Afro-Marxist capitals. The "Leninist core" of the state is the object of particular support. The construction of a vanguard party, the state communications apparatus, and the organs of state security are spheres in which the Soviets are prepared to offer their experience and counsel. Indeed, the military Marxist-Leninists are ceaselessly exhorted by the Soviets to proceed with demilitarization of power through a Leninist party; interestingly, in both Somalia and Ethiopia more than half a decade elapsed between the first affirmation of scientific socialist doctrine and the convening, at Soviet urging, of an organizational congress for a Leninist official party (1976 in Somalia, 1980 in Ethiopia). Cuban and East German partners have offered important help with the Leninist core; the East Germans have specialized in fashioning state security agencies.

Only the Afro-Marxist states have accepted the Leninist model for a ruling party. This form of Soviet relationship is not visible in the instance of the mass parties of the populist socialist states. Even in Egypt, where for a time in the late 1960s the Soviet presence was pervasive, the relationship hinged much more heavily upon military linkages.

The most significant case of an important political relationship spanning ideological lines is the flowering of Soviet–Nigerian relationships during the civil war. In the first years of independence, Nigeria was exceedingly suspicious of Soviet activity in Africa; not till 1962 were formal diplomatic ties even established. Soviet Nigerian analysts, in the First Republic years, had developed a curious ethnoideological analysis of the bitter regional conflicts that dominated the political scene. The NCNC, whose ethnic base lay in Iboland, was viewed as the most progressive (an intriguing mirror image of Western stereotypes of the adaptable, achievement-oriented Ibo). The AG, with its Yoruba base, was seen as a compradore bourgeoisie formation, while the NPC was viewed as feudal. Some nimble reinterpretation of the data, when the civil war broke out, found the progressive Ibo undergoing metamorphosis into a reactionary national bourgeoisie, while the compradores and feudalists were discovered to contain unsuspected progressive features.[17] The arms aid and diplomatic support provided in the hour of greatest need, when the West was ambivalent, laid the foundation for an enduring relationship that, while not intimate, was nonetheless quite solid.

The truly special relationship is symbolized by a special treaty of friendship and cooperation. To date, these agreements have been signed only with Egypt (1972), Somalia (1974), Mozambique (1977), Angola (1977), Ethiopia (1978), and Congo (1981). Egypt and Somalia have since abrogated their treaties.

The intense levels of Sino-Soviet hostility introduce the Chinese factor as a significant vector in Soviet political relationships in Africa. The counter-Chinese theme in Soviet policy at times rivals the counter-Western dimension. The development of a major Chinese diplomatic presence in a given capital is an irritant for Moscow, irrespective of the ideological orientation of the country concerned.

On the American side, several factors seem to be at play in governing the relative closeness of political ties. Ideological affinity has certainly been one: relations over time have been generally closer with "moderate" than with "radical" regimes. Liberia and prerevolution Ethiopia had special status, partly as countries with no former metropole. The United States' deep involvement in Zairian affairs since 1960, which was partly a consequence of the crisis that accompanied independence, transformed the country into a cold war battleground. There was almost certainly no other African country in which the Central Intelligence Agency was so heavily involved.[18] In the Carter era, a special effort was deployed toward states such as Nigeria and Tanzania, which enjoyed a leadership role within the African concert of nations. In the Kissinger years of intensely personal diplomacy, a ramifying matrix of special links was created with Egypt, built initially on the intimacy of the relationship between Sadat and Kissinger.

With the exception of Zaire, Tunisia, and Morocco, United States links with the francophonic states have generally been less close, a fact not unrelated to the pervasiveness of the French connection with these states. Thus, the United States has been a quite secondary partner to the beacon of African capitalism, Ivory Coast. The American disposition to defer to France has been set aside primarily in cases where France was unable to sustain a privileged relationship—as in Guinea or Tunisia.

Particularly in the Kissinger period, ties with a number of the more radical states became badly frayed. Relations with Congo-Brazzaville were severed in 1965 and not resumed until 1978. The ambassadorial post in Benin fell vacant after the declaration for Marxism-Leninism, and relations remained downgraded to the chargé level in 1979. Angola had not yet been recognized by the United States·in 1981, while only quite minimal linkages existed with Mozambique, Ethiopia, and Libya (the latter severed in 1981).

In the late 1970s, some quiet efforts were made to cultivate effective relations with some of the radical states. A senior diplomat was named as ambassador to Brazzaville, while discreet but successful efforts were made to overcome the initial suspicions of Guinea-Bissau and Cape Verde. These moves, patiently lobbied by the "regionalist" cohort within the diplomatic establishment, had their limits: repeated Angolan overtures for normal relations met no response.

THE MILITARY SPHERE

In the military sphere, Soviet activity has been particularly striking. By the 1970s, the USSR was the major purveyor of heavy equipment in Africa. Most equipment transfers were on a commercial basis, though terms were frequently easy and delivery swifter than for Western suppliers.[19] However spotty the reputation of Soviet civil merchandise, no one doubted the quality of the tanks, missiles, and aircraft available from Moscow. In recent years, the Soviets have increasingly demanded hard currency for their arms; the CIA estimates that 10 percent of Soviet hard cur-

TABLE 5.3. Soviet, East European, and Cuban Military
Technicians in Africa, 1978

Country	Soviet Union and Eastern Europe	Cu
Algeria	1,000	1,
Libya	1,750	200
Morocco	10	
Angola	1,300	19,000
Equatorial Guinea	40	150
Guinea	100	200
Guinea-Bissau	65	140
Mali	180	
Mozambique	230	800
Other	500	485

NOTE: Over 60 Soviet military personnel were reported expelled from Nigeria in August 1979.
SOURCE: Central Intelligence Agency, *Communist Aid in Non-Communist Less Developed Countries 1978*, ER 79-10412U, September 1979, p. 4.

rency earnings came from arms sales by 1978.[20] Recent examples are the $100 million sale of MIG 21s to Zambia in 1980 and the $2 billion arms relationship with Libya that began in 1974.

The list of Soviet arms clients tilted toward the populist socialist and Afro-Marxist states, but included ambiguously socialist Zambia and capitalist Nigeria, as well as the unclassifiable Uganda of Idi Amin. In 1978, half of the two dozen African states with combat aircraft had purchased Soviet planes: Algeria, Egypt, Libya, Sudan, Congo-Brazzaville, Ethiopia, Nigeria, Somalia, Uganda, Mozambique, Guinea, and Mali.[21] Complex equipment requires Soviet logistical support and ensures entry to the armed forces through training programs.

There is a striking reluctance on the part of even the Afro-Marxist states to meet Soviet desires for littoral naval and air facilities. Soviet needs for base and access rights stemmed from concerns of strategic significance: support positions for its Middle Eastern policy; bunkering, especially in the Mediterranean and Indian Ocean, for its global fleet deployment;[22] overflight and similar transit facilities for rapid deployment of equipment to potential crisis zones; and air base access for aerial surveillance of sea routes, especially for the detection of Polaris submarines. For the most part, much more than mere ideological affinity has been involved in cases where various forms of military use rights have been granted; usually, in these instances, the Soviets also served as active partner in the defense of the host country against external or internal foes.

Egypt was the first country to accord significant facilities. Though its ties with the Soviet bloc dated from the Czech arms deal of 1955 and the Soviet pledge of 1958 to build the Aswan Dam, a really comprehensive military relationship emerged only after the calamitous defeat of the Egyptian army in the June 1967 war—at a time when the Nasserian moment of socialist enthusiasm on the social and economic fronts had already passed its peak. There had been only five hundred Soviet military advisers before the 1967 war, but in the months that followed the number multiplied to several thousand. Nasser, in desperate straits, badly needed massive Soviet aid to rebuild his shattered armed forces. It was at this juncture that he granted the Soviet request for full and automatic access to Egyptian naval ports; the request had been rejected in 1964 and 1965 when extensive arms supply accords and economic aid protocols were negotiated. A secret five-year agreement providing full naval base rights as well as airfield facilities was signed in April 1968.[23] In 1969–70, the Soviet position was momentarily further entrenched when Egypt had to call upon Soviet missile crews to force an end to the Israeli bombing raids deep in Egypt that accompanied the "war of attrition." This leverage soon vanished when Sadat chose a different strategic route for the defense of Egyptian interests (and gradually reverted to a liberal-market economy); in July 1972, Sadat abruptly terminated the mission of the Soviet military advisory group, which was cut overnight from some fifteen or twenty thousand to about one thousand. The base rights themselves were withdrawn in 1976, when Sadat completed the expulsion of Soviet personnel and denounced the friendship and cooperation treaty of 1971.[24]

Somali cession to the Soviets of a naval and air base complex at Berbera (Somalia) in the early 1970s was likewise motivated more by the Somalia–Ethiopia territorial dispute than by Marxism-Leninism as regime doctrine. These rights were annulled in 1978, when Soviet–Cuban intervention on the Ethiopian side turned the tide against the Somalis in the Ogaden. De facto Soviet air and naval base rights were a corollary of the large-scale military backing, in collaboration with Cuba, provided to the MPLA regime in Angola in 1975 and to Ethiopia in 1978.

Transit facilities have at times been made available to the Soviets by Congo-Brazzaville and Mali in connection with southern African liberation movement support operations. Also, Guinea granted air base rights near Conakry in the 1970s. These facilities were used primarily for maritime surveillance. In this instance, the ideological shift away from populist socialism by Touré in 1978 does appear to be correlated with the cancellation of these rights.

An intriguing ideological gloss was placed upon the military connection in a Soviet commentary of 1973:

The advantage of the army as against political parties is obvious if one compares the sources for financing the parties, which are limited and not always reliable, with the resources allocated to maintaining the army. . . . The army is a state organization, which receives the funds for its support entirely from the state budget. It does not need to worry about the business situation in the country, nor about the financial power of the bourgeoisie. . . . In other words, as distinct from political parties, the army . . . is an institution paid for not by any one or other class grouping, but by the whole nation. . . . It also differs from plain civilian institutions in that the character of its hierarchy and of its discipline is incomparably more rigorous. This has meant that a politically active officer corps has been able with great success to use the army for its own political aims.[25]

American military relationships with Africa have been far less significant than those of the Soviet Union. Military aid to Africa, never very large, dwindled to inconsequential levels by the 1970s. From 1950 to 1967, military aid to the continent totaled $227 million. Ethiopia was by far the largest recipient. By 1968, the continental total was only $25 million.[26] Such defense-related aid programs as the "security supporting assistance" had little impact in Africa: the continent received from 1 to 5 percent of total outlays in this category from 1976 to 1979.[27]

Several determinants explain patterns of American military relationships with Africa. Certainly ideology plays an important part; programs are concentrated among the moderate, market-economy states. Conversely, radical states stand out for their absence from the list.[28] This nonappearance can be understood both in terms of American reluctance to collaborate in the security field with such states and of the ready access these countries have to Soviet supply. No doubt at least as important is the fear and suspicion such states have of permitting the United States access to their security establishments, thereby creating a potential Trojan horse for imperialism.

Moderation alone, however, does not explain all the variance. Some patterns are explicable in terms of de facto compensation for base rights; Morocco, Libya (before Qadafy), and Ethiopia (before Mengistu) certainly pried significant sums of both military assistance and economic aid in return for the granting of military facilities. This consideration disappeared from the picture in the 1970s, only to suddenly reappear in the post-Afghanistan scramble for military support points to ensure the security of the Middle East oil fields.

In the two African states that had no metropole (Liberia and Ethiopia), the United States played a major tutelary role in nurturing the armed forces. Analogous military support was provided to Zaire, in collaboration with Belgium. The Egyptian and, to a lesser extent, the Sudan linkages are explicable in terms of the proximity of these two countries both to the Middle East crisis zone and to heavily Soviet-supplied neighbors. The training programs and—in the Moroccan case—heavy equipment sales are partly stimulated by the magnitude of Soviet supply to Algeria and Libya.

Conversely, the very restricted military relationships with a number of moderate states reflect a tacit division of labor with the former colonial powers. This premise, a policy constant since the 1960s, was succinctly stated with relation to economic ties by then Assistant Secretary of State for African Affairs David Newsom in 1973; it applies with equal force to the military realm:

The United States does not desire—even if it had the capabilities and resources to do so—to replace the former colonial powers in trade and economic relations with African nations. . . . We continue to believe, however, that the traditional ties of language, education and business that link these nations with the metropole nations in Europe are important to both partners.[29]

Particularly in former French and British colonies, the armed forces grew out of imperial constabularies, with the first generation officer corps enjoying intimate relationships with the metropolitan military institutions. These initial arrangements, barring some disruption in overall relations, are characterized by strong inertia.

ECONOMIC AID

In the field of economic aid, the Soviet effort is remarkably parsimonious. Even the Afro-Marxist states have been treated to the skimpiest of servings. A sudden upsurge of total economic commitments to the third world—from $875 million in 1977 to $3.7 billion in 1978—is misleading because more than half of this sum went to a gigantic $2 billion phosphate development in Morocco. In the late 1970s, there was increasingly open discontent

TABLE 5.4. United States Military Assistance to Africa, 1950–78

($ thousands)*

Country	FY 1950–FY 1968	FY 1969	FY 1970	FY 1971	FY 1972	FY 1973	FY 1974	FY 1975	FY 1976	FY 1977	FY 1978
Libya	12,624										
Morocco	28,300	1,294				7					
Tunisia	23,331	2,713	2,666	4,768	1,494	1,792	1,603	1,822	228	31	20
Benin	55										
Cameroon	239										
Ethiopia	113,133	10,312	9,307	10,497	9,421	8,796	10,208	11,431	3,354	1,680	
Guinea	810										
Ivory Coast	54										
Liberia	4,318	237	226	274	111	107	13	4		3	
Mali	1,865										
Niger	52										
Senegal	2,646										
Upper Volta	57										
Zaire	19,031	2,027	1,318	27							

*Excludes training.
SOURCE: Department of Defense, Foreign Military Sales and Military Assistance Facts, December 1978, pp. 17–18.

across the ideological spectrum with both the scope and quality of Soviet economic assistance.

Table 5.5 reveals that a Marxist-Leninist option is by no means a certain cue triggering a flow of Soviet and East European aid. While Mozambique, Angola, and Ethiopia have significant numbers of Communist economic technicians augmenting the military support received, there is not the remotest resemblance to the $2–$3 billion of aid supplied annually to Cuba. Indeed, Ethiopia's Afro-Marxist regime was still drawing on credits extended as far back as 1959 to the imperial government of Haile Selassie. Madagascar, Benin, and Congo-Brazzaville in particular received inconsequential levels of aid. The biggest concentration of Soviet bloc technicians was in Libya (mostly Bulgarians) and Algeria, in connection with large public sector contracts rather than with aid per se. Further limiting the impact of Soviet aid are the widespread complaints about the quality and congeniality of the contingent of Soviet technicians. Usually housed in compounds, where internal surveillance can be maintained, Soviet technicians often have limited command of the working languages of the host countries and have restricted social interactions. For different reasons, this negative appraisal does not extend to the Chinese and Cuban personnel: the former, though self-secluded, are admired for their personal austerity, while the latter are far more convivial and socially attuned to the African environment.

Sheer financing difficulties play an important part in constraining the scale of Soviet economic aid.[30] The local costs of the technical assistance contingent must somehow be paid without debiting Soviet foreign exchange reserves. The sale of Soviet goods on local markets to raise these funds has often proved difficult, given the consumer resistance to many Soviet products.

Other factors besides "revolutionary democratic" commitment by the recipients clearly enters the calculus. In maintaining a near-universal diplomatic presence, the Soviets are automatically under pressure, even from nonsocialist states, to match the (inadequate) levels of Western aid. The counter-Chinese reflex also comes into play; in sub-Saharan Africa, Chinese credits and grants from 1954 to 1978 were more than twice as great as those of the Soviets, and they led to the building of such prestigious showcases as the Tazara railway from Dar es Salaam to the Zambian copperbelt. This challenge cannot go unanswered.

The emergent Soviet need for access to African resources is becoming a more tangible factor. The $2 billion Moroccan phosphate deal is only the most spectacular example. The thirty-year loan to Guinea in 1973 was evidently dictated by Soviet resource needs (bauxite, in this instance). A number of small economic aid agreements have been made with littoral states as leverage to obtain concessions for fishing rights for the giant Soviet trawler-factory fleets.

Whatever the ideology of the host country, Soviet aid is generally tied to public sector projects. No doubt this aid is partly justified in Soviet eyes by the thought that even African capitalists are thereby induced to build socialism in spite of themselves. The giant Soviet iron and steel project in Nigeria falls into this category, although the impact of this intended showcase of public sector enterprise has been diluted by the disconcerting tendency of the completion date to remain poised on an ever-receding horizon; the agreement in principle was struck in 1968, the survey accord was signed in 1970, a site agreement was reached in 1976, and a final go-ahead was given in 1977, but inauguration is still well in the future.[31]

If Soviet aid programs have been a general disappointment to most African states, American aid has hardly been characterized by its munificence. From 1946 to 1971, some $2.6 billion of the $37 billion provided to developing nations in loans and grants went to Africa.[32] There was a short-lived surge in the New Frontier days, when African development aid reached $326 million in 1963, a total that permitted Secretary of State Rusk to claim that "On a per capita basis, Africans get a larger share of the combined economic assistance of the United States and

TABLE 5.5. Communist State Economic Credits and Grants to African States, 1954–78

($ millions)

Country	1954–78			1977			1978		
	USSR	Eastern Europe	China	USSR	Eastern Europe	China	USSR	Eastern Europe	China
Algeria	716	524	92						
Mauritania	8	10	87						
Morocco	2,098	170	35				2,000	89	
Tunisia	96	210	97		35	57			
Angola	17	88		6	6		1	76	
Benin	4		44						
Botswana			20						
Cameroon	8		71						
Cape Verde	3	1	2				3		
Central African Republic	3		14						
Chad	5		50						
Congo	28	60	75		3				
Equatorial Guinea	1								
Ethiopia	105	95	102		23			45	
Gabon		2	25					2	
Gambia			17						
Ghana	94	105	42	1					

Kenya	48		18						
Liberia	20		23			23			
Madagascar	90	23	89				6		
Mali			100				1		
Mauritius	5		35						
Mozambique	5	17	60		5	12		2	
Niger	2		52						
Nigeria	7	80							
Rwanda	1		22						
São Tomé			18						
Senegal	8	35	60						
Seychelles			4						4
Sierra Leone	28	6	41						
Somalia	164	240	155						18
Sudan	65		82			62		24	
Tanzania	38	23	362	18				3	
Togo			45						
Upper Volta	6		51						
Zaire			103						
Zambia	9	62	331					12	
Egypt	1,440	890	134		95				

SOURCE: Central Intelligence Agency, Communist Aid Activities in Non-Communist Less Developed Countries 1978, ER 79-10412U, September 1979, pp. 7–10.

Europe than any other area of the world."[33] No sooner was this modest peak reached than it came under challenge: in an ill-conceived effort to develop a widely accepted justification for a long-term aid program, President Kennedy created a study commission headed by Lucius Clay to examine assistance programs for third-world countries. The Clay Commission, narrowly interpreting its mandate to consider aid in terms of "its optimum contribution to strengthening the security of the U.S. and the Free World," concluded that Africa was not situated on the "frontiers of freedom" and had to take a back seat in the face of the "sharp, hard criterion of immediate strategic interests." In devising aid programs for the many sovereignties of balkanized Africa, the United States was trying to do "too much for too many." African states should look to the former colonial masters for their development needs; Africa was "an area where the Western European countries should logically bear most of the necessary aid burden."[34] When one adds to these authoritative sentiments the rising distractions of the Indochina crisis and the fact that aid appropriations had to run the gauntlet of a House committee chaired by the hostile, myopic, and venal Louisiana Congressperson Otto Passman, the steady real decline of African aid that persisted from 1964 until 1976 is easily understood.

Those who supported a continuation of aid experimented with various devices to keep the program alive. In the early 1960s, "development emphasis" countries that were to be showcases of American development assistance were designated; these included Tunisia, Nigeria, Zaire, Liberia, Ethiopia, and the East African Community states. Ambassador Edward Korry headed another commission in 1966 to chart a path through the years of penury. The commission isolated ten countries where "development prospects are best or where there is a special U.S. interest or relationship."[35] Regional cooperation was stressed; in the 1970s, "basic needs" and the "rural poor" entered the AID lexicon. While the African share of aid did increase from 5 percent in 1976 to 10 percent in 1979, the total remained exceedingly small; Israel alone, during these years, received four to five times as much aid as all of Africa—except, by the end of the decade, Egypt, which after Camp David likewise received more than the other fifty countries combined.

By the late 1970s no individual country, with the exception of Egypt, was receiving very much economic assistance. The original "development emphasis" list had long since ceased to stand out. Some countries, such as Gabon and Nigeria, were deemed too wealthy to require aid. Others, such as Amin's Uganda or Equatorial Guinea, had dropped from the aid roster because of the sanguinary character of the regimes (till 1979). About 40 percent of the development assistance total was targeted upon two broad regional programs: the Sahel program, which emerged as a regionally conceived international aid effort at long-term remedy of the disaster conditions experienced in the drought conditions of the early 1970s;[36] and the Southern African program, which was aimed at compensating those who experienced economic damage from the spillover of the liberation struggles. From 1979 on, the situation declined further when Congress failed to enact aid appropriations, leaving funds blocked at the previous year's level. The prospects were even gloomier for the 1980s, as economic aid ranked high on the hit list of Reagan administration budgeteers.

No simple correlation was evident between "moderate states" and aid distribution. While assistance programs were maintained with states that enjoyed historically close ties (Liberia, Zaire), efforts were also made to sustain at least minimal relationships with Afro-Marxist states through the economic assistance medium (Ethiopia, Benin). At the same time, some premium in aid seemed available to states that reduced the proximity of their Soviet ties (Egypt, Somalia, Sudan). Aid patterns also demonstrated some deference to French sensitivities about entitlement to a privileged, if not exclusive, relationship with erstwhile colonies. All of these factors crisscrossed the ideological spectrum and diluted its explanatory power.

TOTAL 5.6. American Development Assistance in Africa

	Total economic assistance ($ millions)		
Country	1978	1979	1946–67
Sahel program			
Cape Verde	10.2	3.5	
Chad	15.4	9.0	7.4
Gambia	1.8	2.5	7.0
Mali	12.7	13.5	18.6
Mauritania	7.6	7.9	3.4
Niger	12.3	9.8	12.9
Senegal	17.2	14.4	27.8
Upper Volta	16.1	13.2	9.6
Southern Africa program			
Angola	0.5		
Botswana	17.9	15.7	5.1
Lesotho	9.0	10.3	2.1
Malawi	0.2	3.9	14.0
Mozambique	6.1	8.2	
Swaziland	13.1	4.6	0.1
Zambia	39.2	15.5	49.2
Other			
Benin	0.8	1.9	10.5
Burundi	1.8	3.9	6.8
Cameroon	12.7	8.1	28.3
Central African Republic	0.8	0.5	4.4
Comoros			
Congo	0.6	0.9	2.1
Djibouti	0.8	1.0	
Ethiopia	7.2	14.9	222.3
Gabon		0.2	7.0
Ghana	10.1	21.0	209.9
Guinea	13.9	8.5	71.4
Guinea-Bissau	4.8	2.9	
Ivory Coast	0.2	0.2	32.8
Kenya	31.4	22.1	59.7
Liberia	5.4	6.8	208.5
Madagascar	1.1	3.6	12.5
Mauritius	0.2	3.5	0.5
Nigeria			207.2

| Country | Total economic assistance ($ millions) | | |
	1978	1979	1946–67
Other			
Rwanda	3.2	5.6	6.1
São Tomé	0.1	0.2	
Seychelles	0.1	0.4	
Sierra Leone	5.1	6.5	36.2
Somalia	16.6	15.9	68.5
Sudan	19.8	40.0	127.4
Tanzania	25.4	20.4	56.4
Togo	2.5	3.7	13.2
Zaire	28.4	27.4	372.8

SOURCES: AID congressional budget submission, FY 1980; Immanuel Wallerstein, "Africa, the United States, and the World Economy: The Historical Bases of American Policy," in *U.S. Policy toward Africa*, ed. Frederick S. Arkhurst (New York: Praeger, 1975), p. 23.

TRADE AND INVESTMENT

A major limiting factor in the Soviet Union's African relationships is the weakness of trade flows. In 1976, only three African states numbered the Soviet Union among their top five trading partners (Egypt, Somalia, and Cameroon). A significant fraction of African exports to the Soviet Union are in payment for arms deliveries (Egypt, Somalia, most recently Ethiopia). Not only was Africa overall a very minor commercial partner for the USSR, but the rate of trade growth there was slower than with any other major region.[37]

Several reasons may be adduced for this slender volume of trade. The Soviet Union does not need most African primary commodities. Soviet planners do not wish to promote coffee or cocoa consumption; tea is the national beverage. Nor do the Sovi-

TABLE 5.7. Overall Soviet Trade with Africa, 1970–76

| | (f.o.b., $ millions) | | | | |
	1970	1973	1974	1975	1976
African exports to the USSR	485	630	830	980	860
Soviet exports to Africa	580	660	840	800	730

SOURCE: United Nations, *Statistical Yearbook*, 1977.

ets want African edible oils, petroleum, or most minerals. Some of these agricultural commodities have been taken in order to foster politically desirable trade relationships (for example, Ghanaian cocoa in the early 1960s) or in payment for weapons (Egyptian cotton, Ethiopian coffee). However, such arrangements do not form the basis for a solid trading partnership.

On the African end, interest in Soviet products (except armaments) is also limited. The merchandise has a probably exaggerated reputation for shoddiness, and Western trademarks for such widely marketed items as bicycles, sewing machines, vehicles, and the like are well established. Given the Soviet penchant for barter arrangements, the difficult in establishing a long enough list of saleable Soviet items singularly complicates the picture. Soviet oil and in a few cases (for example, Algeria) heavy industrial machinery are exceptions, but the days of USSR petroleum exports appear to be drawing to a close.

As noted above, three large commodity deals, motivated by Soviet commercial needs, have been made: Moroccan phosphate, Guinean bauxite, and—with nearly all of the littoral states—fish. The latter, in fact, hardly figures at all in international trade transactions because the accords negotiated authorize the Soviet trawler fleets to simply sweep the coastal waters in return for a tiny fraction of the haul and some assistance to local fisheries. The actual Soviet take is unknown, and many observers believe it far exceeds the agreed levels.[38] The African states have no means of monitoring the activities of the fleets or of patrolling their two-hundred-mile "economic zones" to pre-

TABLE 5.8. American Trade with Africa

| Country or region | ($ millions, f.a.s. value) | | | |
| | 1965 | | 1976 | |
	Exports	Imports	Exports	Imports
World	27,346	21,366	114,997	120,677
Africa	1,224	875	5,206	12,639
South Africa	438	225	1,348	925
Nigeria	74	59	770	4,938
Algeria	21	5	487	2,209
Libya	64	31	277	2,243
Angola	13	48	35	264
Egypt	31	158	810	93
Gabon	5	10	46	190
Ghana	36	59	133	155
Ivory Coast	11	46	64	248
Zaire	70	38	99	189

SOURCE: Gordon Bertolin, "U.S. Economic Interests in Africa: Investment, Trade, and Raw Materials," in *Africa and the United States*, ed. Jennifer Seymour Whitaker (New York: New York University Press, 1978), p. 31. Reprinted by permission.

vent Soviet factory trawlers (and for that matter those of the Japanese and others) from hauling away everything their nets can scoop up. There is a growing sentiment among coastal states, irrespective of ideology, that the offshore waters are being dangerously overfished by the Soviets and others.

American economic relationships with Africa are much more extensive, both in volume and scope. They include not only trade but also investment and lending and resource dependency for a number of rare minerals. In global terms African economic ties with the United States are of less magnitude than those with other world regions, but they have grown rapidly in importance in the last two decades.

On the trade side, the most swiftly expanding components have been oil and natural gas imports from Africa and agricultural exports to the continent. Both of these were inconsequential until the 1970s; the decline of American domestic oil

TABLE 5.9. United States Direct Private Investment in Africa, 1976

| | (Cumulative book value, $ millions) | | |
Country or region	Investment	Earnings on investment	Earnings as % of investment
Total, all areas	137,244	18,843	13.7
Africa, total	4,467	794	17.8
South Africa	1,665	202	12.1
Libya	362	214	59.1
Liberia	348	45	12.9
Nigeria	341	192	56.3
Other	1,750	140	8.0

SOURCE: Gordon Bertolin, "U.S. Economic Interests in Africa: Investment, Trade, and Raw Materials," in *Africa and the United States*, ed. Jennifer Seymour Whitaker (New York: New York University Press, 1978), pp. 24, 27. Reprinted by permission.

production on the one hand and the widespread African crisis of food production on the other have created this exchange dynamic. Other American imports from Africa are largely primary commodities: coffee, cocoa, chrome, cobalt, platinum, industrial diamonds. Exports to Africa—which in the 1970s fell far behind imports—include some industrial and consumer goods and technology.[39]

Investment has been heavily concentrated in the oil and mineral extraction field, which in 1976 accounted for two-thirds of all United States direct investment in Africa. The major exception is South Africa, where American equity, held by over three hundred large corporations, covered a broad industrial front; South Africa in 1976 accounted for 37 percent of all American investment in Africa, with Libya, Liberia, and Nigeria lagging far behind with about 8 percent each. Zaire ($250 million), Gabon ($170 million), and Kenya ($150 million) are other recipients.[40]

Another important and rapidly growing dimension of economic interrelationship is private bank lending. From inconsequential levels in 1970, this form of capital flow took on massive proportions in the 1970s, with huge liquidities available in first

Eurodollar, then petrodollar markets. A major fraction of the earnings of some internationally oriented banks, like the two Rockefeller institutions Chase Manhattan and Citibank, came from overseas transactions, especially LDC (less developed country) lending. The majority of these loans carried some form of guarantee, and the interest rates were higher. The pattern of bank lending appears to favor capitalist-oriented states—leading the ranks of the heavily over-borrowed countries at the end of the 1970s were Zaire, Gabon, and Ivory Coast, with South Africa also a favored bank client. However, populist socialist regimes such as Algeria and Tanzania had borrowed heavily as well. By the 1970s, neither populist socialism nor Afro-Marxism was viewed by the banks as a barrier to lending. Much more important than ideology were such factors as the stability of the regime, the reliability of its pledges, the competence of its management, and assured high value export commodities to "secure" repayment.

An emergent theme in the African–Western economic nexus is the recognition of the dependency of industrial economies on sundry mineral commodities for which Africa is a major supplier. The "limits to growth" literature in the early 1970s had prepared the way for this new awareness, and the traumatic shock of the 1973 Arab oil embargo, reapplied by subsequent OPEC pricing policies, dramatized the phenomenon. While Western consumers could doubtless forego, if need be, the beverage commodities (coffee, cocoa, tea), industry would be crippled by the sudden interruption of such African minerals as manganese (steel hardening; 44 percent of United States imports from Africa in 1975); chromium (stainless steel; 36 percent of American imports from Africa in 1975); cobalt (heat-resistant, high-performance alloys and magnets; 59 percent of American imports in 1975 originated in Africa). Gold, antimony, industrial diamonds, columbium, platinum group, and of course oil are other commodities for which African supply is crucial.[41] Western Europe is dependent on Africa for yet other minerals, such as copper and uranium.

Given the nature of the economic relationships—which, as we have seen, are closely linked on all fronts to African primary commodities—we see that geology has been far more important than ideology in shaping their contours. Investment is more sensitive to political considerations than trade. The great concentration of investment in South Africa is surely attributable to the staunchly capitalist orientation of the state, which is bound to the peculiar combination of a highly industrial economy and a racial oligarchy that sustains an artificially large pool of socially powerless low-wage labor. In the rest of Africa, outside the raw materials sector, multinational capital has been relatively timid; American investors face not only entrenched colonial capital in the mercantile and light industrial sectors but deep-seated nationalism even in some African capitalist states (Nigeria, Zaire from 1972 to 1975). Significant multinational entry outside the petroleum–mineral sphere is visible only in a handful of countries: Kenya, Zaire, Nigeria, perhaps now Egypt. There is more interest in contracted services (major construction projects, management contracts), on the whole, than in real equity investment; profits levied on the transaction are immediate and secure. In the words of one analyst, "both multinational corporations and African governments are still in a period of probing each others' powers, limitations, capabilities, and trustworthiness, which accounts for the relatively slow growth of American investment in independent Africa." [42]

In the raw materials sphere, mines of colonial vintage have for the most part been nationalized: iron in Mauritania, copper in Zaire and Zambia, diamonds in Sierra Leone, among others. New projects outside the southern African zone have been relatively limited and are concentrated in countries that are either especially congenial to Western investors (Gabon, Niger, Zaire) or willing to concede virtually complete enclave autonomy (for example, in Guinea). The very long lead times, the large sums that must be immobilized in creating the infrastructure, the high political uncertainties, and the volatility of prices for many metals (for example, copper) create a very large risk factor. In this context, Afro-Marxism may be viewed as an additional peril: no major new Western mineral development project (except oil) has been launched in any of these states, although one must immediately add that only Angola is resource-rich.

Petroleum is clearly a special case. Lead times are much less, and the requisite infrastructure for deposits in coastal or offshore zones is simpler. Production costs are extremely low compared to the market value, especially after 1973. The profitability figures in table 5.9 are enlightening in this respect; even though both Libya and Nigeria have nationalized the majority holdings of the oil operations, investors are reaping windfall gains. The proceeds from oil at the present time provide ample room for both the state and the oil companies to derive rich benefits. Further, the phenomenal cash flow makes it easy for the nationalizing state to reimburse fully and swiftly the equity that is forcibly acquired. While this does not make the "seven sisters" partisans of nationalization, it certainly reduces its sting. Negotiations between an oil company and the host government are thus not a zero-sum game; from this perspective, one may understand that populist socialism and Afro-Marxism do not appear to be a major inhibition for Western oil companies.

AFRICAN INTERNATIONAL AFFILIATIONS: IDEOLOGY AND CONSTRAINED CHOICE

Thus far, our primary focus has been upon Soviet and American policies toward Africa. We need now to reverse the perspective and ask how far ideology intervenes to explain African preference in external relationships.[43] Does the Afro-Marxist state desire maximum reliance on a Soviet partnership and minimal ties with the West? Does the African capitalist regime fear Soviet ties and cling to Western linkages?

The significance of the distinction in world view should not be minimized. Anti-imperialism is a fundamental postulate of scientific socialism. From this perspective, the United States is the fount of contemporary imperialism. At the same time that the Afro-Marxist states do not wish to affiliate with the socialist commonwealth of states (COMECON), they do not regard the Soviet bloc as simply the mirror image of the Western capitalist states. Precisely because Soviet ties are not entangled with "international capitalism," they are of a different nature and not associated with the same profit-siphoning mechanisms held to be inherent to capitalism. While none would go so far as to concur in the oft-repeated Castro claim that relationships with the Soviet Union can never be "exploitative" for the weaker partner, the wellsprings of the political and economic behavior of the capitalist and socialist states are viewed as different.

For the populist socialist, the asymmetrical image of Soviet and American policy motivations is less marked, but the philosophical aversion to capitalism and its perceived linkage to imperialism is pronounced. There is strong distrust of the contemporary instrumentalities of the international capitalist structure, the giant banks and the multinational corporations. The intensely nationalist undercurrents and radical impulses also intervene. A development pattern tributary to external capitalism is believed to secrete within the walls of the polity crippling obstacles to the establishment of a prevailing vision of a self-reliant, autonomous, socialist society.

For the market-economy state, the chimeras are reversed. State policy reasoning departs from political economy postulates similar to those in Western states. Aggressive bargaining may be necessary to forestall too heavily skewed a balance of advantage between external capital, and the national state and indigenous business. But for most, distrust of ultimate Soviet motivations is greater; relations with the Soviet Union are usually flavored by the fear that the Soviets would prefer a regime that is oriented differently.

At the same time, these divergent perspectives are partly

crosscut by the common themes in African diplomatic perspective noted in table 5.2. Nonalignment is a cardinal principle for virtually all states. While the concept is quite elastic, stretching from the intimacy of the French connection of an Ivory Coast or a Senegal to the habitual backing of Soviet positions in international forums for an Angola or an Ethiopia, adherence to the precept does provide a common reference point. The doctrine of nonalignment exerts some pressure toward equilibrating Western and Eastern ties; conversely, exclusive American or Soviet partnership forfeits nonalignment and unduly circumscribes the already limited room for autonomous diplomacy. Nationalism as well is a central value to nearly all regimes. Total reliance upon either great power is a self-imposed limitation on sovereignty. Further, Afro-Marxists and African capitalists are side by side in the uphill struggle for a New International Economic Order. With or without a theory of imperialism, virtually all African nations believe that the overall pattern of North–South relationships is profoundly inequitable. Since economic linkages with Western industrial states are vastly more important than those with the Soviet bloc, North–South litigation essentially juxtaposes African and Western interests.

In the political realm, nearly all African states desire minimally correct diplomatic relations with both superpowers, as a mark of nonalignment and badge of sovereignty. The specific configuration of regional political concerns and the perception of threats to the survival of the regime or even of the state play a crucial role. The Horn is an evident example: Somalia began building a politico-military relationship with the Soviet Union in the 1960s under a market-economy regime, when the United States refused to provide military assistance because of the threat posed by Somali irredentism to Ethiopia and Kenya. When the Soviets seized the opportunity to build an intimate politico-military relationship with Ethiopia in 1977, the Somalis, by then officially Afro-Marxists, ruptured their Soviet ties and sought backing from the West. Nigerian relations with the Soviet Union first became significant when the Soviets offered arms supply and diplomatic support during the civil war, at a time when United States policy offered only lukewarm backing. The solidity of Angolan linkages with the Soviet Union and Cuba is not due simply to the official commitment to scientific socialism, but rather is founded upon the decisive military aid provided during the civil war in 1975–76, while the United States (along with South Africa, Zaire, and others) armed the MPLA adversaries. Luanda's suspicions of the United States are sustained by the fear that covert aid to the UNITA guerrillas may be resumed, as has been openly proposed in some quarters in Washington. The humiliating snubbing of the Soviets and their East European partners at the Zimbabwe independence ceremonies in 1980 is explicable in terms of the aid that the Soviets provided to Robert Mugabe's rival-partner, Joshua Nkomo.

Commitment to southern African liberation has also been an overarching theme in African diplomacy that affects political relationships with the major powers. On the one hand, the unambiguous Soviet backing of African liberation and the Soviet role as purveyor of arms to (selected) guerrilla movements are critical and valued resources, both for the movements concerned and for those states most heavily involved in the southern African struggle. On the other hand, it is believed by African states that Western countries have a degree of potential leverage over the white redoubts that is not available to the Soviets. The perceived leverage provided the basis for periodically close diplomatic cooperation between the West (the "Western contact group" in Namibia, Britain and the United States in Zimbabwe) and the African "front-line" states (Angola, Botswana, Mozambique, Tanzania, and Zambia, themselves an ideological cross section). Although Afro-Marxist Angola and Mozambique played a crucial part in the negotiations on Namibia and Zimbabwe, respectively, forcing major concessions on the respective guerrilla movements, the suspicion lingered that the heavy engagement of Western capital in South Africa would in the final analysis prevent full American support for African liberation, especially in South Africa itself.

The well-documented record of both superpowers, as well as of France, in promoting changes in regime and funding dissident groups likewise plays a part in political relationships. The abortive Communist coup in Sudan in 1971—and the presumed Soviet support for it—brought about a sharp curtailment of Sudanese relationships with the Soviet Union. Such events as the mercenary invasion of Benin in 1977, the Bob Denard (a French mercenary) coup in the Comoros in 1978, the incursion by Portuguese mercenaries into Guinea in 1971, and the invasion of Shaba by Angolan-based "Katanga gendarmes" in 1977 and 1978 sustain a psychosis of potential subversion in most African capitals. The balance of evidence suggests that both the Soviet Union and the United States are much less attracted to such strategies now than they were in the first years of African independence; suspicions nonetheless persist.

In the military realm, ideology apart, African states face important constraints in choices of weapons suppliers. For heavy weapons, such as planes and armor, a given decision has long-term implications in terms of qualifying personnel to operate the equipment, logistical and maintenance systems, and access to spare parts. African states frequently have a different concept of their security needs than do potential suppliers; regimes may also face heavy internal pressures from their military establishments for more advanced weaponry. Arms purchases from the United States must run a gauntlet of bureaucratic and congressional approval; Soviet supply may be more swiftly negotiated and may possibly involve more favorable commercial terms. A case in point was the controversial $100 million aircraft deal that Zambia signed with the Soviet Union in 1980: this purchase came after the Zambian security forces had been repeatedly humiliated by Rhodesian raids that had knocked out crucial rail and road bridges as well as Zimbabwean camps. The United States and Britain had declined to sell such equipment, contending that it was unnecessary and that Zambia could not afford it. The regime faced dangerous discontent within its armed forces and a sense of its helplessness in the face of eventual South African military threats. This made the Soviet purchase appear necessary in spite of the unattractive commercial terms.[44]

In the economic realm, choices are exceedingly narrow. There is simply no alternative to primarily Western linkages in trade and in access to capital. Aid has been meager from all sides and overall has tended to decline in real terms. The Afro-Marxist states, which in the mid-1970s had hopes for a much more generous supply of Soviet assistance, have found not only that the amounts are disappointingly small, but that Soviet execution of aid projects has fallen far short of expectations. Western aid has been equally unsatisfying: its high administrative costs and tendency to circulate benefits back to the donor country in the form of payments for services and supply have become conventional wisdom. What is perhaps most curious is that, despite the many disillusionments, aid continues to be earnestly solicited on all sides.

The tightly circumscribed choices available in international economic relationships considerably reduce the impact of ideological perspective. Afro-Marxist states as well as market-economy ones offer investment guarantees to Western capital-holders. Machel, suggesting that necessity might be virtuous, argues that "Foreign capital has experience working in socialist countries in Europe, Asia, and Latin America. It will have the opportunity to find out that here, just as in those countries, it will be able to make profits at the same time that it is contributing to the construction of socialism."[45] Further, the now widespread appreciation that the Soviet Union, in its commercial dealings, promotes unequal relationships as relentlessly as do multinational corporations, has nullified any ideological assumptions that trading terms from COMECON are inherently more advantageous than those of Western states. The notoriety of the fishing accords, the Guinean bauxite affair, and other instances of sharp Soviet mercantile practice have put African states on guard in their Soviet dealings.

DOES IDEOLOGY MATTER? THE QUERY REVISITED

We may now return to the broader questions with which we began this chapter. Does African ideological choice play a decisive role in shaping external ties? Do the great powers interpret African regimes and events as functions of the doctrinal orientations of particular regimes?

The response is clearly affirmative in part. The Soviet Union is attracted by the "revolutionary democratic" choice of some African states, a category that includes both Afro-Marxism and populist socialism. What is perceived in the late 1970s as a trend toward socialist orientation is viewed as the African dimension of a broader historic trend. As Gromyko puts it, "The present international situation is characterised by increasing orientation towards socialism. This positive process has become possible owing to the growing consciousness of the peoples in the developing countries, and to the support they receive from the socialist countries."[46] The United States, conversely, is clearly more comfortable with regimes that are committed to a market-economy ideology: Ivory Coast and Kenya are viewed as exemplary cases. American officialdom for the most part is persuaded that these economic premises are most likely to produce sustained growth. Despite the real and partly successful effort to build civil relationships with Afro-Marxist states since 1977, there can be no doubt that the ties with Gabon or Cameroon are simpler and more multiplex than those with Mozambique or Congo-Brazzaville.

Military supply and training links likewise reflect, to a significant extent, the ideological gamut. For both donor and recipient the security apparatus is the most sensitive sector of the state, and both parties must have a clear sense that the relationship will serve their special interests. There are instances where arms supply crosses ideological lines—especially on the Soviet side, where this is a more salient aspect of policy. Nigeria and Zambia are cases in point. In both instances, the purchaser sought the weapons under the sense of a mortal threat to the polity.

Economic relationships also show some ideological impact. This is most visible in the Western investment field, excepting petroleum, where a clear preference for the more congenial "investment climate" provided by market-economy states is perceptible. Bank lending, however, seems less influenced by ideology. Both Soviet and American aid show an interactive effect from African ideology. The preference for "moderate" states has been somewhat more pronounced on the American side than has Soviet exclusivity in the direction of the Afro-Marxist contingent. However, the relative modesty of both aid programs limits the significance of this factor.

However, while ideology is indisputably a significant vector, it is powerfully crosscut by other determinants, both for the great powers and for the African states. Both the Soviet Union and the United States desire a universal presence; to sustain it, both must find formulas for encouraging friendly ties with regimes on the yonder side of the ideological divide. Both the Soviet Union and the United States define African policy in a global perspective; broader strategic considerations may well override regional ideological factors. Areas contiguous to the Middle East and the southern Africa sphere have a geopolitical importance that goes far beyond immediate considerations of revolutionary democracy or market economy.

Nonideological factors are particularly strong in the economic realm. The Western industrial world—and perhaps in the future the Soviet bloc as well—is critically dependent on a number of African resources; their geographical distribution has only an accidental relationship to ideology. Historically, and for a long time to come, African trading relationships have been overwhelmingly with the West. The pressing contingencies of external payments balances and the large share of state revenues that is in most instances tied to export taxation make these linkages imperative. Afro-Marxist Angola is as totally dependent for state revenue and foreign exchange on its Western oil sales as Afro-capitalist Zaire is on its copper.

Soviet economic national interests are clearly dominant in a number of its largest aid and credit accords. The $2 billion phosphate deal with Morocco, which is viewed by many observers in Africa as a veritable Western gendarme, is a spectacular example. So, closely examined, was the 1973 bauxite deal in Guinea; though Touré was a somewhat erratic populist socialist, the terms of the accord were so heavily weighted toward Soviet commercial advantage that proletarian internationalism entirely disappears from view.

On the part of the great powers, a residual skepticism as to the solidity of African ideological commitments is also involved. Both are aware that startling reversals are possible—the sudden declarations for Marxism-Leninism of military regimes of Benin and Madagascar, the realignment in the Horn in 1977–78, the many oscillations of Sékou Touré. This underlying fluidity to African politico-ideological alignments means that no situation— at least up to the present—is ever irreversible. It is true that the sudden and unexpected extension of the Brezhnev doctrine of the limited sovereignty of socialist states to Afghanistan in December 1979 created new uncertainties—especially in Ethiopia and Angola, where significant Communist military detachments were garrisoned and where Soviet bloc personnel had most extensively entrenched themselves in the security apparatus of the state. The possibility that the Soviet Union would not permit a reversal of the Afro-Marxist option—which, on the basis of their acceptance of summary expulsion from Egypt and Somalia in 1976 and 1978, respectively, could have been dismissed before

Afghanistan—now must be considered. It remains unlikely, however, and would certainly transform the whole pattern of international relationships in Africa were it attempted.

On the African end, there are also significant factors at work that are at variance with the ideological determinant. The universal acknowledgement of nonalignment as a goal, the importance attached to a concerted African standpoint on many international issues, the priority accorded by nearly all states to African liberation and racial equality all exert a pressure to overcome doctrinal polarities. The very nature of the spectrum confers special influence and authority on those states—such as Tanzania and Nigeria—that tend toward the political middle and can thus broker the differences between "moderates" and "radical anti-imperialists."

Ideology, then, takes us some distance to an understanding of African international relations. But only a small part of the way. A complete conception of the overall pattern demands our consideration of the various factors that interact with ideology and partly countervail it: growth, equality, autonomy, human dignity, participation, and capacity expansion. These are discussed in the next chapter.

6

By Way of Conclusion: A Preliminary Appraisal of Ideology and Performance

THE LIMITS OF EVALUATION

I now turn, by way of conclusion, to the humbling task of tentatively appraising the consequences of ideological choice. I have argued that the three streams of development philosophy categorized as Afro-Marxism, populist socialism, and market-economy capitalism do constitute contrasting policy paradigms. The differing configurations of values do influence overall policy patterns. While none of the three developmental world views is so homogeneous as to yield a single and authoritative policy pattern, there are common and recurrent characteristics of each pathway. What, then, may be said about the outcome? Do all roads have a common ending? Or are there major differences in development performance that are common to the cluster of states that have persistently followed a given avenue?

As the first chapter stressed, such an appraisal must necessarily be multidimensional—and quintessentially subjective. A set of six criteria was proposed to guide the judgment: growth, equality, autonomy, human dignity, participation, and capacity expansion. However, each of these measures, on close inspection, proves to be complex and quite resistant to meaningful "operationalization" in terms of a single numerical indicator (or even a cluster of them). I shall accordingly confine myself to discursive analysis—which evidently contains its own flaws of imprecision and subjectivism. In defense, it is argued merely that this evaluative discussion is preliminary and tentative—a contribution to a debate, rather than a final verdict.

GROWTH

Growth cannot be considered as the sole measure of performance, yet neither can it be set aside. Certainly no African leader would dismiss it. Indeed, without growth none of the other goals can be achieved. As a point of departure, table 6.1 presents World Bank calculations of overall GNP change.

The figures for the Afro-Marxist group are not fully relevant, as only Congo and Somalia among this group thus identified themselves before 1975. The relatively impressive figures for Algeria, Congo, and Nigeria partly reflect ballooning oil prices and require deflation—especially in the case of Nigeria, for which petroleum has become a relatively more important component of the total economy. Angola and Mozambique suffered the enormous initial disadvantage of the flight of the European segment of the populace (about 440,000 in Angola and 200,000 in Mozambique), who monopolized many of the technical skills and took with them their liquid capital. In the populist socialist group, only a fraction of the stagnation in Ghana can be attributed to an ideological experiment, which ended in 1966. Mali as well partly detached itself from this group after 1968.

Thus far, rapid growth has eluded the Afro-Marxist states. There are as yet no signs of the rapid, forced-draft growth that did accompany Stalinist economic policies in the Soviet Union, Eastern Europe, North Korea, and China (though not in Cuba or Indochina). Some analysts might argue that the soft-option version of Marxism-Leninism fails to impose the rigorous discipline and ruthless means that were the nether side of Stalinism. Others might doubt whether the contemporary African state has sufficient power to enforce such policies—and that any truly se-

TABLE 6.1. Real GNP Growth Rates in Selected African States, 1960–76

Country	Per capita GNP 1976 ($ millions)	Real per capita GNP growth, 1960–76	Real per capita GNP growth, 1970–76
Afro-Marxist group			
Angola	310	2.8	−0.6
Benin	180	0.0	1.0
Congo	530	1.3	2.6
Ethiopia	100	1.9	0.2
Madagascar	200	−0.1	−2.3
Mozambique	150	1.4	−4.3
São Tomé	360	n.a.	−5.3
Somalia	110	−0.3	−0.6
Populist socialist group			
Algeria	1,010	1.8	3.8
Egypt	280	1.9	3.1
Ghana	370	−0.2	−0.7
Guinea	210	1.4	0.7
Mali	100	0.9	0.5
Tanzania	180	2.6	1.7
African capitalist group			
Ivory Coast	650	3.3	1.9
Kenya	250	2.6	0.9
Nigeria	400	3.5	5.4

SOURCE: *World Bank Atlas 1978*, p. 14.

rious effort would lead to a Cambodia rather than to 10 percent growth rates. Yet this verdict must remain tentative, as the time frame is too short—and the two states with the best potential resource base and ultimate prospect of success, Angola and Mozambique, have been so incapacitated by civil war on the one hand and the Zimbabwe spillover on the other, that fair appraisal is really precluded. Mozambique in the 1980s will be a crucial testing ground; the 1980 political settlement in Zimbabwe removed a critical obstacle. The FRELIMO regime began with more coherent leadership and more popular support for its ideological options than did most other Afro-Marxist states. The success or failure of Mozambique in building a strong economy on scientific socialist premises will have profound repercussions throughout the continent. The relative effectiveness of the Benin regime should also be noted since it has been achieved without the benefit of mineral exports. The Marxist-Leninist regime has nonetheless often performed better economically than its sundry predecessors, though the results are modest.

In the populist socialist group, Algeria, Egypt, and Tanzania have performed respectably on growth criteria for a large part of the time. Algeria has used its hydrocarbon revenues to build a substantial industrial sector. Egypt did fairly well through much of the Nasser period, though serious difficulties were encountered in the final years of populist socialism. The exceptionally heavy burden of defense expenditures borne by Egypt, especially after the 1967 war, deserves part of the blame. The Tanzanian economy, which enjoyed reasonable success during the first decade of independence, was badly dislocated by the excesses of the mass villagization campaign in 1973–76 and by unfavorable weather. The heavy costs of the Uganda invasion of 1979 added a further handicap. Nonetheless, the growth performance over the years has been quite respectable, particularly in the absence of any mineral development.

While these three experiments in populist socialism could claim reasonable growth success, Ghana, Guinea, and Mali had mediocre results. Similar patterns were observable in the three states: all committed large amounts of public investment funds to singularly ill-chosen state-run industrial projects that were intended as a motor force for both socialism and development. Likewise, the socialist-inspired rural policies were so unfavorable to the smallholder population that a demoralized peasantry as well as petty rural capitalists sought relief in smuggling or raising crops that were saleable outside the state marketing

˜he contrast between these two groups of populist
.es suggests the conclusion that a singularly mis-
of choices, not an indelible flaw in the ideology, was
ın the cases of failure.

.erms of growth, Ivory Coast and Kenya clearly do stand
ɔlid accomplishment has been sustained over time in both
₃, with the Ivory Coast record somewhat stronger. The
ɔwth has healthy roots in the rural sector and has not been in-
.ᵤenced by mineral bonanzas in either case. The potential of the
statist model of nurture capitalism for high growth is further
confirmed by the figures for neo-Victorian Malawi (3.2 percent
real per capita annual increase in 1960–76), likewise an agrarian
economy. Market-economy Botswana also shows good figures
(6.0 percent annual per capita growth rate for the same period),
although mineral expansion has been important here. The imminent end of this phase of capitalist growth has been regularly
predicted by its critics: Amin argued more than a decade ago that
Ivory Coast was merely exploiting the opportunities for "easy"
growth utilized by Ghana early in the century.[1] The more recent World Bank study likewise forecast a more difficult period
ahead.[2] Growth indeed slowed at the end of the 1970s in both
Kenya and Ivory Coast; the former experienced serious external
payments problems, while the latter faced a high external debt
and costly disappointments in its sugar scheme. Whether expansion at the earlier rate can be resumed is uncertain.

While the market-economy formula clearly can produce
positive growth results, there is no guarantee that it will do so.
Imperial Ethiopia and Liberia under Tubman and Tolbert had
only a mediocre record, especially in the 1970s. And we have examined at some length in chapter 4 the calamitous case of Zaire.
Nigeria is also an ambiguous case in growth terms: though the
raw figures seem impressive, they conceal the escalating dependency upon oil and the disheartening stagnation of the agricultural economy.

EQUALITY

The simplest and most widely touted policy trade-off is between growth and equality. Related to the ideological criterion—and crudely stated—this hypothesis would hold that African capitalism would produce both high growth and high inequality, while the various forms of socialism would yield much better results on the equality front but at the price of a mediocre growth record. Do the data support this proposition?

The first response is that the evidence concerning income distribution patterns is both too sparse and too unreliable to permit unqualified judgments. A very important fraction of the revenues accruing to the dominant politico-commercial class in many countries is in a twilight zone (if not an underworld) of illicit transactions, corrupt levies, and fringe mercantile activities that falls completely outside the national income accounts. An extreme case is the Shaba (Zaire) regional commissioner cited by Gould, whose state salary represented only 2 percent of his earnings.[3] The evidence ingeniously gleaned by Cohen from the Official Gazette on Ivorian urban property speculation by the political elite is another edifying example.[4] At the other end of the scale, the real revenues of participants in the urban "informal sector," or the smallholder sphere, are not very adequately measured. Conclusions on this score, then, are necessarily exploratory.

One major recent study on a global scale advances the contrary argument that redistribution is indeed compatible with growth. Chenery and his collaborators further demonstrate that high growth rates have been combined with low inequality levels in a number of countries spanning the ideological spectrum: Yugoslavia (Marxist-Leninist), Tanzania and Sri Lanka (populist socialist), Taiwan, South Korea, and Costa Rica (capitalist).[5] Third-world experience is thus diverse in the actual relationship between growth and distribution. A strategy is suggested for rendering the growth and equality goals compatible: maximize GNP growth; redirect investment to poverty groups, by giving them access to such assets as skills, land, and credit; redistribute income through fiscal policy; and transfer existing assets (especially land) to the poor.[6] Can these happy results be achieved in Africa? Do any of the ideological paradigms foster or inhibit their realization?

In certain respects, the Afro-Marxist and populist socialist states have to their credit forceful measures betokening a real egalitarian commitment. These include stiff regulations inhibiting the accumulation of wealth and capital by the political and bureaucratic leadership and less reliance on expatriate cadres with very high income and consumption expectations. The anticapitalist ethos of these regimes attaches a great stigma to buccaneering mercantile activity by the political elite. In states such as Mozambique, Tanzania, and Guinea-Bissau, the austere—even puritanical—public ethics are quite tangible. In such instances as Algeria and Congo-Brazzaville, most observers find the austerity ethos less pervasive; public buildings in Brazzaville are adorned with red banners declaring "*à bas les enveloppes*" (down with bribes); the smoke of these moral exhortations implies that some glowing embers of bureaucratic extortion must exist. The greater reliance, especially by the Afro-Marxist states, on Soviet bloc technicians—whatever their other limitations—does avoid the costly role model of Western personnel, whose opulent life-style fixes a set of expectations for the top African stratum that can be achieved only through high inequality levels.

In Ethiopia, the land reform of 1975—which preceded the choice of Marxism-Leninism—did have a revolutionary effect on rural inequality. In Egypt and Algeria as well, important land reform measures were taken to eliminate the most extreme forms of agrarian inequality by removing the top layer of large operators. In both cases, the evidence casts doubt on whether the poorest rural strata have benefited very much—but certainly a significant group in the middle levels of rural society has. In Mozambique, Angola, and Guinea-Bissau, socialist regimes have made real efforts to bring a better life to peasant sectors that were either totally neglected (Guinea-Bissau) or harshly oppressed under Portuguese rule. The policy priority accorded to rural well-being is beyond dispute; the effects of the strategies pursued remain to be demonstrated.

Chenery et al. stress the use of fiscal policy for redistributive purposes, while warning that this must not be pursued to the exclusion of growth-oriented resource use. However, in a wide array of African states fiscal policy—far from being redistributive—is a veritable suction pump drawing resources out of the peasant sector. Irrespective of ideology, many states have relied very heavily on taxation of external trade, in particular exports; the incidence of the such taxes, for agricultural commodities, is entirely upon the rural producers. Pricing policies and state-directed marketing structures have also served to transfer resources from rural smallholders to the state and the urban sector. Thus the effective rate of taxation of the poorest segment of the population—the peasantry—may be 50 percent or more, while the top income brackets are often only lightly taxed—particularly for their transactions in the "underground economy," which escape the fiscal net altogether. In policy discourse, such tax issues have never been correlated with ideological principle; no one has ever suggested that high export taxes have anything to do with either socialism or capitalism. Of the states examined, only Kenya stands out for its relatively low levels of rural taxation (if we include in this concept pricing policies as well as direct and indirect fiscal levies).

More generally, policies that bring about stagnation of rural marketed production are probably by nature inegalitarian. Conversely, rising rural output—if it is not merely expanded plantation production—does raise the incomes of the poorest segment of the populace. Viewed from this angle, the effective agricultural policies in Ivory Coast and Kenya partly mitigate the high degrees of inequality visible at the top of the social scale. In the Ivory Coast, Ivorian farmers in the perennial crop zones of the south have experienced major gains. The northern savanna has much less potential, but the remarkable increase in cotton production suggests some benefits here as well. The lowest end of the social scale tends to be occupied by foreign migrants—those who truly are the victims of inequality.

A careful study of rural incomes in Tanzania, where distributional equities have received unusually high policy attention, reveals that in the first decade of independence there was a steady decline in real returns to farmers. At this juncture, evidence of a production crisis led to sharp increases in agricultural price levels; also, personal income taxes on the bottom strata were effectively ended in 1974. Over time, average farm family total incomes remained about 55 percent of the average wage-earner income; however, the absolute gap widened from Tsh. 1,484 per family in 1964 to 3,243 in 1975. While these findings confirmed the view that returns to the rural sector were inadequate, they still probably illustrated a higher level of equity for the peasantry than in most other states.[7]

Another dimension of inequality is the basic urban wage level. This is generally fixed by the state; the employment structure is such that a substantial fraction of workers fall in the unskilled laborer category and probably receive the basic minimum wage. Recent ILO data again suggest that the relationship between regime ideology and real wage patterns is not very close.

A significant aspect of state action in the equality field is the provision of basic services to the population at large. Of these, the most universally desired in recent years are education and health. Again, what stands out from available statistical information is the absence of correlation between ideology and performance. All regimes accept the urgency of education; indeed, all are under equal pressure from a population that now recognizes the intimate link between education and social mobility. While Somalia and Mozambique have truly dramatic achievements to their credit in the mobilization of resources for education, so also Nigeria audaciously committed itself to achieving universal pri-

TABLE 6.2. Changes in Real Minimum Wages in Selected
African States, 1963–74

Country	Consumer price index (1963 = 100)	% change in real minimum wages
Burundi	157.8	−36.6
Cameroon	155.7	−14.9
Central African Republic	186.0	−19.4
Chad	182.0	9.9
Congo	154.6	75.5
Gabon	155.8	7.0
Ghana	281.5	−59.0
Ivory Coast	172.0	26.2
Kenya	160.0	30.4
Liberia	178.7	−44.0
Libya	160.6	121.7
Madagascar	168.7	−30.5
Mauritania	185.9	−31.8
Morocco	146.6	77.4
Niger	166.3	−33.2
Senegal	144.1	46.8
Tanzania	199.6	13.6
Togo	151.0	−12.6
Tunisia	150.8	13.4
Zaire	699.7	−53.5
Zambia	193.8	−17.4

SOURCE: Susumu Watanabe, "Minimum Wages in Developing Countries: Myth and Reality," *International Labour Review* 113 (May-June 1976): 353.

mary education by 1976 (it was not fully realized, but massive outlays were made), and Ivory Coast has made imaginative use of televisual instructional methods in rural areas. Tanzania as well pushed for universal primary education by 1977.

Possibly there is a linkage between socialist preference and high priority for adult literacy campaigns. The three most noteworthy instances of large-scale adult education projects are in Afro-Marxist Somalia and Mozambique and populist socialist Tanzania. The Somali campaign, involving the mobilization of the secondary school population, was by most accounts of real significance. In Tanzania, over five million have been enrolled in the adult programs; the persons who took the adult literacy tests in 1977 outnumbered the entire primary school population. Meaningful inroads were made into the illiteracy rate (65 percent literacy in 1977).[8] The impact of the Mozambique campaign is less well known, but it faces much greater obstacles. Unlike Somalia and Tanzania, Mozambique has no single, widely spoken African language; therefore a mass literacy campaign faces the intimidating task of teaching both a new language (Portuguese) and reading skills for it. Arguably the egalitarianism of populist and scientific socialist thought helps explain the resource commitment to adult literacy drives.

A full assessment of the impact of health expenditures on equality would need to undergo more discriminating analysis than is attempted here. An effectively egalitarian health care delivery system would disperse health facilities and personnel through the countryside and stress prevention and mass paramedical services rather than costly advanced medical technology. Thus, while levels of health expenditures do not appear to vary by ideological type, it is possible that market-economy states are more prone to follow the Western medical model of high cost, high quality, and, for a country of meager means, limited access health care.

Performance on egalitarianism, then, draws an ambiguous evaluation. African capitalist states permit very high returns to a relatively narrow segment of African political figures, top functionaries, and businessmen, as well as to expatriate managerial and technical personnel. Afro-Marxist and populist socialist states are likely to inhibit wealth accumulation at the top stratum. For wage earners and smallholders, however, it is much less clear that sluggish growth is compensated for by efficacious redistribution, as appears to have been the case in Cuba.[9] The rural-based economic growth achievements in Ivory Coast and

Kenya make at least arguable the proposition that these states have brought an improvement in the well-being of farmers that is not matched by most of the other cases considered.

One other dimension of the equality issue deserves mention. The African capitalist state appears to be peculiarly susceptible to large-scale corruption, which reaches a level where the state is corroded. Zaire is the extreme case. When the *enrichissez-vous* ethos of capitalism is joined to the use of the state apparatus by the political class to privatize public resources, unrestrained by any operative public ethic, the state risks becoming, in the eyes of its populace, not the night watchman of classical liberalism but the brazen burglar. When this occurs, the hour is at hand when the citizenry will applaud such macabre spectacles as the summary executions of three former heads of state in Ghana in 1979 and of thirteen leading regime figures in Liberia in 1980. While corruption may be found in the Afro-Marxist or populist socialist state, it does not match the virulence of the malady in Zaire or, to a milder extent, in Nigeria.

AUTONOMY

Autonomy and self-reliance are the next criteria to be applied. At issue here is certainly not total economic autonomy, which no state can achieve in an interdependent world, much less an impossible autarchy. Positive performance consists in enlarging the scope of choice and reducing the impact of external constraints on policy options. The essence of autonomy is the possibility of designing a development strategy that is responsive solely to internal value preferences and images of desired future societal arrangements.

For one important school of analysts, the dependency theorists, subordination to the interests of external capitalism is the inevitable fate of the weaker, peripheral state. Further, they would argue, the capitalist developmental strategy is likely to re-

inforce and deepen this peripheralization through the more active welcome to foreign investment and freer rein offered to it.
Probably the most eloquent statement of this thesis is the Leys
monograph on Kenya.[10] Other writers so extend the concept as to
make dependency a condition not only universal but inescap-
able in the framework of the contemporary "international capitalist system"; a case in point is Wallerstein, for whom the Soviet Union is a part of the "capitalist world economy," with
Africa one vast periphery whose states are limited to narrow ma-
neuvering for marginal advantage.[11]

In concrete terms, autonomy seems to be most circumscribed when economic crisis places a polity in receivership.
Large shortfalls of foreign exchange or state revenue create urgent needs for external resources. Such moments of impasse
translate at once into severe political pressures: shortages of
basic imported consumer goods in urban markets; difficulties in
meeting state payrolls; production facilities crippled by lack of
parts and materials; the risk of hyperinflation. Desperation evidently diminishes a state's bargaining power in its dealings with
external sources of succor.

In practice, the boundaries of autonomy do not seem so
rigidly determined as the dependency school would suggest.
Angola, for example, is utterly dependent for 90 percent or more
of its state revenue and foreign exchange on the Gulf Oil enclave
off the Cabinda shores—carefully guarded from regionalist dissidence by Cuban troops. Yet it is difficult to discern that this has
had any impact upon Angolan choices in the blueprints for its
internal development, in its unambiguous endorsement of Marxism-Leninism as regime doctrine, in its anticapitalist orientation
(softened in 1980), or in its close alignment on the international
theses supported by its Soviet and Cuban military patrons. Mozambique, equally dedicated to the Afro-Marxist world view, has
been forced to accept extensive South African involvement in
the management and operation of its key port installations, railway, and hydroelectric grid, to continue the despised practice of

supplying contract mine laborers, and to exercise great discretion in extending sanctuary and support to South African liberation movements. The very fact that there is no analogue to Gulf Oil in Mozambique—and thus a perennial crisis of foreign exchange and state revenue—imposes severe restrictions on choice relative to the regional capitalist stronghold of South Africa. This tributary relationship, however, does not at all apply to Mozambiquan relations to the stronghold of world capitalism, the United States, with which Maputo has only slight relations of trade, aid, technology, or capital.

Of the states we have considered, in many respects the two that are least dependent are Algeria and Nigeria. While Algeria has relatively high debts and Nigeria has extensive foreign capital investment, the strongly nationalist—economically and politically—positions of both have been underwritten by the market strength of oil exporters. Conversely, the trends in international trade toward rising energy and food costs in particular, have increased the vulnerability of most African states.

Another irony is the continued affiliation of two Afro-Marxist states, Benin and Congo-Brazzaville, with the CFA franc system, which places international trade arrangements under externally imposed (and ultimately French) discipline. Yet at the same time this compromise of autonomy averts the more disabling trauma of an inconvertible currency, with the inflation, shortages, and smuggling this is likely to create. This form of dependent tie does not in itself appear to have constrained other ideologically derived policy choices in these two states. However, in the Congo case, the recurrent state revenue crisis generated by the overdeveloped state apparatus and the deficit-ridden public sector does continually place the regime in a mendicant role.

In any case, the 1970s have demonstrated that there is no possibility of trading Comecon dependency for economic linkages with the Western world. Whether or not the Cuban tributary relationship with the Soviet Union is ethically or politically pref-

erable to the Ivory Coast bondage to France, the option to exchange one for the other is not available. The Soviet camp is neither able nor willing to provide markets, capital, or aid on a
significant scale, even to the "revolutionary democratic" states.
All states, whatever their ideology, are faced with the challenge
of optimizing their autonomy and advantages in their dealings
with economically and politically more powerful Western industrial states.

Playing the dependency game does not necessarily require
ideological surrender. Crisis situations, which bring about IMF
stabilization plans and agonizing debt rescheduling negotiations, do result in often stringent, externally imposed conditions.
But most states, at most times, do not find themselves in the
kind of impasse that has beset Zaire since 1975 or Tanzania in
1979–80.

Another important dimension of dependency originates in
the military supply relationship. Here the choices are painful.
Advanced weapons are available only from a handful of major
powers. Once the weapons are obtained, spare parts and often
maintenance and even operating personnel must come from
the same source. This places potent leverage in the hands of the
supplying power, a leverage that is magnified when significant
numbers of military personnel from the external partner are introduced. Some states avert these disabilities by foregoing advanced weaponry and accepting military weakness—an option
that has its own disabilities and exposes the state to other kinds
of external pressures. The Soviet Union has been the major arms
supplier in Africa in recent years, and thus this form of dependency is most visible in those states that are heavily reliant on
the Soviet military relationship. Ethiopia in 1980 is the obvious
extreme example. As noted in chapter 5, these states tilt toward
the socialist end of the spectrum but are found in all ideological
groupings.

In sum, I do not find a close correlation between degree of
autonomy and self-reliance and ideology. On the African capital-

ist side, Ivory Coast has freely chosen a development pathway in close cooperation with France; this relationship accords privileged status to French personnel and capital and is the very model of modern dependency. At this price, the Ivorian economy has achieved remarkable success, above all in contrast to such neighboring states as Ghana and Guinea, which serve as direct reference points for the Ivorian populace. However, the capitalist option can also have a much more nationalist face, as in the Nigerian instance. Nigeria in recent years has combined domestic nurture capitalism with aggressive support of southern African liberation and a tough negotiating posture with foreign capital. Since the oil boom began, Nigeria has become ever more deeply drawn into the international economy. But a strong balance of payments and state revenue situation place Nigeria in a position of strength in its external economic dealings. And Nigeria is not militarily insecure; thus the Soviet supply of advanced aircraft that the Nigerian air force cannot fully operate does not weigh much in policy calculus. Nigeria was thus able to reject defiantly American pressures during the Angolan civil war, to warn the Soviets and Cuba not to overstay their welcome in Africa in 1978, and to abruptly seize British Petroleum holdings in 1979 in punishment for its dealings in southern Africa.

Among the populist socialist states, we observe a comparable gamut of outcomes. Algeria has maintained a radical anti-imperial international posture and has progressively extended its control over the critical sectors of the domestic economy. Similarly, resource-poor Tanzania pursued its socialist experiment quite uninhibited by the "international capitalist system" until the food crisis of the mid-1970s; and then the more general financial crisis of 1979 following the Uganda invasion placed the state in peril of bankruptcy. The first crisis was partly overcome by a remarkable flow of external aid and credit from Western sources and international agencies, which were charmed by the ethical force and transparent sincerity of Tanzanian socialism. While

Tanzania is far from being self-reliant, the diffuse dependency implied by these high levels of external assistance contrasts with the kind of dependency found in populist socialist Guinea. There, a capricious economic management forced the state to pawn repeatedly its most valuable resource, bauxite deposits, to an assortment of external corporate interests (American, Soviet, Swiss, French, Italian, Yugoslav). The terms of these agreements reflected the weakness of a state whose treasury was empty of cash or exchange.

On the Afro-Marxist side, we also see a diversity of outcomes. The Benin regime, while still in the CFA zone, had brought more stable governance and more competent direction to the country than any of its predecessors and also stood in a less demeaningly subservient position to France. Somalia as well had been quite self-reliant, even in its most disastrous venture of invading Ethiopia in 1977. Congo, on the other hand, faced a monthly crisis of meeting the state payroll. Angola and Ethiopia remained dependent upon foreign military contingents to help combat dissident or secessionist forces, themselves externally supported, and Mozambique was squeezed by its South African economic connections.

HUMAN DIGNITY

On the human dignity measure, we may consider direct evidence of repression and indirect indicators such as the appearance of significant refugee populations in neighboring states.[12] In some respects, 1979 appeared to be a turning point in the significance of this performance measure. For the first time, the Organization of African Unity devoted extensive attention to the issue, and a human rights commission was formed. Also, three of the most serious offenders, Amin (Uganda), Bokassa (Central African Republic), and Nguema (Equatorial Guinea), were overthrown. The

TABLE 6.3. Human Rights Observation in Selected African States, 1978–79

Afro-Marxist group	Populist socialist group	African capitalist group
Angola—civil war situation; some allegations of arbitrary arrests, political incarcerations	**Algeria**—since Chadli Bendjedid becomes President, all political prisoners released; generally good human rights record	**Ivory Coast**—very good human rights record
Benin—little brutality or repression; periodic political arrests after plot scares; estimate 25 political prisoners	**Cape Verde**—40 political prisoners arrested 1977; released 1979; good human rights record overall	**Kenya**—fairly good overall record, though under Kenyatta some critics silenced by detention (Ngugi), a few political assassinations (Kariuki); Arap Moi release for all the handful of detainees
Congo—political detainees amnestied 1979, except Yhombi-Opango; no harsh repression but "considerable room for improvement"	**Guinea-Bissau**—very good human rights record	**Nigeria**—very good human rights record
Ethiopia—Extensive violations, especially in urban areas, peaking with Red Terror, December 1977–April 1978; Amnesty International claims at least several thousand, perhaps tens of thousands killed, tortured, imprisoned; some	**Egypt**—very good record in recent years; repression of some groups (Muslin Brotherhood, Communists) under Nasser	
	Ghana—in later Nkrumah years, extensive use of Preventive Detention Act, several hundred political prisoners	
	Guinea—psychosis of the "permanent plot" has brought repeated	

oners; regime opponents at large, though silenced

Mozambique—extensive confinement of opponents in "reeducation" camps; number of detainees unknown but considerable; some death sentences for crimes against "state security"

São Tomé—very good human rights record; several tried on conspiracy charges in 1979, trial "apparently conducted fairly"

Somalia—a "security conscious" atmosphere; exiles claim several hundred political prisoners, Amnesty International identifies 13 "prisoners of conscience"; 17 army officers tried and executed in 1978 for coup attempt

pecially after November 1970 Portuguese invasion), extensive use of torture, fatal to a number of prisoners; in 1978, still about 1,000 political prisoners, some relaxation since

Mali—some violations in early 1960s, most notably in repression of Tuareg dissidence in 1963

Tanzania—extensive violations in Zanzibar, under Karume, though these not really under Dar es Salaam control; Zanzibar abuses end under Jumbe; occasional use of preventive detention legislation, Amnesty International reports several hundred such detainees in 1978, though most of these on criminal, not political, suspicion

SOURCES: House of Representatives, Committee on Foreign Affairs, and Senate, Committee on Foreign Relations, *Country Reports on Human Rights Practices for 1979*, submitted by Department of State, 4 February 1980: House of Representatives, Committee on International Relations, and Senate, Committee on Foreign Relations, *Country Reports on Human Rights Practices*, submitted by Department of State, 3 February 1978.

newly imposed requirement that the Department of State compile an annual public report on the state of human rights around the globe provides an informational starting point.[13]

What stands out above all is that massive and systematic assaults upon human dignity are a function not of ideological strategy but of insecure and paranoid rulers. The quite insignificant role of repression in a number of Afro-Marxist states demonstrates that this option—perhaps because of the "soft," non-Stalinist form of Marxism-Leninism in Africa—does not require *gulag archipelagoes* or the unlimited terror of a Pol Pot. Nor is there support for the O'Donnell argument in the Latin American context that capitalism—international and domestic—can survive only through the creation of a powerful bureaucratic-authoritarian, national-security state strong enough to contain and depoliticize the "popular sectors."[14]

On the Afro-Marxist side, such repression as has occurred in Angola and Mozambique is most closely tied to the incomplete political hegemony that the victorious liberation movement had acquired in key portions of the country during the guerrilla struggle years. In Ethiopia, the revolutionary regime has carried through a more far-reaching social transformation than any other, particularly in rural social and economic relations. Ironically, though, the Red Terror was not directed at recalcitrant landlords, but at an equally revolutionary urban intelligentsia who challenged not the principal options of Ethiopian Marxism-Leninism but the "hijacking" of the revolution by the military. In no other Afro-Marxist capital is the atmosphere of fear and intellectual intimidation so pervasive.

While most regimes were intolerant of open opposition, cooptation rather than coercion was the more frequent tactic in defusing it. Leaders such as Houphouët-Boigny in Ivory Coast developed this technique to a fine art, which—together with the success image of the system—explains the remarkably small security force of only 4,950 men (1978) that the regime required. We might add, however, that not all market-economy states had such generally positive human rights records as those we have considered in detail; Hastings Banda ran a particularly harsh and intolerant authoritarian capitalist state in Malawi. In 1980, Amnesty International published a harsh indictment of human rights violations in Zaire. Infringements of human rights there were "flagrant and gross," with extensive documentation of "political arrests and detention without trial . . . torture, harsh prison conditions and both judicial and extrajudicial executions." [15]

Another significant measure of human dignity lies in the numbers of persons who have fled to neighboring lands. While a small number of persons with internationally transferable credentials, such as doctors, may relocate with little personal hardship, for most persons, especially peasants, the flight abroad represents an act of true desperation. Recent data on the disconcerting number of African refugees is presented in table 6.4.

Only three of the states that have concerned us in this study figure on the refugee list: Angola, Ethiopia, and Guinea. In the first instance, there has been a flow of Angolans into Zaire for a long time, initially during the colonial period largely for economic reasons. The early phase of the liberation struggle was concentrated in the Kongo area of northern Angola, and the violent repression that followed provoked a considerable exodus, many of the refugees becoming permanently resettled. Some additional outflow occurred during the civil war, and Luanda has yet to build a firm base of support in these areas. However, most of this outflow has little to do with postindependence policies or ideology.

The exodus from Guinea, which gathered momentum from the mid-1960s, was triggered both by the capricious political atmosphere (for intellectuals and merchants) and the economic deterioration (for the mass). The political and economic relaxation since 1978 appears to be reversing the flow. The Ethiopian case is more contemporary and more serious; numerically, the exodus includes mainly Eritreans and especially Somalis. The Mengistu regime has been unable to find an alternative to armed

TABLE 6.4. African Refugees

Country of origin	Range of estimates of refugees leaving their country (minimum and maximum)	Comments
Angola	132,000 to 550,000	Nearly all from northern Angola to coethnic Kongo zones in Zaire; dates from colonial period
Burundi	152,000	Mainly triggered by 1972 holocaust
Equatorial Guinea	112,000 to 127,000	Mainly from mainland province to Cameroon, Gabon; probably a number now returning, after Nguema overthrow
Ethiopia	562,000 to 830,000	From Eritrea to Sudan and Djibouti, and from Ogaden to Somalia; latter group rapidly increases to over one million in 1979–80
Guinea	3,000 to 1,000,000	A number return after political relaxation and economic liberalization in 1978
Malawi	15,000	Uncertain figure; many Jehovah's Witnesses
Namibia	23,000 to 33,000	
Rwanda	175,000	Exodus dates from Hutu revolution of 1959–61
South Africa	1,000 to 2,000	
Sudan	14,000 to 16,000	
Uganda	20,000 to 100,000	Before Amin overthrow; some have returned
Zaire	358,000	1978 figure, mostly from Shaba after 1977 and 1978 invasions and subsequent "pacification"; a substantial number have returned
Zimbabwe	102,000 to 140,000	Many now returning after political settlement

SOURCE: Senate, Committee on the Judiciary, *World Refugee Crisis: The International Community's Response*, report prepared by Congressional Research Service, Library of Congress, 96th Congress, 1st Session, August 1979, p. 21.

repression to cope with the separatist aspirations, which have widespread support in these regions. In the Somali case, accusations began to be heard in 1979 that there was a deliberate effort to force ethnic exodus through military harassment, destruction of water sources, and similar heavy-handed measures.

Again, one may note that this regional repression has no relationship to ideology. Both the Somali regime and the Eritrean dissidents claim to be Marxists. None of the other states in question, it should be added, has faced such a mortal threat to its very survival. Secessionism is a threat that virtually all states will meet with force (as, for example, in Nigeria in 1967 or in Angola with the relatively minor Cabinda separatist movement).

PARTICIPATION

Participation has not been highly valued in most African states in the independence era, except in the ritualistic sense of mass turnouts for plebiscitary elections or presidential rallies. The most important contemporary exception is Nigeria, whose exercise in restoring constitutional democratic rule through fair, open, and unrestricted competition is one of the world's most remarkable political experiments. Tanzania pioneered a very different formula for a degree of participation within the single party framework; it permits periodic competition of persons, although not a challenge to the regime's ideological options. This system has been followed by several other states—within our own universe, Kenya and Ivory Coast—with some salutary effects. In both Kenya and Tanzania, there were spectacular defeats for some of the princes of the regime, which no doubt provides some psychological relegitimation of power.

There are some other channels through which significant participation can occur. Bienen makes a persuasive case for the administration itself being an institution of citizen access to the state.[16] Cohen offers a similar brief for the occasional series of "presidential dialogues" carried on by Houphouët-Boigny with diverse social groups in Ivory Coast.[17] The more effective liberation movements—especially FRELIMO—sustain some participative momentum from the high levels of rural involvement indispensable to sustaining the struggle.

However, there are some contrary trends. The transformation of "revolutionary democratic" parties into Leninist vanguard movements based on democratic centralism inexorably makes them weapons for control rather than instruments of participation. The frequent failure of populist socialist regimes to find permanent formulas for "mobilization" has been noted earlier; this had been particularly striking in Nasser's Egypt and Algeria, where repeated efforts to breathe life into the Arab Socialist Union and the FLN have met with failure. In Ethiopia, there was a significant element of participation in the peasant associations formed to self-administer the land reform and, some might argue, in the urban neighborhood associations—though these latter were warped by their functions as "vigilance" committees and intimidation squads. Whether this level of participation can be sustained over time—especially if the long-awaited Leninist party is fully launched—remains to be seen.

An array of states that have a somewhat stronger participation record than the continental norm thus might include Nigeria, Kenya, Tanzania, and Mozambique. All ideological camps are represented on this list. Participation, again, is not a measure that clearly distinguishes the three pathways.

CAPACITY AND PERFORMANCE

The most elusive measure of all is the enlargement of societal capacity. Appraisal in this domain is particularly subjective and speculative; there are no measures beyond the judgmental assessments of knowledgeable observers. And yet the competency of the state is fundamental to all developmental designs. Contrary to Nkrumah's whimsical assertion that capitalism is too complex for Africa, the demands on state capacity are highest for the Afro-Marxist state, with its aspirations for a command economy, comprehensive central planning, and an extensive public sector. However, the African capitalist state as well is committed to broad-front intervention and regulation, a public sector much larger than that of the early industrial European state, and government planning within a market framework. The scope of state action in all three development models places a high premium on the effectiveness and capacity of public institutions.

Further, the relative hegemony of the state over society, traceable to what some have termed the "over-developed colonial state,"[18] sets all development in jeopardy in the event of a highly incompetent state. Neither a market economy nor a socialist economy can function when fettered with a demoralized, corruption-ridden state. The predatory terror regime of Amin destroyed both public and private markets. The sharp decline in state competency observable in the mid and late 1970s in Zaire likewise had a deleterious impact upon the economy.

At the independence day point of departure, all African states faced serious limitations upon their capacities, the product of the domination of colonial status apparatuses by European personnel and the general dereliction of colonial powers in providing advanced training and high-level experience to African personnel. The Africanization of cadres and the rapid expansion of higher education systems were intended to repair these defects. These policies, of course, responded not only to the desire for a competent and self-reliant state, but also to the pressures for social ascent by the new African middle class.

Though all states faced this difficulty, some were more afflicted than others. The transitional crisis of state competency was most severe in the former Portuguese territories, where opportunities for African education had been most restricted. The challenge was compounded by the extreme dislocations attending independence in Mozambique and especially Angola, where the flight of the European population greatly increased the responsibilities that the state was forced to bear. Abandoned enterprises, usually stripped of much or all of their physical capital, had to be taken over by the state. Thus states with few experienced personnel acquired overnight an enormous public sector; the revolutionary skills acquired in the liberation struggle were not necessarily transferable to these administrative responsibilities. At the other end of the spectrum, the coastal West African states (for example, Ghana, Benin, Nigeria, Congo-Brazzaville) greeted independence with greater reservoirs of indigenous managerial talent.

Various formulas for reducing the gap between state capacity and its assigned tasks were available. One was the recruitment of large numbers of foreign personnel, a practice that inevitably involved some compromise of the autonomy goal. Ivory Coast stands out in its persisting recourse to French personnel, who undoubtedly enhanced the competency of the state, but at considerable cost in remuneration and the embedding of French influence within the public sector. Angola and Mozambique also tried to fill the void in state capacity with large numbers of foreign, but not ex-metropolitan, personnel: in the Angolan case, 10,000 Soviet bloc and Cuban economic technicians, and in Mozambique 5,000 young professionals, who, though recruited from both East and West, were expected to be sympathetic to the ideological options of the regime. Other devices were to delegate state activities to local or private bodies or to withdraw the state from particular spheres. Ethiopia, which clearly lacked the state machinery to implement the revolutionary land reform of 1975, simply invited the peasantry to form associations for the execution of the policy. Zaire at various points has assigned to private corporations or even to mission societies such tasks as road maintenance and management of social programs. Mozambique and Angola, in 1980, sought to withdraw the state (at least temporarily) from the vast sweep of the commercial economy they had inherited in 1975.

Again, I do not discern an extensive overlap of patterns of state capacity expansion and ideology. On the African capitalist side, the relative effectiveness of the state apparatus in Ivory Coast and Kenya is generally conceded, though with a significant neocolonial tradeoff in the former instance. Nigeria presents a more mixed picture. At its best, as in the conduct of the 1979 electoral operations, it manifests a remarkable degree of effectiveness. These operations were exceedingly complex, with momentous implications for the legitimacy of the state. Some 47 million voters were registered, exacting rules were applied in the monitoring of the competing political parties, and balloting was conducted on five successive weeks. The striking paucity of challenge to the basic integrity of the process confirms the excellent performance of the administration. In the economic domain, however, the state is blemished by lapses in probity and by the ineffectiveness of its rural development.

Among the populist socialist states, Algeria has overcome the dislocations of the final, self-destructive paroxysm of the colonial settler state and has constructed a reasonably competent government managing a large segment of the economy. Tanzania draws mixed appraisals. Lofchie stresses the demoralization of the public service,[19] while Moris despaired of the capacity of rural administration to fulfill its overwhelming responsibilities.[20] On the other hand, an ILO study in 1978 carefully weighed the arguments that claimed to see a declining competence in the parastatal sector and concluded that these criticisms were unjustified.[21]

Among the Afro-Marxist states, the Benin state has demonstrated reasonable capacity; possibly its human resources have been better used under the more stable conditions achieved under the Kerekou regime. The gap between developmental design and state capacity is most evident in Ethiopia, which has never had a very effective rural administration. The element of class struggle that was involved in the Ethiopian revolution led to the exodus after 1975 of a segment of the top state cadres, who were compromised by their *ancien régime* associations, their ties to the landed aristocracy dispossessed by the *Derg*, or their unwillingness to accept the rigid authoritarianism of military Marxism-Leninism. A more fundamental problem is the political alienation of much of the intelligentsia, despite the ideological sympathy many of them have for the revolutionary goals of the regime. Absent a resolution of these contradictions, prospects are doubtful for the rapid expansion in state capacity required by its scientific socialist doctrine. Mozambique, on the other hand, despite the weaknesses of the state discernible beneath the homogeneous and committed top layer of state and party cadres, may have the leadership, legitimacy, determination, and good fortune to erect a state capable of fulfilling its socialist dream.

FINAL REFLECTIONS

What instruction for the future, then, can be gleaned from two decades of developmental experimentation in Africa? Do the lessons of experience offer a signpost to the future? Does ideology matter?

My reading of the evidence does not lead to a single, unambiguous conclusion. In growth terms, setting aside the large oil producers, only Ivory Coast and Kenya stood out. However, some nonoil states in all camps did perform respectably, Tanzania and Benin, for example. But both Afro-Marxism and populist socialism badly need an inspirational case where the socialist choice is accompanied by dynamic expansion; this did occur in an earlier generation of Communist states, but has eluded the more recent Comecon members (Cuba and Vietnam and its dependencies).

However, the capitalist model is associated with some aspects of the creation of inequality, especially the emergence of high levels of wealth accumulation at the top, both among the African elite and the "foreign estate" that participates in the management of the capitalist economy. Dependency, an appar-

TABLE 6.5. African Growth Rates Compared with Other Selected States

	Real per capita GNP growth, 1960–76		Real per capita GNP growth, 1960–76
Afro-Marxist group		**Other Marxist-Leninist states**	
Angola	2.8	China	5.2
Benin	0.0	North Korea	7.3
Congo	1.3	Mongolia	1.0
Ethiopia	1.9	Yugoslavia	5.6
Madagascar	−0.1	Rumania	8.4
Mozambique	1.4	USSR	3.8
São Tomé	n.a.	East Germany	3.2
Somalia	−0.4	Cuba	1.1
Populist socialist group		**Other populist socialist states**	
Algeria	1.8	Sri Lanka	2.0
Egypt	1.9	Iraq	3.6
Ghana	−0.2	South Yemen (Marxist-Leninist from 1978)	−5.2
Guinea	1.4	Burma	0.7
Mali	0.9	Peru (populist socialist 1968–75)	2.5
Tanzania	2.6		
African capitalist group		**Other third-world capitalist states**	
Ivory Coast	3.3	Brazil	4.8
Kenya	2.6	Mexico	3.0
Nigeria	3.5	Malaysia	3.9
Malawi	3.0	South Korea	7.3
Zaire	1.4	Taiwan	6.2

SOURCE: *World Bank Atlas 1978*, pp. 14–22.

ently simple concept as presented in some of the literature, in reality is a very complex and difficult measure. As I understand it, constraints on autonomy do not have a simple relationship with ideological preference. Nigeria and Algeria appear to stand out as autonomous; in differing ways, states such as Ivory Coast, Congo, and Mozambique are very dependent.

The preservation of human dignity is not incompatible with any of the three model pathways, although it has been seriously compromised in a few of the cases examined—most notably Ethiopia. Elements of participation may be found—along with limits to its exercise—in all three system types, though Nigeria towers above all others on this measure, at least in the euphoria of civilianization and the successful conduct of a very fair and free electoral contest. We were unable to make clear distinctions on the basis of the final criterion, enlargement of state capacity.

Ideological preference does influence, in significant ways, the matrix of policy. At the time of independence, there was little to differentiate Ivory Coast and Guinea or Kenya and Tanzania. The cumulative impact over two decades of sharply divergent visions of the future has made Ivory Coast and Kenya very different from Guinea and Tanzania.

Many other factors, of course, shape the overall developmental outcome: resource endowment, climatic disasters, proximity to conflict zones, energy and food prices. A central place must be accorded as well to such a homely variable as the simple competence of particular regimes. Ideology does make certain choices more likely. Each type contains particular vulnerabilities. But within each framework, a very wide margin of difference arises from the skill, competence, and rationality with which a given strategy is pursued.

Notes

CHAPTER 1

1. Not to everybody at the time of judgment; for contrasting appraisals, see Elliot J. Berg, "Structural Transformation Versus Gradualism: Recent Economic Development in Ghana and the Ivory Coast," in *Ghana and the Ivory Coast*, ed. Philip Foster and Aristide R. Zolberg (Chicago: University of Chicago Press, 1971), pp. 187–230, and Reginald Green, "Reflections on Economic Strategy, Structure, Implementation, and Necessity: Ghana and the Ivory Coast," in ibid., pp. 231–64.

2. Abdoulaye Ly, *Les masses africaines et l'actuelle condition humaine* (Paris: Editions Présence Africaine, 1956).

3. Julius K. Nyerere, *Ujamaa: Essays on Socialism* (London: Oxford University Press, 1968).

4. Useful treatments of early African socialism may be found in William H. Friedland and Carl G. Rosberg, eds., *African Socialism* (Stanford: Stanford University Press, 1964); L. V. Thomas, *Le socialisme et l'Afrique* (Paris: Livre Africain, 1966).

5. Joseph Schumpeter, *Capitalism, Socialism and Democracy*, 3d ed. (New York: Harper & Row, 1950), pp. 59–163.

6. Scientific socialism was, of course, not entirely new on the scene. In many countries, small numbers of intellectuals espoused Marxist-Leninist convictions. Missionary efforts to foster diffusion of these tenets were carried on through the sundry Soviet, East European, and, to some extent, Chinese embassies, and the metropolitan countries through the respective Communist and other far left parties. For a useful case study of ideological diffusion, see William J. Foltz, "Le Parti Africain de l'Indépendance: Les dilemmes d'un mouvement communiste en Afrique occidentale," *Revue Française d'Etudes Politiques Africaines* 45 (September 1969): 8–35.

7. For an initial overall assessment of these new directions in so-

cialism, see Carl G. Rosberg and Thomas M. Callaghy, eds., *Socialism in Sub-Saharan Africa: A New Assessment* (Berkeley: University of California Institute of International Studies, 1979); Richard L. Sklar, "Socialism at Bay" (Paper delivered at annual meeting of African Studies Association, Houston, November 1977).

8. So named by one of Amin's former collaborators, Henry Kyemba, *A State of Blood* (New York: Ace Books, 1977).

9. E. A. Brett, "Relations of Production, the State, and the Ugandan Crisis," *West African Journal of Sociology and Political Science* 1, no. 3 (January 1978): 249. On the Amin debacle, see also David Gwynn, *Idi Amin: Deathlight of Africa* (Boston: Little Brown, 1977); David Martin, *General Amin* (London: Faber and Faber, 1974); International Commission of Jurists, *Uganda and Human Rights* (Geneva, 1977).

10. *West Africa* 3191 (11 September 1978): 1775.

11. *Washington Star*, 2 September 1978.

12. Crawford Young, "Zaire: The Unending Crisis," *Foreign Affairs* 57, no. 1 (October 1978): 169–85.

13. Susumu Watanabe, "Minimum Wages in Developing Countries: Myth and Reality," *International Labour Review* 113 (May–June 1976): 353.

14. Of this now immense literature, we may note in particular the numerous writings of Samir Amin, especially *Unequal Development* (New York: Monthly Review Press, 1977) and *Accumulation on a World Scale: A Critique of the Theory of Underdevelopment* (New York: Monthly Review Press, 1974); Colin Leys, *Underdevelopment in Kenya* (Berkeley: University of California Press, 1974); Walter Rodney, *How Europe Underdeveloped Africa* (London: Bogle-L'Ouverture, 1972); Peter Gutkind and Immanuel Wallerstein, eds., *The Political Economy of Contemporary Africa* (Beverly Hills: Sage Publications, 1976).

15. James H. Mittelman, "The Dialectic of National Autonomy and Global Participation: Alternatives to Conventional Strategies of Development—The Mozambique Experience," *Alternatives* 5 (1979–80): 316.

16. Anatoly Gromyko, "The Present Stage of the Anti-Imperialist Struggle in Africa," *Social Sciences* 10, no. 4 (1979): 4. Gromyko is director of the USSR Africa Institute.

17. It should be noted that this term is my own and is used to connote the distinctiveness of Marxism-Leninism in Africa; it is never used by persons of such ideological persuasion about themselves.

18. Simon Kuznets, *Modern Economic Growth* (New Haven: Yale University Press, 1966).

19. Gunnar Myrdal, *Asian Drama*, 3 vols. (New York: Pantheon, 1968).

20. Irma Adelman and Cynthia T. Morris, *Economic Growth and Social Equity in Developing Countries* (Stanford: Stanford University Press, 1973).

21. Hollis Chenery, *Redistribution with Growth* (London: Oxford University Press, 1974).

22. Arthur Okun, *Equality and Efficiency: The Big Tradeoff* (Washington: Brookings, 1975).

23. Harry Eckstein, *The Evaluation of Political Performance: Problems and Dimensions* (Beverly Hills: Sage Publications, 1971).

24. Leonard Binder et al., *Crises and Sequences of Political Development* (Princeton: Princeton University Press, 1971).

25. See the interesting discussion in W. Edward Clark, *Socialist Development and Public Investment in Tanzania 1964–1973* (Toronto: University of Toronto Press, 1978), pp. 6–10.

26. Chenery, *Redistribution with Growth*, suggests a somewhat different strategy for using the growth measure in a more effective way, by disaggregating GNP change by income level and weighting that accruing to the lowest deciles.

27. For a useful discussion of the participation concept, see Myron Weiner, "Political Participation: Crisis of the Political Process," in Binder et al., *Crises and Sequences*, pp. 159–204.

28. Samuel Huntington, *Political Order in Changing Societies* (New Haven: Yale University Press, 1968).

29. Nelson Kasfir, *The Shrinking Political Arena* (Berkeley: University of California Press, 1976).

30. James S. Coleman, "The Development Syndrome: Differentiation-Equality-Capacity," in Binder et al., *Crises and Sequences*, p. 79.

31. The concept of the modern bureaucratic-authoritarian state is developed initially by Guillermo O'Donnell, *Modernization and Bureaucratic Authoritarianism* (Berkeley: University of California Institute of International Studies, 1973) (and modified by other works since). It should be noted that his model applies to the relatively developed states of Argentina, Uruguay, Brazil, and Chile, where preservation of a capitalist economy appeared to require the forcible demobilization of the "popular sectors," with state management assured by a technocratic bureaucracy. Thus defined, African states do not really fit the "bureaucratic-authoritarian" model.

32. This argument is developed in Crawford Young, "The State and

the Small Urban Center," in *The Small Urban Center and African Development*, ed. Aidan Southall (Madison: African Studies Program, University of Wisconsin-Madison, 1979), pp. 313–33.

CHAPTER 2

1. Among the now vast literature on the Cuban revolution, I find particularly persuasive the analysis of Jorge I. Dominguez, *Cuba: Order and Revolution* (Cambridge: Harvard University Press, Belknap Press, 1978).

2. I am not including such ephemera as the bizarre Comoros regime of Ali Soilih (1975–78) or the sanguinary Equatorial Guinea regime of Macias Nguema (1968–79), although these unlamented leaders were occasionally quoted as cloaking their capricious rule in Marxism-Leninism. In both instances the chaotic (Comoros) or terrorist (Macias Nguema) personalism of actual governance, not to mention its paranoia and incompetence, excludes according serious weight to these episodic verbalizations. "Emperor" Jean-Bedel Bokassa of the Central African Republic briefly declared himself a "scientific socialist" in 1970 and dispatched a mission to Moscow to see what reward that might bring. The delegation returned empty-handed, and the regime's Marxism-Leninism quickly vanished.

3. See the official history of the Mongolian Communist Party, which makes clear how arduous the struggle was to impose Communism upon a society of nomadic Buddhist herders. William A. Brown, *History of the Mongolian People's Republic* (Cambridge: East Asian Research Center, Harvard University, 1976).

4. See the exhaustive study by Robert Scalapino and Chong-Sik Lee, *Communism in Korea*, 2 vols. (Berkeley: University of California Press, 1972).

5. Dominguez, *Cuba: Order and Revolution*, carefully evaluates the nature and limits of Soviet influence in the Cuban strategy. See also Carmela Mesa-Lago, ed., *Cuba in the 1970s* (Albuquerque: University of New Mexico Press, 1974).

6. Alexander B. Woodside, *Community and Revolution in Modern Vietnam* (Boston: Houghton Mifflin, 1976).

7. *Le Monde*, 5 October 1978.

8. The most careful study of the Chinese role in Africa remains Bruce D. Larkin, *China and Africa 1949–1970* (Berkeley: University of California Press, 1971). On the Cuban role in Africa, see especially Jorge

I. Dominguez, "Cuban Foreign Policy," *Foreign Affairs* 57, no. 1 (October 1978): 83–108.

9. In *Sub-Saharan Africa*, ed. Rosberg and Callaghy, pp. 143–44.

10. Amilcar Cabral, *Revolution in Guinea* (New York: Monthly Review Press, 1969). See also the comparison between Leninism and populism by Jowitt, "Scientific Socialist Regimes in Africa: Political Differentiation, Avoidance, and Unawareness," in *Sub-Saharan Africa*, ed. Rosberg and Callaghy, pp. 151–59.

11. Edward Alpers, "The Struggle for Socialism in Mozambique, 1960–1972," in *Sub-Saharan Africa*, ed. Rosberg and Callaghy, pp. 267–95, argues that the main lines of the Marxist-Leninist commitment were in place by 1972.

12. See the useful analysis of recent trends in Soviet analysis of African politics by Milena Charles, "The Changing Vision of the African Working Class—A Component of Soviet Strategy in Black Africa?" *Journal of Modern African Studies* 16, no. 4 (December 1978): 695–700. For a current Soviet statement, see also N. Kosukhin, "Revolutionary Democracy: Its Ideology and Policies," *Social Sciences* 10, no. 4 (1979): 50–63.

13. Marina and David Ottaway, *Ethiopia: Empire in Revolution* (New York: Africana Publishing Corporation, 1978), pp. 169–70.

14. P. I. Manchkha, "Communists, Revolutionary Democrats and the Noncapitalist Path of Development in African Countries," *Current Digest of the Soviet Press*, 27, no. 51 (21 January 1976), quoted by Jowitt, in *Sub-Saharan Africa*, ed. Rosberg and Callaghy, p. 150.

15. The most valuable recent studies on Congo-Brazzaville are Hugues Bertrand, *Le Congo* (Paris: Francois Maspero, 1975) and Samuel Decalo, "Ideological Rhetoric and Scientific Socialism in Benin and Congo-Brazzaville," in *Sub-Saharan Africa*, ed. Rosberg and Callaghy, pp. 231–64, and *Coups and Army Rule in Africa* (New Haven: Yale University Press, 1976).

16. Bertrand, *Le Congo*, pp. 77–90.

17. Ibid., pp. 106–15.

18. Jan Vansina, in research in a small up-country community of three hundred in the mid-1960s, found that every adult had made the 100-mile journey to Brazzaville and had kinsmen there; a number made the journey every weekend. Knowledge of political events was high. Personal communication.

19. According to Decalo, in *Sub-Saharan Africa*, ed. Rosberg and Callaghy, p. 257. Other sources identify him as a Makoua (Fort Rousset); Bertrand lists him as a Kouyou cousin of Ngouabi, *Le Congo*, p. 22.

20. Decalo, *Coups and Army Rule*, provides an excellent account of this period, pp. 123–72.

21. Ibid., p. 164.

22. Ibid., pp. 158–59.

23. *Africa Contemporary Record, 1974–75*, pp. B576–77.

24. Ibid., 1976–77, p. B493.

25. Decalo, in *Sub-Saharan Africa*, ed. Rosberg and Callaghy, p. 258.

26. Watanabe, "Minimum Wages in Developing Countries," p. 353.

27. *World Bank Atlas 1978*, p. 14.

28. This information derives from a World Bank study of the logging industry.

29. Central Intelligence Agency, *Communist Aid to Less Developed Countries of the Free World 1977*, ER 78-1047 8U, November 1978, p. 5.

30. Decalo, in *Sub-Saharan Africa*, ed. Rosberg and Callaghy, p. 260.

31. Bertrand, *Le Congo*, p. 64.

32. *Africa Contemporary Record, 1976–77*, p. B493.

33. Bertrand, *Le Congo*, pp. 188, 256.

34. Ibid., p. 189.

35. Ibid., p. 221.

36. According to World Bank data. This is far from the only explanation for the falling forestry output; exploitative and wasteful harvesting techniques by the French lumber companies, which have creamed the accessible southern forests, is a major factor.

37. ELF maintained that the oil pools were smaller than anticipated, while the potash company claimed that the orebody was undulating rather than flat, making extraction costs much higher than anticipated. The providential floods in 1977 provided a devoutly wished for pretext to abandon the project. In 1980, there were indications that an American corporation might reopen the mines, and oil output prospects heightened.

38. *Africa Contemporary Record, 1975–76*, p. B472.

39. The best accounts of Benin (Dahomey) politics in the pre-1972 period are Dov Ronen, *Dahomey* (Ithaca: Cornell University Press, 1975); Decalo, *Coups and Army Rule*, pp. 39–85.

40. For convincing detail, see Decalo, *Coups and Army Rule*, pp. 53–57.

41. Ibid., p. 54.

42. Ibid., p. 79.

43. Most observers believe that the alleged tryst was a fabrication and that Aikpe was the victim of an assassination. See Decalo, in *Sub-Saharan Africa*, ed. Rosberg and Callaghy, p. 243.

44. Ibid., p. 236.

45. See Charles Bettelheim et al., *La construction du socialisme en Chine* (Paris: Maspero, 1968). Bettelheim had been a prime architect of the disastrous initial plans for Guinea and Mali in 1959–61. See also Marcelle Genné, "La tentation du socialisme au Benin," *Etudes Internationales* 9, no. 3 (September 1978): 383–403.

46. *Africa Contemporary Record, 1976–77,* p. B550.

47. Genné, "La tentation du socialisme," pp. 391–92.

48. Ibid., p. 397.

49. Ibid., p. 395.

50. Decalo, in Rosberg and Callaghy, eds., *Sub-Saharan Africa,* p. 240.

51. Genné, "La tentation du socialisme," pp. 393–94.

52. Ibid., p. 401.

53. As of 1979, the United States still had only a chargé d'affaires in Cotonou, despite the advent of the Carter Administration, which had a less serious allergy to Marxist regimes, and repeated entreaties by Benin to appoint a regular ambassador.

54. *Africa Contemporary Record, 1974–75,* p. B631.

55. CIA, *Communist Aid to Less Developed Countries . . . 1977,* p. 5.

56. *World Bank Atlas 1977.*

57. *Africa Contemporary Record, 1976–77,* p. B558.

58. On contemporary Madagascar, useful sources include Robert Archer, *Madagascar depuis 1972* (Paris: Editions de l'Harmattan, 1976); Louis Molet, "Madagascar depuis 1972," *Afrique et Asie Modernes* 113 (1977): 39–51; Philippe Leymarie, "Le Fokonolona: la voie malgache vers le socialisme?" *Revue Française d'Etudes Politiques Africaines* 112 (April 1975): 42–62; Philippe Leymarie, "Madagascar: comment repartir?" *Revue Française d'Etudes Politiques Africaines* 116 (August 1975): 15–17; Philippe Hugon, "L'evolution économique de Madagascar de la 1ère à la séconde république," *Revue Française d'Etudes Politiques Africaines* 143 (November 1977): 26–57; F. Bezy, "La transformation des structures socio-économiques à Madagascar (1960–1978)," *Cultures et Développement* 11, no. 1 (1979): 83–116; Georges Seira-Ratsimandisa, "Théorie et pratique du 'Fokonolona' moderne à Madagascar," *Canadian Journal of African Studies* 12, no. 1 (1978): 37–58.

59. Jean Poirier, "Les groupes ethniques de Madagascar," *Revue*

Française d'Etudes Politiques Africaines 100 (April 1974): 31–40; Virginia Thompson and Richard Adloff, *The Malagasy Republic* (Stanford: Stanford University Press, 1965), pp. 258–65.

60. Leymarie, "Le Fokonolona," pp. 42–43.

61. Ibid., pp. 45–47. The ambitious and strong-willed Resampa acquired many enemies over the years. To the French community, he was a dangerous instrument of American interests; to the Malagasy left, he was an unreliable agent of American imperialism; to the Merina, he was a cotier militant who conspicuously chose to speak French rather than Malagasy on various occasions.

62. Hugon, "L'evolution économique de Madagascar," p. 33. Archer, *Madagascar depuis 1972*, pp. 46–53, argues that the exclusion of Merina elites by Tsiranana has been exaggerated by some analysts; he points out that most department heads were from the Tananarive Merina bourgeoisie, while the territorial service had more cotier elements.

63. Archer, *Madagascar depuis 1972*, pp. 63–76.

64. Ibid., pp. 38–47.

65. Leymarie, "Le Fokonolona," pp. 49–58.

66. Hugon, "L'evolution économique de Madagascar," p. 33.

67. Archer, *Madagascar depuis 1972*, pp. 30–45.

68. *Africa Contemporary Record, 1974–75*, p. B221.

69. Archer, *Madagascar depuis 1972*, pp. 93–120.

70. Ph. L., "Madagascar: comment repartir?" p. 15.

71. *Africa Contemporary Record, 1976–77*, p. B251.

72. Hugon, "L'evolution économique de Madagascar," p. 49.

73. Archer, *Madagascar depuis 1972*, pp. 140–45.

74. CIA, *Communist Aid to Less Developed Countries . . .* 1977, p. 17; ibid., 1978, p. 26.

75. In Archer, *Madagascar depuis 1972*, p. 181. For a pessimistic appraisal, see *Washington Post*, 8 March 1981, p. A19.

76. Philippe Decraene, "Specificités somaliennes," *Revue Française d'Etudes Politiques Africaines* 115 (July 1975): 29–40. See also Basil Davidson, "Somalia in 1975: Notes and Impressions," *Issue* 5, no. 1 (Spring 1975), and the more extended study by Decraene, *L'expérience socialiste somalienne* (Paris: Berger-Levrault, 1977).

77. The classic monograph on Somali society is I. M. Lewis, *A Pastoral Democracy* (London: Oxford University Press, 1961).

78. Quoted in David Laitin, "Somalia's Military Government and Scientific Socialism," in *Sub-Saharan Africa*, ed. Rosberg and Callaghy, p. 174.

79. CIA, *Communist Aid to Less Developed Countries* . . . *1977*, pp. 3, 5, 11.

80. I am indebted to William J. Foltz for this observation.

81. Laitin, in *Sub-Saharan Africa*, ed. Rosberg and Callaghy, p. 197.

82. Ibid., pp. 200–01.

83. Decraene, *L'expérience socialiste somalienne*, pp. 168–69.

84. Ibid., pp. 90–91.

85. Philippe Decraene, "Notes sur la voie socialiste somalienne," *Revue Française d'Etudes Politiques Africaines* 137 (May 1977): 54–78.

86. Ibid., pp. 69–70.

87. See the valuable discussion on these points by Laitin, in *Sub-Saharan Africa*, ed. Rosberg and Callaghy, pp. 181–90.

88. Ibid., p. 203.

89. I am indebted to Foltz for this observation.

90. Decraene asserts, however, that this claim is made only by regime oppoents and is inaccurate: *L'expérience socialiste somalienne*, p. 156.

91. *Africa Confidential*, 14 February 1979.

92. *World Bank Atlas 1977*.

93. In *Sub-Saharan Africa*, ed. Rosberg and Callaghy, p. 198.

94. Ottaway and Ottaway, *Ethiopia*, p. 190.

95. P. T. W. Baxter, "Ethiopia's Unacknowledged Problem: The Oromo," *African Affairs* 77, no. 308 (July 1978): 295.

96. On the Ethiopian land system, see John Cohen and Dov Weintraub, *Land and Peasants in Imperial Ethiopia* (Assen, Netherlands: Van Gorcum and Co., 1975); Allen Hoeben, *Land Tenure Among the Amhara of Ethiopia* (Chicago: University of Chicago Press, 1973).

97. Baxter, "Ethiopia's Unacknowledged Problem," pp. 291–92.

98. For an Oromo-oriented perspective, see Baxter, ibid. The pan-Oromo consciousness, Baxter argues, was forged by their increasing incorporation into the Ethiopian state and their participation in the army, the bureaucracy, the university, and even parliament. Among other things, this national involvement made Oromo elites aware of their numerical strength. For Oromo, "An Amhara is one who, all in all, assumes that Amharic culture is so obviously superior to the other cultures of Ethiopia that all Ethiopians should seek to acquire that culture." (p. 289). There are strong signs of a rapid deepening and mobilization of Oromo identity, a process in which the Oromo Liberation Front plays an important role. They now lay claim to an independent "Oromia" state.

See "A Letter to Cubans in Harar" (from the Oromo Liberation Front), *Horn of Africa* 2, no. 1 (1978): 10–14.

99. On Somalis in Ethiopia, see Richard Greenfield, "The Ogaden: Province or Colony?" *West Africa* 3142 (26 September 1977): 1965–68 and *West Africa* 3143 (3 October 1977): 2017–19.

100. Donald N. Levine, *Greater Ethiopia: The Evolution of a Multi-ethnic Society* (Chicago: University of Chicago Press, 1974), p. 26.

101. Tom Farer, *War Clouds on the Horn of Africa*, 2d ed. (New York: Carnegie Endowment for International Peace, 1979), p. 50.

102. Ottaway and Ottaway, *Ethiopia*, p. 67.

103. Ibid., pp. 71–77.

104. John Harbeson, "Socialist Politics in Revolutionary Ethiopia," in *Sub-Saharan Africa*, ed. Rosberg and Callaghy, pp. 345–72. See also the excellent analysis of the Derg in Ottaway and Ottaway, *Ethiopia*, pp. 128–48.

105. Ibid., p. 136.

106. See, for example, the intriguing Oromo Liberation Front appeal to the Cubans, "A Letter to Cubans in Harar."

107. One of the rare articles on this island state is Laurie S. Wisenberg and Gary F. Nelson, "Sao Tome and Principe: Mini-state with Maxi-problems," *Africa Report* 21 (March–April 1976): 15–17.

108. For the most comprehensive treatment of Angolan nationalism and the conquest of independence, see John A. Marcum, *The Angolan Revolution*, 2 vols. (Cambridge: MIT Press, 1969, 1978).

109. Kevin Brown, "Angolan Socialism," in *Sub-Saharan Africa*, ed. Rosberg and Callaghy, p. 302.

110. Basil Davidson, "In Angola Now," pt. 4, *West Africa* 3135 (8 August 1977): 1631. This and the three preceding parts offer a very upbeat interpretation: pt. 1, *West Africa* 3132 (18 July 1977): 1472–73; pt. 2, *West Africa* 3133 (25 July 1977): 1518–22; pt. 3, *West Africa* 3134 (1 August 1977): 1578–79.

111. Davidson, "In Angola Now," pt. 4, p. 1631.

112. See the series by David Lamb in the *Los Angeles Times*, 25–27 May 1980.

113. CIA, *Communist Aid to Less Developed Countries . . . 1978*, pp. 7, 21.

114. *New York Times*, 8 February 1981.

115. Radio Luanda, broadcast transcript, 31 May 1980.

116. This is already visible in the divergent appraisals now extant. For examples of optimistic assessments, see Allen Isaacman, "Mozam-

bique since Independence," *Africa Report* 26, no. 4 (July–August 1978): 4–9; Thomas Henriksen, "Marxism and Mozambique," *African Affairs* 77, no. 309 (October 1978): 441–62; and the contributors to a special number of *Issue* [8, no. 1 (Spring 1978)] devoted to Mozambique. For the pessimistic view, see Tony Hodges, "Mozambique: The Politics of Liberation," in *Southern Africa in Crisis*, ed. Gwendolen M. Carter and Patrick O'Meara (Bloomington: Indiana University Press, 1977), pp. 48–88.

117. Mittelman, "The Mozambique Experience," p. 318. This is the best documented assessment of postindependence Mozambique to date, by an author sympathetic to the FRELIMO orientation, yet careful and balanced in his analysis. See also, by the same author, "Mozambique: The Political Economy of Underdevelopment," *Journal of Southern African Affairs* 3, no. 1 (January 1978): 35–54.

118. This is the argument of Edward Alpers, in *Sub-Saharan Africa*, ed. Rosberg and Callaghy, pp. 267–95.

119. John Saul, *The State and Revolution in Eastern Africa* (London: Heinemann, 1979), pp. 67–77.

120. Isaacman, "Mozambique since Independence," p. 5.

121. Mittelman, "The Mozambique Experience," p. 318.

122. Allen and Barbara Isaacman, "Mozambique on the Road to Economic Recovery," *Africa Report* 25, no. 3 (May–June 1980): 6.

123. Ibid., p. 7.

124. Saul, *Revolution in Eastern Africa*, pp. 429–44.

125. Isaacman, "Mozambique since Independence," p. 6.

126. CIA, *Communist Aid to Less Developed Countries . . . 1977*, p. 18.

127. See the rather nuanced appreciation of the repression issue in Mozambique in Department of State, *Country Reports on Human Rights Practices for 1979*, Joint Committee Print, Committees on Foreign Affairs and Foreign Relations, 96th Congress, 2d Session, 1980, pp. 133–36. Mittelman argues that the persistence of fragments of capitalism makes some degree of coercion inevitable and that the relatively modest degree of repression relative to the colonial era is indicative of a clearly positive direction: "The Mozambique Experience," pp. 319–20.

CHAPTER 3

1. There were of course other currents of socialist thought, in countries such as South Africa, Sudan, and the Mahgreb. Until indepen-

dence loomed, however, these remained encapsulated within particular territories and frequently were expounded primarily by European intellectuals (South Africa, Algeria).

2. For useful summaries of African socialism—their admiring tone often reflects the preeminence of this diffuse creed—see Friedland and Rosberg, eds., *African Socialism*, and Thomas, *Le socialisme et l'Afrique*.

3. Julius Nyerere, *Ujamaa: Essays on Socialism* (London: Oxford University Press, 1968), pp. 3–4.

4. Leopold Sédar Senghor, *On African Socialism* (New York: Frederick A. Praeger, 1964), pp. 67–103. On Senghor's thought, see also Irving L. Markovitz, *Leopold Sédar Senghor and the Politics of Negritude* (New York: Atheneum, 1969).

5. Quoted in Charles A. Micaud, *Tunisia: The Politics of Modernization* (New York: Frederick A. Praeger, 1964), pp. 142–43.

6. Nyerere, *Ujamaa*, pp. 76–77.

7. An early challenge to this view was entered by Igor Kopytoff, "Socialism and Traditional African Societies," in *African Socialism*, ed. Friedland and Rosberg, pp. 53–62.

8. Among the many critics on this score, see Bernard Magubane, "The Evolution of the Class Structure in Africa," in *Political Economy of Africa*, ed. Gutkind and Wallerstein (Beverly Hills: Sage Publications, 1976), pp. 169–97.

9. These characteristics do not necessarily rule out "pragmatism," particularly at the level of personal transactions by leaders. Nkrumah, Nasser, and Nyerere all were equipped with immense charm in private negotiations and often a good deal of personal flexibility. But *radical* seems a reasonable characterization of their public personalities.

10. Nyerere, *Ujamaa*, pp. 2–3.

11. See the various contributions in Ghinta Ionescu and Ernest Gellner, eds., *Populism: Its Meaning and National Characteristics* (London: Weidenfeld and Nicolson, 1969).

12. A classic example of this adulation is William E. Smith, *Nyerere of Tanzania* (London: Victor Gollancz, 1973); herein originated the oft-cited Nyerere phrase, "We must run while they may walk."

13. The intrinsic interest of the Tanzanian experience is reflected in the vast literature devoted to it. Among the more important studies are Joel D. Barkan and John J. Okumu, eds., *Politics and Public Policy in Kenya and Tanzania* (New York: Praeger Publishers, 1979); Dean E.

McHenry, *Tanzania's Ujamaa Villages* (Berkeley: University of California Institute of International Studies, 1979); Jannik Boesen et al., *Ujamaa—Socialism from Above* (Uppsala: Scandinavian Institute of African Studies, 1977); Francis Hill, *Ujamaa: Mobilization and Participation in Tanzania* (London: Frank Cass, 1978); Lionel Cliffe et al., *Rural Cooperatives in Tanzania* (Dar es Salaam: Tanzania Publishing House, 1975); P. M. Van Hekken and H. V. E. Thoden Van Velzen, *Land Scarcity and Rural Inequality in Tanzania* (The Hague: Mouton, 1972); Cranford Pratt, *The Critical Phase in Tanzania 1945–1968* (Cambridge: Cambridge University Press, 1978); James R. Finucane, *Rural Development and Bureaucracy in Tanzania: The Case of Mwanza Region* (Uppsala: Scandinavian Institute of African Studies, 1974); Clyde Ingle, *From Village to State in Tanzania: The Politics of Rural Development* (Ithaca: Cornell University Press, 1972); Issa G. Shivji, *Class Struggles in Tanzania* (London: Heinemann, 1976); Samuel S. Mushi, "Revolution by Evolution: The Tanzanian Road to Socialism" (Ph.D. diss., Yale University, 1974); Justin H. Maeda, "Popular Participation, Control, and Development: A Case Study of the Nature and Role of Popular Participation in Tanzania's Rural Development" (Ph.D. diss., Yale University, 1976); Michael F. Lofchie, "Agrarian Crisis and Economic Liberalisation in Tanzania," *Journal of Modern African Studies* 16, no. 3 (1978): 451–75; Philip Raikes, "Rural Differentiation and Class Formation in Tanzania," *Journal of Peasant Studies* 5, no. 3 (April 1978): 285–325; Helge Kjekshus, "The Tanzanian Villagization Policy: Implementational Lessons and Ecological Dimensions," *Canadian Journal of African Studies* 11, no. 2 (1977): 269–82; W. Edmund Clark, *Socialist Development and Public Investment in Tanzania* (Toronto: University of Toronto Press, 1978); L. Cliffe and John Saul, eds., *Socialism in Tanzania*, 2 vols. (Dar es Salaam: East African Publishing House, 1957); Henry Bienen, *Tanzania: Party Transformation and Economic Development* (Princeton: Princeton University Press, 1970); Bismarck U. Mwansasu and Cranford Pratt, eds., *Towards Socialism in Tanzania* (Toronto: University of Toronto Press, 1979); Goran Hyden, *Beyond Ujamaa in Tanzania* (Berkeley: University of California Press, 1980).

 14. Pratt, *Criticial Phase in Tanzania*, p. 175.

 15. United Republic of Tanzania, *Report of the Presidential Special Committee of Enquiry into Co-Operative Movement and Marketing Boards* (Dar es Salaam: Government Printer, 1966), pp. 2–3.

 16. Pratt, *Criticial Phase in Tanzania*, pp. 1–8.

 17. Shivji, *Class Struggles in Tanzania*, pp. 79–99.

18. Nyerere, *Ujamaa*, pp. 15–16.

19. *Towards Socialism in Tanzania*, ed. Mwansasu and Pratt, pp. 19–45.

20. Clark, *Socialist Development in Tanzania*, p. 112. The Clark analysis of public sector expansion and performance is especially valuable. On the bank nationalization, see James H. Mittelman, "Underdevelopment and Nationalization: Banking in Tanzania," *Journal of Modern African Studies* 16, no. 4 (December 1978): 597–618.

21. Clark, *Socialist Development in Tanzania*, p. 117.

22. Ibid., pp. 98–172.

23. Lofchie, "Agrarian Crisis," pp. 458–59.

24. Pratt, *Criticial Phase in Tanzania*, pp. 227–65.

25. Lofchie, "Agrarian Crisis," p. 458.

26. David Court, "The Education System as a Response to Inequality," in *Politics and Public Policy*, ed. Barkan and Okumu, p. 222.

27. Nyerere, *Ujamaa*, pp. 44–75.

28. On the Kilimanjaro aspect, see Joel Samoff, *Tanzania: Local Politics and the Structure of Power* (Madison: University of Wisconsin Press, 1974).

29. Ruth Besha, "Education for Self-Reliance and Rural Development," mimeographed, Institute of Education, University of Dar es Salaam, 1973. Cited by Court, in *Politics and Public Policy*, ed. Barkan and Okumu, pp. 224–25.

30. Ibid., p. 226.

31. Green, in *Towards Socialism in Tanzania*, ed. Mwansasu and Pratt, p. 26.

32. United Republic of Tanzania, *Report of the Presidential Commission on the Establishment of a Democratic One Party State* (Dar es Salaam: Government Printer, 1965).

33. Lionel Cliffe, ed., *One Party Democracy* (Nairobi: East African Publishing House, 1967), provides an exhaustive study of these elections and demonstrates their important effect in relegitimizing the party.

34. Most notably by Bienen, *Tanzania: Party Transformation*; Finucane, *Rural Development in Tanzania*; Samoff, *Tanzania: Local Politics*.

35. Pratt, in *Towards Socialism in Tanzania*, ed. Mwansasu and Pratt, p. 199.

36. See, for example, Saul, *Revolution in Eastern Africa*, pp. 185–86; *Towards Socialism in Tanzania*, ed. Mwansasu and Pratt, pp. 202–03.

37. Nyerere, *Ujamaa*, p. 25.

38. Joel Samoff, "Crises and the Transition to Socialism in Tanzania" (Paper delivered at Conference on International Relations and Third World Development, University of Denver, June 1979), p. 13.

39. Nyerere, *Ujamaa*, p. 33.

40. Ibid., p. 120.

41. Mushi, "Revolution by Evolution," pp. 158–66.

42. McHenry, *Tanzania's Ujamaa Villages*, pp. 91–105.

43. Mushi, "Revolution by Evolution," pp. 351–52.

44. Ibid., pp. 346–54.

45. Boesen et al., *Ujamaa—Socialism from Above*, p. 170; Kjekshus, "Tanzanian Villagization Policy," p. 270.

46. Boesen et al., *Ujamaa—Socialism from Above*, p. 166.

47. Maeda, "Popular Participation," pp. 171–78.

48. Mushi, "Revolution by Evolution," pp. 363–65.

49. Ibid., p. 365.

50. Shivji, *Class Struggles in Tanzania*, is representative of this school.

51. Pratt, *Criticial Phase in Tanzania*, p. 217.

52. Mushi, "Revolution by Evolution," p. 367.

53. James Scott, *The Moral Economy of the Peasant* (New Haven: Yale University Press, 1976).

54. Mushi, "Revolution by Evolution," pp. 407–19.

55. Kjekshus, "Tanzanian Villagization Policy," p. 451; Raikes, "Rural Differentiation in Tanzania."

56. Maeda, "Popular Participation," pp. 185–235.

57. Lofchie, "Agrarian Crisis," p. 451.

58. Shivji, *Class Struggles in Tanzania*, pp. 106–10.

59. Samoff, "Crises and the Transition to Socialism in Tanzania," p. 12.

60. Lofchie, "Agrarian Crisis," p. 453.

61. Ibid., p. 463.

62. Ibid., pp. 464–65.

63. Bifuko Baharanyi, whose doctoral dissertation was presented to the Université Nationale du Zaire (Lubumbashi) in 1980.

64. Goran Hyden, "Administration and Public Policy," in *Politics and Public Policy*, ed. Barkan and Okumu, pp. 96–101. This style is characterized by periodic "frontal attacks" on reform, where the "ambition is to maximize as many social values as possible through policies which serve to mobilize new resources for the achievement of these very values," and a disposition to embark on major policies without having full knowledge of the consequences.

65. Green, in *Towards Socialism in Tanzania*, ed. Mwansasu and Pratt, p. 37.

66. Ibid., p. 39.

67. Alex Radian, *Resource Mobilization in Poor Countries: Implementing Tax Policies* (New Brunswick: Transaction Books, 1980), p. 8.

68. Boesen, in *Towards Socialism in Tanzania*, ed. Mwansasu and Pratt, pp. 138–43.

69. Quoted in ibid., p. 229.

70. Hyden, in *Politics and Public Policy*, ed. Barkan and Okumu, p. 97.

71. Quoted in Michael Clark, *Algeria in Turmoil* (London: Thames and Hudson, 1960), p. 17.

72. Clement Henry Moore, *Politics in North Africa* (Boston: Little Brown, 1970), p. 82.

73. David and Marina Ottaway, *Algeria: The Politics of a Socialist Revolution* (Berkeley: University of California Press, 1970), pp. 16–17.

74. Robert B. Revere, "Revolutionary Ideology in Algeria," *Polity* 5, no. 4 (Summer 1973): 484.

75. Ottaway and Ottaway, *Algeria*, pp. 117–24.

76. Arslan Humbaraci, *Algeria: A Revolution that Failed* (London: Pall Mall Press, 1966), p. 95.

77. For example, Humbaraci, *A Revolution that Failed*; Gerard Chaliand, *L'Algérie est-elle socialiste?* (Paris: Maspero, 1964).

78. Tony Smith, "The Political and Economic Ambitions of Algerian Land Reform, 1962–1974," *Middle East Journal* 29, no. 3 (Summer 1975): 263.

79. *Africa Contemporary Record, 1974–75*, p. B4.

80. For an examination of these texts, see John R. Nellis, "Socialist Management in Algeria," *Journal of Modern African Studies* 15, no. 4 (December 1977): 529–54; Peter Knauss, "Algeria's Agrarian Revolution: Peasant Control or Control of Peasants?" *African Studies Review* 20, no. 3 (December 1977): 65–78; Smith, "Algerian Land Reform"; John Waterbury, "Land, Man, and Development in Algeria," American University Field Service, *Fieldstaff Reports*, 1973.

81. Nellis, "Socialist Management in Algeria," p. 537.

82. Waterbury, "Land, Man, and Development," pt. IV, p. 1.

83. See, for example, K. C. Ammour and J.-J. Moulin, *La voie algérienne* (Paris: Maspero, 1974).

84. Jean Leca, *L'Algérie politique: Institutions et régime* (Paris: Fondation Nationale des Sciences Politiques, 1975), p. 74; sixteen of the twenty-six were military figures, and eight of the ten civilians were for-

mer *Armée de Libération Nationale* fighters. See this same source for a good analysis of the paradoxical marriage of populism and the administrative state.

85. Ottaway and Ottaway, *Algeria*, p. 61.

86. Ibid., p. 67.

87. Quoted in ibid., p. 270.

88. Humbaraci, *A Revolution that Failed*, p. 88.

89. Ottaway and Ottaway, *Algeria*, pp. 264–66; Nellis, "Socialist Management in Algeria," pp. 532–33.

90. Nellis, "Socialist Management in Algeria," p. 537.

91. *Africa Contemporary Record, 1974–75*, p. B18.

92. Nellis, "Socialist Management in Algeria," p. 538.

93. Quoted in ibid., p. 541.

94. "Point de la situation sur la gestion socialiste des entreprises," Algérie Presse Service, Bulletin Economique (Algiers, 10 May 1975), pp. 31–32. Quoted in Nellis, "Socialist Management in Algeria," p. 549.

95. Ibid., p. 547.

96. Ibid., pp. 547–54.

97. On agrarian socialism in Algeria, in addition to literature already cited, see Thomas L. Blair, *"The Land to Those Who Work It"*: *Algeria's Experiment in Workers' Management* (Garden City, N.Y.: Doubleday & Co., 1969); Ian Clegg, *Workers Self-Management in Algeria* (London: Penguin Books, 1971); Gerard Duprat, *Révolution et autogestion en Algérie* (Paris: A. Colin, 1973); Dj. Sari, "L'evolution de la production agricole en Algerie," *L'Afrique et l'Asie Moderne* 114 (1977): 12–24.

98. Ottaway and Ottaway, *Algeria*, p. 63.

99. Blair, *Land to Those Who Work It*, pp. 74–75; Sari, "L'evolution de la production agricole," pp. 13–16; Smith, "Algerian Land Reform," p. 266; Gerard Viratelle, *L'Algérie algérienne* (Paris: Editions Ouvrières, 1970).

100. Ottaway and Ottaway, *Algeria*, p. 61. Blair, *Land to Those Who Work It*, p. 128, gives a figure of 150,000 at the time of launching *autogestion*.

101. Cited in Knauss, "Algeria's Agrarian Revolution," p. 69.

102. Ibid., p. 70.

103. Ibid., p. 76.

104. Ibid., p. 74.

105. Ibid., pp. 70–76. See also Jean Leca and Jean-Claude Vatin, "Le systéme politique algérien (1976–1978)," *Annuaire de l'Afrique du Nord, 1977*, pp. 58–63.

106. Leca, *L'Algérie politique*, p. 90.

107. Ibid., p. 89.

108. Ibid., pp. 140–86; Ottaway and Ottaway, *Algeria*, pp. 57, 140–43, 206–10.

109. Quoted in Nellis, "Socialist Management in Algeria," pp. 531–32.

110. Moore, *Politics in North Africa*, p. 131.

111. John P. Entelis, *The New York Times*, 12 December 1979. Entelis was a Fulbright professor at the University of Algiers in 1977–78 and a harsher critic of the Algerian regime than most observers.

112. *Africa Contemporary Record, 1976–77*, p. B6.

113. *Annuaire de l'Afrique du Nord, 1977*, (Paris: Editions du Centre National de la Recherche Scientifique, 1978), p. 547.

114. Nellis, "Socialist Management in Algeria," p. 534, based upon Algerian statements and the *Quarterly Economic Review of Algeria*.

115. Leca, *L'Algérie politique*, p. 446.

116. See Lars Rudebeck, *Guinea-Bissau: A Study of Political Mobilization* (Uppsala: Scandinavian Institute of African Studies, 1974); Rudebeck, "Socialist-Oriental Development in Guinea-Bissau," in *Sub-Saharan Africa*, ed. Rosberg and Callaghy, pp. 322–44; Tony Hodges, "Guinea-Bissau: Five Years of Independence," *Africa Report* 22, no. 1 (January–February 1979): 4–9; Denis Goulet, *Looking at Guinea-Bissau: A New Nation's Development Strategy*, Agricultural Development Council, occasional paper no. 9, 1978.

117. See, for example, Basil Davidson, *The Liberation of Guiné* (Baltimore: Penguin Books, 1969).

118. For insight on the Cabral contribution, see Amilcar Cabral, *Revolution in Guiné* (London: Stage 1, 1969), and the valuable analysis of Cabral's thought by Henry Bienen, "State and Revolution: The Works of Amilcar Cabral," *Journal of Modern African Studies* 15, no. 4 (December 1977): 555–68.

119. Rudebeck, in *Sub-Saharan Africa*, ed. Rosberg and Callaghy, p. 326.

120. Bienen, "State and Revolution," pp. 560–61.

121. Ibid., p. 568.

122. Quoted by Rudebeck, *Sub-Saharan Africa*, ed. Rosberg and Callaghy, p. 327.

123. Hodges, "Guinea-Bissau: Five Years of Independence," p. 7.

124. Ibid., p. 5.

125. Ibid.

126. *West Africa* 3311 (12 January 1981): 62–63.

127. Bob Fitch and Mary Oppenheimer, *Ghana: The End of an Illusion* (New York: Monthly Review Press, 1966).

128. Roger Genoud, *Nationalism and Economic Development in Ghana* (New York: Praeger, 1968).

129. See their contributions in Foster and Zolberg, eds., *Ghana and the Ivory Coast*.

130. Tony Killick, *Development Economics in Action* (London: Heinemann, 1978), p. 25.

131. Kwame Nkrumah, *Ghana: The Autobiography of Kwame Nkrumah* (Edinburgh: Thomas Nelson and Sons, 1959), p. vii.

132. Killick, *Development Economics*, p. 34.

133. Ibid., p. 38.

134. Quoted in ibid., pp. 45–47.

135. W. Scott Thompson, *Ghana's Foreign Policy 1957–1966* (Princeton: Princeton University Press, 1969), pp. 46–48.

136. Kwame Nkrumah, *Consciencism* (London: Heinemann, 1964).

137. Kwame Nkrumah, *Class Struggle in Africa* (New York: International Publishers, 1970).

138. Cited in Colin Legum, "Socialism in Ghana: A Political Interpretation," in *African Socialism*, ed. Friedland and Rosberg, pp. 142–43.

139. The extent of stratification in the cocoa areas is frequently exaggerated. The agricultural census of 1970 showed that the average farm was 12.3 acres; cocoa growers numbered 290,000 and farmed 3.5 million acres. At the top were 5,000 relatively large operators who often traded cocoa and whose farms averaged 50.2 acres. For thorough data on the cocoa sector, see R. A. Kotey, C. Okali, and B. E. Rourke, *The Economics of Cocoa Production and Marketing* (Legon: University of Ghana, 1974).

140. For details on the Volta Dam project, see Walter Birmingham, I. Neustadt, and E. N. Omaboe, *A Study of Contemporary Ghana* (London: George Allen & Unwin, 1966), vol. 1, pp. 391–410.

141. Killick, *Development Economics*, p. 249.

142. For a compelling presentation of this argument, see "Imperialism and the Volta Dam," *West Africa* 3270–73 (24 March, 31 March, 7 April, 14 April 1980): 518–23, 571–73, 611–14, 655–60.

143. Marvin P. Miracle and Ann Seidman, *State Farms in Ghana*, Land Tenure Center #43, University of Wisconsin, 1968, p. 19.

144. Killick, *Development Economics*, pp. 192–93.

145. Dennis Austin, *Politics in Ghana 1946–1960* (London: Oxford University Press, 1964), p. 173.

146. For an exhaustive study of the Ghanaian cooperative movement, see the forthcoming doctoral dissertation by Tim Rose, University of Wisconsin-Madison.

147. Col. A. A. Afrifa, *The Ghana Coup 24th February 1966* (London: Frank Cass, 1967), p. 87.

148. Bjorn Beckman, *Organising the Farmers: Cocoa Politics and National Development in Ghana* (Uppsala: Scandinavian Institute of African Studies, 1976), p. 107.

149. De Graft-Johnson Report, quoted in Killick, *Development Economics*, p. 191.

150. Killick, *Development Economics*, pp. 171–72.

151. From a survey of 750 farmers conducted by Rose.

152. These calculations may be found in Kotey, et al., *Economics of Cocoa Production*, p. 53.

153. Figures appear in *West Africa* 3191 (11 September 1978): 1775.

154. Among the useful sources on the Guinean experience, Claude Rivière, *Guinea: The Mobilization of a People* (Ithaca: Cornell University Press, 1977), is the most convincing recent work. See also Ladipo Adamolekun, *Sekou Toure's Guinea* (London: Methuen, 1976); B. Ameillon, *La Guinée: Bilan d'un indépendance* (Paris: Maspero, 1964); Henri de Decker, *Nation et développement communautaire en Guinée et au Sénégal* (Paris: Mouton, 1968); Fernand Gigon, *Guinée: Etat-pilot* (Paris: Plon, 1959); Ruth Schachter Morganthau, *Political Parties in French-Speaking West Africa* (Oxford: Clarendon Press, 1964); William Derman, *Serfs, Peasants, and Socialists* (Berkeley: University of California Press, 1973); R. W. Johnson, "Sekou Toure and the Guinean Revolution," *African Affairs* 69 (October 1970): 350–65; Victor D. DuBois, "The Decline of the Guinean Revolution," *American Universities Field Staff Reports*, West Africa Series 8, nos. 7–9 (1965).

155. Rivière, *Guinea*, pp. 90–92.

156. On the dynamics of the perennial plot, see ibid., pp. 121–40.

157. Ibid., p. 196.

158. Adamolekun, "The Socialist Experience in Guinea," in *Sub-Saharan Africa*, ed. Rosberg and Callaghy, pp. 75–76.

159. Rivière, *Guinea*, p. 190.

160. De Decker, *Nation et développement*, p. 88.

161. Ibid., pp. 93–94; Rivière, *Guinea*, pp. 117–18.

162. William Derman, "Cooperatives in the Republic of Guinea: Problems of Revolutionary Transformation," in *Popular Participation in Social Change: Cooperatives, Collectives, and Nationalized Industry,*

ed. June Nash, Jorge Dandler, and Nicholas S. Hopkins (The Hague: Mouton, 1976), pp. 420–27.

163. Ibid., p. 427.

164. Ibid. Derman's earlier book paints a very favorable picture of the social and political role of the PDG.

165. Rivière, *Guinea*, pp. 181–82.

166. Ibid., p. 180.

167. *Jeune Afrique* 927 (11 October 1978): 73. By 1979, after two years of bitter renegotiation, the Soviets agreed to somewhat improve the price formula, though this remains well below the world market level. The Soviets maintain that the price reflects the low grade of the ore.

168. Rivière, *Guinea*, p. 180.

169. For a chilling account of Boiro and its "cabinets techniques," see *Jeune Afrique* 814–15 (13–20 August 1976); *Le Monde*, 19 December 1978.

170. Lansine Kaba, "Rhetoric and Reality in Guinea," *Africa Report* 23, no. 3 (May–June 1978): 47.

171. See the accounts of these events in ibid., pp. 43–45, and in Tamar Golan, "Returning to the Fold," *West Africa* 3172 (1 May 1978): 843–44.

172. Of particular value in elucidating the Malian socialist experiment is the study by William I. Jones, *Planning and Economic Policy: Socialist Mali and her Neighbors* (Washington: Three Continents Press, 1976); see also Guy Martin, "Socialism, Economic Development and Planning in Mali, 1960–1968," *Canadian Journal of African Studies* 10, no. 7 (1976): 23–47; x x x, "L'expérience socialiste malienne et ses faiblesses," *Revue Française d'Etudes Politiques Africaines* 37 (January 1969): 40–50; Claude Meillassoux, "A Class Analysis of the Bureaucratic Process in Mali," *Journal of Development Studies* 6, no. 2 (January 1970): 99–105; Samir Amin, *Trois expériences africaines de développement: le Mali, la Guinée, et la Ghana* (Paris: Presses Universitaires de France, 1965); Nicholas S. Hopkins, *Popular Government in an African Town: Kita, Mali* (Chicago: University of Chicago Press, 1972); and Kenneth Grundy, "Mali: The Prospects of 'Planned Socialism,'" in *African Socialism*, ed. Friedland and Rosberg, pp. 175–93.

173. Quoted by Grundy, in *African Socialism*, ed. Friedland and Rosberg, pp. 176–77.

174. Martin, "Socialism in Mali," p. 35.

175. Amin, "Trois expériences africaines," pp. 117, 128–29.

176. Jones, *Planning and Economic Policy*, pp. 113–24.

177. Ibid., pp. 225–54.

178. Claude Meillassoux, *Urbanization of an African Community: Voluntary Associations in Bamako* (Seattle: University of Washington Press, 1968), p. 32.

179. Martin, "Socialism in Mali," p. 44. This class interpretation of Malian socialism was first put forward by Meillassoux in "A Class Analysis."

180. Jones, *Planning and Economic Policy*, p. 305.

181. Ibid., pp. 264–65.

182. Ibid., pp. 299–305.

183. Ibid., p. 335.

184. *World Bank Atlas 1978*, p. 14.

CHAPTER 4

1. In *Crises and Sequences in Political Development*, Binder et al., pp. 76–77.

2. Charles E. Lindblom, *Politics and Markets* (New York: Basic Books, 1977), p. 116. For an earlier similar argument from a very different political perspective, see Friedrich A. Hayek, *Road to Serfdom* (Chicago: University of Chicago Press, 1944). It can indeed be argued that those African regimes that have continuously permitted open political competition with multiple parties—Gambia, Botswana, Mauritius—all fall in the African capitalist category.

3. Huntington, *Political Order in Changing Societies*, pp. 192–263.

4. See, for example, G. O'Donnell, "Reflections on the Patterns of Change in the Bureaucratic-Authoritarian State," *Latin American Research Review* 13, no. 1 (1978): 3–38.

5. This argument was first developed by Hamza Alavi, "The State in Post-Colonial Societies: Pakistan and Bangladesh," *New Left Review* 74 (July–August 1972): 59–83.

6. Sayre P. Schatz, *Nigerian Capitalism* (Berkeley: University of California Press, 1977), pp. 1–3.

7. Among the extensive literature generated by the Ivorian experiment, see Berg and Green, in *Ghana and the Ivory Coast*, ed. Foster and Zolberg; Bastiaan A. den Tuinder, *Ivory Coast: The Challenge of Success* (Baltimore: Johns Hopkins University Press, 1978); Michael A. Cohen,

Urban Policy and Political Conflict in the Ivory Coast (Chicago: University of Chicago Press, 1974); Samir Amin, *Le développement du capitalisme en Côte d'Ivoire* (Paris: Editions du Minuit, 1967); Bonnie Campbell, "The Ivory Coast," in *West African States: Failure and Promise,* ed. John Dunn (Cambridge: Cambridge University Press, 1978).

   8. *World Bank Atlas, 1978,* p. 14.

   9. Den Tuinder, *Ivory Coast,* p. 3.

   10. Campbell, in *West African States,* ed. Dunn, p. 92.

   11. Den Tuinder, *Ivory Coast,* p. 7.

   12. Cited in another generally critical article, Alexander G. Rondos, "Ivory Coast: The Price of Development," *Africa Report* 24, no. 2 (March–April 1979): 4.

   13. In *West African States,* ed. Dunn, p. 72.

   14. Amin, *Le développement du capitalisme,* p. 91; on coffee and cocoa acreage, see den Tuinder, *Ivory Coast,* pp. 39–40.

   15. I am indebted to an Ivorian scholar, Luc Kouamé, for this observation.

   16. Den Tuinder, *Ivory Coast,* p. 44.

   17. Ibid., p. 45; Rondos, "The Price of Development," p. 5.

   18. For comparable Ghana figures, see Fitch and Oppenheimer, *Ghana: The End of an Illusion,* p. 41.

   19. Den Tuinder, *Ivory Coast,* p. 46.

   20. The foregoing details are drawn from ibid., pp. 228–45.

   21. Rondos, "The Price of Development," p. 6.

   22. In *West African States,* ed. Dunn, pp. 114–15.

   23. Richard Stryker, "No Easy Choice: Development Trade-offs under Neo-Colonialism," typescript, 1977.

   24. See the trenchant rebuttal to Rondos by Jon Woronoff, "Ivory Coast: The Value of Development," *Africa Report* 24, no. 4 (July–August 1979): 13–19.

   25. Stryker, "No Easy Choice," p. 9.

   26. In *West African States,* ed. Dunn, p. 108.

   27. Den Tuinder, *Ivory Coast,* p. 154.

   28. Arthur Lewis, *Politics in West Africa* (New York: Oxford University Press, 1965), p. 24.

   29. In *West African States,* ed. Dunn, p. 115.

   30. Hollis Chenery et al., *Redistribution with Growth* (London: Oxford University Press, 1974), pp. 8–9.

   31. Den Tuinder, *Ivory Coast,* p. 135.

   32. *Jeune Afrique* 1013 (4 June 1980).

   33. Sessional Paper #10, Kenya Parliament, *African Socialism and*

its Application to Planning in Kenya (Nairobi: Government Printer, 1965).

34. Among the rich assortment of materials on Kenya, see especially Leys, *Underdevelopment in Kenya*; E. A. Brett, *Colonialism and Underdevelopment in Kenya* (London: Heinemann, 1972); John W. Harbeson, *Nation-Building in Kenya: The Role of Land Reform* (Evanston: Northwestern University Press, 1973); Carl G. Rosberg and John Nottingham, *The Myth of Mau Mau: Nationalism in Kenya* (New York: Praeger, 1966); John Burrows et al., for the World Bank, *Kenya: Into the Second Decade* (Baltimore: Johns Hopkins University Press, 1975); Peter Marris and Anthony Sommerset, *African Businessmen* (London: Routledge and Kegan Paul, 1971); Barkan and Okumu, eds., *Politics and Public Policy*; Henry Bienen, *Kenya: The Politics of Participation and Control* (Princeton: Princeton University Press, 1974); Cherry Gartzel, *The Politics of Independent Kenya* (London: Heinemann, 1970); David Leonard, *Reaching the Peasant Farmer: Organization Theory and Practice in Kenya* (Chicago: University of Chicago Press, 1977); Geoff Lamb, *Peasant Politics* (Sussex: Julian Friedman Publishing, 1974); Gerald Holtman and Arthur Hazlewood, *Aid and Inequality in Kenya* (London: Overseas Development Institute, 1976).

35. *African Socialism*, p. 7.

36. Ibid.

37. Leys, *Underdevelopment in Kenya*, p. 145.

38. Quoted in ibid., p. 145.

39. I subscribe here to the central thesis in the classic study of Kenyan nationalism by Rosberg and Nottingham, *The Myth of Mau Mau*.

40. Particular stress on the locational factor is made by Edward W. Soja, *The Geography of Modernization in Kenya* (Syracuse: Syracuse University Press, 1968), pp. 24–26.

41. Leys, *Underdevelopment in Kenya*, p. 58.

42. Government of Kenya, *A Plan to Intensify the Development of African Agriculture in Kenya* (Nairobi: Government Printer, 1955), quoted in Harbeson, *Nation-Building in Kenya*, pp. 34–35.

43. Leys, *Underdevelopment in Kenya*, p. 57.

44. Ibid., p. 62.

45. Ibid., pp. 75–76.

46. Ibid., p. 115.

47. On the settlement schemes, in addition to the excellent analysis in ibid., pp. 63–117, see also Harbeson, *Nation-Building in Kenya*, pp. 135–260.

48. *Report of the Mission on Land Settlement in Kenya* (Van

Arkadie Report) (Nairobi: 1966), cited in Leys, *Underdevelopment in Kenya*, p. 74.

49. Ibid., p. 74.

50. Burrows et al., *Kenya: Into the Second Decade*, p. 455.

51. Leys, *Underdevelopment in Kenya*, pp. 115–16.

52. Burrows et al., *Kenya: Into the Second Decade*, p. 455.

53. On Kenya cooperatives, see Goran Hyden, *Efficiency versus Distribution in East African Cooperatives* (Nairobi: East African Literature Bureau, 1973); Frank W. Holmquist, "Peasant Organization, Clientelism, and Dependency: A Case Study of an Agricultural Producers Cooperative in Kenya" (Ph.D. diss., Indiana University, 1975).

54. S. E. Migot-Adholla, "Rural Development Policy and Equality," in *Politics and Public Policy*, ed. Barkan and Okumu, p. 164.

55. Ibid., p. 162. It will be recalled that a significant number of the largest farms were still European.

56. Burrows et al., *Kenya: Into the Second Decade*, p. 189.

57. Ibid., pp. 197–98.

58. Ibid., p. 172.

59. Bienen, *Kenya*, p. 39.

60. Inter alia, see Kathleen A. Staudt, "Agricultural Policy, Political Power, and Women Farmers in Western Kenya" (Ph.D. diss., University of Wisconsin-Madison, 1976); Leonard, *Reaching the Peasant Farmer*; Jon R. Moris, "The Agrarian Revolution in Central Kenya: A Study of Farm Innovation in Embu District" (Ph.D. diss., Northwestern University, 1970); Robert Chambers, *Managing Rural Development* (Uppsala: Scandinavian Institute of African Studies, 1974).

61. Jon R. Moris, "An Appraisal of Rural Development in Kenya," unpublished paper (Nairobi, 1969). Cited in Bienen, *Kenya*, p. 189.

62. Ibid., p. 184.

63. Leys, *Underdevelopment in Kenya*, p. 119.

64. Ibid., p. 123.

65. Nicola Swainson, "State and Economy in Post-Colonial Kenya, 1963–1973," *Canadian Journal of African Studies* 102, no. 2 (1978): 371–72.

66. Ibid., pp. 366–70.

67. For example, warnings of the threat posed by deteriorating conditions for rural landless and urban unemployed are to be found in Barkan, "Comparing Politics and Public Policy in Kenya and Tanzania," in *Politics and Public Policy*, ed. Barkan and Okumu, pp. 3–42; Burrows et al., *Kenya: Into the Second Decade*, pp. 4–6; Bienen, *Kenya*, pp. 183–96.

68. Odinga came in from the cold under Moi and was placed in charge of cotton marketing.

69. See the revealing exposé of the "royal family" and its business transactions in *Sunday Times*, 10, 17, 24 August 1975.

70. As suggested in the relatively sympathetic portrayal by Vincent B. Khapoya, "Kenya under Moi: Continuity or Change?" *Africa Today* 27, no. 1 (1980): 17–32. The author does point to Kikuyu overrepresentation in the cabinet.

71. Sources I have found particularly valuable on the Nigerian political economy include Schatz, *Nigerian Capitalism*; Peter Kilby, *Industrialization in an Open Economy: Nigeria 1945–1966* (Cambridge: Cambridge University Press, 1969); Gavin Williams, ed., *Nigeria: Economy and Society* (London: Rex Collings, 1976); David B. Abernethy, *The Political Dilemma of Popular Education* (Stanford: Stanford University Press, 1969); Robin Cohen, *Labour and Politics in Nigeria 1945–1971* (London: Heinemann, 1974); H. A. Oluwasamni, *Agriculture and Nigerian Economic Development* (Ibadan: Oxford University Press, 1966); Polly Hill, *Studies in Rural Capitalism in West Africa* (Cambridge: Cambridge University Press, 1970); Gerald K. Helleiner, *Peasant Agriculture, Government, and Economic Growth in Nigeria* (Homewood, Ill.: Richard D. Irwin, 1966); Jerome C. Wells, *Agricultural Policy and Economic Growth in Nigeria 1962–1968* (Ibadan: Oxford University Press, 1974); Eno J. Usoro, *The Nigerian Oil Palm Industry* (Ibadan: Ibadan University Press, 1974); Sara S. Berry, *Cocoa, Custom, and Socio-Economic Change in Rural Western Nigeria* (Oxford: Clarendon Press, 1975); Wolfgang Stolper, *Planning without Facts* (Cambridge: Harvard University Press, 1966); Wouter Tims, *Nigeria: Options for Long-Term Development* (Baltimore: Johns Hopkins University Press, 1974); B. J. Dudley, *Instability and Political Order* (Ibadan: Ibadan University Press, 1973); Richard Sklar, *Nigerian Political Parties* (Princeton: Princeton University Press, 1963); James S. Coleman, *Nigeria: Background to Nationalism* (Berkeley: University of California Press, 1958); John P. Macintosh, *Nigerian Government and Politics* (Evanston: Northwestern University Press, 1966); Keith Panter-Brick, ed., *Soldiers and Oil: The Political Transformation of Nigeria* (London: Frank Cass, 1978).

72. Gavin Williams, "Nigeria. A Political Economy," p. 43.

73. F. A. Baptiste, cited in Gavin Williams and Terisa Turner, "Nigeria," in *West African States*, ed. Dunn, p. 147. In 1980, Awolowo (still claiming socialism as doctrine) retorted to critics who were wagging their fingers at some of his land purchases that socialism does not mean poverty.

74. A. A. N. Orizu, quoted in Coleman, *Nigeria: Background to Nationalism*, p. 297.

75. On the *Agbekoya* tax revolt, the most important postindependence upsurge of radical rural populism, see Christopher Beer, *The Politics of Peasant Groups in Western Nigeria* (Ibadan: Ibadan University Press, 1976).

76. Williams and Turner, in *West African States*, ed. Dunn, p. 153; Helleiner, *Peasant Agriculture*, pp. 34–35; Tims, *Options for Development*, pp. 69–76.

77. Kilby, *Industrialization in an Open Economy*, p. 9.

78. Tims, *Options for Development*, p. 70.

79. Kilby, *Industrialization in an Open Economy*, p. 15.

80. Tims, *Options for Development*, p. 73.

81. Leon Dash, in *Washington Post*, 24 January 1980.

82. Kilby, *Industrialization in an Open Economy*, p. 11.

83. Schatz, *Nigerian Capitalism*, p. 6.

84. Ibid., p. 6.

85. Quoted in Panter-Brick, *Soldiers and Oil*, p. 156.

86. Ibid., pp. 59–61.

87. Ibid.

88. Kilby, *Industrialization in an Open Economy*, p. 32.

89. Schatz, *Nigerian Capitalism*, pp. 56, 167–97.

90. Tims, *Options for Development*, p. 4.

91. Williams and Turner, in *West African States*, ed. Dunn, p. 171.

92. Oluwasamni, *Agriculture and Nigerian Economic Development*, p. 132.

93. Usoro, *Nigerian Oil Palm Industry*, p. 3.

94. Ibid., p. 60.

95. Cited in ibid., p. 86.

96. Helleiner, *Peasant Agriculture*, p. 106.

97. Usoro, *Nigerian Oil Palm Industry*, p. 115.

98. Helleiner, *Peasant Agriculture*, pp. 163, 195–97.

99. Berry, *Cocoa, Custom, and Socio-Economic Change*, pp. 193–94.

100. *Commodity Yearbook*, 1949, 1977.

101. Helleiner, *Peasant Agriculture*, p. 163.

102. Ibid., pp. 119–20.

103. Wells, *Agricultural Policy*, pp. 212–61.

104. This is the conclusion of Schatz, *Nigerian Capitalism*, p. 30, and, more emphatically, Williams and Turner, in *West African States*, ed. Dunn, pp. 166–72.

105. A survey of Ahmadu Bello university students taken in 1973

asked respondents to rank social categories in terms of possible "suffering" or "exploitation": 62.7 percent ranked farmers first and only 3.2 percent placed urban workers at the top of the list. Paul Beckett and James O'Connell, *Education and Power in Nigeria* (London: Hodder & Stoughton, 1977), p. 132.

106. See, for example, the study of the condition of the urban poor in Ibadan by Peter C. W. Gutkind, "From the Energy of Despair to the Anger of Despair," *Canadian Journal of African Studies* 7, no. 2 (1973): 179–98.

107. Otto Klineberg and Merisa Zavalloni, *Nationalism and Tribalism Among African Students* (Paris: Mouton, 1969), p. 58. A similar view of politicians emerges in the more recent survey of Beckett and O'Connell, *Education and Power.*

108. Most notably first Prime Minister Abubakar Tafewa Balewa, Generals Muritala Muhammad and O. Obasanjo, and President Shehu Shagari were generally believed to be men of high personal integrity. President Azikiwe was tainted by the scandals associated with his African Continental Bank, although this was prior to his elevation to the presidency. General Yakubu Gowon was accused by some close observers, though not all, of complicity in the 1972 cement scandal and was overthrown partly because he tolerated dishonesty on the part of most of his military state governors.

109. See the monumental study of political trials in Nigeria and two other African states by H. Marshall Carter, "Political Justice: The African Experience: Studies in Nigeria, Uganda, and Zambia" (Ph.D. diss., University of Wisconsin-Madison, 1973).

110. *World Bank Atlas, 1978,* p. 14.

111. Yves de Schaetgen, "L'économie gabonaise," *Revue Française d'Etudes Politiques Africaines* 90 (June 1973): 67–94.

112. Ibid., p. 86.

113. For more detail, see Guy Gran, ed., *Zaire: The Political Economy of Underdevelopment* (New York: Praeger, 1980); Crawford Young, "Zaire: The Unending Crisis," *Foreign Affairs* 57, no. 1 (Fall 1978): 169–85.

114. For a much fuller account, see the forthcoming study on the Mobutu era by Crawford Young and Thomas Turner. Two particularly interesting sources are Kamitatu Massamba, "Problematique et rationalité dans le processus de nationalisation du cuivre en Afrique Centrale: Zaire (1967) et Zambie (1969)" (Ph.D. diss., Institut d'Etudes Politiques de Paris, 1976); J. Ph. Peemans, "The Social and Economic Development

of Zaire since Independence: An Historical Outline," *African Affairs* 74, no. 295 (April): 148–79.

115. The Economist Intelligence Unit noted in 1971 that the first significant syndicated bank loan, in November 1970, organized by Bankers Trust, was "unusual" in that it was intended for road and bridge construction; the resort to private bank finance for such infrastructure investments was generally believed to be too costly. *Quarterly Economic Report, Zaire, Rwanda, and Burundi*, 1 February 1971.

116. Benoit Verhaegen, "Universities, Social Class, and Economic Dependency" (Paper delivered at Rockefeller Foundation conference on the African university and development, Bellagio, Italy, August 1978).

117. U.S. Senate, 96th Congress, 1st Session, *U.S. Loans to Zaire*. Hearing before the Subcommittee on International Finance of the Committee on Banking, Housing, and Urban Affairs, 24 May 1979, p. 7.

118. Ward B. Saunders, "Imperialism and the Volta Dam: A Reply," *West Africa* 3280 (2 June 1980): 958.

119. *Washington Post*, 13 November 1979.

120. The private participants were Amoco Minerals, 28 percent; Charter Consolidated, 28 percent; Mitsui, 14 percent; Omni Mines and *Bureau de recherches géologiques et minières* (both French), 3.5 percent each; Leon Tempelsman & Son, 2 percent, as agent fee. The Zaire state held 20 percent, in return for the concession. Amoco Minerals, long restive about the repeated delays in the project, sold its holdings to French interests in 1979.

121. *Washington Post*, 1 January 1980.

122. On 30 November and radicalization, see Michael G. Schatzberg, *Politics and Class in Zaire: Bureaucracy, Business and Beer in Lisala* (New York: Africana, 1980); Edward Kannyo, "Political Power and Class Formation in Zaire: The 'Zairianization Measures,' 1973–1975" (Ph.D. diss., Yale University, 1979).

123. This, for example, is the central thrust of the Gran argument, *Zaire: The Politicial Economy of Underdevelopment*.

124. James Mayall, "Africa in the International System: The Great Powers in Search of a Perspective," *Government and Opposition* 14, no. 3 (Summer 1978): 354.

125. Jonathan Kwitny, *Wall Street Journal*, 2 July 1980, p. 1.

126. David J. Gould, *Bureaucratic Corruption in the Third World* (New York: Pergamon Press, 1980).

127. Monseigneur Kabanga, *Je suis un homme*, Archêveché de Lubumbashi, March 1976.

128. These comments were made in a public lecture delivered at the American Cultural Center in Lubumbashi in January 1975.

CHAPTER 5

1. Gromyko, "Present Stage of the Anti-Imperialist Struggle," p. 24.

2. On Soviet policy in Africa, see especially Robert Legvold, *Soviet Policy in West Africa* (Cambridge: Harvard University Press, 1970); Warren Weinstein, ed., *Chinese and Soviet Aid to Africa* (New York: Praeger, 1975); Christopher A. Stevens, *The Soviet Union and Black Africa* (London: Macmillan, 1976); Robert Kanet, *The Soviet Union and the Developing Nations* (Baltimore: Johns Hopkins University Press, 1974); Oye Ogunbadejo, "Ideology and Pragmatism: The Soviet Role in Nigeria, 1960–1977," *Orbis* 21, no. 4 (Winter 1978): 803–30; W. Scott Thompson, *Ghana's Foreign Policy 1957–1966* (Princeton: Princeton University Press, 1969); Charles B. McLane, *Soviet-African Relations* (London: Central Asian Research Bureau, 1974); United States Senate, Committee on Foreign Relations, *Perceptions: Relations between the United States and the Soviet Union* (Washington: Government Printing Office, 1979); "The USSR and Africa," *Problems of Communism* 27, no. 1 (January–February 1978): 1–50. Important sources on American policy in Africa include Waldemar A. Nielsen, *The Great Powers and Africa* (New York: Praeger, 1969); Waldemar A. Nielsen, *African Battlelines: American Policy Choices in Southern Africa* (New York: Harper & Row, 1965); Frederick S. Arkhurst, ed., *U.S. Policy toward Africa* (New York: Praeger, 1975); Rupert Emerson, *Africa and United States Policy* (Englewood Cliffs, N.J.: Prentice-Hall, 1967); Jennifer S. Whitaker, ed., *Africa and the United States: Vital Interests* (New York: New York University Press, 1978); Helen Kitchen, ed., "Options for U.S. Policy towards Africa," *Foreign Policy and Defense Review* 1, no. 1 (1979); Henry Bienen, "U.S. Foreign Policy in a Changing Africa," *Political Science Quarterly* 93, no. 3 (Fall 1978): 443–64; William J. Foltz, "United States Policy toward Southern Africa," *Political Science Quarterly* 92, no. 1 (Spring 1977): 47–64; Rene Lemarchand, ed., *American Policy in Southern Africa: The Stakes and the Stance* (Washington: University Press of America, 1978); Robert M. Price, *U.S. Foreign Policy in Sub-Saharan Africa: National Interest and Global Strategy* (Berkeley: University of California Institute of International Studies, 1978).

3. R. Ulianovsky, *Socialism and the Newly-Independent Nations* (Moscow: Progress Publishers, 1974), p. 21. Cited in the fine exegesis of

Soviet Africanist writings of the early 1970s by Marina Ottaway, "Soviet Marxism and African Socialism," *Journal of Modern African Studies* 16, no. 3 (September 1978): 477–86.

4. V. F. Stanis, ed., *The Role of the State in Socio-Economic Reforms in Developing Countries*, p. 27. Cited in Ottaway, "Soviet Marxism and African Socialism," p. 482. A major exception to the proletarian weakness is southern Africa, where Soviet analysts note with interest a potentially promising working-class base; Milena Charles, "The Changing Vision of the African Working Class—A Component of Soviet Strategy in Black Africa?" *Journal of Modern African Studies* 16, no. 4 (December 1978): 695–700.

5. V. Solodovnikov, "Problems of Non-Capitalist Development," in Research Center for Africa and Asia, Bulgarian Academy of Sciences, *Developing Countries on the Non-Capitalist Road* (Sofia: 1974), p. 23, cited in Ottaway, "Soviet Marxism and African Socialism," p. 480. Elizabeth Kridl Valkenier finds in her survey of recent Soviet writings on the noncapitalist pathway a growing acceptance of a large private sector in the transitional period, reminiscent of the NEP era in the Soviet Union: "Development Issues in Recent Soviet Scholarship," *World Politics* 32, no. 4 (July 1980): 485–508.

6. L. Rathenan and H. Schilling, "The Non-Capitalist Development in Asia and Africa—Balance, Problems, Prospects," in *Developing Countries on the Non-Capitalist Road*, cited in Ottaway "Soviet Marxism and African Socialism," p. 480. It should be noted that the works scrutinized by Ottaway were all written before 1975, when the Afro-Marxist state became an important phenomenon.

7. Nikolai Kosukhin, "Revolutionary Democracy: Its Ideology and Policies," *Social Sciences* 4 (1979): 51.

8. Ibid., p. 52.

9. Gromyko, "Present Stage of the Anti-Imperialist Struggle," p. 29.

10. Kosukhin, "Revolutionary Democracy," pp. 53–54.

11. Ibid., p. 55.

12. Ibid., pp. 55–56.

13. Freidel Trappen and Ulbricht Weishauft, "Aktuelle Fragen Des Kampfes um Nationale und Social Befrieng in Subsaharischen Afrika," *Deutsche Aussenpolitik* 24, no. 2 (February 1979): 30. I am indebted to Melvin Croan for drawing this citation to my attention.

14. See the valuable critique of this debate by a moderate "globalist," Donald Zagoria, "Into the Breach: New Soviet Alliances in the Third World," *Foreign Affairs* 57, no. 4 (Spring 1979): 733–54.

15. Elliot J. Berg, "Socialism and Economic Development in Tropical Africa," *Quarterly Journal of Economics* 78 (November 1964): 549–72.

16. Remarks of the Honorable David D. Newsom, Undersecretary of State for Political Affairs, before the Subcommittee on African Affairs of the House Committee on Foreign Affairs, 18 October 1979, typescript. It is interesting to note that his list was the same as that of Gromyko.

17. Ogunbadejo, "Ideology and Pragmatism," pp. 806–11.

18. See the chapters by Rene Lemarchand and Stephen Weissman in Lemarchand, *American Policy in Southern Africa*; John Stockwell, *In Search of Enemies* (New York: W. W. Norton & Co., 1978); United States Senate, Select Committee to Study Governmental Operations, *Alleged Assassination Plots Involving Foreign Leaders*, 94th Congress, 1st Session, 20 November 1975; Stephen Weissman, *American Foreign Policy in the Congo 1960–1964* (Ithaca: Cornell University Press, 1974).

19. For an intriguing glimpse at patterns of Soviet military relationships, see Gad Toko, *Intervention in Uganda: The Power Struggle and Soviet Involvement* (Pittsburgh: University of Pittsburgh Center for International Studies, 1979). The author, a former Ugandan air force officer who attended training schools in the Soviet Union, reports that the initial supply of old model Soviet aircraft were gifts, but spare parts had to be purchased. Little inventory was maintained for parts, which meant that frequent entreaties had to be made for a renewal of supply, which was used as leverage.

20. Central Intelligence Agency, *Communist Aid Activities in Non-Communist Less Developed Countries, 1978*, ER 79-1041 2U, September 1979.

21. For a complete list of major military equipment, see International Institute for Strategic Studies, *Military Balance 1978–1979* (London: 1979). See also the annual yearbooks of the Stockholm International Peace Research Institute (SIPRI).

22. Chester A. Crocker, "The African Dimension of Indian Ocean Policy," *Orbis* 20, no. 3 (Fall 1976): 637–68.

23. Alvin Z. Rubinstein, *Red Star on the Nile* (Princeton: Princeton University Press, 1977), pp. 6–46.

24. Ibid., pp. 188–202.

25. Quoted by David Morrison, *Africa Contemporary Record, 1976–1977*, p. A78.

26. Nielsen, *The Great Powers and Africa*, pp. 367–68.

27. House of Representatives, Committee on Foreign Affairs, Subcommittee on Africa, *Foreign Assistance Legislation for Fiscal Years*

1980–81 (Part 6), Hearings and Markup, 96th Congress, 1st Session, 1979, p. 6.

28. A good illustration is the list of countries sending military personnel for training programs in the United States in 1978 and 1979; this included Egypt (35), Morocco (395), Tunisia (249), Chad (3), Ghana (95), Kenya (52), Liberia (38), Mali (4), Senegal (18), Sudan (64), Upper Volta (8), and Zaire (129). Department of Defense, *Security Assistance Programs FY 1980*, pp. 20–21.

29. Quoted in Arkhurst, *U.S. Policy toward Africa*, p. 75.

30. Stevens, *The Soviet Union and Black Africa*, pp. 74–100; on Soviet aid, see also Warren Weinstein, ed., *Chinese and Soviet Aid to Africa* (New York: Praeger, 1975); Alvin Z. Rubinstein, ed., *Soviet and Chinese Influence in the Third World* (New York: Praeger, 1975).

31. Ogunbadejo, "Ideology and Pragmatism," p. 822.

32. William R. Cotter, "How Much Does the U.S. Really Give Africa?" *Africa Report* 17, no. 8 (September–October 1972): 17–20.

33. Quoted in Emerson, *Africa and United States Policy*, p. 41.

34. Ibid., p. 56; Nielsen, *The Great Powers and Africa*, pp. 298–99.

35. Nelson Kasfir, "Interdependence and American Commitment to Promote Development in the Third World: Africa—The Hardest Cast," in *American in an Interdependent World*, ed. David A. Baldwin (Boston: University Press of New England, 1976), p. 229.

36. Michael Glantz, ed., *The Politics of National Disaster* (New York: Praeger, 1976).

37. United Nations, *Statistical Yearbook*, 1977.

38. One report indicates the Angolans receive only 4–6 percent of the fish netted by Soviet trawlers in Angolan waters. To boot, the Soviets were paying only $.96 a pound for Angolan coffee delivered to meet arms and other debts, when the world price was $2.14: David R. Smock and Norman N. Miller, "Soviet Designs in Africa," *American Universities Fieldstaff Reports*, Africa 17, 1980, p. 12.

39. For a succinct resume, see Gordon Bertolin, "U.S. Economic Interests in Africa: Investment, Trade, and Raw Materials," in *Africa and the United States*, ed. Whitaker, pp. 21–59.

40. Ibid., p. 23.

41. For full documentation, see House of Representatives, Committee on Interior and Insular Affairs, Subcommittee on Mines and Mining, *Sub-Saharan Africa: Its Role in Critical Mineral Needs of the Western World*, 96th Congress, 2d Session, 1980.

42. Bertolin, in *Africa and the United States*, ed. Whitaker.

43. On African diplomatic perspectives, see Ali A. Mazrui and Hasu

H. Patel, *Africa in World Affairs: The Next Thirty Years* (New York: The Third Press, 1973); Yashpal Tandon and Dilshad Chanderana, *Horizons of African Diplomacy* (Nairobi: East African Literature Bureau, 1974).

44. *Africa Confidential* 21, no. 11 (21 May 1980).

45. Quoted in Mittelman, "The Mozambique Experience," p. 326.

46. Gromyko, "Present Stage of the Anti-Imperalist Struggle," p. 424.

CHAPTER 6

1. Amin, *Capitalisme en Côte d'Ivoire.*

2. Den Tuinder, *Ivory Coast.*

3. Gould, "Zairian National 'Development.'"

4. Cohen, *Urban Policy and Political Conflict,* pp. 43–46.

5. Chenery et al., *Redistribution with Growth,* p. xv.

6. Ibid., pp. 38–49.

7. International Labour Office, *Towards Self-Reliance* (Addis Ababa: Jobs and Skills Programme for Africa, 1978), pp. 162–163.

8. Ibid., p. 198.

9. Dominguez, *Cuba: Order and Revolution,* makes a carefully documented case for the high effectiveness of the Castro regime in delivering social services and meeting basic needs, while failing to achieve significant economic growth. The exodus of refugees in 1980 provided interesting confirmation of this. The great majority were urban, in good part blue collar, a group that was not so socially and economically disadvantaged under the *ancien régime.* Few came from rural areas, where the Castro regime has made basic social amenities available for the first time.

10. Leys, *Underdevelopment in Kenya.*

11. Immanuel Wallerstein, "Dependence in an Interdependent World: The Limited Possibilities of Transformation within the Capitalist World Economy," *African Studies Review* 17, no. 1 (April 1974): 1–26.

12. Another dimension of the human dignity issue is deprivation of basic rights to economic livelihood and social well-being. We have considered this aspect under the equality theme; here we are concerned with political repression.

13. The Department of State human rights report is obviously a document drafted in a political context and is affected by the anticipated offense that critical findings will give to governments with whom friendly ties are sought. Even when discount is made for these con-

textual considerations, it remains the most comprehensive survey available. I do not believe its African reporting is heavily influenced by a priori judgments of regime ideologies.

14. O'Donnell, "Reflections on the Bureaucratic-Authoritarian State."

15. Amnesty International, *Human Rights Violations in Zaire* (London: Russell Press, 1980), p. 1.

16. Bienen, *Kenya.*

17. Cohen, *Urban Policy and Political Conflict.*

18. Alavi, "The State in Post-Colonial Societies."

19. Lofchie, "Agrarian Crisis," p. 457.

20. Quoted by Pratt, in *Towards Socialism in Tanzania,* ed. Mwansasu and Pratt, p. 229.

21. ILO, *Towards Self-Reliance,* pp. 123–29.

Index